WITHDRAWN

Social Security and Welfare

INTRODUCING SOCIAL POLICY
Series Editor: David Gladstone

Published titles

Perspectives on Welfare
Alan Deacon

Risk, Social Policy and Welfare
Hazel Kemshall

Comparative Social Policy: Theory and Research
Patricia Kennett

Education in a Post-welfare Society
Sally Tomlinson

Social Security and Welfare: Concepts and Comparisons
Robert Walker

Reconceptualizing Social Policy
Amanda Coffey

Social Security and Welfare

Concepts and Comparisons

ROBERT WALKER

Open University Press

Open University Press
McGraw-Hill Education
McGraw-Hill House
Shoppenhangers Road
Maidenhead
Berkshire
SL6 2QL

email: enquiries@openup.co.uk
world wide web: www.openup.co.uk

and Two Penn Plaza, New York, NY 10121-2289, USA

First published 2005

A catalogue record of this book is available from the British Library

ISBN 0 335 20934 3 (pb)   0 335 20935 1 (hb)

Library of Congress Cataloging-in-Publication Data
CIP data has been applied for

Typeset by RefineCatch Ltd, Bungay, Suffolk
Printed in Great Britain by Bell and Bain Ltd, Glasgow

Contents

Series Editor's Foreword   x
Acknowledgements   xii

Part 1: Objectives   1

1   Words, Meaning and the Importance of Context   3
    Words matter   4
    The liberation of difference   9
    The importance of context   13
        Liberal welfare regimes   15
        Social democratic welfare regimes   15
        Conservative welfare regimes   16
        Additional welfare regimes   17
    Closing summary   19
    Further reading   19

2   Aims and Objectives   21
    Systems and schemes   21
    System aims, policy objectives and functions   23
        Aims   23
        Objectives   24
        Functions   27
    Examples of aims   29
        Alleviation of poverty   29
        Income maintenance and replacement   30
        Promoting social cohesion   31
        Protection against risk   32

Redistribution 33
Compensation 34
Promotion of economic efficiency 35
Behavioural change 35
On objectives 36
An important extension 39
Closing summary 40
Further reading 40

3 **Functions and Constraints** 42
Types of function 43
Provision for need 43
Maintenance of circumstances 45
Developing potential 47
Changing behaviour 48
Remedying disadvantage 51
Reproducing disadvantage 51
Producing disadvantage 52
Types of constraint 55
Political 55
Economic 56
Social 57
Administrative 58
Closing summary 59
Further reading 60

Part 2: Mechanisms 61

4 **Financing** 63
Why financing is important 63
Rationale for social spending: limits on individual saving 66
Funding mechanisms 69
Insurance 71
Collective transfers 78
Closing summary 86
Further reading 87

5 **Allocation and Administration** 88
Routes to entitlement 88
The insurance route 89
The citizenship route 90
The means-tested route 91
Institutions 93
National government 93

Sub-national government 94
Social partnerships 95
Private insurance and pensions 99
Contractors 100
Benefit administration 102
Entry and application 102
Verification and decision-making 104
Payment, review and sanction 106
Appeals 108
Closing summary 110
Further reading 110

Part 3: Effectiveness 111

6 Income Replacement and Compensation 113
Income replacement 117
Determining replacement rates 118
Assessing replacement rates 119
Compensation 122
Income loss 124
Lowered living standards 126
Loss of participation 127
Assessment 127
Closing summary 130
Further reading 130

7 Tackling Poverty, Guaranteeing Sufficiency 131
Defining adequacy 133
Determining the adequacy standard 136
Normative judgement: budget standards 137
Attitudinal assessment 138
Arbitrary determination 141
Dynamism 144
Assessing adequacy 145
Closing summary 149
Further reading 149

8 Redistribution of Income 150
Vertical redistribution 150
Purpose 150
Mechanisms 151
Measurement 154
Horizontal redistribution 163

Territorial redistribution 167
Life-course redistribution 170
Closing summary 174
Further reading 174

Part 4: Efficiency 175

9 Target Efficiency 177
Concepts and measurement 179
Internal targeting efficiency 180
External targeting efficiency 183
Benefits to the non-needy 187
Mismatch in target populations 187
Population and benefit dynamics 189
Fraud and abuse 190
Mal-administration 190
Measurement error 191
Reasons for unmet need 191
Inadequate benefit levels and limited coverage 191
Low take-up 193
Closing summary 199
Further reading 200

10 Economic Efficiency 201
Shaping economic structures 202
Altering incentives 203
The unemployment trap 207
The poverty trap 208
The savings trap 211
Behavioural responses 212
Benefit dependency and duration 213
Reservation wages 215
Work-rich, work-poor families 215
Uncertainty and risk 216
Policy responses 218
Directing behaviour 218
Structural reform 222
Closing summary 228
Further reading 228

11 Administrative Efficiency 229
Intermediate outcomes 230
Delivery and volume 230

Speed of service   231
Accuracy and adequacy   231
User efficiency   232
Access   232
Quality of treatment   235
Security   237
Management of resources   239
Personnel   239
Information technology   246
Performance management   247
Internal audit   248
External audit   251
Closing summary   251
Further reading   252

Part 5: Contemporary Influences   255

12 Individualization and Social Change   257
Individualization   257
Diversity   260
Gender relations   261
Racial and ethnic diversity   264
Diversity of lifestyles   267
Employment and family   268
Solidarity   271
Closing summary   274
Further reading   275

13 Globalization and Internationalism   277
Globalization   277
Policy competition   279
Flexible labour markets   282
Migration   285
Internationalism   288
Policy learning   288
International organizations and supra-national governance   292
Social security on a global scale?   299
Further reading   300

Postscript   301

Glossary   303
Bibliography   314
Index   334

Series Editor's Foreword

Welcome to the sixth volume in the Introducing Social Policy series. The series itself is designed to provide a range of well informed texts on a wide variety of topics that fall within the ambit of social policy studies.

Although primarily designed with undergraduate social policy students in mind, it is hoped that the series – and individual titles within it – will have a wider appeal to students in other social science disciplines and to those engaged on professional and post-qualifying courses in health care and social welfare.

The aim throughout the planning of the series has been to produce a series of texts that both reflect and contribute to contemporary thinking and scholarship, and which present their discussion in a readable and easily accessible format.

It is extremely appropriate that such a series should include a volume concerned with social security. Income maintenance services generate issues not only of policy and management, but also of principle and quality of life. They are redolent with historical imagery – as the continuing pervasive influence of the Poor Law of earlier centuries attests. They raise questions in the present about justice, comprehensiveness, sufficiency and targeting; as well, of course, as the relationship between work and welfare. And, for the future, there is especially the impact of an ageing population and the risk of financial insecurity in old age, as well as the impact of globalisation on national social security systems.

These sorts of issues are all too often discussed in a national policy myopia, characterised by legal detail relating to conditions and entitlements. Not so this text by Robert Walker. He has chosen deliberately to discuss the working and effectiveness of the British system in a genuinely comparative context. Central to his approach is what he terms, in his opening chapter, 'the liberation of difference', and the exploration of divergent responses to common human needs and risks on which he then impressively embarks.

He does so against a framework of clearly defined concepts around which the book is organised. Here tooo this volume is distinctive in the clarity with which it discusses divergent aims, different methods of funding, management and allocation, and alternative (and often competing) measures of efficiency, effectiveness and outcome.

In his final section Walker turns his attention to the inter relationship between social security and, on the one hand, changing lifestyles and family structures and, on the other, the proceses of globalisation, flexible labour markets and cross-national migration. The issues he raises in this section suggest that the study of social security is dynamic. It is not only about then and now, or a particular country's experience. The changes he describes – and the responses they evoke – will shape all our wellbeing, now and in the future.

David Gladstone, University of Bristol.

Acknowledgements

There are many people to thank and no one else but myself to blame.

Jennifer Park is my love, inspiration and harshest critic without whom I could neither work nor write. My son and daughter, Oliver and Melissa, have likewise made incredible sacrifices when work so often took over family life.

Colleagues who have proved an inspiration to me are too many to name, but I must mention Karl Ashworth, Jonathan Bradshaw, Andreas Cebulla, Alan Deacon, Tony Fitzpatrick, Dave Greenberg, Karen Kellard, Stephen Jenkins, Lutz Leisering, Jane Millar, Gill Pascall, David Piachaud, Mike Reddin, Bruce Stafford and Michael Wiseman. Bruce Bradbury, Ginger Brown, Dong-Myeon Shin, Deuk Yung Ko and Sook-Yeon Won have also made specific contributions to research for this book for which I am very grateful.

Finally, I have learned much from the students that I have had the privilege to teach and who market-tested the material included in this volume: Laura Bailey, Catherine (Kate) Brooks, Clare Collins, Melissa Cox, Penny Dexter, Ameet Gadhoke, Neil Heath, Jasmin Howell, Kiera Hughes, Kirsty Jeeves, Zoë Jackson, Jane Lim, Sarah McLaughlin, Michael Mitchell, Sophia Odidison, Maggie Orr, Claire Parkinson, Janey Reynolds, Alice Rogen, Jessica Sale, Lean Shaw, Michele Smailey, Donovan Snape, Richard Walker, Guillia Ward and Debbie Webster.

PART 1

Objectives

chapter

one

Words, Meaning and the Importance of Context

This is a book about concepts rather than facts. While facts are of interest to the student of policy, they are less important than concepts. Facts change so rapidly that books are out of date before they are published. Indeed, the pace of policy change frequently defeats even the most sophisticated search engines scanning the World Wide Web; the result is that the naïve and not so naïve Web-user can take as current fact policies that have already been superseded.

Concepts have a longer shelf life than facts. While policy analysts and academics are constantly seeking to define more discriminating concepts and techniques, the evolutionary process is positively sedate compared with the advance of policy. More importantly, facts acquire their meaning through their juxtaposition with concepts. The untold billions of pages that constitute the World Wide Web are no more than silent noise until the Web-user provides the search engine with a combination of concepts – key words. Likewise, policies and policy systems only become comprehensible when they are defined and described in relation to concepts such as aims and objectives, cost and cost effectiveness, efficiency and opportunity costs. Throughout the text, key concepts are printed in bold and defined when first introduced, as well as being included in the glossary.

Moreover, facts are necessarily located in place and time and are also limited by time and place. Concepts, by contrast, travel comparatively well, albeit not perfectly, across time and jurisdictions. (**Jurisdiction** is the term applied to the territory over which the authority of a government is exercised.) Indeed, it is through the application of common concepts to the study, interpretation and evaluation of policies in different jurisdictions that it becomes possible to assess and understand the potential and limitations of policy ideas and opportunities.

The aim of this book, therefore, is to offer readers a set of conceptual tools that will enable them to define and assemble facts better to understand the design, implementation and effectiveness of a subset of social policies: those that have to do with social security and welfare.

Words matter

Social Security and Welfare, the title of the book, is a play on words. It exploits ambiguity both to attract and deceive while simultaneously revealing the confusion that can result from using words that mean different things to different people. It is important to clear up any misunderstanding by defining the constituent terms that will be used as consistently as possible throughout the remainder of the volume.

Social security has a rather specific meaning in the United States of America (USA) and in most countries of continental Europe. In these countries, **social security** describes cash benefit systems that are run or sponsored by government and funded primarily from contributions of workers and their employers with payments being made to needy people based on their contribution records. In Britain, the terms **insurance** or **contributory benefits** are often used interchangeably to refer to these kinds of benefit. The basic state retirement pension scheme in Britain is contributory or insurance-based, as are the majority of benefits in Germany, the core old-age, survivors and disability (OASDI, 'I' for Insurance) programme in the USA and analogous schemes in Sweden and Korea.

In Britain, the term social security is much more encompassing. Indeed, it is so wide-ranging and contested that some years ago Michael Hill (1990) suggested that social security should be defined as the policy responsibilities of the UK Department of Social Security. Although there may have been some merit in this suggestion at the time, the department was abolished in 2001 and most of its functions taken over by the new Department of Work and Pensions. (These developments serve as further evidence of the dangers of relying too heavily on policy facts.) In addition to social insurance schemes, the British use the term social security to embrace both means-tested and non-contributory benefits. **Means-tested benefits** are schemes under which people can claim if their income and other resources fall short of a prescribed standard; **non-contributory benefits** are schemes under which people are entitled to benefit on the basis a contingency, such as a disability, without the requirement for contributions and irrespective of the level of their resources. Both are generally funded from general taxation. Means-tested benefits are also called **social assistance**: indeed, this is the term usually used to refer to means-tested benefits throughout continental Europe and by international agencies such as the Organization for Economic Cooperation and Development (OECD) and the International Labour Organization (ILO). In the USA these kinds of scheme, most notably Transitional Assistance for Needy Families (TANF), formerly Aid for Families with Dependent Children (AFDC), and sometimes food stamps, are often called 'welfare' (see below). Australia is unusual in that virtually all benefits are means-tested, albeit sometimes with a high eligibility threshold.

In British academic circles, although less frequently in popular debate, certain components of a worker's remuneration package – **occupational benefits** such as sickness benefits and occupational retirement pensions – are included within the concept of social security. The logic for doing so is that these benefits serve the same functions as sickness benefits and pensions provided by the state and may serve as alternatives to state provision. In fact, in Britain, occupational pensions have historically served to supplement state pensions that are low by international standards. Occupational benefits of this kind have until recently been somewhat less important in most other parts of the world and have tended to be treated as a form of deferred wage rather than a component of social security provision.

It is increasingly important to recognize that individual cash benefits can be delivered through the tax system. The main purpose of income tax is to raise revenue for governments to spend. However, an important maxim is that people should be taxed according to their ability to pay. Often, this means that the percentage rate of tax that people pay increases with income and, frequently, that account is taken of other financial demands on the taxpayer's income. For example, in many countries a person's tax liability will be reduced if they have children or are paying interest on a home loan. This is often achieved by providing a **tax allowance**, a stipulated amount of income that is tax free (or taxable at an unusually low rate), which serves to reduce a person's tax liability. Sometimes, however, tax authorities go further and provide **tax credits** – nominal or actual payments to taxpayers. Where tax credits are nominal, they serve to offset tax liabilities, thereby reducing people's tax bills. However, in the case of so-called **refundable tax credits**, tax authorities will pay out money if the value of the tax credits accorded to a person exceeds their tax liabilities. Refundable tax credits are analogous to payment of social assistance.

So far, this discussion of meanings has focused on cash benefits in implicit opposition to the delivery of services. It is now important to make this distinction explicit, although there are complications in doing so. First, benefits are often no longer paid in cash. Instead, they are frequently delivered directly into recipients' bank accounts through automatic credit transfer. In Britain, for example, legislation has recently been introduced to compel banks to create facilities for achieving this. Elsewhere there are examples of electronic benefit transfer 'debit' cards, allowing benefit recipients to use hole-in-the-wall banking technology to draw on their 'benefit account' (Kellard 2003).

Secondly, in some countries benefits are paid **in kind**, that is in the form of goods or services rather than in cash. Perhaps the best-known example of this is the Food Stamps programme available to low-income individuals and families in the USA. Until quite recently, food stamps took the form of vouchers that were issued to recipients after a means test and could be exchanged for food in certain shops. Nowadays it is increasingly the norm for electronic benefit transfer to be used, with shopkeepers 'swiping' the recipient's food stamp card to deduct the purchase amount from the purchaser's food stamp account. In some parts of Britain, too, benefits to meet exceptional needs have been paid in the form of vouchers for such items as cookers and beds that were only exchangeable in certain stores; the intention in this case was to ensure that awards were spent for the purposes requested and that value for money in the purchase of those goods was assured (Walker *et al.* 1992).

Thirdly, in many Nordic and European continental countries, cash social assistance payments have traditionally been delivered as one element in a package of social work services. Whereas in Britain, social workers have sought to avoid further complicating their multiple roles as advocate, counsellor and support worker by the addition of paymaster, their counterparts in Germany and Sweden have embraced the opportunity of working with families in the round and have not infrequently used their control of finance as an instrument to stimulate behavioural change (Minas and Stenberg 2000; Adema *et al.* 2003). Moreover, recent trends from so-called passive benefit regimes to proactive ones that prioritize speedy return to employment – typified by the Mutual Obligation Initiative in Australia (Howard 2003), TANF in the USA (Wiseman 2003a) and the New Deal policies in Britain (Walker and Wiseman 2003a) – are making benefit receipt conditional on participation in services such as job training and work experience (Chapter 10).

Despite these complexities, there is still a useful distinction to be drawn between social security provisions, the principal aim of which is to provide cash and cash-like payments to individuals and families, and social welfare systems that deliver assistance in the form of services.

In this book, therefore, the focus is on policies that aim to deliver cash and quasi-cash payments to individuals and families. The generic definition of social security is taken to include:

• contributory (social insurance) benefits;
• non-contributory cash benefits;
• social assistance (means-tested) benefits; and
• tax credits.

It embraces benefits designed and delivered through the public, private and not-for-profit sectors or any combination of the three. The term social assistance is reserved for means-tested benefits.

To return to wordplay, welfare also has multiple meanings. As noted above, it has long been used in the USA to describe means-tested provision, especially TANF, and has often carried negative connotations with, in recent years, welfare often being contrasted with the positive word 'work' (Weaver 2000). To an American audience *Social Security and Welfare* fairly adequately describes the scope of the policies covered in this book.

Elsewhere in the world, welfare has more often than not been seen as synonymous with well-being or, as in the case of the term *'welfare state'*, with systems run or coordinated by government that are intended to enhance individual and collective well-being. More recently, with UK politics acting as a conduit of American ideas into Europe and political spinners borrowing the advertising industry's love of alliteration, the mantra of 'welfare to work' has entered the policy vocabulary with the risk that the word welfare will come to be devalued (Peck 2001). For the most part, though, policymakers in continental European countries continue to talk of 'activation', rather than 'welfare to work', and of social security and social assistance policies, while bureaucrats in the European Commission talk of 'social protection' (cash benefits and health insurance). Among both these communities the term welfare is used to refer to the socially integrative welfare state that is widely viewed as a defining characteristic of modern European culture.

Among economists, welfare has many further meanings, often of a technical nature (Broadway and Bruce 1984). At heart, however, the concepts that economists grapple with closely mirror the lay conception of well-being and have to do with how such well-being can be measured and maximized. Economists conceptualize **individual welfare** in terms of individuals' preferences as revealed by the choices that they make within a given income and price regime. The presumption is that, given free and informed choice, individuals will choose the bundle of goods and services that maximizes their own utility or satisfaction. **Social welfare** is then taken to be the sum of individual welfare. The economics gets complicated when the choices of individuals are dependent on, and influence, the choices of others; when choices have to be made without information, when price regimes are not fixed and in conditions of uncertainty; when individuals express preferences that do not accord with self-interest or are not readily susceptible to measurement in money terms; and when individuals differ in their pattern of preferences such that, for example, one person's ideal social distribution of resources meets with the disapproval of another. These are, of course, situations that often arise in real life.

Throughout the remainder of this volume, the term **welfare** is used to refer to the goals of social security systems and to measures of the performance of systems, schemes or programmes. Distinctions are made between, first, the welfare or well-being of individuals and families, and increments to that well-being that are attributable to the receipt of social security provision, and secondly, between individual well-being and that of societies as a whole. In the latter case, usage of the term welfare is closely aligned to that of welfare economists, referring to the extent to which maximum social benefit is attained.

Case Study 1.1 Social security in the UK

The social security system reflects the highly centralized, unitary nature of the British state, an electoral system that often provides governments with large majorities (and, hence great power) but for comparatively short periods, and an adversarial political culture in which consensus is often lacking.

The mix of contributory, non-contributory and social assistance benefits is largely delivered through the local offices of a single, national government department (the Department for Work and Pensions), with certain other benefits being administered by local government under tight central regulation. In recent years, a number of benefits have been transformed into refundable tax credits that are delivered by the tax authorities (Inland Revenue) under the direct control of HM (Her Majesty's) Treasury. One deviation from uniform national coverage is the separate administration of social security in Northern Ireland, and the recent creation of a Scottish parliament and a Welsh assembly may bring further change.

Partly a product of history (the origins of British social security can be traced to at least the sixteenth century), the benefit system is very complex, with around 40 separate schemes. While some benefits have proved durable (e.g. industrial injuries benefits), most tend to be frequently changed, a consequence of a succession of governments of different political hues and the ease with which a powerful executive can implement reform. Most benefits are paid in cash rather than in kind (recent work activation policies depart from this pattern) and Britain enjoys a universal, free at the point of use, health system that is administratively separate from social security.

The major area of social security provision not delivered by central government comprises occupational – and, to a lesser extent, private insurance – retirement pensions. At their height in 1967, 53 per cent of the workforce was covered by occupational pensions. This is a legacy of the Beveridge Report that shaped the post World War II social settlement. Beveridge, a Liberal, believed that the state should meet only basic needs (relieving poverty), leaving individuals scope to supplement incomes through personal savings. Social insurance benefits remain low by continental European standards but are enhanced by social assistance additions that make the British system heavily reliant on means testing, a feature characteristic of liberal welfare regimes.

Despite the competence of the Department for Work and Pensions being limited to Great Britain, comparative national statistics are often produced for the UK which is the unit of analysis adopted in this book. Unless otherwise stated, 'Britain' and the 'UK' are used interchangeably to refer to the UK.

Comparison 1.1 Population size and demographic structure, 2002

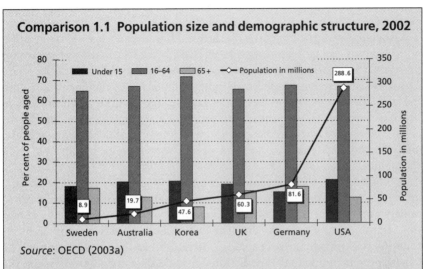

Source: OECD (2003a)

The six case study countries vary markedly in size – the US population of almost 289 million is nearly 29 times that of Sweden. They differ rather less in terms of age composition. One in six people in Germany and Sweden are aged 65 or over and, while South Korea has a comparatively young age profile, the number of elderly people is predicted to increase very rapidly (Comparison 12.3).

The liberation of difference

The wordplay encapsulated in the title *Social Security and Welfare* has revealed the varying meaning carried by words in different countries and contexts. This, in turn, should awaken awareness to the fact that things are done differently in different places.

This diversity of policy has arguably had a stultifying effect on the development of the academic discipline of social policy. It has tended to reinforce the natural inclination to study policy within jurisdiction boundaries and has caused comparative policy studies to be relegated to a sub-discipline. If the career trajectory of social policy graduates is to take them into their own local or national public service, it is seemingly self-evident that they should learn things relevant to that system rather than learning about diversity abroad. So rigid has been this fascination with the local that the discipline of social policy is not widely recognized internationally. The study of social security is largely the preserve of lawyers across much of continental Europe. There is still only one chair of social policy in the whole of Germany, and in the USA social policy is largely taught on public policy programmes in which economics is frequently the dominant perspective.

Associated with the emphasis on the local has been a focus on description with analysis being undertaken from within the normative frameworks prescribed by particular national states. Social policy, including the study of social security, has tended to be interested in the particular rather than the general; that is, it has been ideographic rather than nomothetic and hence not concerned with the identification of general principles, theories or laws. The reverse is true of economics, which may explain why many of the analytic concepts that are applied across jurisdictions are drawn from economics.

In contrast to the ideographic study of social policy, a systematic approach would seek to evolve and apply general principles so as better to understand the operation and effectiveness of policies and systems. Within this framework, the rich diversity of policy objectives and policies found across jurisdictions becomes a virtue rather than a distraction. The experiences in individual jurisdictions provide data for analysis while the diversity of experience furnishes those data with variation that allows hypotheses to be tested and refined, and the different ways of doing things to be compared and evaluated. Under this scenario local and national differences are doubly liberating. First, they allow general principles to be adduced and cumulative learning to take place. Secondly, they draw attention to the fact that there are different and sometimes better ways of attaining particular policy goals. Such liberation is likely to further the international trade in policy ideas that is increasing apace, while drawing attention to the likely limits of direct transfer of policies from one jurisdiction to another (Chapter 13; Rose 2001).

This book is intended as a modest contribution to the systematic approach to social policy and to the analysis of social security, while still being compatible with existing modes of teaching. Its focus is on the exposition of concepts rather than the generation of new knowledge. The organizing principle is that of pluralistic evaluation, which postulates that policies can (and indeed, should) be evaluated with respect to the multiplicity of objectives held (at different times) by various social groups and political actors (Smith and Cantley 1985; Ritchie and Lewis 2003). This perspective encourages the integration of concepts drawn from economics, social policy, sociology and social psychology and facilitates the discussion of issues that have applicability across the frontiers of narrow national debates (Walker 1988).

Case Study 1.2 Social security in the USA

The USA is often considered the archetypal liberal welfare regime and its social security policies are generally consistent with this view. Benefit expenditure is low by international standards – less than half that of Sweden in per capita terms and only two thirds that of the UK – and social insurance was established comparatively late. Insurance was introduced in 1935, under President Roosevelt, to cover for old age, unemployment and blindness and, in 1956, expanded to embrace other forms of disability. Old Age, Survivors and Disability Insurance (OASDI) has grown since 1935 and now covers 96 per cent of all jobs. Medicare is a health insurance scheme for persons aged over 65. It is funded from a payroll tax on current employees, participant contributions and federal general tax revenue.

Social assistance is categorical in form with separate schemes for people lacking resources due to old age or disability (Supplemental Security Income, SSI), families with dependent children (TANF), low-paid workers (Earned Income Tax Credit), certain people with health needs (Medicaid) and individuals at risk of hunger (Food Stamp Program). There is no national assistance programme for childless able-bodied persons of working age (although they can receive food stamps) and, since 1996, federally funded TANF payments have been restricted to a lifetime maximum of 60 months (although states can exempt 20 per cent of their caseloads from this limit and exceed it using their own revenues). Consistent with the strong US work ethic, TANF requires many recipients to participate in 'work activities' which is leading to increased social assistance spending on services.

The federal structure of the USA complicates provision. Whereas OASDI and SSI are primarily federal programmes, TANF is state run, with block grant federal funding covering a variable proportion of the cost. States also have powers to supplement federal provisions – including providing General Assistance for persons ineligible for federal programmes – resulting in considerable geographic variation in the nature and level of provision. Six cabinet-level federal departments, including Health and Human Services, Labor and Agriculture, are engaged in policy and provision, responsibilities are often shared with and between agencies at state level, and service delivery may be undertaken by non-governmental organizations. This pluralism, combined with the shifting balance of power between the president and the legislature, slows policymaking, and programmes have generally proved to be long-lasting. Most recent political debate has concerned 'welfare' – often equated with TANF which is largely received by lone mothers and disproportionately by people of colour. This debate has been vigorous, embracing issues of morality, personal responsibility and individual behaviour.

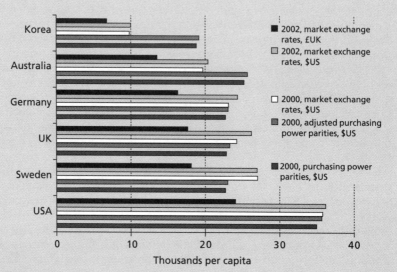

Comparison 1.2 Per capita gross domestic product (GDP)

Legend:
- ■ 2002, market exchange rates, £UK
- ☐ 2002, market exchange rates, $US
- ☐ 2000, market exchange rates, $US
- ▨ 2000, adjusted purchasing power parities, $US
- ■ 2000, purchasing power parities, $US

X-axis: Thousands per capita (0, 10, 20, 30, 40)

Countries: Korea, Australia, Germany, UK, Sweden, USA

Source: OECD (2003a) and DoL (2003)

Per capita gross domestic product (GDP) – economic production divided by population size – provides a measure of a country's income. The chart makes comparisons in two years, 2000 and 2002. For the latter year, the amounts for each country are converted into US dollars and pounds sterling using market exchange rates to facilitate comparison. On this basis, Sweden, the UK and Germany have quite similar levels of income ($27k, $26.2k and $24.4k respectively). Australia has a little less ($20.3k), Korea a lot less ($10k) and the USA a lot more ($36.2k).

For year 2000 it is possible to take account of differences in the cost of living between countries using purchasing power parities. Because these figures are based on different sources, a correction factor has to be incorporated in the analysis. Comparing per capita GDP for 2000 converted using market exchange rates with that converted using adjusted purchasing power parities indicates differences due solely to the choice of conversion factor. Taking account of living costs in this way reveals that Australians ($25.7) enjoy a higher standard of living than the wealthiest Europeans ($23.3k for the UK) and that Koreans are not that far behind ($19.2). The figures using purchasing power parities published by the US Department of Labor (the bottom bars in the chart) confirm this even though based on different data.

The importance of context

A systematic approach to the analysis of social security does not deny the importance of local institutions and political and social context. Rather, social security benefits are viewed as the administratively shaped response to socially agreed objectives that are themselves the politically mediated outcome of ideological and class struggles in reaction to socially recognized risks and problems. A systematic analysis of benefit provisions and their effectiveness would therefore necessarily entail much more than a passing acquaintance with the economic, social and political institutions that both characterize and help to define the jurisdiction or jurisdictions under study. It is for this reason that most of the case studies and examples presented in this book are drawn from just six countries: Australia, Germany, Sweden, South Korea, the UK and the USA. In this way it is hoped that the reader will acquire at least sufficient contextual understanding to judge the validity and robustness of the distinctions being drawn. However, readers are urged to extend their knowledge by reference to the articles and books included in the sections on further reading.

The choice of countries is informed by the prevailing wisdom concerning welfare regimes. Welfare regimes refer to the different ways in which countries – or jurisdictions – organize economic production and transfers within the context of a capitalist market economy. Regimes are characterized by sets of collective values, aims, institutions and policies that are combined in integrative and distinctive ways and that shape political responses to change. The theory is that countries adopting the same regime are in many respects of substance more similar to each other than to countries or jurisdictions following different regimes. Moreover, while regimes are not static, their evolutionary path is much dependent on prior policy choices and existing institutions. Consequently, countries belonging to one regime type are likely to act similarly in response to change and perhaps differently from countries with other kinds of welfare regime.

There is considerable agreement that at least three distinctive welfare regimes can be identified (Figure 1.1). Esping-Andersen (1990) has called these the *liberal, social democratic* and *corporatist* or, latterly (Esping-Andersen 1999), *conservative welfare regimes* respectively, while Titmuss (1974) labelled essentially the same groupings as the 'residual', 'institutional redistributive' and 'industrial achievement' models of social policy (Goodin *et al.* 1999). There is much less agreement as to how many other meaningfully distinct regime types there are, and some dissent as to whether the concept has empirical validity in addition to its heuristic value (Arts and Gelissen 2002).

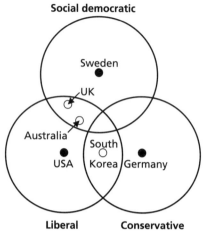

Figure 1.1 Welfare regimes and countries

Table 1.1 summarizes the dimensions along which regimes have been defined and the features that characterize the three prototypical regimes. Figure 1.1 reveals that the USA, Sweden and Germany, three countries featured in this volume, are respectively model examples of the liberal, social democratic and conservative regimes.

Table 1.1 Characterizing welfare regimes

	Liberal	*Social democratic*	*Conservative*
Role of:			
Family	Marginal	Marginal	Central
Market	Central	Marginal	Marginal
State	Marginal	Central	Subsidiary
Welfare state:			
Dominant mode of solidarity	Individual	Universal	Kinship Corporatism Etatism
Dominant locus of solidarity	Market	State	Family
Degree of decommodification	Minimal	Maximum	High (for breadwinners)
Characterization	Residual	Universalist	Social insurance

Adapted from Esping-Andersen (1999)

Liberal welfare regimes

Liberal regimes are individualistic, giving pride of place to the concept of liberty, often defined as freedom from interference by other human agents, notably the state. Liberal economic ideals value highly the role of the free market and only reluctantly sanction regulation to reduce market imperfections. It follows that resource allocation is largely left to the market not least because liberal economic theory suggests that this generally rewards individuals in terms of their marginal contribution to social welfare. Where individuals fail to thrive economically because of market imperfections, these are likely to be tackled at source, for example through macroeconomic policies to enhance labour demand. If people are unwilling to make an economic contribution this is treated as a matter of choice, but alternative provision is only made available when individuals are genuinely unable to contribute for reasons beyond their control. Wherever possible, collective welfare is provided through the market and where not, the residual provision is limited to a few approved risks, tightly regulated and targeted so as to exclude 'undeserving' claims and to prevent undue reliance on state funds. Priority is given to measures that offer relief from poverty rather than maintain incomes, foster social solidarity or promote equality.

Social democratic welfare regimes

Historically and ideologically, social democratic regimes were born out of opposition to liberal policies and prioritize the concept of equality above that of freedom. In its purist form, the objective is to seek and exploit political equality in order to achieve economic and social equality in the form of a classless society. More pragmatically, goals of equality may be expressed in terms of **social citizenship** – the ability to fully participate – or reduced to the concept of equal opportunity rather than equality of outcome. A central tenet of social democratic regimes is that equality, however defined, cannot be achieved with an unfettered market and that the role of the state, in regulating the market and promoting social welfare, is paramount.

Social democratic mechanisms for attaining these goals are the maintenance of full employment, universalistic provision and the marginalization of assistance based on the assessment of financial need. The state seeks to guarantee that men and women are able and motivated to work, willingly providing employment within the public sector and childcare to help attain desired outcomes. Welfare provision is generous, comprehensive in the risks covered, universal and uniform with flat-rate benefits. Private provision, on the other hand, is actively discouraged with services that elsewhere are bought and sold in the market place being **'decommodified'** –

that is, allocated and often delivered by the state rather than the market. As an intention and a result, receipt of a public service or benefit becomes both a right and a badge of citizenship, a statement of equal worth and solidarity. Redistribution of income from richer individuals to the less well off is achieved through the tax system (the redistributive potential of the benefit system is weakened by universal flat-rate provision) and a virtual circle is created in which high public expenditure and employment can be sustained by high taxes progressively levied on a large labour force.

Conservative welfare regimes

The origins of conservative or corporatist regimes can be traced to the patterns of reciprocity established in feudal times, to **etatism** – the attempt by nineteenth-century European monarchs to foster national allegiance as a bulwark against socialist ideas – and to the social teachings of Roman Catholicism, perhaps most notably the Papal Encyclical *Rerum Novarum* in 1891.

A central value is **social cohesion**, a stable, national collective defined around a nested hierarchy of social groups, with the family at the bottom and the nation state at the top. The principal collective response mechanism is that of **risk pooling**, sharing the cost of responding to the occurrence of a contingency between group members based on the principle of **subsidiarity**, with responsibility for pooling being allocated to the lowest group in the hierarchy that is capable of bearing the risk in question. When the family cannot cope, social protection is typically organized by occupational group, guild or industrial sector and is based on social insurance principles or, in the case of people excluded from these structures, by local communities administering social assistance. Often the degree of decommodification is great but support for the family was historically provided first to the breadwinner, the male in patriarchal societies. The female homemaker was initially to be supported through informal contacts with the local community and was only latterly awarded corporate protection via her dependent status on her employed husband.

With the corporate structures substituting as necessary for the patriarchal family, the role of the state is that of promoting the welfare of its citizens through regulation and, where appropriate, facilitation. This is evident in the underwriting and financial support of social insurance schemes and in tripartite management of the economy, together with representatives of employers and employees. The goal of such management is not primarily the promotion of competition, as it is under a liberal regime, but negotiated compromise and collaboration for the common good. Tripartite wage bargaining is the archetypal example of this corporatist activity, but it extends to collective workforce training, labour force reduction to stem unemployment and, indeed, to virtually all aspects of economic and social management.

Additional welfare regimes

Various authors have suggested adding additional regimes to the basic three. Leibfried (1992), Ferrera (1996) and others propose that Mediterranean countries constitute a fourth regime characterized by very marginal social assistance and the perverted use of benefits and employment to solicit and retain political power. The former feature, which – with the encouragement of the European Commission – is becoming less marked, is arguably a manifestation of the reliance on the family[1] that characterizes conservative regimes, while the latter is merely a rather extreme example of electoral practices common elsewhere (see Chapter 2).

A more persuasive case can be made for an Antipodean welfare regime, although the differences between Australia and New Zealand are large and have been increasing as New Zealand has moved more quickly towards a predominantly liberal regime (Castles 1996). However, Australia arguably still differs from the classic liberal regime. Although its social security system relies almost exclusively on social assistance, the income threshold is so high as to be considered inclusive rather than stigmatizing. Moreover, despite erosion of the wage arbitration system, enough remains of its egalitarian objectives to argue that the labour market is itself a producer of welfare. This, combined with rights-based access to medical treatment and a redistributive benefit system, means that the Australian welfare system fosters social cohesion by promoting equity above equality, treating everybody the same by applying means testing almost universally. In doing this, Australia is virtually unique and serves as a rich source of alternative policy strategies. It is for this reason that Australia features in this book.

Finally, there are the countries of South East Asia that were once called the 'tiger economies'. These tend to blend elements of liberal and conservative regimes and are characterized by commitments to full employment, regulated labour markets and comparatively restricted income distributions. Paternalistic employment practices are facilitated by authoritarian and often nationalistic political regimes with Confucianism frequently substituting for Catholicism as the source of support for, and reliance on, the family as the foundation of social welfare outside the labour market. Esping-Andersen (1999) recognizes that the welfare systems of these countries do not fit easily into any of the three basic regime types, but is reluctant to exchange

---

1 Esping-Andersen (1999) demonstrates empirically, albeit on a comparatively limited test, that Mediterranean countries do not differ significantly from other continental European countries in terms of either the benefits and services directed to families, or the welfare burden they are expected to deliver.

parsimony for greater precision of description. However, as with Australia, the hybrid nature of welfare systems in South Asia means that they are a rich source of policy case studies and so the Republic of Korea is featured in this volume (hereafter referred to as South Korea or Korea).

It is important not to become too intellectually attached to the regimes discussed above. They are simplified models of a complex reality. Differences between countries within the same regime can be significant and **path dependency**, the propensity for regimes to be self-perpetuating as values and institutions limit policy choices, is not immutable. Britain, for example, which today is best characterized as a liberal regime more clearly belonged to the social democratic model in the 1950s (Esping-Andersen 1999).

What is important is that context matters in the systematic analysis of social security. While the concepts introduced in this volume have universal applicability, their use and interpretation have to take cognizance of, and be sensitively attuned to, the complex matrix of values and institutions that characterize individual jurisdictions and for which the term 'welfare regime' is convenient shorthand.

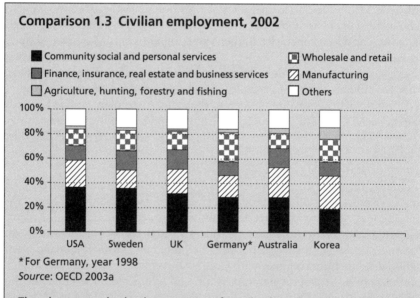

Comparison 1.3 Civilian employment, 2002

Legend:
- Community social and personal services
- Finance, insurance, real estate and business services
- Agriculture, hunting, forestry and fishing
- Wholesale and retail
- Manufacturing
- Others

Countries (x-axis): USA, Sweden, UK, Germany*, Australia, Korea

*For Germany, year 1998
Source: OECD 2003a

The chart reveals the importance of service-based employment to all six countries. The USA, Australia, the UK and Sweden all have around 70 per cent of people employed in wholesale and retail sectors and in community and financial services. Germany and Korea have the largest manufacturing sectors while almost one in ten Koreans is still employed in agriculture or fishing.

Closing summary

This book is about social security, cash and quasi-cash payments organized collectively by governments, private companies and not-for-profit organizations, and about social welfare, a generic goal of social security policies. Unlike many books on social security, it is not primarily a descriptive account of provision; instead, it introduces concepts that may be used creatively to assess the extent to which social security systems are contributing positively to social welfare.

Providing a kitbag of concepts and analytic techniques rather than facts, the intention is that the book should be more valuable to the reader as a source of transferable and testable ideas and less bounded than others in both jurisdiction and time. Hopefully, it should also be more valuable to the reader as a source of transferable and testable ideas and less susceptible than the author to the ageing process.

Nonetheless, analysis cannot be divorced from either context or social values; both constitute objects of study for social security analysts. Moreover, however objective the analyst, context and values help to inform the objectives and mode of analysis, and influence the attitudes and opinions of author and reader alike. Therefore, case studies and international comparisons accompany the discussion of ideas to encourage the reader to reflect on how concepts can be employed better to understand the many worlds of social security provision.

Further reading

McKay and Rowlingson (1999) introduce some of the basic social security terminology, albeit from a largely British perspective, while Arts and Gelissen (2002) review and stimulate thinking about regime theory.

Descriptions of the social security systems of over 170 countries can be found on the social security worldwide database maintained by the International Social Security Association. The database is accessible, at a charge, in English at: http//:www-ssw.issa.int/sswen. Broadly the same information is also available free of charge via the US Social Security Administration (SSA) on: http://www.ssa.gov/policy/docs/progdesc/ssptw/

More detailed descriptions of the social security systems of member states of the European Union were published annually until 2001 by the European Commission, being derived from the Mutual Information System on Social Protection (MISSOC) with the title *Social Protection in the EU Member States and the European Economic Area*. The 2001 report is available at: http://europa.eu.int/comm/employment_social/missoc2001/index_en.htm

Very useful statistical and other information relating to social security provision in the six study countries can be found at the following government websites that can be accessed directly or via a portal on the US Department of Labor website: http://www.bls.gov/bls/other.htm#International

- *Australia*: http://www.abs.gov.au
- *Germany*: http://www.destatis.de/e_home.htm
- *South Korea*: http://www.nso.go.kr
- *Sweden*: http://www.scb.se
- *UK*: http://www.statistics.gov.uk/
- *USA*: http://www.bls.gov

National social security departments also usually have helpful websites.

chapter
two

Aims and Objectives

This chapter is about ambitions. The remainder of the book is about establishing whether such ambitions are realized.

It is also a chapter about distinctions. There are important distinctions to be drawn between social security systems and social security schemes, between system aims and policy objectives, between different kinds of aim and objective and between aims, objectives and functions. Each distinction is tackled in turn before asking the question 'Whose aims and objectives are they anyway?'.

Systems and schemes

The first distinction is between single social security schemes, programmes or benefits and entire, jurisdiction-wide systems of social security provision. Within any given jurisdiction, the **social security system** is defined as the full set of social security provisions operative within that jurisdiction. The discussion of welfare regimes in Chapter 1 was conducted at the level of systems. Occasionally reference is made to social assistance systems; by analogy a social assistance system comprises all means-tested provisions within a given jurisdiction.

If social security systems are comprised of individual schemes or programmes, what constitutes a scheme or programme? Unfortunately this apparently simple question has no simple answer. There is not even a universally accepted term to describe what is to be defined: a 'social security scheme', a 'benefit', a 'benefit scheme', a 'benefit programme' or (in the USA) a 'program' or even a 'policy' are all used by different authors in different contexts to describe the same thing.

In an ideal uncomplicated world, a social security scheme would have a unique name, a clearly articulated objective or a prioritized set of objectives, a specific target group – the eligible population – with well-defined eligibility criteria to determine who falls within the target group, and a set of entitlement rules that specify the amount of benefit to which eligible claimants are entitled. It would also have an administrative organization dedicated to the promotion and delivery of benefit, a transparent and coherent funding mechanism, and a structure of political accountability for the design, implementation, monitoring and funding of the scheme. In reality, this is frequently not the case.

In Britain, for example, Jobseeker's Allowance comprises two fundamentally different benefits that can in certain circumstances be paid simultaneously to the same individual. One component is a contributory benefit paid out to unemployed persons based on social security contributions that they have previously made. It is ostensibly funded from the UK National Insurance Fund and serves partially to replace income lost due to unemployment. No account is taken of children or adult dependants that the claimant might have. The other component (income-based Jobseeker's Allowance) is funded from direct taxation and is a form of social assistance benefit (and hence means tested) that seeks to relieve or prevent poverty arising from unemployment. Both kinds of benefit are payable when contributory Jobseeker's Allowance is insufficient to lift the claimant household above the income threshold for receipt of social assistance. In such circumstances, the claimant receives a single payment comprising both components of Jobseeker's Allowance. Moreover, before 2001, different ministers in separate government departments were politically accountable for each of the two components of benefit. Since 2003, recipients of the income-based component with dependent children also receive a separate refundable tax credit (Child Tax Credit) administered through the tax system (Inland Revenue) to cover child costs, an item previously met through income-based Jobseeker's Allowance.

A second example of the complexity of real-world social security provision is taken from Germany. Common legislation provides two forms of unemployment benefit: *Arbeitslosenversicherung* and *Arbeitslosenhilfe*. Both are administered through the same administrative structure comprising the Federal Labour Institute (*Bundesanstalt für Abreit*), the labour offices of the regions or *Länder* (*Landerarbeitsämter*) and local labour offices. *Arbeitslosenversicherung* is financed by contributions from employers and employees, with any deficits underwritten by the federal government. Payment of *Arbeitslosenversicherung* lasts for up to three years, after which a person moves to *Arbeitslosenhilfe*, which is means tested and financed from federal taxation.

Such complexity makes the consistent use of terms difficult. The convention adopted throughout the remainder of this book is to use the term 'benefit' or 'tax credit' to refer to the lowest-level, discrete component within hierarchies of benefit provision. The terms **benefit scheme** or **tax credit scheme** are used to describe groups of benefits or tax credits that are administered together under a common rubric. Very often a scheme will have a specific name deriving from legislation or common usage. 'Policies' is the collective term used for both schemes and benefits. Under these conventions, Jobseeker's Allowance and Child Tax Credit are schemes, contributory and income-based Jobseeker's Allowance are benefits; *Arbeitslosenversicherung* and *Arbeitslosenhilfe* together count as a scheme, but individually are benefits. A social security *system*, as already defined, describes all the social security schemes, benefits and tax credits operative within a single jurisdiction.

System aims, policy objectives and functions

Aims and objectives both have to do with purpose. **Aims** are the purposes ascribed to a social security system. Policy **objectives** are the counterpart of aims but apply to individual benefits, tax credits and schemes. **Functions**, which can relate to systems or policies (schemes, benefits and tax credits), have to do with outcomes, whether intentional or unintentional.

Aims

System aims were mentioned during the discussion of welfare regimes in Chapter 1. Indeed, the fact that certain countries appear to prioritize some of the same aims and others different ones gave rise to the notion of regimes, while the sharing of aims is used as one criterion by which countries are empirically grouped together into regime types. However, one of the reasons why regime types are contested is that aims are rarely explicitly stated, sometimes appear to be mutually incompatible and change over time.

System aims are the embodiment of political intent and provide the ongoing rationale for social security provision. They reflect, but also help to shape, the collective identities of nations and jurisdictions. As such, they represent the evolving endpoint of a political process that involves clashes of values and ideas, and conflicts between various vested interests and power groups. Their origins can be traced by historians while their continued existence is deduced from analysis of the language and content of current political debate, perhaps supported by opinion polling. Explicit statements are usually available only at times when reform is proposed or in the preamble to legislative change. In these circumstances, aims, often derived from earlier statements propounded in the context of previous reform, are restated either to show that the changes proposed are consistent with the aims or that circumstances are such that the aims themselves need to be changed or reformulated.

A couple of examples will suffice taken from Britain and Australia. The 1942 Beveridge Report encapsulated the aims of the post World War II welfare state in Britain in almost poetic language: the need was to slay the five giants of want, disease, ignorance, squalor and idleness (unemployment) on the road to reconstruction (Cmnd. 1942). Transformed by time and experience, this vision translates into the more prosaic language of the current aims of the Department for Work and Pensions (Cm. 2003: 133–4):

1 Ensure the best start for all children and end child poverty in 20 years.
2 Promote work as the best form of welfare for people of working age, while protecting the position of those in greatest need.
3 Combat poverty and promote security and independence in retirement for today's and tomorrow's pensioners.
4 Improve rights and opportunities for disabled people in a fair and inclusive society.

A second example is provided by the recent review of Australian social security provision for people of working age which resulted in the '*Australians Working Together*' reform package, announced in the 2001/2 budget. The review report (RGWF 2000: 4) specified the following 'three key aims':

1 A significant reduction in the incidence of jobless families and jobless households.
2 A significant reduction in the proportion of the working age population that needs to rely heavily on income support.
3 Stronger communities that generate more opportunities for social and economic participation.

System aims, therefore, are revealed most authoratively in official statements. But they are more than mere statements of political intent. While system aims are not uncontested, they nevertheless articulate principles that in a democracy command the support, or at least the passive consent, of a large portion of the electorate. They help to establish the paradigm within which policy development takes place and that, in turn, provides the *raison d'être* for benefit and tax credit schemes and shapes their objectives.

Objectives

Policy objectives are generally easier to identify and specify than system aims. This is partly because they are associated with particular schemes and benefits and so are often less nebulous. Policy objectives will almost certainly be specified in legislation or in the policy statements or interpretative guides that may accompany it. They are also frequently included in a more popular form in publicity material and on application forms. However, as will be explained in a later section, certain kinds of objective are less likely to be widely publicized even though they may be equally significant to the designers of the policy.

Objectives are set by policymakers and are not collectively owned in the way that system aims generally are. More so than system aims, policy objectives are statements of political aspiration and intent and are subject to the vagaries of ideological fashion and the ramifications of political infighting. They establish the rationale for benefit or tax credit schemes and, very importantly, provide the criteria against which performance can be assessed. Even so, objectives are seldom specified with the precision desired by policy evaluators. The latter would insist that objectives be formulated in a way that facilitated performance measurement, meaning that both the nature and the degree of change to count as success would need to be specified, preferably in numerical form, in advance of implementation. In reality this is rarely the case.

Objectives are typically expressed as aspirations rather than numerical targets (so-called performance objectives), although there are exceptions. In Britain, the New Deal for Young People, a work activation programme linked to benefit receipt, was introduced in 1997 with the explicit objective of moving 250,000 young unemployed people off benefit and into work. Similarly, the Swedish government set the objective of halving the numbers receiving social assistance between 1999 and 2004 (Eklind and Löfbom 2002). The objectives set for the main US social assistance scheme, TANF, are more typical, although indirect mention is made of numerical targets:

1 Provide assistance to needy families so that children may be cared for in their own homes or in the homes of relatives.
2 End the dependence of needy families on government benefits by promoting job preparation, work and marriage.
3 Prevent and reduce the incidence of out-of-wedlock pregnancies and establish annual numerical goals for preventing and reducing the incidence of these pregnancies.
4 Encourage the formation and maintenance of two-person families. (WMCP 2000)

In order to assess the performance of policy against stated objectives it is invariably necessary to look beyond the primary legislation to find more precise information from which to assemble evaluative criteria that facilitate measurement. An often fruitful source is the assumptions made by governments when attempting to forecast the cost of new policies which frequently contain projections of caseload and per capita benefit cost.

However, it is important to bear in mind that policies seldom have a single objective and to recognize that the priority given to specific objectives may evolve over time in a way that is not explicitly recognized.

Case Study 2.1 Social security in Sweden

Sweden is a constitutional monarchy with considerable power vested in local government, comprised of some 20 counties and 289 municipalities; together they raise 46 per cent of total taxation (compared with about 5 per cent in Britain and 13 per cent in Germany). Counties have responsibility for regional economic development and healthcare, but generally have no authority over municipalities that are largely responsible, among other functions, for the funding and delivery of social assistance. Social insurance is a national responsibility, split between unemployment insurance, administered by the trade unions under the supervision of the National Labour Market Board (*Arbetsmarknadsstyrelsen*), and other social insurance provided by the National Social Insurance Board (*Riksförsäkringsverket*) through about 330 local offices.

Until recently, Swedish social security had enjoyed considerable stability due to popular support and the dominance of the Social Democratic Party that has been in power, with the exception of two brief interludes, since 1932. However, the origins of Swedish social security extend back to at least 1913 when the world's first universal old age pension scheme was introduced. The system of provision expanded in coverage and generosity, especially during the period from the 1940s until the early 1990s, largely based on social insurance principles. In 1996, Sweden devoted 35 per cent of its GDP to social protection and, although this had fallen to 32 per cent by 2000, Sweden still spends more on social welfare than any other country in Europe (Eurostat 2003). Social insurance is mainly funded by employer contributions.

Swedish welfare has long been based on a high employment–high benefits model. High levels of both employment and economic participation serve to provide a large tax base as well as industrial production. Active labour market policy – the so-called Rehn-Meider model developed in the 1950s – limits unemployment and facilitates structural change. Universal public services and comprehensive benefits contribute to social well-being but also provide employment and, in the case of benefits such as parental insurance and child allowances and services like good-quality childcare, serve to enhance labour supply. As the early use of activation policies implies, conditionality has always been a strong component in the Swedish model and is evident in the local delivery of social assistance (*socialbidrag*) through social work offices (Hort 2001).

Recession in the early 1990s, combined with a brief spell under a Conservative government, resulted in significant changes to the Swedish social security but not to fundamental restructuring. Eligibility criteria have been made more restrictive and replacement ratios have been reduced. The most substantial change was the introduction of a new old-age pension system in January 2001. In essence, although to oversimplify, this added to a reduced flat-rate pension and a pay-as-you-go earnings-related pension, a fully funded component (*premiereservsystem*) and increased the contribution to the total cost made by employees.

A British example serves to illustrate this point. Family Credit, an in-work, means-tested benefit available to workers with dependent children, was introduced in 1988 to increase the financial incentive for unemployed people to return to work and to reduce the number of people reliant on out of work benefits. In its first months it served mainly as a transitional benefit with most people ceasing to claim benefit after 12 or 18 months. Over time the number of people receiving benefits for longer periods accumulated in the caseload and the benefit increasingly began to function primarily as a form of long-term wage support or subsidy (Walker 1993). When this was recognized, the benefit was increasingly presented principally as a measure that served to support a flexible, competitive labour market (Walker and Wiseman 1997). Furthermore, in 1998 when the scheme was adapted and re-badged as Working Families Tax Credit (WFTC) by a new Labour government, it was promoted as a measure to address child poverty and social exclusion (HM Treasury 1998).

While the objectives of social security schemes are often easier to identify than system aims, they may still be complex and defy simple measurement. They are also likely to change more rapidly than aims.

Functions

Whereas aims and objectives are statements of intent, functions are defined outside the political process and have to do with outcomes irrespective of the stated policy objective or system aim. A function is an analytic concept concerned with the change brought about by a policy or an entire system. The change may relate to the behaviour or well-being of the recipient individual or family, or to the consequences of the policy or system for the society or jurisdiction as a whole. Whereas aims and objectives are always desirable, at least for those who promote the policy, functions can be both positive and negative. Aims and objectives are finite and typically modest in number. Functions are limited only by intellectual capacity and the paucity of theory and evidence.

There is sometimes an apparent coincidence between aims and objectives on the one hand and functions on the other. An example is when the objective of a benefit scheme is to relieve poverty and the scheme can be shown to be providing relief from poverty. In this case, the scheme is attaining its objective by functioning to relieve poverty. However, if the scheme were to prove unsuccessful, the objective or intent would remain the same, even though the scheme did not function to provide relief from poverty. Moreover, the same scheme could function in many other ways. It might reduce work incentives, enforce social control and/or exacerbate social exclusion, none of which may have been intended, desired or predicted by the designers of the scheme. The different functions of social security are discussed in Chapter 3.

To summarize, aims relate to social security systems, objectives to benefit schemes and functions to both. Aims and objectives are intentions (or sometimes mere aspirations) which are forged through the political process and established prior to the implementation of policy, although they may sometimes be modified thereafter. Functions are determined on the basis of evidence concerning the outcomes of policy once it has been implemented.

Comparison 2.1 Social security spending as a percentage of GDP

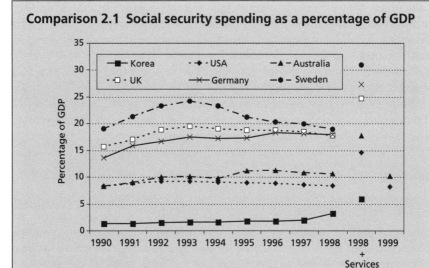

Source: OECD (2003b)

Social security spending on cash benefits is highest in the European countries and lowest in South Korea.

The trends represent the combined effects of changes in social security spending and in GDP (national income). Increased per capita spending in the early 1990s reflects economic recession (as is also true of the increase in South Korea between 1997 and 1998). Falls in per capita spending in Sweden after 1993 are due to increased economic growth but also austerity measures implemented by a Liberal-led coalition government.

For 1998, the graph compares spending on cash benefits with a total that includes spending in kind, notably on health insurance. Expenditure is markedly greater in each case but the rank order of countries does not change, except for Britain and Germany. Health insurance (and other services) constitute a bigger proportion of the total in Germany than in Britain).

Examples of aims

Discussion of regimes in the last chapter partly revolved around the priority given to the alleviation of poverty, redistribution of income and fostering social cohesion as aims of welfare state provision. They warrant a slightly fuller examination here as aims of social security systems. Promotion of economic efficiency, protection against risk, compensation and behavioural change are other aims that deserve mention.

It is important to acknowledge first that mature social security systems are characterized by multiple aims, and secondly that policy measures established in pursuit of one aim may effect other changes as well. In so far as social security systems differ in their aims, the differences are typically ones of emphasis – the priority given to one aim rather than another. Even then, differences may only be matters of degree.

The secondary impacts of policy measures are often profoundly important. It is difficult, for example, to conceive of any set of policies that succeed in alleviating poverty that do not result in (or result from) some redistribution of income or assets. Such secondary consequences may be recognized and promoted as subsidiary aims. If not, they are best considered to be functions of a system.

Alleviation of poverty

Modern social assistance systems and some social security systems have their origins in the aim of alleviating poverty. Before the Reformation the dispensation of charity to the poor was often in the hands of the church in Christian cultures and remains the responsibility of religious authorities in some Islamic societies (Jawad 2002). Responsibility shifted first to local communities and then to national authorities, although in many countries the administration of social assistance remains with local jurisdictions (Eardley *et al.* 1996; Bolderson and Mabbett 1997). An early secular codification of society's responsibility for the poor is available in the English Poor Law of 1601. This instigated a poor rate (or tax) levied on property owners, the proceedings from which were then allocated to the poor by local 'overseers'. Able-bodied poor people were expected to work in return for subsistence and shelter provided in a Poor Law workhouse. Over time, the practice of **outdoor relief**, cash payments to people living outside the workhouse, became increasingly important and survived despite attempts to abolish it in the 1834 Poor Law Amendment Act. The current UK Social Security Advisory Committee is the direct descendant of the Poor Law commissioners (Donnison 1982).

Poor Law principles were exported throughout large parts of the British Empire and matured into modern social assistance schemes. Similar schemes evolved throughout Europe, although they often mixed cash payments with a greater emphasis on service provisions, in some cases leaving a larger role for charitable, frequently church-based, organizations to make supplementary cash donations. In modern regimes, social assistance systems both establish a *de facto* poverty line or minimum standard of living and provide the mechanism through which individuals and their families can enjoy the right to such a standard based on citizenship or residence.[1]

Over time, the relief of poverty has been supplanted by other more socially ambitious aims in many economically developed countries, with social security schemes providing benefit levels much above the poverty threshold established by social assistance. Indeed, in most modern regimes the aim of poverty relief, as opposed to poverty prevention, has been relegated to the status of an objective of residual social assistance schemes and is explicitly addressed by the state almost exclusively via this policy mechanism. (Domestic charities often continue to complement social assistance schemes by providing poverty relief.) In Britain, though, some social security and non-contributory benefits are set at levels below the social assistance threshold, which means that they have routinely to be supplemented by social assistance payments. Many British families are therefore supported at the *de facto* poverty threshold by a combination of social security and social assistance schemes (Walker with Howard 2000).

Although societies have successfully reduced the need to prioritize poverty relief, it remains an objective of social assistance schemes as the minimum, socially acceptable response to economic need (Chapter 7). Structures of social assistance are often the first forms of social security to be put in place and are being actively promoted by international organizations in increasingly coordinated attempts to tackle poverty on a global scale (Chapter 13). Likewise, in another context, the unanticipated collapse of the Korean economy in the late 1990s precipitated the rapid development of a social assistance scheme. Moreover, social assistance systems have proved remarkably robust in the face of financial pressure and fiscal constraint. The USA is probably the only country to revoke the right to such protection (by, in 1996, imposing limits on the time for which TANF could be received).

Income maintenance and replacement

A more ambitious aim than poverty relief is that of maintaining income in the event of prescribed contingencies. Income lost due to a contingency such as disability or unemployment is replaced with social security payments. The reference point to which benefit levels relate is not a

---

1   This general principle does not apply in Australia. There, most schemes are means tested, but because different means tests apply to different schemes which pay out benefits of varying generosity, no single minimum standard is established.

socially defined minimum but the standard of living that the social security recipient formerly enjoyed. Benefits with income maintenance as an objective are typically **earnings-related** – that is, levels of payment are fixed as a proportion of former earnings.

Income maintenance is an objective that is frequently though not universally associated with insurance schemes in jurisdictions characterized by conservative regimes. This reflects the fact that the objective is consistent with other welfare goals discussed below, notably the promotion of social inclusion and, to a lesser extent, the sharing of risk. However, setting benefits in relation to prior living standards lessens the redistributive impact of social security provision.

Promoting social cohesion

A feature of many social security systems in continental Europe is the emphasis given to fostering social cohesion. The systems bind diverse sociodemographic groups together in a web of mutual support and obligations that helps to define the nature of citizenship, nationhood and national culture.

Germany is the classic case and provides a good example of the role of etatism, discussed in Chapter 1, in the birth of social security provisions (Mommsen 1981). To simplify a complex history, Bismarck in the late nineteenth century used three tools to unify Germany: an imperialistic foreign policy; tariffs and economic support to protect agricultural interests and to promote industrial growth; and social security to provide the emergent working class with protection against the risks of industrialization. Bismarck also believed that providing economic protection to the working class in the name of the Kaiser would protect the state against the destructive forces of socialism. Social insurance schemes covering sickness (introduced in 1883), accident (1884) and old age and invalidity (1889) created a fabric of integration and mutual solidarity within the workplace and across industries. This '*Soldaten der Arbeit*' survived even the Third Reich and remains a cornerstone of German social security. Benefits that replace or maintain incomes, rather than simply protect against poverty in the event of job loss or ill health, also help to create common interests across different income groups and classes.

A common characteristic of systems that prioritize social cohesion is **universalism** – that is, schemes are universally available to anybody in prescribed circumstances irrespective of their particular characteristics such as social position or income. This contrasts with systems that seek primarily to relieve poverty in that these are often **selective**, providing benefits only to people in or at risk of poverty. Even under universal systems not everyone necessarily gains directly from social security since not all persons will need to claim benefit. Contributions to the cost are therefore often compulsory.

Protection against risk

The social insurance systems established in nineteenth-century Germany were based on the premise that the process of industrialization had placed virtually everybody at economic risk and that insurance brought individual and collective security. This pooling of risk is often an important aim of social security systems although, as will be discussed in Chapter 5, there are various mechanisms by which this can be achieved.

However, risk is rarely equally shared. The unskilled are much more at risk of unemployment than the highly educated, while poor people are generally at greater risk of dying young than the more affluent. This can limit the degree of social solidarity that it is possible to achieve because those who are least at risk have least to gain through insurance. Nevertheless, the advance of the welfare state has in many countries been marked by the gradual expansion of collective schemes, with rights being extended from workers to their dependants and the merging of generous schemes for civil servants and the middle class with provisions originally implemented to benefit the working class. France is one country where the fragmentation of social security provisions is still evident, with separate schemes for different industries and types of worker clearly illustrating the boundaries of *solidarité* in French society (Hantrais 1996). Likewise, similar differentiations are present in the much younger Korean old-age pension system with separate, generally superior, schemes for public sector employees, private schoolteachers and military personnel.

Redistribution

As previously noted, redistribution is a necessary consequence or function of social security. Nevertheless, it is quite often also explicitly stated as an aim, usually in the context of achieving greater social justice.

Vertical redistribution entails transferring income between different income groups. **Positive vertical redistribution** is achieved if income is transferred from the rich to the poor in the fashion of Robin Hood and is most closely identified with social democratic regimes. Until the Swedish insurance system was reformed in 1999, pensioners received a standard flat rate benefit even though contributions were fixed as a percentage of earnings (up to a fixed maximum), thereby ensuring that formerly low-waged workers received a higher return than their higher paid counterparts. The Australian system of universal means-tested pensions funded from general taxation also results in considerable positive redistribution.

Horizontal redistribution is the transfer of resources to people who have high demands on their budgets irrespective of their incomes. A classic example is Britain's Child Benefit, which is paid to all families if they have dependent children, but horizontal redistribution is an aim more typical of systems in conservative regimes in which the family is supported financially as the principal agent of social welfare.

Case Study 2.2 Social security in Germany

The German welfare state is built on social insurance principles that can be traced to accident funds established by miners in the Middle Ages. Laws were enacted in 1883, 1884 and 1889, as part of Bismarck's creation of modern Germany, which introduced compulsory insurance for workers (and some salaried employees) to cover health, accident and pensions. These measures remain the nucleus of the German social security system. Coverage was extended to most salaried workers in 1911, when provisions were also added with respect to old age, invalidity, widows and orphans. Insurance was introduced to cover unemployment in 1927 and long-term care in 1995. The continuation of special insurance funds for groups such as miners, railway workers and seamen is a legacy reflecting the origins of social and state provision.

The centrality of social insurance is evident in the post World War II constitution that provides for a democratic and social federal state, with solidarity and personal responsibility being the underlying principles of the social state. The constitution also establishes roles for the social partners, government, employers and trade unions, which continue to shape social security. Tripartite wage agreements between the social partners establish industry-wide wages. They are represented in the governance of the statutory state insurance schemes that are jointly funded by employer and employee contributions (except for accident insurance, the cost of which is met solely by employers), underwritten and sometimes also subsidized by federal government. Statutory health insurance, which covers 90 per cent of the population (the remainder insure privately), is typically provided through local, company or guild health insurance funds and provides free primary and secondary healthcare and prescription treatment.

Insurance provision, which lies within the competence of the federal government, is complemented by universal child benefits and payments for young people in education after the age of 16 and is underpinned by social assistance, the latter being provided and funded by the states (*Länder*) and municipalities.

Sluggish economic growth since reunification in 1990 and a rapidly ageing population have caused considerable concern about the continued viability of the pay-as-you-go funding of pensions. Indeed, it is a current goal of the German federal administration to replace statutory pensions with capital-based old-age provision. Insurance benefits are generally indexed to wages and increased annually but, as an economy measure, were up-rated in line with prices in 2001 and 2002.

Benefits, such as insurance schemes that encourage people to save, perhaps for retirement, aim to effect **life-course redistribution** by facilitating people transferring surplus income from periods of their lives when they are comparatively prosperous to times of relative shortage. This is the 'Moses principle' of saving for the seven thin years. The British system achieves much more redistribution across the life-course than vertical or horizontal redistribution (Falkingham and Hills 1995), and this may be so for other jurisdictions, although life-course redistribution is rarely articulated as an explicit aim.

Debates about the purpose of redistribution are complex and often culturally nuanced relating to different conceptions of social justice. Nevertheless, to oversimplify, social security is more often used to promote equality of outcomes in social democratic regimes and to ensure equality of opportunity in conservative and liberal regimes. In the former case, social security is used explicitly to reduce income and associated inequalities resulting from social factors and sometimes from natural endowments. However, an important caveat is often applied even in social democratic countries: namely, that the circumstances of those who stand to benefit should be due to factors beyond their control. This is justified on grounds of fairness, prevailing public attitudes and economic efficiency in that to do otherwise would encourage fecklessness (Le Grand 1999).

In the case of equality of opportunity, people receive equal support but without any guarantee that final incomes will be equal (or, even, that inequality will be noticeably reduced). The principle here is that barriers to individuals fulfilling their potential should be removed but that substantial limits should not be placed on what each person can attain and retain since, among other things, doing so might reduce economic efficiency. Education has long been viewed as a mechanism for promoting equality of opportunity but not for ensuring equality of outcome, since the intellectually talented are likely to be more successful in the economic race. However, social security provisions are now increasingly also being used to equip people to progress better in paid employment. This reflects a growing consensus across welfare regimes that work is 'the main vehicle through which individuals and families gain a sense of dignity, worth, self-respect, a stake in society and escape from poverty' (Plant 1999: 61).

Compensation

For analytic purposes it is helpful to recognize the aim of compensation, although it has close affinity with the aim of horizontal redistribution and is more often evident as the objective of a benefit scheme rather than the aim of a social security system. Compensation can be made with respect to extra costs or loss incurred due to specified contingencies. Disability benefit schemes are quite often designed to meet the additional costs attributable to disability. So, for example, the Australian Disability Pension includes a mobility allowance, carer payment and telephone allowance. Benefit rates are also sometimes adjusted in recognition of regional variations in living costs: a remote areas supplement is therefore available for some Disability Pension recipients in Australia.

Turning to compensation for loss, this is most evident in the calculation of entitlement for work injury benefits which often reflect the degree of incapacity (UK, Germany) or the loss of earnings (Sweden, USA). Incapacity benefits are also sometimes set according to degree of incapacity (Sweden) or loss of earning capacity (Germany). In Germany, job creation schemes (*ABM*) linked to receipt of unemployment benefits and providing market rate incomes reflect both the personal and social cost of economic reintegration since reunification.

Promotion of economic efficiency

Social security provision can be used explicitly to promote economic efficiency, both as a tool of macroeconomic management and as an instrument of microeconomic policy. Expenditure in the low point of an economic cycle simultaneously protects the incomes of people who are unemployed and injects needed additional demand into the economy. The origins of social security in the USA in the 1930s were explicitly tied to this agenda in the attempt, under President Roosevelt's leadership, to stimulate demand during the Great Depression and this strategy became a tenet of Keynesian economic management that held sway internationally in the post World War II era. Social security can also facilitate economic restructuring by reducing the personal and social cost of unemployment attached to downsizing anachronistic industries. The Thatcher governments in Britain in the 1980s made explicit use of unemployment to reduce inflation and curb the power of the trade unions – a policy made possible by the very benefits that should have been abolished according to vocal exponents of the monetarist theories that were being pursued (Hayek 1949; Minford *et al.* 1983). A little later, the German government employed pension policy to promote early retirement as a mechanism to reduce the size of the labour market, reduce unemployment and fight stagflation (Clasen *et al.* 1998) while, today in Britain, social security is being used to increase labour market flexibility as part of a wide-ranging modernization agenda (Walker and Wiseman 2003b).

Behavioural change

Finally, it is important to recognize that social security is very often a mechanism by which governments seek to achieve a more profound social aim, namely that of effecting a change in people's behaviour. Bismarck sought to prevent social unrest and the advance of socialism. Pension contributions make people save for retirement when they might prefer to spend their income on current consumption. Family benefits have been used to try to increase birth rates (in Britain and Australia following World War II), while 'family cap' provisions currently employed by certain US states seek to discourage out of wedlock births by not meeting the additional costs of any children conceived when in receipt of TANF. The recent proliferation of proactive social assistance policies in the USA and Britain and active labour market policies in Germany and Sweden seek to encourage personal responsibility and adherence to the work ethic. Britain has even begun to experiment with using social security as a quasi-legal sanction, denying certain benefits to families deemed to have engaged in antisocial behaviour. Arguably, the aim of such systems of provision is to promote individual virtue by persuading or coercing people to behave virtuously (Deacon 2002).

On objectives

As noted already, policy objectives tend to be more specific than system aims. The first distinction to be made is between primary and secondary objectives. **Primary objectives** are those that would provide sufficient cause to establish a benefit scheme where none existed. **Secondary objectives** are a response to the inadequacies of existing provision.

Primary objectives can be very similar to the aims discussed in the preceding section and are equally, if not more, diverse: preventing poverty, socializing risk, fostering social inclusion, promoting social integration and social well-being, reducing inequality, changing behaviour etc. Their additional specificity arises from being linked to particular benefit and/or tax credit schemes that have to be politically justified and defended. Logically, all social security schemes require at least one primary objective to justify their continued existence.

Very often, though, proposals for benefit reform are driven by secondary objectives. These are sometimes called iatrogenic (the adjective was originally used to describe a disease or health problem caused by a medical treatment – Walker 2004), and are extremely heterogeneous. They can be a response to the failure of previous schemes or to the unintended consequences such schemes may have had, such as the creation of perverse incentives. They may be a reaction to problems incurred in implementation and administration – perhaps undue expense or complexity – or to changes in the policy environment: unwelcome interaction with new social provision, social developments or a shift in the ideological paradigm resulting in different priorities.

TANF, the primary US social assistance benefit discussed previously (p. 25), provides a good illustration of a mix of primary and secondary objectives. The first objective, 'to provide assistance to needy families' is a primary one, although this is complicated by the prior intent to enable 'children [to] be cared for in their own homes or in the homes of relatives'. This is presumably seen as preferable to providing care in institutions at public expense as might have happened under the seventeenth-century Elizabethan Poor Law in Britain, a policy model that was later exported to the USA.

The second objective, 'to end the dependence of needy families on government benefits by promoting job preparation, work and marriage' is clearly iatrogenic, reflecting a belief that the previous benefit (AFDC) had encouraged recipients not to work and had increased illegitimate births.

The third and fourth objectives are secondary objectives masquerading as primary ones. In itself, paying a benefit to both one- and two-parent families is unlikely to attain either of the objectives of preventing or reducing the incidence of out of wedlock pregnancies or encouraging the formation and maintenance of two-person families. On the other hand, extending a benefit previously available only to single-parent families, as was generally the case with AFDC, to two-parent families might succeed in reducing financial incentives not to marry, or to remain with, a partner.

A second distinction is to be made between **principal objectives** and **subordinate objectives**, differentiated on priority. This reflects the fact that policymakers often try to address multiple policy concerns when designing and implementing social security or tax credit schemes. In so doing, there are trade-offs to be made between the various policy objectives since it is seldom possible to design a policy that has maximum purchase on more than one objective. For example, imagine a policy that seeks to eradicate poverty while maximizing social cohesion. The first objective could be achieved most effectively by paying poor people a benefit exactly equal to the amount by which their initial income falls short of the poverty line. This would ensure that no one was in poverty and do so with the minimum of benefit expenditure (although the administration costs involved in locating and assessing every poor person could be high – Chapters 7 and 11).

The second objective, maximizing social cohesion, is more nebulous with no obvious 'best fit' solution. What is clear, however, is that paying benefits to all poor persons irrespective of why they lack income and meeting the cost by taxing everybody else is unlikely to foster social cohesion. Taxpayers will begrudge their 'hard-earned' income being spent on 'undeserving' poor people, while 'deserving' poor people will feel stigmatized through association and suffer the general hostility of taxpayers.

In making the trade-offs between objectives that are necessary when designing policy, policymakers give priority to principal objectives over subordinate ones. Logically and linguistically there can only be one principal objective within a given set – all others have to be subordinate. Choices, though, often need to be made between subordinate objectives, and some will be prioritized over others. Frequently, policymakers weight certain key objectives above all others and the distinction between principal and subordinate objectives is intended to reflect this.

So far the assumption has been that policy objectives are clearly stated and for public consumption. Such is the nature of practical politics that this is not always the case, which leads to a further distinction between **open** and **covert objectives**. Primary, secondary, principal and subordinate objectives can all sometimes be covert and these various distinctions are well illustrated by the aforementioned introduction of Working Families Tax Credit (WFTC) in Britain in 1998. When objectives are covert, public evaluation of the policy is necessarily partial and the policy architects may consider policies successful that to the public appear to be failing. Thus, the Social Fund, a cash-limited system of loans and grants introduced in Britain in 1988, survived with minimal change because it capped escalating expenditure on one-off exceptional needs even though official evaluations showed it not to target the most needy.

An important extension

It is appropriate now to return to the assertion that the aims of a system belong to society and policy objectives to policymakers, because reality is more complex. Aims are only socially owned to the extent that all sections of the public believe that they have voices that are heard and acted upon which, in turn, depends on the effectiveness of democratic institutions. Moreover, irrespective of the openness of democracy, some groups are likely to believe, rightly or wrongly, that they are impotent, with the result that system aims are likely to be forever contested.

The same is, if anything, truer of policy objectives. The classic model of policymaking is that policymakers first devise objectives, then design and implement the policy and finally monitor and evaluate it against the original objectives. In reality, policymakers are but one of the groups active in the policy domain. The populace is engaged as individual consumers of the policy – as benefit recipients, but also as taxpayers, employees, employers, voters and, even, as policy administrators. These same individuals play a role as passive or active members of interest groups: trade unions, employers' organizations, professional associations and user and welfare advocacy groups. The policy community is also differentiated between those in power and those in political opposition, and, within government, it may be necessary to distinguish between spending departments and those responsible for administering government finance.

These various actors are likely to differ in their understanding of what a policy was intended to achieve, what they would want it to achieve and how they personally had been (or might be) affected by it. They may also be a position to exert a direct or indirect influence, usually miniscule and distant but sometimes substantial and immediate, on the implementation, effectiveness and long-term viability of the policy.

Case Study 2.3 Overt and covert policy objectives: a British example

WFTC replaced Family Credit in 1998 (Walker and Wiseman 1997). Both schemes channelled resources to low-income families with children in which at least one person worked full time (defined to be more than 16 hours weekly). WFTC was more generous with only 55p being deducted from benefit for every pound (£1) increase in income compared with 70p in the case of Family Credit. Whereas Family Credit was assessed by the then Benefits Agency and usually paid as a benefit cheque to the non-working parent who was deemed to be the principal carer of the children, WFTC was assessed and paid through the tax system (generally as an addition to the principal worker's wage).

The table below lists overt and covert objectives for WFTC. The former included boosting the incomes of low-waged families and encouraging lone parents into paid employment as primary objectives, and improving financial incentives (the high taper and income tax meant that 130,000 Family Credit recipients received less than 10p from each extra pound earned) and boosting take-up (the tax system was thought to be less demeaning and stigmatizing) as secondary ones.

However, WFTC also provided a subsidy to employers to create employment (thought to be politically unpopular) that it was hoped might serve to lessen employers' opposition to the introduction of a national minimum wage. In public accounting terms, the policy change reduced public spending *and* tax (WFTC counted as a tax break not benefit expenditure), which US experience with the Earned Income Tax Credit suggested meant that redistribution to raise the incomes of low-paid families could be increased with minimal political opposition. The tax authorities were also thought to be more able to be 'tough on fraud' than the benefit administration.

Type of objective

		Primary	Secondary
Over	Principal	Increase income of low-waged families	Improve financial incentives
	Subordinate	Encourage lone parents into paid employment	Raise take-up
Covert	Principal	Subsidize employers	Increase redistribution
	Subordinate		Tackle fraud

Therefore, in analysing and evaluating social security it is important to assess the degree of consensus concerning system aims and policy objectives. Likewise, it is essential to appreciate the distinction between the **internal objectives** of those responsible for the design of a policy and the **external objectives** of other stakeholders who might, on occasion, like to change it.

Closing summary

This chapter has focused on the *raison d'être* for social security, distinguishing between the aims of social security systems and the objectives of individual schemes.

Numerous distinctions have been introduced. The most important are those between primary objectives, which supply the basic justification for any scheme, and secondary ones that often provide the subject matter of political debate and the rationale for policy change; between principal and subordinate objectives that differ in terms of the priority attached to them; and between overt and covert objectives, the former featuring in public discourse, the latter being known only to architects of a policy.

Aims and objectives of social security are important to everyone. If attained, significant numbers of people stand personally to benefit; if not, resources are misused. Without clear objectives, performance cannot be properly assessed nor political accountability exercised. However, aims and objectives are usually contested and rarely immutable, changing over time and according to perspective.

Further reading

Fitzpatrick (2003) provides an excellent brief overview of the issues that are further elaborated in McKay and Rowlingson (1999).

The following provide useful accounts (in English) of the national policy context, provision and debates in the case study countries.

- *Australia:* Aspalter (2003); Jones (1996); Saunders (1994).
- *Germany:* Schmid (2002); Lange and Shackleton (1998); Lee and Rosenhaft (1997); Clasen and Freeman (1994).
- *South Korea:* Kwon (2002); Shin (2000); Kyung-Suk (1998).
- *Sweden:* Timonen (2003); Swenson (2002); Kautto *et al.* (2001); Olsson (1993).
- *UK:* Millar (2003).
- *USA:* Gilbert and Parent (2004); Wiseman (2003a); Weil and Finegold (2002).

Books rapidly become dated and websites of government departments and international agencies can be useful. The OECD Public Management and Governance

Programme (PUMA) hosts a website (currently being further upgraded) describing the institutional structures of all six case study countries, listing recent developments and providing links to national agencies:

* http://www1.oecd.org/puma/country/australia.htm
* http://www1.oecd.org/puma/country/germany.htm
* http://www1.oecd.org/puma/country/korea.htm
* http://www1.oecd.org/puma/country/sweden.htm
* http://www1.oecd.org/puma/country/uk.htm
* http://www1.oecd.org/puma/country/us.htm

chapter

three

Functions and Constraints

This chapter is about outcomes but also about constraints.

The aspirations and ambitions discussed in Chapter 2 are not always achieved, in part because of constraints on the effective design and implementation of policy. What is achieved is a set of **outcomes,** observable products of a policy implementation. This set embraces the possibility that there is no change or no measurable outcome associated with a policy. Outcomes determine the function or functions that a social security system or scheme is said to have.

Whereas social security systems are accorded aims and policy objectives, functions can apply to both systems and policies. Whereas system aims belong to societies and policy objectives belong, at least at first pass, to policymakers, functions belong to no one, except perhaps to policy analysts. Aims and objectives are normative; functions are neutral or objective accounts of the consequences of policy and system outcomes. Whereas aims and objectives imply intentionality, functions apply to outcomes irrespective of any intention.

Constraints sometimes mediate between aims and functions, helping to explain why aims and objectives are not met. They also set the bounds to what is achievable, both politically and economically.

This chapter divides into two parts. The first identifies a set of the most important functions of social security. A full set, although finite, would be very large. The second part of the chapter presents a selection of the most significant constraints.

Types of function

Some of the major functions of social security provisions are listed in Table 3.1, which is adapted from the work of Spicker (1993). They are organized according to whether they appertain to individuals or to a collectivity such as the jurisdiction in which the system or policy is located, or to subdivisions of it such as communities or neighbourhoods. Functions listed at the top of Table 3.1 are more likely to be considered positive than those at the bottom.

Provision for need

Perhaps the most familiar function of social security is to meet the financial needs of individuals and families. This is not the place for a detailed discussion of the concept of need, its relationship to well-being or the means by which needs can be established (for that see Chapter 7). However, certain points should be noted and for once it is worth stating the obvious: social security systems do not meet every financial need; they are neither designed nor function in this way. Most people, most of the time, rely directly on the labour or capital markets to generate the financial resources with which to meet their needs, or do so indirectly through dependency on the people with whom they live.

Social security is generally designed to meet the needs of a **target population**, comprising those people who are deemed eligible for benefit because they have insufficient income from paid employment, home-production or assets. Social security may not meet all the financial needs or wants as defined by members of the target population, only those prescribed by

Table 3.1 Functions of social security

Function	Individual	Collective
Provision for needs	Humanitarian	Social welfare Economic development
Maintenance of circumstances	Protection	Reproduction
Development of potential	Capacity	Solidarity Integration
Changing behaviour	Rewards Deterrent	Social control
Remedying disadvantage	Cure Compensation	Equality Social justice
Reproduction of disadvantage	Perpetuation	Reproduction
Production of disadvantage	Punishment	Social division

Adapted from Spicker (1993)

legislation or by social security officers exercising authorized discretion. The definition of **prescribed needs**, the needs that social security is designed to meet and the degree to which it meets them, is socially determined within each jurisdiction. So, too, is **capability**, the reason or reasons why a person is unable to access sufficient funds of their own and which legitimate their claim for benefit. Moreover, both needs and capabilities are likely to be contested and to feature repeatedly in political debate about the adequacy of provision and legitimacy of claims.

Although target populations, prescribed needs and capabilities are politically and specifically determined for each social security system and scheme, the corresponding analytic concepts used to determine function are less tightly circumscribed. Account is typically taken of all persons within a jurisdiction and of all the needs that social security could theoretically be used to meet. In principle, this enables a comparative assessment of function to be made, establishing how well a system or scheme provides for need relative to other systems or schemes. This is different from asking how well a scheme or system fulfils its objectives (the substance of policy evaluation), which requires performance to be measured against stated objectives interpreted in terms of the politically agreed target population, prescribed needs and capabilities.

Turning from individual need to ways in which social security can benefit the wider community, Spicker (1993) highlights social welfare and economic development. These two functions have already been considered as objectives of social security in Chapter 2. With respect to social welfare, suffice to say that policymakers from conservative and social democratic regimes in Europe in particular are apt to view the individual financial security afforded by the state as a litmus test of civilized modern society. This perspective is epitomized by T. H. Marshall's portrayal of a historic progression in the development of human rights from legal rights through political rights to the social rights enshrined in social security (Marshall and Bottomore 1992). The survey evidence is that citizens also value this security highly, although their willingness to fund its cost has fluctuated over time (Hills 2001).

Certain aspects of social security can be beneficial for the economy. For example, unemployment and many means-tested benefits are countercyclical in nature, with expenditure on them increasing as the economy falters and falling when the economy grows, thus aiding economic stability. However, such benefits account for only a comparatively small portion of total spending (varying from 19 per cent in Britain in 1992/3 to about 14 per cent in 1998/9 – UK Archive 2003). Equally, there is some limited evidence and much debate that suggests that social security provisions may reduce employment rates and saving ratios to the detriment of economic performance. These issues are discussed in more detail below and in Chapter 10.

Maintenance of circumstances

Another function that social security can have is to maintain income when a persons's circumstances change adversely. Indeed, in the literature, the term 'income maintenance' is occasionally used synonymously with social security. While this usage is inappropriate, since it excludes other functions such as meeting need and remedying disadvantage, it reveals the importance of social security as a means of protecting individuals against substantial falls in their incomes. The term social security itself, as Spicker (1993: 105) notes, carries connotations that in a modern welfare state 'people ought to be able to feel secure'. This means not only that people are protected from poverty but also that they should be relieved from at least some of the hardships that might result from a deleterious change in circumstances.

To the extent that people receive any additional social security following a drop in income, some degree of income maintenance is necessarily achieved. However, certain countries – Germany in particular – have chosen to prioritize income maintenance by the use of **earnings-related benefits**, setting benefit levels as a proportion of former wages, thereby providing equivalent protection irrespective of prior economic status. This approach limits the fall in incomes experienced by people with previously high incomes (in a way that flat-rate benefits do not) and can have the strategic objective of soliciting support for state social security from affluent groups who could afford to purchase private insurance. The goal is to foster social cohesion but this is achieved at the expense of replicating in the benefits system inequality that was generated in the labour market.

Earnings relation illustrates how complex the functions of social security can be at a societal level: maintaining privilege and inequality while pursuing the political aim of building social cohesion through the development of common interests. Another way in which social security fosters the maintenance of circumstances at the societal rather than an individual level is through generating the solidarity between generations that allows societies to survive by reproducing themselves. While parenthood can bring boundless pleasure, it is not without financial and other costs. Given that society needs to reproduce itself in order to replenish the labour force and perpetuate economic development, many governments have chosen to subsidize parenting through the social security system.

Systems of cash support for children are perhaps most developed in France (where they had their origins as wage supplements paid by employers to male employees with children). However, they exist in varying forms in four of the six countries featured in this book although, since 2002, benefits in Australia have been integrated with the tax system and are dependent on income. Even the exceptions, Korea and the USA, provide free primary and secondary education, although the high levels of child poverty found in these countries, when compared with Europe, are consistent with the contention that the personal costs of social reproduction can be very high if not widely shared.

Retirement and old-age pensions can similarly strengthen bonds between generations since they are often partly if not entirely funded from tax and other payments made by current employees. In this way, workers fund the pensions of past workers, implicitly acknowledging that the former's ability to do this is partly due to the latter's earlier economic contribution to society. This intergenerational bond is under threat in some countries due to the growth in the pensioner population relative to the number of workers and the need, therefore, to increase taxes to maintain the value of the pensions paid (Chapter 12).

Developing potential

Social security can help foster individual development in a number of ways. It may, for example, enable benefit recipients to avoid the scarring effects of poverty. Linked to labour market policies, social security has also been used explicitly to enhance the employability of working-age benefit recipients and to propel them towards, what in the USA is termed, **self-sufficiency** – that is, securing a wage or other self-generated income above the means-tested threshold. This linkage is called **activation** in Europe and **proactive** or active **welfare** in the USA and Britain, and makes benefit receipt conditional on participation in measures to enhance employability, including various mixes of training, assisted job search and work experience. One variant of activation, prevalent in the USA and spreading in Europe, is **workfare,** in which receipt of social assistance is made conditional on mandatory participation in specified programmes of work or work experience (Lodømel and Trickey 2001). The evidence suggests that these kinds of policy can often succeed in lessening the time that people spend out of work and increase total earnings in the short term (Ashworth *et al.* 2004a). It is less evident that earnings gains are sustained (but see Greenberg *et al.* 2004) or that many people climb very far in the labour market (Dickens 2002; Holtzer 2002; Wavelet and Anderson 2002).

At a macro level, many commentators have observed that social security provisions serve the needs of the economy, although, as noted in Chapter 2 and discussed in detail in Chapter 10, this view is contested. Titmuss (1974) referred to the 'handmaiden role' of welfare, with education and training schemes providing a skilled and healthy labour force. Social security benefits can be similarly beneficial to employers. Unemployment benefits and state redundancy payments lessen the costs to industry of downsizing and relocation, in-work benefits lower wage costs, and state retirement pensions lessen the administration and set-aside costs for employers of providing adequate pensions. Suffice to say here that, while there is little evidence that economic performance is much greater in corporatist or social democratic

Case Study 3.1 Social security in Australia

Australia is a federal state, or commonwealth, comprising six states, two mainland territories and a number of island territories. However, control of social security policy is vested mainly with the commonwealth government, notably with the Department of Family and Community Services with secondary involvement of the Departments of Employment and Workplace Relations, Health and Ageing, and Veterans' Affairs. Since 1997, most social security benefits have been delivered through Centrelink, a statutory authority that provides services on behalf of commonwealth departments and other agencies.

Social security provision dates back to 1909, with the introduction of age and invalid pensions. A plethora of new benefits were introduced between 1940 and 1945, but there were few further developments until the 1985 Social Security Review, since when the system has been subject to continuing revision. Australia is unusual in relying almost entirely on means-tested provision, sometimes explained with reference to the aspirations of the early settlers for independence and self-reliance. Assistance is categorical, not universal, with separate systems of benefits for people not expected to work, unable to work or unable to find work. Although eligibility for benefits extends well up the income distribution, poverty relief is the main policy objective. Except during the Whitlam governments (1972–75), when Supporting Mothers' Benefit was introduced and the means test for old-age pensioners briefly abolished, there has been little active support for social democratic principles of progressive taxation, equity and social justice.

Labour governments (1983–96), influenced by fiscal crisis, neo-liberal economics and a vociferous anti-welfare lobby, sought to constrain expenditure growth, increasing targeting with assets tests and the means testing of Family Allowance Supplement for working families. Consistent with the principle of 'reciprocal obligation' that they espoused, policies were transformed from passive to active with, for example, the introduction of the 'Newstart' activation policy for the unemployed, the Jobs, Education and Training ('JET') programme for lone parents and a child support scheme to compel non-custodial parents to contribute to support of their children. Perhaps most radically, the Howe Labour government implemented a compulsory private superannuation system of old-age support.

The 1996 Liberal coalition selectively abolished Labour's activation policies as too expensive, created Centrelink, privatized the Commonwealth Employment Service and introduced workfare (Work for the Dole) for young unemployed claimants. Following the McClure review, which reported in 2000, the government has commenced reform under the banner 'Australians Working Together' based on the principles of individualized service delivery; a simple and responsive income support structure; strong incentives; mutual obligation; and social partnerships (RGWF 2000). Reforms introduced to date include the introduction of personal advisers in Centrelink, Working Credit to encourage income support claimants to start work by allowing them to keep more of their benefit when working and annual interviews for recipients of Parenting Payment.

regimes with extensive social security systems that in ones with residual liberal-style provision, there is no strong evidence to the contrary (Goodin *et al.* 1999; Andersen 2002).

Turning from economic to social and political potential, some governments – notably those with conservative welfare regimes – have sought to use social security to build social cohesion and nationhood based on shared interests and mutual dependency. The part played by social security provisions in the unification of Germany under Bismarck in the nineteenth century has already been cited (Chapter 2), but social security was also important in facilitating the reunification of Germany after the fall of the Berlin Wall (Leisering and Leibfried 1999). Similarly, social security is used as a symbolic characteristic of citizenship in the political strategy of South Korea to distinguish itself from communist North Korea.

Analogous processes are apparent at a supra-national level. The European 'social model', which embraces a central role for social insurance underpinned by a social assistance safety net, is promoted both as a unifying mechanism within the European Union and as a litmus test of national commitment to European institutions. In this context, the liberal-leaning character of British social security with the prevalence of means testing serves to impede Britain's further integration into the European project.

Changing behaviour

In Chapter 2 it was shown that governments sometimes explicitly use social security to change the behaviour of individuals and companies. Social security provision can also result in unintended behavioural changes. It is time to introduce three concepts that will feature later in this book: work disincentives, moral hazard and adverse selection.

In a world without welfare benefits, a person without income would have to work, borrow or steal to make ends meet. Providing benefits to the person without income might obviate the need to steal or borrow but could also reduce the incentive to take a paid job. **Work disincentives** describe a situation where the availability of social security benefits could reduce the personal utility or welfare accruing from paid work. It should always be remembered that the existence of disincentives, or, indeed, the presence of positive incentives, does not necessarily translate directly into changes in behaviour (Chapter 10). However, it is often erroneously assumed that they do (Marmor *et al.* 1990).

Different kinds of incentive can disrupt social and private insurance (Walker *et al.* 1995). A person who is aware that they would be penniless if they lost their job might be keener to avoid putting their job at risk than someone who stood to receive social security benefit in the event that they became jobless. This is **moral hazard**, the term applied to situations in which reducing the consequences of a risk event if it occurs increases the likelihood that the event will in fact occur. **Adverse selection** occurs when people who are objectively more at risk disproportionately take out insurance, typically because they have prior knowledge of the extra risk that they face. An example is somebody insuring against joblessness after learning that they are to be made redundant. Of course, simple adverse selection of this kind will usually be ruled out by the terms and conditions of well-designed insurance policies, but the phenomenon is insidious and occasionally impossible to prevent. Whereas moral hazard applies to both social and private insurance schemes, adverse selection is more prevalent with respect to the latter.

Concern about the societal effects of the pattern of incentives and disincentives has dominated much of the ideological debate about welfare for the last 30 years and has been important since the origins of welfare. The UK Poor Law offers numerous examples. The principle of dependant liability under the 1601 Poor Relief Act placed a prior obligation on parents to care for their children and vice versa before making a claim on parish relief. The 1662 Act of Settlement enabled parishes to return destitute persons to their original parish to stop migration of the destitute from poor to more affluent parishes. The proposal of Speenhamland parish in 1795 to supplement the wages of working poor people to enable them to buy bread was tarnished by accusations that employers were restricting wages and effectively pocketing the supplement as a subsidy. The 1834 Poor Law Amendment Act introduced the principle of less eligibility, insisting that those receiving help had to be worse off than the lowest-paid worker – an explicit attempt to tackle work disincentives.

The modern debate is brilliantly summarized in Alan Deacon's (2002) book in this series, *Perspectives on Welfare*, with particular reference to Britain and the USA. To simplify, recent reforms in both countries can be traced to the belief that people respond to incentive structures created by the provision of social security. Where these structures mean that people gain little financially from working, they choose not to work, either because this is the rational action to take – the view of Charles Murray (1984) in the USA and Frank Field (1995) in Britain – or because person-kind is feckless and short-sighted – as Lawrence Mead, a former US Republican adviser, believes. Two competing policy responses follow from this analysis. The first is to cut or end all welfare provision – the Murray view. The second, proposed by Mead and Field, is to police behaviour to ensure that benefit recipients actively engage in job search, training, work experience or, indeed, paid work whenever they are able to do so, a strategy pursued recently in Australia, Britain and the USA.

Evidence for the existence of the behavioural effects of social security and the effect of policy to ameliorate them are discussed in Chapter 10.

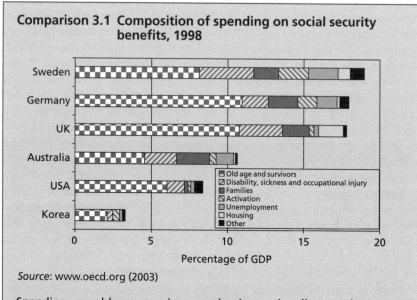

Comparison 3.1 Composition of spending on social security benefits, 1998

Percentage of GDP

Source: www.oecd.org (2003)

Spending on old-age pensions predominates in all countries, except Sweden, where more spending is in the form of services, and Australia, which has a youthful population due to recent immigration.

The insurance-based, employment-focused orientation of the Swedish and German regimes is reflected in high spending on activation measures. Britain, and to a lesser extent Sweden, spend relatively more than other countries on disability benefits and, in the former case, this has become a matter of political concern. High spending in Britain on housing reflects a decision in the 1970s to support low-income householders directly rather than to subsidize social housing *per se*.

The USA and South Korea are notable for the lack of family benefits (to meet the costs of childrearing). In contrast, spending on family benefits is comparatively high in Australia.

Remedying disadvantage

Social security can function to remedy disadvantage. This function is closely related to the aim of compensation discussed in Chapter 2. At the individual level, compensation may be paid with respect to loss of income, loss of faculty (perhaps indirectly causing a fall in income) or reduced well-being arising from a number of causes. Such causes include accident, disability, caring responsibility and, on occasion (as with the Educational Maintenance Allowance in Britain), participation in education. Moreover, benefits may be paid to meet additional expenses arising from such contingencies as well as loss of income. How far social security provisions succeed in meeting the losses or expenses incurred is an empirical question (Chapter 6).

In looking to establish how far social security remedies disadvantage at a societal level, the focus tends to shift towards rectifying injustice or inequality. Distinctions were drawn in Chapter 2 between equality of opportunity and equality of outcome and between vertical, horizontal and territorial redistribution, while techniques for measuring redistribution are discussed in Chapter 8. Suffice to draw attention to the value bias inherent in the use of the terms *positive* and *negative* redistribution, with the former indicating a reduction in inequality and the latter an increase. These terms reflect policy rhetoric that tends to emphasize the reduction of equality as a policy objective, although this is not always how social security functions. Indeed, occasionally politicians are explicit about their intent to increase inequality, as when earnings-related unemployment benefit was abolished in Britain in 1982 in an attempt to increase work incentives (an iatrogenic objective). More often, negative redistribution occurs inadvertently while prioritizing other objectives or as the result of a covert policy goal.

Reproducing disadvantage

It is important to recall the distinction between aims and objectives, which imply intentionality, and functions that do not. There are comparatively few instances in history in which policies were enacted deliberately to cause harm and even fewer where the harm was widely sanctioned ahead of implementation. Germany, under the Nazi regime, may be an example. However, this is not to say that social security is never harmful either to societies as a whole or individuals within them.

A further distinction is called for between the *perpetuation* and the *creation* of harm or disadvantage. Earnings-related benefits, as already discussed, provide an example of the former and others are considered in this section. There are perhaps fewer instances of social security actually creating disadvantage, although some important ones are considered in the next section.

The classic social divisions of class, age, gender and ethnicity all furnish examples of the ways in which social security provisions can function to perpetuate disadvantage. British pension provision relies on a combination of state and private schemes including occupational pensions provided by employers for 46 per cent of the workforce. From their beginnings, occupational pensions were included in packages of remuneration to attract and retain staff and were targeted on high-productivity employees to the detriment of low-skilled workers. However, even within the public sector, which often pioneered good employment practice, occupational pensions were typically only available initially to white-collar employees. The result, as Richard Titmuss (1963) noted 40 years ago, was to create 'two nations in old age', one comprised of pensioners with occupational pensions who enjoyed comparative prosperity, the other made up of people with minimal resources who were often forced to claim social assistance to top up their basic state pension.

Gender differentials are maintained by social security systems that, for example, prioritize work history as a criterion for benefit receipt, since women typically earn less and engage in paid work for shorter periods than men, even in countries such as Sweden that has long encouraged female employment. Instances of the perpetuation of ethnic disadvantage are legion, ranging from the absence of publicity in minority languages, through regulations that fail to acknowledge cultural differences to overt direct and indirect discrimination. Despite international conventions, such as the International Convention for the Protection of the Rights of All Migrant Workers and Their Families, migrants and refugees can often find themselves at a disadvantage (see Chapter 13). In the USA, recent immigrants are not eligible for means-tested food stamps until they become US citizens. In Britain, asylum seekers are not allowed to work and until recently received social assistance in the form of vouchers rather than cash. In Germany, refugees are excluded from mainstream social insurance provision by token of not having a contribution record and are heavily reliant on social assistance provision, constituting a majority of recipients in some towns (Buhr and Weber 1998).

Producing disadvantage

Age provides examples at the cusp between the creation and perpetuation of disadvantage. A principal mechanism is the imprint left on the life-chances of successive generations by the development of social security provisions. Each generation born or entering the labour market during the great expansion of welfare systems in Europe, the USA and Australia between World War II and the 1980s accessed better provisions than the one that preceded it. The effects of this expansion are most obvious in the strong negative correlation between incomes and age found among pensioner populations in most of these countries. Members of the oldest cohort will have belonged to less generous pension schemes and may well have been able to contribute for less time than people in later cohorts. As a result, they receive less pension and have seen its value more eroded by inflation.

The reverse process has taken hold with the gradual erosion of welfare provisions triggered by stagflation and monetarist ideologies in the 1980s and more recently by fears of rising **dependency ratios** – the ratio of the number of people above retirement age and children to the number of people of working age (Chapter 12). Examples are the raising of the US retirement age to 67, to be fully achieved by 2026, the planned upward equalization of pension ages at 65 for men and women in Britain and the reduction in the **replacement ratio** (the ratio of benefits to former earnings afforded by social security schemes) in Sweden and Germany. These changes mean that later generations will have to contribute for longer than earlier ones to receive similar or even lower benefits. In fact, the generation that may well have gained most from the post World War II welfare state was the one that created it. Members of this generation enjoyed high benefits on retirement paid for by generations still in employment and avoided the contributions necessary to fund the pensions of people retiring before they did.

Real disadvantage can be created by the design and implementation of social security provision. Two examples of the former suffice. First, the interaction of means-tested benefits and taxation can create a **poverty trap**, a situation in which a person may experience a fall, or only a relatively small increase, in net income following a rise in gross pay due to a reduction in benefit and increased income tax. Secondly, people can be negatively affected by the **savings trap**; this occurs when the income that people save serves later to cause them to be ineligible for means-tested benefits or to have lower entitlement. As a result, the people affected never recoup the consumption forgone in saving. (Poverty and savings traps are discussed in more detail in Chapter 10.)

Disadvantage arising from implementation can take many forms. Poor administration can create hassle and inconvenience. Misadministration can result in people being wrongly denied benefit or paid the wrong amount. Even perfect administration can do harm, as when the very fact of claiming benefit is perceived to be stigmatizing. There are three types of stigma that can occur simultaneously. **Felt stigma** is the sense of worthlessness or worse that people feel as a result of claiming benefit. **Active stigma** refers to the attitudes and actions of people not claiming benefit that reveal their contempt for benefit recipients. **Purposive stigma** is stigma created by institutions in order to deter applications. Stigma is further discussed in Chapter 9.

To summarize, functions describe the outcomes of social security systems and policies for individuals and collectivities such as communities or jurisdictions. They do not relate directly to the intentions of policymakers and can be both beneficial and detrimental.

Types of constraint

Constraints may be viewed as one set of reasons why the observed outcomes and functions of social security differ from the aims and objectives, the aspirations of policymakers and policy actors. Constraints may also be

Case Study 3.2 Social security in South Korea

East Asian countries differ from their Western counterparts in that governments tend more actively to prioritize and direct economic development, to regulate provision rather than providing or funding it, to rely on community, firm and family rather than any guarantee of social rights and to favour social insurance as a mode of funding.

Korean social security effectively began with the military government that took power after a *coup d'état* in 1961. Lump Sum Retirement Pay was introduced in 1961 and industrial accident insurance in 1963. A pilot health insurance scheme followed in 1965 which, reformed in 1987 and 1999, now in conjunction with non-contributory, means-tested provision, covers the entire population. A National Pension Programme, proposed and overtaken by the oil crisis in 1973, was reintroduced in 1988; a funded scheme, financed by employer and employee contributions, it covered only a minority of the working population.

Until democratization in 1987, social security was partly a device used by successive authoritarian governments for securing political legitimacy. Democracy and the 1997/8 Asian economic crisis changed the dynamics of the political debate. Unemployment insurance (introduced in 1995) was extended in 1997 and 1999 and the National Basic Livelihood Security Law (NBLSL) was passed, replacing the public assistance programme established in 1961 with Minimum Living Standard Guarantee (MLSG). NBLSL provided assistance to people of working age for the first time and shifted from an absolute to a relative conception of minimum living standard, thereby tripling the number of people who received social assistance from 540,000 in 1999 to 1.51 million in 2000. In 1998, the National Pension Scheme (NPS) was extended to cover urban informal workers and the self-employed that had previously been excluded, but prospective pensions were lowered (decreasing income replacement rate from 70 to 60 per cent in the case of average income earners). It is intended to introduce a system of occupational pensions by 2005 and to further reform the national pension system, changing the lump sum system of payment on retirement so as to reinforce the NPS as an old-age income security programme.

Despite these developments, public spending on social security remains low and tax rates are the second lowest in the OECD. The 1997/8 crisis stimulated the establishment of a tripartite commission of government, employers and trade unions, but industrial relations remain poor and trade union officials risk imprisonment for activities that are legitimate elsewhere. While the major industrial conglomerates (*Chaebols*) provide exceptional security to the third of the labour force that they employ, a third of workers have daily or temporary employment and are largely excluded from benefits, being dependent on support from extended families. Some commentators have suggested that such phenomena reflect Confucianist philosophy and others that Confucianism has been exploited to justify secular political and economic goals.

construed as the set of factors that a Solomon of policymaking would take account of in designing a policy to work perfectly. In reality, of course, there are no Solomons and the lack of omniscience of the policy community means that there are far more factors that can cause policies to have different consequences from those intended than are typically taken account of in advance.

The sets of constraints thus conceived are large and beyond the scope of an introductory chapter in an introductory text. No more can be done but to identify four broad groups of constraint: political, economic, social and administrative, some of which will receive fuller attention in later chapters.

Political

This is the territory of political science and no attempt is made to encapsulate the content of a discipline in a handful of paragraphs. However, insights from political science are vital to understanding social security because it is through the political process that political will is expressed, social aims are constructed and social security policies put in place. Without politics – and without political will – there would be nothing for social security analysts to analyse.

Policy in democracies results from collective decision-taking that is shaped by the working relationships between the various political institutions defined, or allowed for, in a national constitution (Shugart and Carey 1992; Esaisson and Heidar 2000; Moberg 2003). The ease with which a policy idea can become law or otherwise be implemented is therefore conditional not only on the quality of the idea but also on the balance of power between political institutions and the location of the idea with respect to these institutions. An idea originating within the majority party in a highly centralized, parliamentary democracy (as in Britain) based on simple majority voting rather than proportional representation, is typically more likely to reach the statute book than one conceived by a local, leftist lobby or pressure group operating in a federal presidential system with an incumbent right-wing president.

Political constraints are legion. Suffice to say that, other things being equal which they seldom are, opposition to a policy idea is likely to be least when certain conditions apply. There is consensus that the reform appropriately addresses a problem that is generally acknowledged to be important. The reform reduces public expenditure or, at least, is cost neutral while simultaneously creating many gainers and very few vocal losers (unlikely without an increase in expenditure). Finally, the reform represents a development of existing policies, requires minimal institutional reform and is consistent with the prevailing ideology and regime type. Even where these conditions apply, there may be other constraints such as lack of popularity of the incumbent administration, the point in the election cycle, competing policy demands and the adroitness or otherwise of those lobbying for reform or charged with tasks such as policy presentation, coalition building and legislative management.

Economic

Economic constraints impinge on social security from three directions. First, and most self-evidently, resources are required to fund social security. In the last analysis, resources are finite and impose an irrevocable check on what can be spent on social security. However, for the most part the resources available for social security are determined through the political process. With sufficient will and political skill, 'extra' resources can usually be found. They can be 'manufactured' by capturing and utilizing the benefits of economic growth that typically generates extra government revenue or by imposing extra taxation, encouraging or enforcing extra saving, increasing government borrowing or diverting resources from other areas of expenditure. Each strategy has different political and economic implications.

These economic implications serve to define the second set of economic constraints on social security. As discussed in Chapter 10, there is much controversy as to whether social security expenditure itself harms the economy. Taking a short-term perspective, resources spent on social security cannot be spent on other beneficial government projects and thus may have economic as well as political costs. However, in the longer term, social security spending may reduce demands on other areas of expenditure by, for example, promoting better health through reducing the incidence of poverty and thereby curtailing demands on health sector expenditure. The principal macroeconomic concern, though, is that by requiring extra taxation, thereby reducing work incentives and creating other market distortions, social security provision may curtail economic growth. At a micro level, the design of individual schemes is also often shaped by the desire to avoid creating perverse incentives and distorting economic behaviour while at the same time achieving the most efficient use of resources.

The third kind of economic constraint is that which an ailing or changing economy imposes on social security not only by limiting available resources but also by increasing the demands on social security. The sharp economic collapse of the Asian 'tiger' economies in the late 1990s offers a good example. Unemployment in Korea rose from 2.6 per cent in 1997 to 6.8 per cent in 1998, unemployment insurance protected less than one in eight workers and the Livelihood Protection social assistance system reached only 60 per cent of people in absolute poverty (Kim 2003). In response, a new social assistance system (Basic Guarantee) was introduced in 1999 and coverage of unemployment benefit has been extended (OECD 2000).

Another example of the impact of economic change, albeit operating over a longer timeframe, is provided by the doubling of social security expenditure as a proportion of GDP that occurred in Britain between 1971 and 1999. This has been linked to the process of **de-industrialization**, the decline of manufacturing employment relative to work in the service sector, associated with increased productivity and changed production methods (Walker with Howard 2000). Although implicated directly only in expenditure on unemployment and disability benefits, it also provided the context for increased spending on retirement pensions.

Social

Social constraints on the design and effectiveness of social security are closely linked to, although not synonymous with, political ones. To function effectively, social security provisions need to accord with prevailing social norms and behaviours. To the extent that they do not, some individuals will seek to counter the effect of the provisions and may try additionally to mobilize political forces to change the offending policies. When policies are explicitly designed to alter the behaviour of the majority of the population, people will need to be convinced of the value that will accrue to them from changing their behaviour or be aware of, and approve of, the gains for other people. Policies to alter behaviour may also be socially viable if the majority agree that a minority of people need to change their ways.

Three kinds of consideration serve as examples. First, policies need to be consistent with people's values and attitudes in order to function as planned. In the USA, lone parents are expected to work if their children are all aged more than 12 months (or less in some states). This reflects a strong commitment to the work ethic, the fact that married mothers typically work and the acceptance of a punitive element within social assistance (Ellwood 1988; Weaver 2000). In Britain, there is more collective moral uncertainty concerning the desired trade-off between the immediate care needs of children and the positive role model of an employed mother with the result that lone parents are not compelled to work until their children are above school age (Millar 2003).

Secondly, policies need to be compatible with prevailing social institutions. The nuclear family predominates in Britain and, in the context of social security, financial liability is not presumed to extend across generations or typically beyond related people living in the same household (except in the case of child support payments from absent parents). This contrasts with Germany where parents are, for the purposes of social assistance, deemed financially liable for their adult, non-resident children, although the extent to which this obligation is still enforced varies from locality to locality. In Britain, no financial assistance is available for second wives in polygamous marriages since polygamy is illegal but, reflecting migration from countries where polygamy *is* legal, additional benefits are allowable provided the polygamous marriage was contracted in such a country.

Thirdly, policies generally need to work with the grain of accepted and acceptable behaviour. Ignoring this constraint contributed to the initial failure successfully to implement the 1991 Child Support Act in Britain that transferred assessment of the child support maintenance required from a parent without the day-to-day care of their children from the courts to the social security system. The Act imposed a strict formula for assessment that replaced earlier settlements agreed through the courts, including those that involved a cash-sum payment in lieu of regular maintenance. It therefore meant new financial demands on parents without care, many of whom had no access to their children or contact with their former partner. This provoked individual outrage, the formation of pressure groups and eventual change in the law. In the USA, similar policies attracted much less resistance.

Administrative

The fourth set of constraints on social security is well encapsulated by the provocative truism that policy is what is implemented rather than what is enacted. However ambitious the aims or sophisticated the design of a policy, success is dependent on how it is implemented or, indeed, on whether it can be successfully implemented at all. Negative income tax schemes, for example, which seek to integrate taxation and social security delivery into a single process, paying out cash to those whose needs exceed their ability to pay and taking tax from those with incomes in excess of needs, are fine in theory but almost always impossibly complex to implement (Chapter 10).

Social security implementation requires that definitions of need are given practical expression with sufficient precision to avoid injustice and harm but with enough robustness for calculations to be made quickly and accurately by hand or computer a million times over. It entails payments worth billions of pounds, dollars or euros being issued and accounted for with the minimum of loss or fraud. It depends on the successful management of thousands of staff, trillions of paper trans-actions and millions of telephone and face-to-face interactions with applicants and recipients. It requires vast information technology systems, sophisticated marketing and outreach, and the flexibility to accommodate change and to phase transitions with the minimum of adverse impact on new and existing recipients. In sum, it almost seems that the successful implementation of social security is dependent on an oxymoron: a flexible, creative and personalized bureaucracy (Chapter 11).

To summarize, constraints help to explain why the aims of social security and objectives of individual policies are formulated as they are, establishing the boundaries of what is politically, socially, economically and administratively possible. They also help to explain when and why policies are successful or unsuccessful in meeting their objectives.

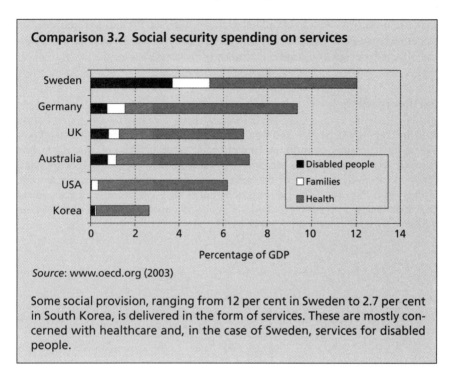

Comparison 3.2 Social security spending on services

Source: www.oecd.org (2003)

Some social provision, ranging from 12 per cent in Sweden to 2.7 per cent in South Korea, is delivered in the form of services. These are mostly concerned with healthcare and, in the case of Sweden, services for disabled people.

Closing summary

Whereas Chapter 2, on aims and objectives, was about the goals that jurisdictions and their policymakers hope to achieve through social security provision, this chapter on functions and constraints has been concerned with outcomes: what happens as a result of social security policy. As such, it epitomizes the book as a whole, the objective of which is to help readers to determine what can be achieved by social security, what has been accomplished and how.

It has been established in this chapter that the functions of social security are very varied and differ for individuals, communities and the jurisdictions within which policies operate. Social security policies and systems can function in benevolent or malevolent ways, enhancing or reducing individual and social well-being.

What systems and policies achieve, how they function, and indeed which policies are introduced and can be sustained, are all subject to a multitude of political, social, economic and administrative constraints. Such constraints limit the actions of policymakers and influence the degree to which aims and objectives are met. Sometimes policymakers are aware of these constraints in advance, sometimes they become apparent later and sometimes they are unknown or unrecognized even by analysts. One of the goals of the systematic study of social security is to appreciate better the constraints on the effective design and implementation of policy.

Further reading

Paul Spicker (1993), McKay and Rowlingson (1999) and Fitzpatrick (2003) all provide useful accounts of the functions of social security, although the distinction between aims, objectives and functions is not always made explicit. Moberg (2003) offers an up-to-date model of the policy process in democratic countries, while Walker with Howard (2000) discuss constraints on social security in the context of Britain and Weaver (2000) provides a punch by punch description of the way in which welfare reform in the USA is shaped by political processes.

PART 2

Mechanisms

Financing

This chapter is about ways of doing things.

Specifically it is concerned with the means by which resources are raised to fund social security provision intended to fulfil the various aims and objectives discussed in Chapter 2. How these resources are allocated to individuals and families is the subject of Chapter 5. Methods of raising and allocating these funds are inevitably affected by the constraints considered in Chapter 3, some being associated with particular welfare regimes.

The chapter divides into three sections of unequal length. The first justifies the priority given to funding over the allocation and delivery of services in the ordering of chapters. The second briefly rehearses the circumstances in which individual saving might need to be supplemented by social security resources. Finally, each of the main funding strategies is outlined in turn: two kinds of insurance – private and social – and four forms of collective transfers organized by families, community organizations, employers and government.

At heart, the chapter is about the extent to which the response to individual financial risk is collectively shared.

Why financing is important

For the most part, benefit payments to individual social security recipients are small, a matter of tens or very occasionally a few hundred pounds, euros, won or dollars per week. Typically, such payments are made to families and individuals who, if not poor, are far from prosperous. They are likely to make the difference between not making ends meet and getting by, rather than conferring great prosperity even when they succeed in fostering social inclusion and cohesion. However, when cumulated across individuals' lifetimes, the sums involved begin to look substantial. In Britain, a country not noted for its generous provision, lifetime receipts have been estimated to average £126k (2004 prices) and to account for 18 per cent of all the gross income received during the average person's life (Falkingham and Hills 1995).

When spending is summed across all people currently receiving social security, the aggregate sums are colossal, measured in terms of billions of dollars. From Comparison 2.1 (see p. 28) it can be seen that in Sweden, the UK and Germany almost one fifth of the entire domestic income is channelled through social security. Even in the USA, the archetypal liberal regime characterized by limited provision, 8 per cent of GPD is attributable to social security spending. Furthermore, in most advanced industrial or post-industrial economies, government spending on social security far exceeds that on education, health or defence.

Social security, therefore, is large-scale governance entailing vast expenditure that somehow has to be funded. Social security, in some countries, is also big business. In Britain, members of the National Association of Pension Funds held £650 billion in assets in 2002 and paid benefits to 4 million pensioners (NAPF 2002). In 1999, over £930 billion – 29 per cent of UK personal sector wealth – was invested in long-term insurance products and the Association of British Insurers (ABI 2002) claimed that every day UK insurance companies paid out £135 million compared with £110 million paid by the UK government in state pensions. Insurance companies own about 21 per cent of UK ordinary shares listed on the London Stock Exchange, while company pension funds own another 18 per cent.

Not only is spending on social security large, financing and resources are inextricably linked to provision in ways that have no parallels in other areas of the welfare state. Whereas the funding on, say, education is translated into teachers, school buildings and books, and that on transport results in the building of roads, railways and airports, spending on social security results in nothing concrete or tangible, except for the miniscule proportion that is spent on social security offices and the bureaucracies that staff them. Rather, what is achieved is a redistribution of cash resources, usually in the form of income, from non-recipients to social security beneficiaries. Social security 'spending' changes the amount of income that individuals themselves have to spend, when they are able to spend it and, occasionally, as in the case of food stamps in the USA, what they are able to spend it on. Social security recipients have more income to spend than would otherwise be the case. Net contributors to social security, who pay more in tax and other social security contributions than they receive in social security payments, have lower incomes and less to spend. Changes in circumstances mean that net contributors may later become net recipients and vice versa.

Social security, therefore, is primarily a mechanism that redistributes resources, notably income, and hence consumption. As already noted in

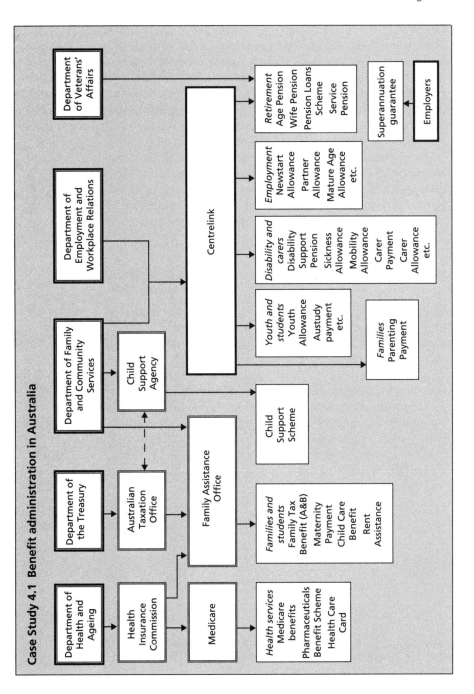

Case Study 4.1 Benefit administration in Australia

Chapter 3, this is irrespective of whether redistribution is set as a specific objective. To the extent that recipients of social security typically have lower initial incomes than net contributors, social security is progressive, redistributing resources from the better off to the less well off, and is typically much more important than taxation in reducing income inequality (Chapter 8). Perhaps as important, from the perspective of financing, social security can also serve to redistribute resources over the life-course from periods of comparative affluence to ones of shortage.

So funding is important, not only because of the enormous scale of resources that are devoted to social security provision, but also because, in essence, social security is a mechanism for reallocating finance and spending power between individuals or families or between the same individuals or families at different times to fulfil a range of social objectives.

Rationale for social spending: limits on individual saving

Setting to one side for the moment the multiple aims and objectives assigned to social security, Figure 4.1 demonstrates the key problem that social security is designed to address with reference to an individual or family: the income, or resources more broadly defined, of the individual or family falls short of some acceptable level for a period. For the most part, individuals and families plan to avoid this contingency by means of personal saving. In simple terms, income received in excess of spending in periods of comparative prosperity is set aside to cover periods of need. There are two basic ways of achieving this: **hoarding**, holding onto money in the form of cash or marketable assets; and **investment**, lending the money to others to invest in profitable activities with a view to gaining interest on the saving (the 'principal').

Hoarding is the simpler strategy. Forget the idea of hiding cash under the

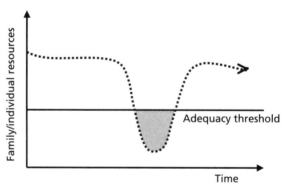

Figure 4.1 A case for social security

mattress or floorboards, hoarding is an activity in which everybody engages in the short term. The task of household budgeting involves putting money aside for the purchases that have to be made. However, as a longer-term strategy hoarding is risky. Money under the mattress or elsewhere can easily be stolen, lost or, indeed, spent. Moreover, in times of inflation, savings held in cash lose their value. As a hedge against inflation, people may hold their money in gold or in works of art, but for many families this is not a practical proposition. In any case, saving in the form of assets does not provide a complete guarantee against inflation. Furthermore, it means incurring transaction costs associated with buying and selling the goods, and reduced liquidity – that is, it is more difficult to access the value of the savings at times of crisis.

With the important exception of owner-occupied housing, most long-term saving is in the form of direct or indirect investment. In the modern world, the number of savings vehicles available is legion. They range from interest-yielding current accounts and savings accounts with banks and building societies, through unit trusts – in which members jointly invest in a portfolio of companies – and 'with profits' life insurance policies, to direct investment in the stock market, not to mention various savings mechanisms run or sponsored by government. By paying interest, these forms of personal savings provide a hedge against inflation and are inherently less risky than hoarding. However, as illustrated by the ending of the investor boom in so-called 'dot.com' internet companies in 2000 and the collapse in share values in the aftermath of 11 September 2001, investments are not immune from risk. Moreover, entry costs are higher than for hoarding, requiring some financial literacy on the part of savers, and there is generally some loss in liquidity.

While there are risks that attach to the accumulation and retention of savings, there are more important reasons why the conundrum represented by Figure 4.1 cannot always be resolved by personal saving alone: the amount of savings accumulated has at least to equal the shortfall in income. Figure 4.2 illustrates this graphically. Savings equal the average income forgone in each time period (T_1) multiplied by the number of periods in which saving occurs (R_1). Savings (R_1T_1) need to exceed the shortfall in income (R_2T_2), defined as the average shortfall each period (R_2) multiplied by the number of periods (T_2), and must also precede it. Even if this is the case, the family whose predicament is schematically portrayed in Figure 4.2 will still experience a substantial fall in living standards. Often, of course, as in the case of young families, periods of high need precede periods of high income. Moreover, for the most part, the amount (R_2) and length of income shortfall (T_2) are unknown and essentially unknowable, as is the period (T_1) over which saving is possible before the crisis event occurs.

The personal dilemma exhibited in Figure 4.2 requires a social or collective response. This may be a government response but can, in certain

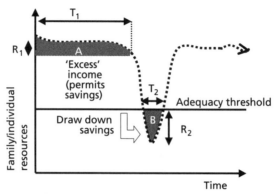

Figure 4.2 Personal savings

circumstances, be provided through private sector insurance. Either way, the response can take one of three forms (Figure 4.3). First, it can seek **prevention** by entirely making good the shortfall in income. Secondly, it can provide **relief** by bringing the income up to a socially acceptable minimum standard, or thirdly, it can offer **amelioration** or **income support** by partially making good the income loss at a higher level than the basic minimum. Which strategy is adopted will depend on the precise objectives of the benefit scheme, whether it is public or private, and on the nature of the existing welfare regime.

The likelihood that social security provision will be available for individuals or families finding themselves in the situation portrayed in Figure 4.1 will depend much on the reasons for their predicament. Other things being equal, they are more likely to receive support if they have been unable, rather than unwilling, to make provision for themselves, or if their circum-

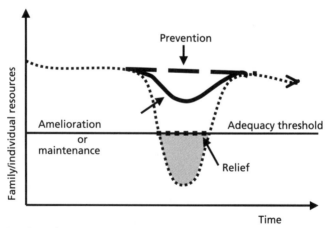

Figure 4.3 Social security strategies

stances are widely shared or socially created. As long ago as 1899, Rowntree (1901) demonstrated that the risk of poverty was highest during childhood and childrearing, times when many mouths had to be fed but few family members were available to work, in old age when frailty made paid employment impossible, and at times of economic recession when unemployment was high (Figure 4.4). The same is true today save for the existence of social security schemes to cover unemployment, sickness, retirement and old age and to meet the additional costs of childrearing (although neither South Korea nor the USA has a universal system of family support – see Comparison 3.1, p. 50).

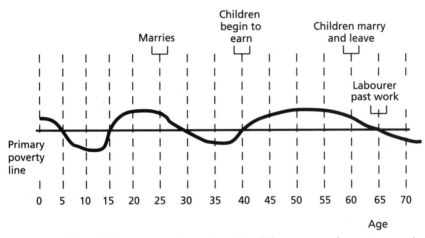

Figure 4.4 Shared income trajectories: the life-course of a nineteenth-century labourer
Source: Rowntree (1901)

In summary, even in advanced economies where there is a plethora of opportunities for saving, events and circumstances arise in most people's lives when personal savings prove inadequate and a collective response is required.

Funding mechanisms

There are two broad collective responses to meeting the kind of individual financial contingency portrayed in Figure 4.1: insurance and collective transfers. **Insurance** provides that, in return for the payment of a sum (called a 'premium' or sometimes a 'contribution'), a third party will pay out a sum of money in the event of an insured, pre-specified contingency. Insurance can be organized by commercial, for-profit companies, by not-for-profit organizations and by governments. The first is more evident in liberal welfare

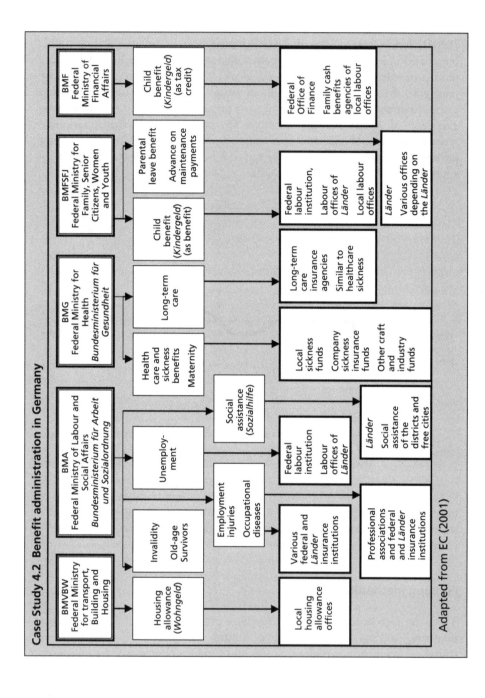

Case Study 4.2 Benefit administration in Germany

Adapted from EC (2001)

regimes, the last in conservative ones, while the advance of commercial capitalism has largely superseded not-for-profit insurance. **Collective transfers** require that two or more individuals agree to make a payment to one or more of their number when a particular contingency arises. For the most part, transfers can be effected only by government or informal collectives rather than by commercial companies. Government transfers are most often associated with liberal regimes where much provision is means tested and funded from general government revenues, but can be important in social democratic regimes, notably Denmark, where tax-funded benefits are a symbolic and practical manifestation of social solidarity.

The different kinds of insurance and transfers have varying characteristics that make them more practical and effective in some circumstances than others. The costs of providing for individual financial contingencies are also differently apportioned between the persons who are party to the agreement. The characteristics and funding implications of each of the main strategies are discussed next.

Insurance

Commercial or private insurance

Private insurance is a contractual financial relationship in which one party (the insurer) seeks to make a profit by providing a service (offering financial security against a specified risk) to the other (the insured). As already noted, commercial insurance is a vast industry that continues to expand as insurers identify additional risks against which they can provide insurance.

Private insurance not only offers the security that personal saving cannot, it can also be more efficient from a social perspective. Figure 4.5, which plots the resources and saving of three people, illustrates why. For Person A, to avoid having inadequate resources resulting from a drop in income – labelled P – they would previously have needed to save an amount equal to the total shaded area (A1 + A2 + A3). However, if two people took out insurance, thereby sharing or pooling the risk, each person would only need to pay half as much in premiums to cover the contingency that one of them suffered a shortfall in resources. If three people took out insurance, premiums would fall again to a third of the savings required from a single individual. Rather than each person having to save the equivalent of P or A1 + A2 + A3, they need only pay the equivalent amount (A3 + B3 + C3) *in total*.

For private insurance to be viable, the insurance company has to set the premiums to cover not only the underlying risk, as illustrated in Figure 4.5, but also administration costs and a margin for profit. However, providing the per capita costs are less than the amount A1 + A2 (in Figure 4.5) insurance still provides an attractive alternative to individual saving.

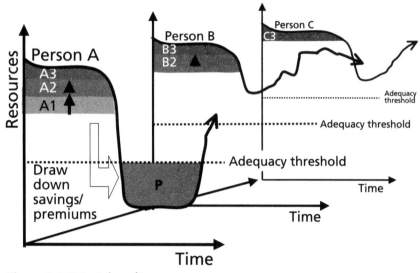

Figure 4.5 Principles of insurance

Leaving aside health insurance, the largest involvement of private insurance companies in social security provision is in the area of retirement pensions, whether provided as *occupational benefits*, through employers able to pool risks across all employees, or in the form of *personal pensions*, direct to individuals. In the early years, the major component of the 'risk' insured was that of living long enough to need, or to be able, to retire. With the increase in life expectancy, the major risk now relates to the length of time for which a person will draw a pension. (The fact that private pensions are insurance rather than saving is evidenced by the fact that a pension ceases on the death of the insured person – or their dependant if dependants are insured – irrespective of the length of time for which the pension has been paid.)

There are, however, serious limits to the scope of private insurance. First, for insurers to fix premiums, they have to be able to quantify the risk, the probability of its occurrence and the size of the loss or shortfall in income incurred. If two of the three people in Figure 4.5 experienced a shortfall in resources, the insurance scheme would fail since claims would exceed the revenue generated through premiums. In reality, insurance companies capitalize on the rule of large numbers, in that the proportion of their clients making a claim will closely approximate to the proportion of all people experiencing an insurable event. Premiums are invariably based on the historic incidence of risks, which means that, for risks to be insurable, they have to remain reasonably stable over time.

Secondly, the risks insured need to be independent. If all three people insured in Figure 4.5 suffered loss at the same time, perhaps because they were all affected by a recession or earthquake, the insurance claims could not be met. (In Figure 4.5 all the people did experience a simultaneous fall in income but only one had inadequate resources as a result.)

Thirdly, the incidence of risk has to be comparatively low, otherwise premiums will need to be very high, approaching the sums required in personal saving (and perhaps exceeding them to allow for administration and profit).

Fourthly, differential premiums related to the level of risk have to be acceptable. This is because private insurance works by pooling people who confront similar levels of risk and who pay similar premiums. Pooling people in noticeably different risk categories would necessitate charging individuals at low risk comparatively high premiums. Such people would be attracted away to schemes offering lower premiums by pooling low-risk individuals, causing premiums to rise for those people at greater risk who remain, who might then find themselves unable to afford the premiums charged. Differential premiums require that insurers can accurately distinguish between people who are at high risk from those who are not. However, if such distinctions cannot be made, all levels of risk are pooled.

Fifthly, people insured should not know more about the level of risk than the insurers. If people seeking insurance have superior knowledge, then adverse selection (discussed in Chapter 3) may occur, resulting in disproportionate numbers of people most at risk taking up insurance. This could lead to insolvency of the insurance scheme but is more likely to result in individuals knowing themselves to be at high risk paying unjustifiably low premiums while others were charged higher premiums to cover the large number of payouts.

Finally, for private insurance to work, it must be possible to keep the consequences of moral hazard at a sustainable minimum. The phenomenon of moral hazard (people changing their behaviour and increasing their level of risk because they have insurance) was discussed in Chapter 3.

The workings of the market therefore limit the ability of private insurance to provide universal protection. Firms will not chance their viability by insuring risks that cannot be assessed and competition conspires to increase insurance costs for those most at risk. Sometimes governments act to alter the market rules or parameters in order to help expand the role of the private sector. Strategies used include subsidies, making insurance compulsory and government underwriting of private schemes.

Car accident insurance is a classic example of the second strategy employed by many governments. Compulsion here reduces the scope for adverse selection by ensuring that everyone, not just those most at risk, joins the scheme, thereby lowering premiums overall. Since 1992, Australia has applied this strategy to pension provision by requiring employers to provide and contribute to occupational pensions for all employees earning more than a low earnings threshold and by encouraging employees to make additional contributions (Bateman and Piggott 2001).

The use of subsidies is seen in the provision of tax incentives in Britain and the USA (Emmerson and Tanner 2000; CBO 2003) to encourage the growth of private pension schemes. These incentives take many forms, including offsetting employer and employee contributions against tax, non-taxation of pension accrual and provision for tax on pensions to be levied at favourable rates, or for some components of pensions (such as, in Britain, lump sums) to be paid tax free. All aim to make 'saving for' or 'contributing to' a pension more attractive to workers and employers.

When governments underwrite private schemes, they become the insurer of last resort. If an insurance company fails, governments are sometimes prepared or forced to meet the cost of the outstanding liabilities. In the inflationary era of the 1970s and 1980s, when pension funds found it difficult to increase pension payments in line with inflation, the British government met part of the cost of doing so.

So, while private insurance has distinct advantages over personal saving, the inability to pool groups of people exposed to different levels of risk may make insurance too expensive for persons facing the highest risk. Even allowing for intervention by governments, some contingencies may be uninsurable. This is the case when the risk cannot be assessed, varies over time or is too vulnerable to adverse selection. Unemployment is generally considered to be a case in point (Rejda 1994; Walker *et al.* 1995; Burchardt and Hills 1997). Finally, there is also the risk that insurance companies will become insolvent because of incompetent management, fraud or other reasons.

Not-For-Profit insurance

Many commercial insurance companies have their origins in **mutual,** member-owned organizations that, in turn, in Europe, had their roots in medieval guilds. Moreover, although the trend has been for mutual insurers to convert into commercial companies, as recently as 1999, six of the world's largest ten insurers were mutual organizations (Birkmaier and Laster 1999).

The early mutual associations were based on **pay-as-you-go** principles – namely that current contributors met the costs of current beneficiaries – which made them inherently unstable. However, quite rapidly sound actuarial principles were applied so that premiums could be mathematically determined – the Equitable began this practice in London in 1756 to be followed, in 1778, by the *Hamburgische Allegmeine Versorgungs-Anstalt* in what today is Germany (Hansmann 1998).

The attraction of mutual organizations stemmed from the need of prospective customers, especially those taking out life insurance, to have confidence in the long-term integrity of the insurer in an uncertain world. Because mutual insurers were owned by their policyholders, they had little incentive to behave opportunistically. Indeed, they were rather more likely to veer on the side of caution, building up reserves which could be liquidated if favourable circumstances allowed and returned to their policyholders. In the early nineteenth century, the first Australian and US insurers were commercial (stock) companies, but mutual insurers entered the market in the middle of the century and rapidly proved to be more stable and successful. The advantage for mutual organizations insuring shorter-term risks – a cooperative of German farmers in Süderauerdorf provided mutual insurance against fire as early as 1537 – is that neighbours or workgroups often possess a clearer appreciation of the risks than commercial insurers and may be less likely to cheat on each other.

These latter considerations were important in the growth of insurance provided by the early trade unions to cover sick pay, accident benefits and unemployment. These provisions were often absorbed into state schemes with unions sometimes retaining a role in the delivery of benefits. In Sweden, trade unions administer some 38 unemployment funds under the supervision of the National Labour Market Board (*Arbetsmarknadssttyrelsen*) with unemployment insurance usually being compulsory only for union members.

The reasons for the recent demise of mutual organizations, especially in Europe, have been various. They include: greater longevity that has led to a change in products with the requirement for higher returns on investment to fund, for example, longer periods of retirement; new technology that has lowered the entry costs for new commercial companies that no longer need to have a local presence; and deregulation and the creation of the euro, that have increased competitiveness. However, the drivers of change have been commercial (to raise capital, unlock the value of ownership rights, promote growth through acquisition and increase inefficiency) rather than actuarial.

Government or social insurance

At face value, social insurance organized by governments appears to operate in the same way as private and not-for-profit insurance. People pay premiums – usually called contributions – to insure themselves against risks and receive payments in the event that the insured contingency occurs. However, as Table 4.1 reveals, many differences exist between private insurance and social insurance, of which the most important are that governments can employ compulsion and need not be reliant exclusively on income from past insurance contributions. In addition, the cost of social insurance is typically shared between employees, employers and sometimes government itself. Funding social insurance in this way clearly reduces the direct costs for employees, although it may serve to exclude non-workers and sometimes the self-employed.

Table 4.1 Features of private and social insurance

Social insurance	Private insurance
• Compulsory	• Voluntary
• Prescribed and comparatively limited protection	• Greater protection available depending on preferences and ability to pay
• Benefits prescribed by law (that can be changed)	• Benefits established by legal contract
• Government monopoly	• Competition
• Costs difficult to predict	• Costs more readily predictable
• Full funding not necessary because of compulsory contributions of new entrants and because programme assumed to last indefinitely	• Must operate on a fully funded basis without reliance on contributions of new entrants
• No underwriting	• Individual or group underwriting
• Investments generally in public sector	• Investments in private securities
• Taxing power available to combat inflation	• Greater vulnerability to inflation
• Emphasis on social adequacy	• Emphasis on individual equity
• Possibility of pooling people with different risks	• Pooling only of people with similar risks
• Cost of financing typically spread between insured, employers and government	• Cost of financing borne primarily by insured
• Cost of insurance (contributions) set according to social/political objectives	• Cost of insurance (premiums) to insured related to actuarial risk
• Average contribution less than comparable private premium due to wider pooling	

Adapted and expanded from Rejda (1994)

Compulsion enables pooling to be achieved across diverse risk groups, which extends insurance to cover even those most at risk. This is possible because, although average contributions have to be sufficient to cover the high risks, there is no scope for individuals at minimum risk to leave and secure lower premiums elsewhere. Hence, contributions made by those most at risk can be set actuarially low, while those of other people have to be higher for the fund to remain solvent. Average premiums would be lower than if *everybody* were to secure insurance cover in the absence of compulsion.

Compulsion also means that payments need not be linked directly to contributions. In a perfect market, anyone receiving a lower payout than justified by their premiums would move to a company where they could secure their just desserts. With compulsion, it is possible for governments to fix payments with regard to social adequacy rather than individual equity and hence to engineer vertical or horizontal redistribution of income.

Social insurance is also free from the constraint of **funding**: saving and investing premiums (contributions) today to accumulate assets from which future liabilities can be met. Pension companies, for example, can only pay out in pensions what has been accumulated from premiums paid in the past (and investment income that has accrued from them.) Consequently, companies and their shareholders are trapped by history. If more people retire earlier than was expected, or if interest rates fall on investments, pension rates have to be lowered.

A government can choose to follow the private sector practice of funding. More often, though, they opt for a pay-as-you-go strategy in which benefits paid to current recipients are paid for by current contributors and taxpayers. This offers much greater flexibility in responding to unanticipated events and developments. If demands are higher than expected because of, say, demographic change, high inflation or economic recession, they can be met almost immediately by increasing taxes and contributions.

Inevitably, there are dangers in pay-as-you-go funding which is dependent on current taxpayers being prepared to fund current recipients. This demands a preparedness on the part of the comparatively wealthy to forgo personal spending to meet the living expenses of people receiving benefits. In the context of pensions, it requires the current generation of contributors to be willing to pay for the pensions of the previous one and to have the confidence that future generations will do likewise. Also, flexibility may be exploited by policymakers to avoid taking difficult decisions about long-term strategy and some economists argue, as reported in Chapter 10, that pay-as-you-go funding can negatively affect economic growth.

Who pays?

By way of conclusion, it is appropriate to ask who bears the financial cost of insurance. In the case of private insurance, the insured have to pay premiums and thus forgo or, at least, defer other forms of consumption or saving to do so. Those who need to make a claim on insurance get some or all of their money back and possibly a great deal more depending on the size of their claim. This leaves those who do not make a claim paying most for their security of mind. Indeed, there is evidence that some people are particularly risk averse and over-insure themselves relative to the actuarial risk (Cebulla and Ford 2000); they are likely to bear a disproportionate share of the overall cost of insurance. This will also apply in the case of not-for-profit or mutual insurance.

If claims exceed revenue, then the cost of insurance passes to insurance companies and their shareholders and to the commercial underwriters who share the risk. In the event of the financial collapse of insurance companies, governments may take on some liabilities which passes the cost on to the taxpayer.

In most countries, social insurance is largely funded by contributions made by employed persons and employers. Employers are likely to pass on their social insurance costs to their employees in the form of lower wages, to their customers as higher prices and to their shareholders as lower dividends. This means that employees are likely to pay several times over, via contributions, lower wages and higher prices. The net costs of employees who need to claim insurance benefits are again lower than those who do not and, because social insurance pools differential risks, employees in low-risk groups are likely to pay disproportionately high contributions. To the extent that government tops up insurance funds from general tax revenues, tax-payers, corporate and individual, also carry some of the direct costs of social insurance while the direct benefits that they enjoy may be negligible.

In summary, therefore, insurance has distinct advantages over personal saving, providing higher security at lower overall cost. However, private and not-for-profit insurance is frequently unable to offer cover to the most at risk groups at premiums that they can afford, and some risks, notably those that are either very pervasive or not amenable to reliable measurement, cannot be insured commercially. Because governments can use compulsion and thereby exploit the social advantages that can accrue from pooling people at diverse risk, social insurance can provide cover to more people against a greater range of contingencies with lower average premiums. However, this is achieved to the detriment of the individuals who are least at risk who are compelled to pay dispropor-tionately high contributions. Arguably, though, this latter group shares other benefits attributable to social insurance such as greater social cohesion (see Chapter 2).

Collective transfers

Saving and insurance both rely on individuals and families taking pre-ventative action to protect themselves against the financial consequences of risks that they may encounter in life (including, in the case of life insurance, death). Indeed, they may be compelled by government to take such action.

There are, even so, occasions when individuals are unable, or unwilling, to prepare for the worst by saving or taking out insurance and who deliberately, or unwittingly, depend on other mechanisms to get by at times of crisis. In such circumstances, transfers that can occur in real time without strategic planning are important. These may involve help from families, friends and community organizations as well as government transfers.

Informal transfers

Even in advanced welfare societies, the family remains the pre-eminent source of social security. This is strikingly evident from Figure 4.6. Although relating to the 1980s, it shows that in three countries with contrasting welfare regimes, well over 80 per cent of the income of families headed by a person aged 25–54 derived from the wages earned by the family head and/or their partner. Whatever their other functions, marriage and cohabitation are mechanisms for sharing income and assets, transferring cash and other resources between partners and their children. They provide economies of scale, lessen costs associated with reproduction and offer a modicum of protection at times of financial crisis. Taken overall, the contribution of social insurance or other social security benefits to incomes is negligible in comparison with intra-household transfers. For pensioners, and for the minority of families with working-aged adults who are without paid employment, the role of social security benefits is obviously much greater.

Transfers within the extended family can also be important, especially from parents to children and, later in life, from children to parents. The transfer of property and other assets, especially at death and in the benefactor's later years, is a major mechanism by which families and social classes maintain their financial and social standing. Among the poorest families in Western societies, cash normally exchanges hands only between relatives and even then, to avoid accusations of charity or moral blackmail, such exchanges may take the form of interest-free loans (Clasen *et al.* 1998; Walker and Collins 2003). In East Asia, the priority attached to kinship

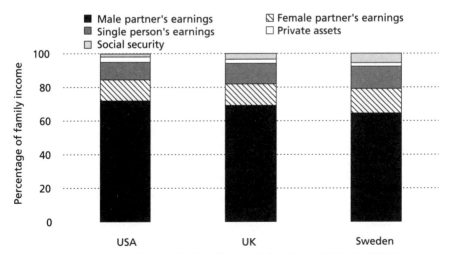

Figure 4.6 Income packages for families with head aged 25–54 (1980s)
Source: Rainwater *et al.* (1986)

under Confucianism is sometimes cited as a reason for the late development of welfare states, although this view is strongly contested by some scholars (White and Goodman 1999).

Such intra-familial exchanges are assumed between people living in the same household when means are assessed for the purposes of social assistance and, in Germany, direct relatives not living with claimants may also be required to make a financial contribution. Non-monetary exchanges between households are more frequent, including informal assistance, bartering, gifts, discounted produce, second-hand clothes and childminding. However, such exchanges are often avoided when families feel that they may be unable to meet unstated and unpredictable obligations and expectations of reciprocity that invariably attach to informal exchange of this kind (Pahl 1984; Nelson and Smith 1999).

It should be noted, therefore, that although informal transfers circumvent the contracted behaviour inherent in saving and insurance, each form of exchange has associated with it quite complex and sometimes arduous obligations.

Community initiatives

Charities have long provided an element of social security. Indeed, as explained in Chapter 2, welfare states in European countries were often created as an alternative to charitable support, seeking to provide the comprehensive coverage that charities are typically unable to offer and to avoid the stigma that attached to charity. While charity is widely despised by low-income families, it is necessarily used when more acceptable sources of support are not available to them (Kempson 1996; Walker and Collins 2003).

Informal exchanges between neighbours can be extended and codified within formal neighbourhood organizations (Kempson 1996; Holman 1998). Sometimes, these organizations are spontaneous in their origins. On other occasions, professionals, often from outside the area, deliberately create them as part of a process of community development (Holman 1998).

Credit unions are a further example of collective initiative to promote social security. They have their origins in Rochdale, England, where, in 1844, a group of weavers founded a cooperative store, and in Germany where a cooperatively owned mill and bakery was founded by Hermann Schulze-Delitzsch in response to crop failures and famine in 1846. In 1850, Schulze-Delitzsch established the first cooperative credit society, known later as a 'People's Bank'. Today credit unions exist in around 100 countries and offer a vehicle for individuals who would usually be excluded from formal financial institutions because of low or irregular incomes to save and gain access to low-cost credit.

Credit unions have much in common with early mutual insurance schemes. Based in local areas, or obliged to have some other collective bond, perhaps through an informal organization, employer or occupation, members are able to hold a limited number of shares – in Britain, shares are valued at a pound and ownership is restricted to £5,000. Dividends on shares typically range between 1 and 3 per cent and it is the ownership of shares that endows members with the right to borrow. Although credit unions are governed by the members themselves, the credit union movement in certain countries espouses a somewhat moralistic agenda in addition to the goal of creating credit at fair and reasonable interest rates. This agenda includes the promotion of thrift, controlling and using members' savings to their mutual benefit, and training members to use money wisely (HM Treasury 1999).

Occupational welfare

Employment offers its own social security. Not only does it provide wages – the main source of household income (see Figure 4.6), depending on the jurisdiction, occupation and status, it also offers a range of other pecuniary and non-pecuniary rewards. These can include health insurance, pensions, car use, childcare, recreational facilities, subsidized meals, discounted travel and goods, to name only the most obvious. With employment comes a virtual welfare state denied to those without employment.

The monetary value and importance of occupational welfare varies according to the nature and availability of government and other provision. In the USA, the most significant part of the employment package after wages is health insurance, since the healthcare system is largely private and medical charges are high. Somewhat similarly in South Korea, employment provided a passport to health insurance until the introduction of comprehensive national insurance in 1999. Private health insurance is less important in Australia, Britain and Germany where healthcare is largely free at the time of use. (Even so, 6.9 million Britons had health insurance in 2000, with 15 per cent of all health spending financed privately.) In Britain, the major occupational benefit is frequently an occupational pension that is typically funded by employer contributions and obligatory deductions from wages. About 35 per cent of employees have an occupational pension, a figure that has fallen steadily from 41 per cent since 1988/9. People with occupational pensions disproportionately hold higher status occupations and/or work in the public sector. Often, on retirement, an occupational pension lifts a person in Britain above means-tested social assistance.

An ironic feature of occupational welfare – or, strictly, of employment – is that it also facilitates access to government social insurance. As noted above, employers as well as employees typically pay contributions, thereby sharing the cost. Moreover, in Germany and other conservative welfare regimes, access to the much higher benefits payable through the social insurance system is a major advantage conferred by employment.

Occupational welfare provides part of the remuneration package received by employees. Some parts of the package might be construed as wages taken in kind. Others, notably social insurance contributions and pensions, are better thought of as deferred wages payable in the future in particular prescribed circumstances. From the employer's perspective, occupational welfare forms part of their current costs and, in so far as is possible, employers will seek to recoup them from the prices charged for the goods or services they sell. Employees may sometimes not even recognize the benefits of occupational welfare, viewing pension contributions simply as wage deductions that reduce current spending power.

Government transfers

Financing benefits directly from general government revenue is a feature of all social security systems, although the degree of variation in importance from one country to another led Esping-Andersen (1990) to use it as one of the criteria by which to categorize welfare regimes (Comparison 4.1). Government almost invariably directly finances social assistance, although in a number of countries, Germany, Sweden and the USA included, funding is shared between different levels of government. In Australia, as already noted, most social security is directly financed by the commonwealth (federal) government and means-tested, while in Britain, the last 30 years have witnessed a growth in non-contributory, directly financed benefits, especially for disabled people, that are not means tested. In many countries, social insurance funds are topped up by government, either as a matter of routine or in crisis situations to prevent insolvency.

Direct government financing has a number of attractions. It allows a quick response to unanticipated contingencies and to new needs created by social change. It readily facilitates up-rating of benefits in line with inflation and, indeed, with wages and productivity, thereby allowing benefit recipients to share in rising social prosperity. It creates the possibility of financial security for people unable to accumulate adequate resources of their own even via social insurance. These would include persons unable to work due to disability, limited skills, childrearing obligations or other barriers including discrimination.

On the other hand, direct finance requires strong government able to raise taxes and to redirect resources to less politically powerful groups within society and hence – within a social democracy – the political mandate to do so. Directly financed schemes – perhaps especially when part of a system of mixed provision – are vulnerable to retrenchment and erosion if tax revenues fall or opinion shifts against government. Rights to directly financed benefits are perhaps more fragile than those based on a contract involving a record of contributions and may be further weakened to the

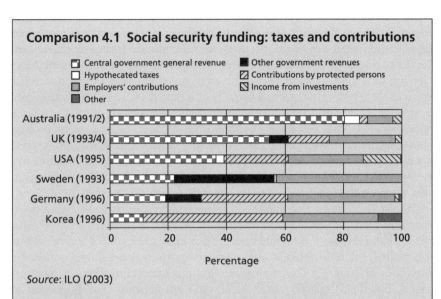

Comparison 4.1 Social security funding: taxes and contributions

☒ Central government general revenue   ■ Other government revenues
☐ Hypothecated taxes   ▨ Contributions by protected persons
☐ Employers' contributions   ◨ Income from investments
▨ Other

Source: ILO (2003)

The graph shows the sources of social security finance for case study countries in the mid-1990s, the latest data available at the time of writing. Broad patterns are clear-cut but care is needed in interpretation of the details, not least because data for Australia, Sweden and the UK are based on earlier accounting conventions than for the other three countries.

The data reveals the widely different emphasis given to contributory benefits, highest in Korea and lowest in Australia, and in the distribution of payments between employers and individual contributors: loaded on employers in Sweden and individuals in Korea.

The role of general revenue funding is the mirror image of insurance. High spending in Australia and the USA is almost entirely disbursed in the form of means-tested benefits; it is tempered in the UK by non-contributory benefits, mostly to disabled people. The prevalence of funding from 'other government sources' in Sweden reflects spending on medical care, pensions and family allowances. Government spending for the USA is not disaggregated and all appears under the heading 'central government general revenue' even though some of this will be raised and disbursed by states.

extent that a sense of shame or stigma attaches to the process of claiming benefits. Certainly, this is true of residual social assistance schemes, although their origins in charitable support and the Poor Law, and the need to undergo a means test, contribute to the stigma. Stigma appears to be less in Australia where almost all social security is funded directly and in Britain for directly funded schemes administered without a means test such as Severe Disablement Allowance.

Governments raise revenue in a plethora of different ways including: direct taxation of the income of individuals and businesses; indirect taxes on sales; excise duties on goods crossing international frontiers; charges on services and goods provided by governments themselves; and investments of varying kinds. This means that the cost of financing social security funded from general revenues is spread broadly and thinly, although not necessarily evenly, across the population as a whole. Very occasionally specific taxes are **hypothecated** – that is, earmarked for spending for specific purposes such as social security. Pay-as-you-go social insurance is sometimes considered a special case of hypothecation, especially where benefits, being not directly related to contributions, make the parallels with pure insurance rather tenuous as is the case in Sweden and the UK.

To conclude, as an alternative to setting aside resources to be called upon when needed, as saving and insurance entails, individuals can rely on reciprocal generosity or obligation, anticipating that others will help out when times are hard. This model of transfers, whether organized within the family or collectively via employers, community organizations or governments, has the attraction of rapid response but depends on a high level of trust between individuals and generations (Chapter 12). As with insurance, the unique contribution that government can make is to compel participation, thereby enabling risk sharing to be more broadly based and, from a societal perspective, correspondingly cheaper.

Case Study 4.3 Benefit administration in the USA

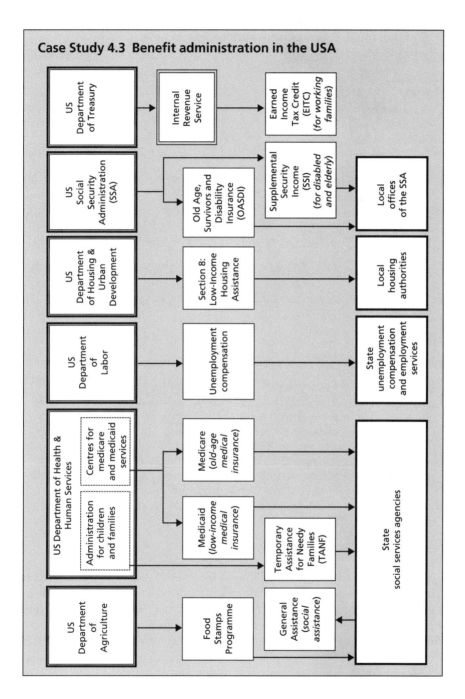

Comparison 4.2 Systems for retirement income

	Australia	Germany	Korea	Sweden	UK	USA
State						
Contributory						
Flat rate					✓	
Earnings related	✓	✓	✓		✓	✓
Non-contributory						
Means tested	✓		✓	✓	✓	✓
Flat-rate universal						
Complementary (Private)						
Mandatory						
Occupational	✓			✓		
Personal				✓		
Voluntary						
Occupational		✓		✓	✓	✓
Personal		✓		✓	✓	✓

Source: ISSA (2003)

The table summarizes the packages of provision for retirement available in each case study country. While a mix of state and private sector pensions are available in each country, countries differ in their reliance on voluntary and compulsory private provision. Korea was due to introduce mandatory occupational pensions in 2003. Sweden abolished flat-rate national provision in 1999 when compulsory, private, fully funded *'premiereservsystem'* accounts were introduced.

Closing summary

Social security, defined generically as in Chapter 1, is invariably the largest area of public spending but contributes little directly to national output or the production of goods and services. Rather, it is a mechanism for pooling risk and redistributing resources from individuals who currently have more to those that have less. In so doing, it provides individuals with a greater degree of financial security against the consequences of many contingencies than most could achieve by personal saving and reduces the collective cost of providing this security.

Social security is achieved through two routes: insurance and transfers. For technical reasons described above, private or commercial insurance cannot cover all eventualities or do so in ways that are affordable to all. Social insurance, provided or orchestrated by government, uses compulsion to enforce risk pooling among people with diverse levels of risk, causing those less at risk to subsidize provision for others.

The largest, protective transfers of resources take place within households and families. These transfers are complemented by more or less formal community transfers, by occupational transfers that benefit those in employment or who have previously had employment, and by social security benefits financed from general government revenues.

The pooling or sharing of risk increases as provision moves from personal saving through private and social insurance to benefits financed from general government revenues. Although there are exceptions, liberal welfare regimes are characterized by greater reliance on family and private insurance, conservative regimes by social insurance and social democratic regimes by making more use of general taxation.

Further reading

Although somewhat dated and narrowly focused on the USA, Rejda (1994) remains a good introduction to the principles of private and social insurance. The reports of the Pension Provision Group (PPG 1998) and O'Connell (2003) are correspondingly concerned with British provision but their respective discussions about the principles and problems of funding old-age pensions are equally applicable to other systems. A report by the Pension Policy Institute (PPI 2003) provides a brief description of pension schemes in the USA and various European countries.

Specialist journals are a useful source of up-to-date information and analysis and have the advantage of being peer reviewed. Important journals to keep abreast of include:

- *American Economic Review*
- *Benefits: Journal of Social Security Policy and Practice* (UK)
- *European Journal of Social Security*
- *Fiscal Studies* (UK)
- *International Social Security Review*
- *Journal of Economic Literature*
- *Journal of European Social Policy*
- *Journal of Human Resources* (US)
- *Journal of Policy Analysis and Management* (US)
- *Journal of Social Policy* (UK)
- *OECD Employment Outlook* (Annual)
- *Review of Income and Wealth*
- *Social Security Bulletin* (US)
- *Social Security Review* (Australia)

chapter

five

Allocation and Administration

This chapter is about the mechanisms through which people receive social security.

In Chapter 4 it was explained how societies find or set aside the resources to meet the shortfall in income of individuals and families who find themselves in certain prescribed circumstances. The intention in this chapter is to describe how these resources are allocated to families and individuals. Simple though the task of allocation may seem, it has spawned some of the largest administrative institutions in the world, involving thousands of staff, vast computer resources and libraries full of legal instruments, instructions and guidance. Given the scale of this welfare enterprise, it is evident that this chapter can provide no more than a basic introduction to the main institutions and issues, a number of which are covered in more detail in later chapters.

The chapter begins by delineating the main routes by which people receive social security benefits. The kinds of institution that have been established to administer social security are described in the next section before outlining the mechanics of welfare administration. How effective the institutions are and the criteria for establishing this are considered in Chapter 11.

Routes to entitlement

A number of definitions are in order. A person is **eligible** for a benefit if they meet all the qualifying conditions and **ineligible** if they do not. The eligible person will be **entitled** (participle of a verb) to the benefit in question if they apply for it. **Entitlement** (a noun) is the amount of benefit that they should receive on application. Figure 5.1 graphically portrays the main routes that people have to negotiate, from becoming eligible for a social security benefit

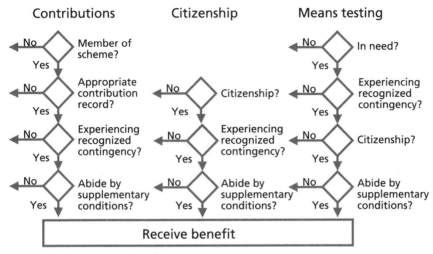

Figure 5.1 Routes to entitlement

to receiving their entitlement. The routes, it will be noted, correspond with the funding strategies discussed in Chapter 4: insurance via contributions and transfers via citizenship and/or means testing.

The insurance route

Figure 5.1 presents the routes to an entitlement as a series of binary decision points relating to qualifying conditions or requirements. Sometime applicants for benefits experience these points as a series of barriers that they have to overcome. The first step on the route to an entitlement is for a person to become an **applicant,** by making an application for benefit. In Figure 5.1, it is assumed that all people make an application. The reasons why many people in fact do not take this step are considered in Chapter 9.

The first qualifying condition on the insurance route to benefit is that the applicant belongs to the insurance scheme. With private insurance, the applicant will generally need to be able be produce a legal document naming them as a policyholder. For social insurance, the applicant may similarly need to produce some evidence that they are members of the scheme, often a unique social security number. Sometimes people may be entitled to benefits as dependants of the policyholder or because they are otherwise named on the insurance policy.

More often than not, applicants will need to have made a prescribed number of premium payments or contributions during a delimited period in order to be eligible for benefits. The reason for this is often to limit the scope for adverse selection or moral hazard. Sometimes, however, these requirements are waived for the purposes of social security. For example, in

Germany and Britain individuals are credited with contributions during periods of sickness and unemployment without which they would later be denied receipt of invalidity benefits.

Entitlement to benefit is also dependent on the applicant having genuinely experienced the insured risk. For unemployment benefit, for example, the person will typically need to have lost their job involuntarily, possibly after a minimum period of employment. Likewise, for accidental injury insurance, the injury will need to have been acquired in circumstances covered by the policy.

Finally, it is highly probable that the applicant will need to abide by a set of supplementary conditions, often designed to avoid abuse of the scheme. In the case of social insurance to cover unemployment, for example, applicants may need to be prepared to actively engage in looking for work, to take jobs offered to them or to engage in training or work experience. This is so in all six of the case study jurisdictions.

The qualifying conditions are imposed to protect schemes against abuse and fraud and to help ensure their financial viability. They also serve to make schemes more exclusive, which will often benefit existing policyholders and contributors by limiting the level of premiums that they have to pay. As a corollary, of course, the conditions limit the number of people and risks that are covered. Moreover, the conditions can sometimes serve systematically to deny access to particular groups. When, for example, entitlement to social insurance is based on employment contributions it can disadvantage people with short or interrupted work histories such as women, young people and migrants.

The citizenship route

Instead of membership of an insurance scheme, applicants via this second route will need to demonstrate citizenship or, for schemes based on residency rather than citizenship, that they have been resident in the jurisdiction for a prescribed time. They will also have to prove themselves to be in circumstances covered by the scheme and may be required to fulfil certain supplementary conditions designed to ensure that their claim is genuine.

The citizenship or residency route to benefit is generally much more inclusive than insurance and, indeed, is sometimes applied because the risks covered are not amenable to insurance. However, while the symbolism of inclusion is strong (with rights to benefit conferred to all by means of legal membership of society), citizenship benefits necessarily exclude some groups, occasionally arbitrarily. Migrants, ethnic minorities and gypsies, for example, may be disadvantaged in this way.

The means-tested route

The third route to entitlement is via means testing which, as explained in Chapter 1, is usually termed social assistance. This route generally couples the occurrence of a particular contingency with the condition that the applicant has income and assets below a prescribed threshold. As a result, social assistance is often the least inclusive route to benefit receipt since large numbers of people may experience the contingency and suffer declines in income and living standards, without falling beneath the means-tested thresholds.

Rigorous supplementary conditions will frequently also apply. These may be designed to ensure applicants are genuinely in need and 'deserving' in the sense that their circumstances are unavoidable and not due to profligacy, fecklessness or other socially unacceptable behaviours. Where claims are judged to be 'undeserving', they may be rejected outright or applicants paid reduced benefit or required to fulfil additional conditions. Supplementary conditions may also be intended to deter unnecessary claims or to assist people to minimize the risk of them ever needing to apply again. The 'workhouse test' applied under the English Poor Law is an eighteenth-century example, requiring that applicants had to endure the humiliation and rigours of entering the workhouse in order to receive benefit. In the USA, the time limit imposed on receipt of TANF is itself a deterrent to claiming and encourages staff to help applicants find alternatives to benefit. Activation and welfare to work policies additionally often compel recipients to engage in activities intended to reduce the length of benefit receipt. In South Korea, eligibility depends on income capacity not actual income (OECD 2000).

Occasionally, conditions of citizenship or residency will also pertain. In the USA, means-tested SSI for old age, blindness and disability is denied to legal migrants arriving after 1996. In the UK, applicants for social assistance are required to fulfil a habitual residency test: in Germany, certain restrictions apply to foreigners while most benefits in Australia are only available to residents.

The requirement for applicants to demonstrate that means are less than a specified minimum obliges them to supply detailed financial information concerning income and usually assets also. Equally, it requires the bureaucracy to establish rigorous methods of checking the authenticity of evidence. Demonstrating need is, in the context of achievement-orientated society, akin to admitting failure and this may in itself limit the number of applications (see Chapter 9).

In summary, the three principal routes by which individuals can gain entitlement to social security (means testing, insurance and citizenship) are characterized by increasing inclusivity. In reality, though, the combination of supplementary conditions and special dispensations can alter this sequence; social insurance is very inclusive in Germany but so, too, is means testing in Australia.

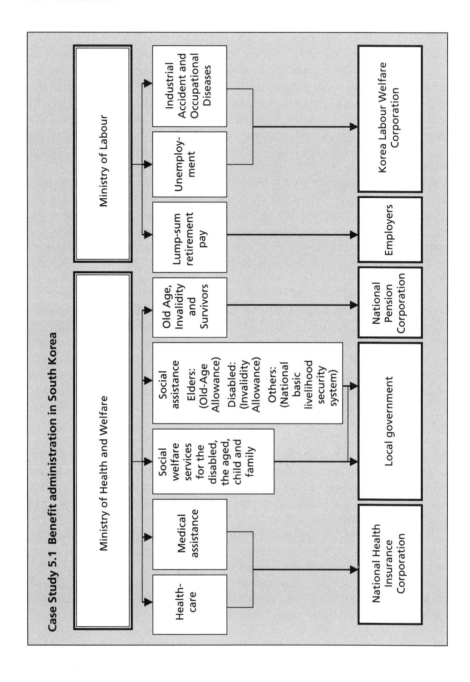

Case Study 5.1 Benefit administration in South Korea

Institutions

There are five broad types of organization involved in social security administration: (1) national and (2) sub-national governments and their executive wings and agencies; (3) 'social partnership' organizations typically constituted under a tripartite board involving government, employers and trade unions; and commercial and mutual organizations that (4) deliver pensions and benefits on an insurance model or (5) are contracted by government to deliver certain social security provisions. The structure and organization of these institutions is naturally shaped by the requirement to deliver social security payments to large numbers of people. They also reflect the basis of entitlement; partnership organizations are more likely to be engaged in delivering social insurance benefits and sub-national governments in administering social assistance. However, the institutions are also moulded by particular welfare regimes and bear the imprint of history because they are rarely replaced but quite often adapted to accommodate exogenous change and new policy directions.

National government

National governments are invariably charged with responsibility for developing strategic social security policy and for regulating, and sometimes stimulating, the activities of sub-national government, private insurance companies and pension funds. Typically, they endeavour with other social security institutions to ensure a comprehensive and coherent pattern of provision. In reality this outcome is rarely achieved due to constraints on central authority, competing interests and political infighting, lack of foresight or political will, technical obstacles or straightforward incompetence. The result is often duplication of provision, poor targeting of policies and unanticipated interaction between benefit schemes that can generate perverse incentives for both social security providers and recipients.

As well as being responsible for policy design, national governments can engage in the delivery of benefits. The extreme case is Britain where almost all social security policies are both national in coverage and delivered by executive agencies of national government. The executive agencies, for example the Pensions Service and Jobcentre Plus, have delegated, though tightly circumscribed authority to determine methods of delivery such as the balance between local offices and centralized processing, but no responsibility for the design of benefit schemes. Chief executives report to the host Department of Work and Pensions headed by a cabinet minister. The Social Security Administration (SSA) in the USA is similar but instead of reporting to a federal department the principal line of accountability is to Congress which also determines strategic policy design. The SSA develops its own mission statements and goals; the costs of benefits and administration are met from payroll deductions (under the Federal Insurance Contributions Act and the Self-Employment Contributions Act) that are accounted for via social security trust funds.

Central government is also likely to play an important role in policy implementation where the delivery of benefits is integrated into the tax system. This is true in Britain, but the USA is the archetypal case. The Earned Income Tax Credit, administered by the US federal Internal Revenue Service, delivers $32.3 billion of benefit to 19.4 million families (Wiseman 2003a). Certain states also implement tax credit schemes of their own.

Sub-national government

The role of sub-national governments in the delivery of benefits reflects the structure of subsidiarity within a jurisdiction – that is, the nature and degree of devolution of responsibility for policy design and implementation to lower tiers of government. It is appropriate to talk of degrees of **devolution** where sub-national governments are responsible for varying aspects of the design and/or financing of social security. **Decentralization** applies where sub-national governments deliver national policies on an agency basis (Bolderson and Mabbett 1997).

Sub-national governments tend to have greatest responsibility for social assistance provisions, which, historically, had their origins at the most local, lowest tier of governance. However, national governments have tended over time – the USA partially excluded – to assume greater control of the parameters of policy, giving higher priority to the goal of **territorial justice** (equal treatment irrespective of place of abode) than to local political accountability.

In Germany, responsibility for social assistance (*Sozialhilfe*) is split between three or more tiers of government. The Federal Ministry of Labour and Social Affairs (*Bundesministerium für Arbeit und Sozialordnung*) provides a broad policy framework and sets the minimum benefit payable. The *Länder*, the second tier of government, determine the standard rates of benefit payable (at 1 July 2000 they varied by only 5 per cent between different *Länder*). The third tier comprises the competent authorities, local authorities (*örtliche Träger*) that are responsible for funding and delivering benefits (although this last responsibility can be delegated to yet smaller units or communes known as *Gemeinde*). The local authorities fund social assistance from local taxes and block grants from the *Länder* and federal government. In effect, the federal government determines the minimum level of benefits but leaves lower tiers of government to administer the scheme and meet most of the cost. In Sweden, where a lowly tier of government (the municipalities) is also responsible for the delivery and funding of social assistance (*socialbidrag*), municipalities are permitted far greater discretion over the levels of benefit paid, albeit under the supervision of the National Board for Health and Social Welfare (*Socialstyrelsen*). In contrast, local authorities in Britain have no policy control over the two schemes that they administer – means-tested Housing Benefit and Council Tax Benefit. Nor, as agents of central government, do they bear any programme costs (except if errors are made).

In marked contrast, US states have unfettered freedom to decide whether to implement and fund social assistance schemes. In 1998, 35 states (including the District of Columbia) ran general assistance programmes, but in nine of these states provision varied between counties and in two other cases assistance was not available throughout all of the state (Gallagher *et al.* 1999). Since 1996, states have also had considerable licence to shape the design of TANF.

By way of conclusion, Table 5.1 locates some of the social security schemes discussed in a matrix defined by which tier of government has responsibility for the design and funding of the schemes. Non-devolved provision, where policy design and funding are a national responsibility, would be located in the top left cell of the matrix. In this case, the financial risk is shared most widely and uniformity of provision is prioritized. If administration costs are borne locally, this provides an incentive for cost-effective implementation. When fully devolved (schemes located in the bottom right-hand cell), local politics and accountability might encourage effective targeting and possibly limit expenditure. Where design is devolved but funding is not, high and inefficient expenditure might be expected. Tensions between central and local government are perhaps most likely when funding is devolved and policy design is not. These tensions are discussed in more detail in Chapter 11.

Social partnerships

Many social partnership organizations engaged in the administration of insurance benefits had their origins in industry-wide agreements drawn up between employers and trade unions, borne out of mutual self-interest (Chapter 4). Government later became involved first as regulator and then as a major financial contributor. They include unemployment funds in Sweden and pensions institutes in Germany. Table 5.2 is analogous to Table 5.1, except that the dimensions indicating tiers of government have been replaced by the distinctions between government and non-government responsibility. Early social partnership organizations would have been located in the bottom right-hand cell, with complete independence from government. Over time, organizations have tended to migrate up the matrix and along the diagonal, reflecting the increased role of the state.

Social partnerships often began as not-for-profit, mutual insurance organizations with contributions set in line with the expected value of

Table 5.1 Devolution of administration

Programme design	*Funding raised*					
	Largely national		*Shared*		*Largely sub-national*	
	Programme	*Administration*	*Programme*	*Administration*	*Programme*	*Administration*
Largely national	UK: Housing Benefit	USA: Unemployment Insurance		UK: Housing Benefit	Sweden: social assistance USA: Unemployment Insurance	Germany: *Sozialhilfe* Sweden: social assistance
Shared	USA: AFDC		USA: TANF			
Largely sub-national				USA: TANF	Germany: *Sozialhilfe* USA: general assistance	USA: AFDC USA: general assistance

benefits. The increased involvement of government has typically been to allow benefits to depart from levels based on actuarial probity. Benefits have also been increased to ensure that they exceed social assistance levels, dependency additions have been introduced and coverage extended to the less well-paid. On occasions, too, governments have had to rescue funds from financial insolvency.

Partnerships are by their nature multiply accountable to the different interest groups represented on their boards of management. Employers, insured persons and beneficiaries may well take different views as to the desirability of higher contributions and the link between contributions and benefits. Governments can have an interest in increasing the coverage of schemes run in partnership to divert people from tax-funded benefits. To the extent that this means pooling people with divergent risks and puts upward pressure on premiums, it is likely to be opposed by employers and existing workers. Equally, non-governmental interests in partnerships may be tempted to exploit the government's position as underwriter of last resort in advocating over-generous benefits and by paying inadequate attention to actuarial considerations. These tensions have been variously resolved (or contained) by varying the powers of participants, both legislatively and through custom.

The varying pattern of responsibility and accountability between social partners can be illustrated with reference to the insurance funds in Germany. As an exemplar of a conservative regime, partnership organizations are a major feature of German welfare provision. The 27 pensions institutes (*Rentenversicherungsanstalten*, LVAs), 900 or more sickness funds (*Krankenkassen*, KKs) and the Federal Employment Institute (*Bundesanstalt für Arbeit*, BA) are all self-administering legal entities under public law. Each institution is allowed to make subsidiary legislation that does not need to be presented to parliament. The boards of pensions institutes comprise equal numbers of employers and employer representatives but, while autonomous, cannot fix pension rates, entitlement conditions or contributions since these are uniform across Germany. The sickness funds, on the other hand, can fix contribution rates because of the uneven risks they carry and, since 1997, workers have been able to choose the funds to which they belong. Unlike the pensions institutes, which receive a 20 per cent federal subsidy, sickness funds are self-financing. The BA, which administers unemployment and child benefits, differs from both sickness and pension funds in that government is represented on both the 17-strong council of governors and the three-person executive board. Although the BA is 90 per cent funded by employer and employee contributions, its budget has to be approved by the federal government.

Table 5.2 Government accountability in social partnerships

Programme design	Funding raised					
	Largely national		Shared		Largely non-government	
	Programme	Administration	Programme	Administration	Programme	Administration
Largely national						
Shared			Germany: KKs		Germany: LVAs, BA	
Largely non-government					Germany: KKs	Germany: LVAs, BA

Private insurance and pensions

Private-sector insurance firms and pension companies are governed by the normal rules of fair trade, competition and financial probity, and mutual and not-for-profit organizations are usually obliged to maintain similar standards, though often through different legislation. However, because the long-term, financial well-being of individuals is so dependent on the activities of these organizations, their relationship to government is typically different and closer than that of firms in other industries.

In Britain, as in the USA and to a growing extent in Australia, private-sector provision is particularly highly developed, reflecting the residual nature of state provision. Some 225 insurance companies are authorized in Britain to provide pensions and life insurance. In 1999, they collected about £116 billion in premiums and paid out £49 billion in pensions and £31 billion on life policies (ABI 2002). In the same year, insurance companies directly employed about 340,000 people. A year later (2000), the capital value of the UK occupational pension industry was estimated to be £825 billion with the top 200 funds accounting for 57 per cent of the total market (UKSIF 2001). In 2000/1, 52 per cent of single pensioners and 72 per cent of pensioner couples received occupational pensions and even greater numbers had investment income, although often not sizeable amounts (Curry and O'Connell 2003).

Government relationships with pension and insurance companies as providers of social security benefits are influenced by a number of concerns: the complementarities and conflicts with state provision; consumer protection; the financial viability of the industry; and their role in the wider economy. In Britain, the post-war welfare settlement brokered by Beveridge sought to provide universal but minimum protection, thereby ensuring a role for supplementary provision. Generous tax regimes succeeded in stimulating occupational pensions schemes provided by employers, and in the 1980s and 1990s a similar device was used to encourage insurance-based individual (or personal) pensions for the 55 per cent of employees without access to an occupational scheme.

As well as coaxing the pension and insurance companies to provide products to their liking, governments have on occasion to use coercion. Sometimes this is because a government's policy goals are antithetical to the interests of the pension industry. The introduction of a state earnings-related pension scheme in Britain 1978 (abolished in 2002), much later than in conservative and social democratic regimes, was resisted by pension funds as anti-competitive, and the legislative compromise allowed members of occupational schemes to opt out of the state scheme provided their occupational pension provided equivalent benefits. Likewise, the pension industry found marketing personal pensions to low-paid workers financially unattractive and, in the late 1990s, the British government compelled employers to contribute to such schemes and in 2001 insisted that pension companies cut their fund management charges to provide low-cost, personal ('stake-holder') pensions.

Legislative coercion is also used by governments in pursuit of consumer protection goals. For example, before the law in Britain was changed in the 1980s, persons moving between pension schemes lost many of their accumulated rights. There is also legislation in Britain governing, for example, the selling of pension products and the ownership and use made by employers of accumulated occupational pension funds.

The relationship between government and the pension and insurance industry is further influenced by the latter's size. How the industry chooses to invest its funds can profoundly influence the nation's long-term economic performance. However, at the time writing the vulnerability of pension funds to stock market performance is an equally important concern. After years when investments were generating surpluses, the collapse in share prices between 2000 and 2002 put pressure on many funds. This accelerated the conversion of occupational pensions from **defined benefit schemes**, which typically fix pensions as a proportion of final salary, to **defined contribution schemes**, where the level of pension is dependent on the returns on investment and on annuity rates at the point of retirement. It also meant that people with personal insurance pensions had to downgrade expectations of their income on retirement. Given that in Britain, unlike many other countries, the improvement in pensioner incomes that occurred in the last third of the twentieth century was largely due to the increasing generosity of occupational and personal pensions rather than state provision, this recent turn of events is a cause for government concern.

Contractors

The final group of organizations involved in the delivery of social security comprises those selling services to government. They are typically in an **agency relationship** with central or local government, being contracted to deliver a policy over which they have no (or limited) influence.

The precise place of such organizations in the panoply of social security provision has varied between jurisdictions and over time. Until recently they have mostly provided supplementary services. In Germany, for example, where cash social assistance (*Sozialhilfe*) is closely related to social work, social work services are typically provided by charities that are reimbursed by the authorities. In Britain, local government, though having only a limited role in social security provision, has nevertheless provided grants to not-for-profit organizations to provide advice and advocacy services for benefit recipients.

Likewise, in the USA some states have long contracted out more service-orientated components of welfare provision such as job search and placement assistance, childcare, transportation, mentoring and specialized

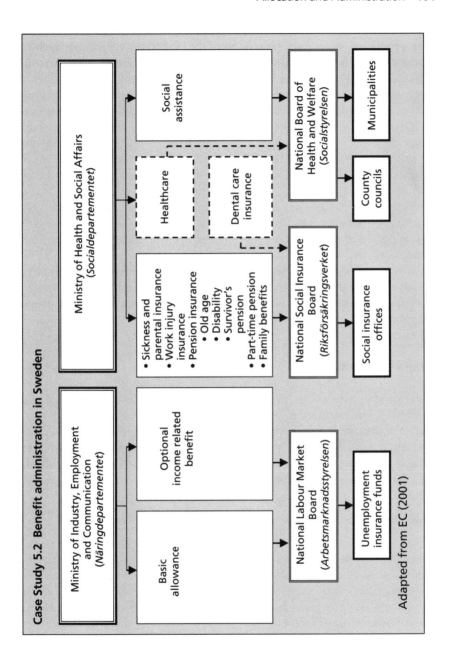

Case Study 5.2 Benefit administration in Sweden

Ministry of Health and Social Affairs
(*Socialdepartementet*)

Social assistance

Healthcare

Dental care insurance

National Board of Health and Welfare
(*Socialstyrelsen*)

Municipalities

County councils

- Sickness and parental insurance
- Work injury insurance
- Pension insurance
  - Old age
  - Disability
  - Survivor's pension
- Part-time pension
- Family benefits

National Social Insurance Board
(*Riksförsäkringsverket*)

Social insurance offices

Ministry of Industry, Employment and Communication
(*Näringdepartementet*)

Optional income related benefit

Basic allowance

National Labour Market Board
(*Arbetsmarknadsstyrelsen*)

Unemployment insurance funds

Adapted from EC (2001)

services for those with mental health and substance abuse problems. However, since 1996 states have been permitted to subcontract case-management activities including the determination of eligibility, and three states, Arizona, Wisconsin and Florida, have contracted out all aspects of TANF administration, with several other states contracting a part. US contractors include commercial firms, such as MAXIMUS and Affiliated Computer Services, and large and small not-for-profit organizations and community groups. Likewise, since the Australian Commonwealth Employment Service was effectively disbanded in 1998, over 200 private and community sector providers (the 'Job Network') have been contracted to provide job brokerage and employment assistance services to those on government benefits. In 2000, the OECD suggested that Korea might do likewise and in Britain, too, there have been moves to contract out case management, and recent legislation allows local authorities to contract out the processing of Housing Benefit applications.

To summarize, public, non-profit-making and commercial organizations are all engaged in the delivery of social security and embedded in complex networks of accountability that differ between jurisdictions and change over time.

Benefit administration

Some of the main components of benefit administration are presented in Table 5.3, differentiating between application processing, infrastructure activities necessary in support of processing, and support services that are frequently provided in addition to, or instead of, cash payments. All three aspects of administration are important, but there is space only to consider the core activity of processing claims.

Entry and application

Points of entry into the benefit system necessarily reflect the institutional structures that in turn are products of history. Private insurance is invariably administered separately from social insurance and assistance, although there are important points of contact. Occupational pensions almost always count as income in the calculation of social assistance payments. Private unemployment insurance often demands payment of state unemployment benefit as evidence supporting a claim.

State provision, too, usually has different points of entry. Insurance benefits are typically administered separately from social assistance, although both kinds of benefits and their administration have been comprehensively merged in Britain while, in Germany, unemployment benefit (*Arbeitslonsengeld*) and its means-tested counterpart (*Arbeitslosenhilfe*) are

Table 5.3 Selected components of social security administration

Application processing	Infrastructure activities	Support and employment services
• Receipt and processing of application	• Policy development	• Child support recovery
	• Collection of premium contributions and taxes	• Substance abuse counselling and treatment
• Verification of supporting documentation	• Compilation and maintenance of contribution/premium records	• Mental health evaluation and treatment
• Calculation of benefit amounts		• Domestic violence evaluation and intervention
• Payment of benefit	• Promotion and advertising of benefits	• Parenting and family support
• Explanation of rights and responsibilities to applicants	• Provision of advice and advocacy services	• Employment orientation and assessment
	• Support of advice and advocacy services	• Supervised job search
• Referral to other resources or benefits	• Advocacy for programme applicants and recipients	• Work experience and on-the-job training
• Administration of case review and appeals	• Staff recruitment, training and management	• Intermediate labour market placement
• Completion and maintenance of case records	• Estate management	• Vocational educational services
		• Post-employment follow-up
• Fraud detection and sanctioning		• Skill enhancement services
• Case management and review		• Employment retention services
		• Provision of supportive services: childcare, transportation etc.

administered together. Sometimes the nature of the contingency and the mode of funding determine the point of entry. So, for example, in Sweden unemployment benefit would be received from a trade-union-administered insurance fund, whereas social assistance would need to be claimed from the municipality.

However, while unemployment benefit in Sweden is delivered through funds administered by trade unions, all other insurance benefits are claimed through local offices of the National Social Insurance Board (*Riksförsäkringsverket*) and such integration is a strategy that has recently been adopted elsewhere. In the USA, there are moves to bring together the delivery of employment services, unemployment benefit and social assistance (TANF). Australia not only integrated provision, with the establishment of customer service centres, but policy design, by merging the

Department of Social Security and the Commonwealth Employment Service to create 'Centrelink'. Since 2002, benefit delivery in Britain has been further refined by organizing provision by client group rather than contingency: all benefits for retired persons being dealt with by the Pensions Agency and those for people of working age through Jobcentre Plus.

Applications have traditionally been taken by post except in the case of social assistance and those benefits for which additional activity is mandated, when personal interviews remain the norm. However, information technology is changing administrative procedures rapidly. In the USA, telephone applications were pioneered by the Social Security Administration, initially for old-age insurance (since validation was available from the administration's own record systems), but now a number of states accept telephone applications for Unemployment Insurance with varying components of the application process being entirely automated. The telephone is the preferred mode of communication in Britain. This reflects customer preferences as well as administrative efficiency but leaves a minority of users without ready telephone access at a considerable disadvantage. Web-based applications are under development (all government services are due to be Web available by 2005) but current practice lags behind aspirations (Kellard 2003).

Verification and decision-making

Once an application and supportive evidence is received, there are three generic steps in determining the outcome of a claim for social security: verification of the evidence, establishing eligibility and determining entitlement. The first step is typically the most resource intensive in that it involves establishing the applicant's identity (often by means of identity or insurance card), circumstances and, for means-tested benefits, income. Examples of the evidence used are given in Table 5.4.

Verification of income is particularly difficult and it is mainly for this reason that social assistance is generally more expensive to administer than social insurance. Nevertheless, the amount of information sought on income and assets varies according to a weakly discernible pattern; it is generally less when the income-related benefit is also **categorical** (that is, eligibility is determined with reference to age or disability) than when not (Bolderson and Mabbett 1997). While the presumption would appear to be that people who are disabled or aged are unlikely to have substantial other income, categorical benefits are also generally more socially acceptable than generic social assistance schemes.

A major difficulty in verification is that the administration requires proof of a negative: namely, that the applicant has no more income or assets than declared, a fact that can never be conclusively established. Positive evidential requirements are often substituted for negative ones. So, in the USA, staff administering food stamps are obliged to check reported income

Table 5.4 Examples of evidence used in determining claims

	Initial claim	*Review*
Institutionally generated evidence	• Contributions record • Address • Others in household • Tax code • Motor vehicle ownership • Vital statistics (births and deaths)	• Date from employers – new hires, wage returns payroll • Tax returns • Income tax data
Claimant generated evidence	• Social security card • Notice of dismissal • Recent payslips • Declaration of income	• Regular signing • Attendance at interviews, training courses etc. • Continuing disability reviews

Source: Bolderson and Mabbett (1997)

against external sources including records of unearned income held by the Inland Revenue Service and employers' quarterly wage returns coded by the State Wage Information Collection Service.

Decisions on eligibility and entitlement are based on interpretative judgement or unfettered discretion, the former characteristic of insurance, the latter more associated with social assistance. **Interpretative judgement** entails following rules to choose between two or more courses of action. The more detailed and prescriptive the rules, the less scope there is for interpretation. Interpretative judgement can be exercised by individuals or collectively by institutions when, for example, legal regulations are accompanied by interpretative text or by examples prepared by a social security administration.

Discretion is exercised when a person or institution chooses between two or more equally valid courses of action, observing the spirit of the legislation but unfettered by rules determining decisions in particular circumstances (Beltram 1984). It should be recognized that 'discretion' used in this way differs from its colloquial usage: 'the capacity to act with prudence and good judgement'. Discretion in this latter sense is to be expected of all social security administrators regardless of whether discretion in the former sense is allowed.

Interpretative judgement and discretion have been associated with the exercise of different kinds of justice: proportional and creative, respectively (Titmuss 1971). **Proportional justice** requires that people be treated equitably, which means that two or more persons whose circumstances are identical will be treated the same, while others whose circumstances are different will be treated differently but to a degree that is proportional and explicit. **Creative justice**, sometimes termed individualized justice, requires a necessarily flexible response to human needs and to the immense variety of complex individual circumstances (Titmuss 1971). Proportional justice demands transparency and published rules that, some have argued, enable applicants to be made aware of their 'rights' (Donnison 1982). Creative justice, on the other hand, permits a personalized response to the individual and the exceptional, but at the expense of weakening the influence or power of the applicant *vis-à-vis* the social security institution.

Discretionary systems are generally more expensive to administer than rule-based ones because they require higher skilled and often professionally trained staff, with time to investigate applicants' circumstances in some detail. Staff-to-applicant ratios need to be higher and, to date, the use of information technology in assessment has been less.

Administrative judgement and discretion are best thought of as 'ideal types' since most decisions taken by social security staff entail elements of both. Pure discretion is comparatively rare even in municipally administered social assistance schemes involving social work input, such as in Sweden or Germany. Pressures on staff time, among other things, mean that decisions come to be codified by either counter-level staff or through detailed management guidance (Chapter 11; Walker *et al.* 1992).

In assessing eligibility, social security staff choose from a number of possible outcomes. They can approve an application, determine entitlement and put a payment into effect. They could reject an application and perhaps refer the applicant to other sources of assistance including charitable institutions. They might defer a decision pending further information. More controversially, they may divert an applicant knowing their claim to be valid. As noted above, the implementation of lifetime limits in the USA, with the introduction of TANF, increased the pressure to deter people from making a claim so as not to deny them the possibility of an award on a later occasion when no alternative was available (Wiseman 2003a). In Germany, the *Länder* have a financial incentive to divert applicants from assistance, part of the cost of which is met locally, to insurance benefits which are federally financed.

Payment, review and sanction

The calculation of entitlement, once judgements have been made as to eligibility, is almost invariably made with computer assistance. So, generally, is the payment of benefit, although methods of payment still vary markedly.

Commercial insurance is apt to make one-off payments in the form of cheques and to pay pensions by credit transfer into recipients' bank accounts. In recent years, social insurance has moved to similar payment methods, although, as of 2003, this process of transition was incomplete in Britain where some payments were still delivered via order books of vouchers to be cashed at post offices. Earned Income Tax Credit in the USA is predominantly paid annually at an end of year tax reconciliation and mailed as a cheque while, in Britain, tax credits can be delivered through the wage packet or by credit transfer. In most countries, payments are generally made monthly, although social assistance offices typically have discretion to pay small irregular amounts in cash, usually in emergencies. Benefits are mostly paid fortnightly in Britain.

Benefits can sometimes be delivered in kind instead of in cash. For the most part, this involves supplementary services such as those listed in Table 5.3, but items such as furniture, clothes and bedding – or vouchers or the money specifically to acquire such items – can be supplied through social assistance schemes in Britain, Germany and elsewhere (although not seemingly in Sweden – EC 2001). Payments of rent and other bills are also sometimes paid directly to landlords or other creditors, although typically only in exceptional circumstances. Food stamps in the USA were initially paid as vouchers to be exchanged for food by participating retailers but are increasingly being paid by electronic benefit transfer, akin to debit cards issued to customers of banks. Other countries are experimenting with this form of payment (Adler and Henman 2001).

While social assistance benefits in Germany and Sweden have always been integrated with social work, the trend over the last two decades has been to link benefit payments with active labour market policies. This means, as noted in Chapter 3, that administrations are increasingly required to deliver jobs or employment experience as well as cash assistance and to provide counselling services and ongoing support. To provide these new services often entails social security administrations contracting with service providers and working more closely with other government agencies, and can lead to mergers, as happened in Britain in 2001, when the Department of Work and Pensions was created from the former Department of Social Security and the Department for Education and Employment. It also means that personnel with labour market expertise, counselling and case management skills need to be recruited or trained to replace or complement staff skilled in the assessment, calculation and payment of cash benefits.

Benefits are put into payment for varying lengths of time and are subject to a range of conditions that typically need to be monitored. As a rule, insurance benefits, especially those relating to old age and disability, are reviewed least frequently: where there are limits on the level of earnings that can be received, reviews of entitlement tend to be conducted annually or perhaps more frequently; where not, benefits may be reviewed more infrequently or even remain in payment indefinitely. Social assistance benefits, though, are often under continuous review since entitlement may depend on weekly or even daily income. Recipients are generally expected to report all changes in circumstances immediately that may trigger reassessment of eligibility and entitlement. To reduce administration costs and work disincentive effects (see Chapters 10 and 11), some income-tested benefits, for example Housing Benefit (*Wohngeld*) in Germany and Tax Credits in Britain, are payable for longer periods with defined changes in circumstances being ignored.

While some reviews of entitlement are integral to the administrative process, others conducted for the purpose of audit or the prevention of abuse may entail re-examining a case and seeking further or alternative evidence (see Table 5.4). Moreover, receipt of social assistance, but also unemployment insurance, is frequently subject to ongoing conditions that applicants have to fulfil, such as active job search, attendance at training classes or regular reporting to the employment or benefit office. Sanctions may take the form of a complete or partial cessation of benefit for varying periods. More commonly, where social assistance benefits are integrated with social work, payment of benefit will be postponed in order to encourage compliance.

Appeals

Most schemes allow applicants to challenge decisions, often on matters of process and administration as well as issues of law. The systems in place differ markedly in status, form and procedure, reflecting the status of the benefit, the basis of entitlement and the legal and constitutional status of the delivery organization. Most systems operate a graded system of review of increasing formality, commencing with a reconsideration of the initial decision, either by the officer who made the original decision or their manager. In the event that the appellant is still dissatisfied, subsequent referral is usually possible to an independent judicial or quasi-judicial body or system. Private insurance and pension funds have typically established industry-wide systems for the redress of grievance and customers can usually also seek satisfaction via the route of customer protection legislation.

It should by now be apparent, even if not so beforehand, that the payment of social security is a non-trivial task. It requires the mobilization of multiple agencies and the deployment of personnel with a diverse range of administrative personal and professional skills. At stake is the financial welfare of millions of social security recipients including some of the most vulnerable members of society. In total, between a twentieth and about a fifth of a nation's domestic product will be used to this end. According to the ILO, in the mid-1990s administration costs comprised 13 per cent of the total in Korea, 2.4 per cent in the USA and 3.6 per cent in Germany.

Case Study 5.3 Benefit administration in Britain

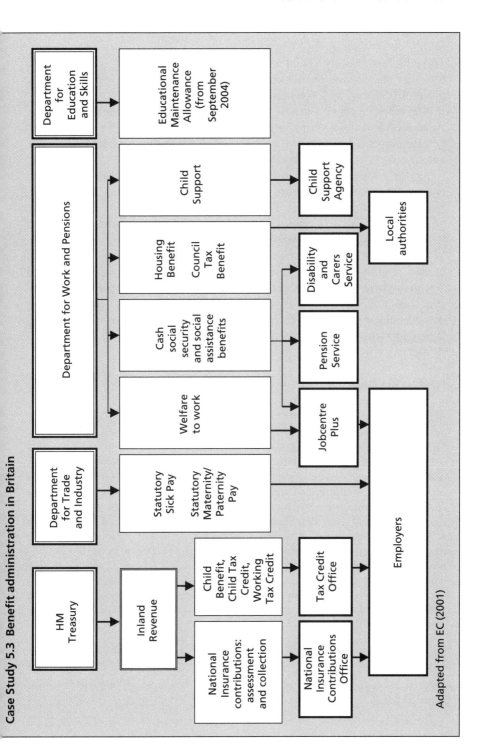

Adapted from EC (2001)

Closing summary

The administration of social security is complex and costly and has led to the creation of some of the world's largest organizations employing many thousands of staff and vast computer resources.

Nevertheless, there are only three routes to claiming benefit: insurance, citizenship and the demonstration of financial need. These, in practice, will be complemented by sets of conditions designed to prevent fraud and abuse and to target resources most effectively.

Similarly, there are only three basic elements in determining an award once an application has been received: validating evidence, determining eligibility and paying benefit. The administrative complexity arises from the need to ensure that decisions are accurate and fair and that the correct benefit is paid to the right people at the appropriate time.

To achieve this aim, a plethora of different institutions has been created in each country involving central and local government, and profit and non-profit organizations embedded in complex networks of legal, financial and transactional relationships. The chapters that follow introduce the conceptual tools necessary to establish how far these organizations succeed in providing modern societies with social security.

Further reading

Bolderson and Mabbett (1997) provide a detailed, primarily descriptive, comparative analysis of the delivery of social security in Denmark, France, Germany, the Netherlands and the USA in the mid-1990s.

Stafford (2003), McKay and Rowlingson (1999) and Wright (2003) offer accounts of social security administration in Britain. Kellard (2003) discusses the development of Britain's use of information technology in benefit administration, while Kelleher *et al.* (2002) report on an early attempt to deliver an integrated work-focused service.

Howard (2003) also describes an attempt to integrate social security with activation but this time in Australia. (Howard undertook the analysis for a PhD thesis; be on the look-out for articles by him.) Hamilton (2002) reviews the effectiveness of recent welfare to work policies in the USA and Bloom *et al.* (2003), in a technically difficult but very significant article, demonstrate the importance of competent administration in determining the effectiveness of policy. Mead (2001) and Riccucci *et al.* (2004) report on the management and administration of social assistance (TANF) in the USA.

 **PART 3**

Effectiveness

chapter

six

Income Replacement and Compensation

This chapter invites the reader to ask whether social security benefits are good enough.

The objectives and functions of social security – the 'why?' questions – were discussed in Chapters 2 and 3, and its funding and delivery – the 'how?' questions – in Chapters 4 and 5. This chapter is the first of four that relate to the question: 'does social security work?', a question that can be asked of entire social security systems or of individual social security schemes. However, it is not the intention to provide the reader with answers. Rather, the aim is to introduce concepts and analytic techniques that the reader can employ to formulate and answer the question for any social security system or scheme. Indeed, it is often instructive to ask the question of different schemes and to compare the results.

Rather than asking whether social security works, the analyst is likely to ask how effective a social security system or scheme is. The term 'effectiveness', when used by economists, 'refers to a simple increase in output following the introduction of an extra unit of input' (Knapp 1984: 77). Does, for example, the provision of a social security system reduce hardship or an extra dollar or pound of benefit reduce the risk of poverty or increase social cohesion? However, the critical requirement is to establish *how* effective social security is, and for this reason it is useful to think of **policy effectiveness** as being a measure of the extent to which a scheme or system attains its objectives.

Conceptualizing effectiveness in relation to objectives transforms the question 'Is it good enough?' from a normative one that can only be answered in terms of the values of the person posing the question, to a critical one that, in theory at least, allows for an objective, empirically verifiable answer. Nonetheless, providing an objective answer is often technically difficult to do.

A helpful metaphor is the thermostat familiar on central heating and air-conditioning systems (Figure 6.1). Using a thermostat entails an awareness of temperature and knowledge of a unit of measurement – for example, degrees centigrade. The user sets a target temperature at which they wish a room to be maintained by the heating or cooling system. The actual temperature compared to the target provides a measure of the effectiveness of the system. Likewise, establishing the effectiveness of a social security scheme requires an understanding of the objective, for example poverty prevention, and a method of measuring this – the **poverty rate**, the percentage of people who are poor. Ideally, there should be a **performance objective** – a precisely specified policy target against which current outcome (the poverty rate) can be measured. In fact, policy targets are rarely explicitly stated (although, in 1999, the British government set a target of eradicating poverty within 20 years) and effectiveness is generally measured by comparing the policy outcome with what had happened before or with outcomes in other jurisdictions.

It will be recalled from Chapter 2 that social security schemes and systems are usually expected to fulfil a range of objectives of varying priority. Not surprisingly, policies are likely to perform better against some objectives than others; given a choice, policymakers will want policies to score highest with respect to the most important ones. Whereas policy effectiveness is an overall assessment made with respect to all objectives, *object performance* is a measure of the effectiveness of a policy with respect to a specific objective.

To return to the thermostat metaphor, the user can usually be confident that the temperature attained is due to the heating or cooling system, although the weather outside could also be a factor. Evaluating social security is not so easy since the particular policy is likely to be just one of a myriad of influences at work and it is very difficult to isolate the impact of the policy alone. Ideally, what is required is the **counterfactual** – the

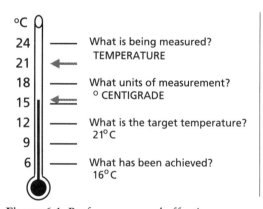

Figure 6.1 Performance and effectiveness

situation that would have obtained had the policy not been introduced. The literature on policy evaluation suggests a number of ways in which the counterfactual could be defined (Walker 2004). It could be another similar jurisdiction, or part of the same jurisdiction where the policy to be evaluated has not been implemented. Differences in outcomes can only confidently be attributed to the policy if everything else about the comparison is identical. Of course, in practice, everything else is unlikely to be identical. Another strategy is to compare outcomes after the introduction of a policy with outcomes beforehand. The difficulty here is that other changes may have occurred apart from implementation of the new policy.

A third approach, considered by some to be the best, entails conducting a policy experiment or demonstration project in which people defined to be eligible to receive the social security benefit are randomly assigned to two groups (Orr 1999). One, the action group, receives the benefit, while the other, the control group, does not. Outcomes for the two groups are compared and any difference observed provides an unbiased estimate of the effect of the policy since all other differences between the two groups are, by definition, random. However, even this approach has its weaknesses. It has to be organized prospectively before a policy is fully implemented. Full implementations, pre-existing schemes or schemes with complete coverage of a jurisdiction cannot generally be evaluated in this way.

Deciding whether a policy is effective is therefore exceedingly difficult. The message is twofold. First, do not assume that a policy is effective merely because the target has been (partially) attained and vice versa; the apparent success or failure may be due to other factors. Secondly, determine the bases upon which measures of effectiveness are established and particularly the robustness of the counterfactual.

Returning to the thermostat metaphor, no mention has yet been made of how the target temperature is set and whether it is adequate. Ambient temperature is essentially a matter of personal taste and some compromise usually has to be negotiated between members of a household, while social conventions apply in public buildings. In democracies, the same is largely true of performance objectives or policy targets such as income replacement or poverty reduction. Targets, explicit or revealed, are more or less sustainable compromises between competing interest groups, variably informed by evidence as to the social and economic consequences of the decisions made.

The remainder of this chapter is devoted to performance objectives relating to two exemplar social security objectives: income maintenance and compensation. (The objectives of alleviating poverty and reducing income inequality are discussed separately in Chapters 7 and 8 respectively.) In each case the concept and mode of measurement is discussed, before reporting on the performance objectives and the extent to which they are achieved. For the most part, no attempt is made to establish the effectiveness of individual policies.

Case Study 6.1 Working-age disability benefit recipients, USA, 1978–2001

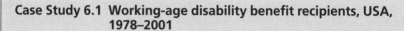

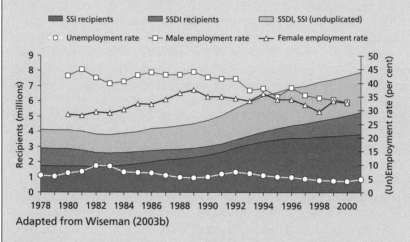

Adapted from Wiseman (2003b)

The chart plots the number of people receiving disability benefits under either the US Social Security Disability Insurance (SSDI) or means-tested Supplemental Security Income (SSI) programmes; the number of recipients, in total, doubled between 1982 and 2001. When SSDI was introduced in the early 1950s, it was conceived as an early retirement scheme and receipt is still conditional on being judged incapable of work. The same disability standard applies to SSI, and the 1300 or so local offices of the Federal Social Security Administration administer both benefits.

The reasons for the increased caseload are complex. Receipt of disability benefits is not time limited and, since less than 0.5 per cent of recipients ever move off benefit, the caseload would be expected to increase over a generation. Moreover, because female economic participation rates have risen, more women have become eligible for SSDI. However, the economic activity rate of persons reporting a disability has fallen with, in the case of men, a particularly marked decline following the passage of the Americans with Disabilities Act in 1990. (See p. 130) Autor and Dugan (2003) suggest the falling economic activity may reflect growing inequality in US wage rates, increasing benefit replacement rates, and generating disincentives for disabled people to seek work.

The imposition of time limits on receipt of Temporary Assistance for Needy Families, together with financial incentives for states to divert recipients from TANF (which states fund) to SSDI and SSI (which they do not), may be a further factor contributing to increased disability caseloads. While disability benefit caseloads are high in areas of high unemployment, the relationship between caseloads and unemployment is negative over time rather than positive, as would be expected if unemployed people were diverting to disability benefits.

Income replacement

Employing social security to maintain living standards by replacing falls in income resulting from prescribed contingencies such as retirement or unemployment is an objective of many insurance-based schemes. As noted in Chapter 2, such schemes are particularly prevalent in conservative welfare regimes. The objective is generally consistent with the aim of fostering social cohesion, since it enables social groups to be included within the same administrative rubric while maintaining the status quo as a result of linking benefits to prior incomes. If social insurance contributions are also income related, the vertical redistribution of income entailed is comparatively limited, especially if measured over long periods. If contributions are not related to income, income maintenance schemes are regressive, re-distributing in favour of the generally better off. The opposite is true if contributions are earnings related and benefits are not.

From the perspective of individual recipients, benefits that offer high levels of income replacement enable them to retain an acquired standard of living and, possibly, to continue to pursue a given lifestyle. This may help them to cope better with the factors precipitating the fall in primary income – for example, unemployment, retirement or childbirth – that are themselves likely to contribute to personal and social stress and lead to the mental illness, marital instability and indebtedness known to be associated with low income (Rafferty and Walker 2003). High benefits may also foster considered and rational decision-taking and adaptation that can have beneficial effects. This is a belief long held by Scandinavian policymakers and echoed recently in US research (Duvå 1976; Scriverner *et al.* 1998). There is growing evidence, for example, that a good match between a person's capabilities and the requirements of the job that they take is likely to benefit career prospects and earnings growth (Kellard 2002; Rangarajan 2002). Such matching can take time and may be hindered by extreme financial pressure. From an economist's perspective, better matching means that the labour market clears more efficiently, allowing for more cost-effective production.

High income replacement is, of course, expensive and raises the spectre of **benefit dependency** – the unnecessarily long-term reliance on benefits (Chapter 10; Deacon 2002). If people can receive almost as much in benefits as they could earn, they might rationally choose to rely on benefits rather than to engage in paid employment.

Determining replacement rates

Setting performance targets for income replacement is not straightforward. It entails the calculation of **replacement rates** which involves expressing benefit entitlement as a percentage of a reference income. The principal issue is choice of the most appropriate reference income. This will differ according to whether priority is given to the objective of maintaining living standards or avoiding perverse incentives. Figure 6.2 illustrates some of the difficulties, plotting the resources of a person who claims benefit after experiencing a long-term fall in earnings, perhaps due to illness. In this not untypical case, setting an earnings-related benefit as a fraction of wage income immediately before the claim would result in a much lower benefit than one based on the person's maximum or average earnings. If concern about disincentives and benefit dependency is a priority, the reference point should not be past income but that which a person could secure by working. Clearly, this is unknown for any individual who is not working and therefore not a very viable basis for setting benefit levels. However, individuals who return to work from benefit generally earn less than they did immediately before claiming because of the erosion of skills and depletion of work experience (McKay *et al.* 1999). This argues for a lower replacement ratio if measured against past earnings.

In general, short-term benefits such as unemployment, sickness and maternity benefits tend to be fixed in relation to recent earnings (often averaged over the latest 12 months); longer-term ones, such as retirement pension, more often reflect a lifetime average or, occasionally, the highest income in any year. The reasons for the difference are complex and vary between jurisdictions. However, concern about disincentives is likely to be the most pertinent factor when fixing rates for short-term benefits and recent wages are likely to be a better predictor of return to work wages than a

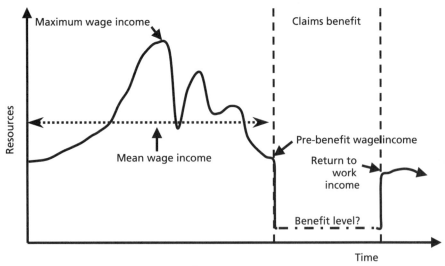

Figure 6.2 Measuring income replacement

lifetime average. With retirement pensions, authorities often attempt to accommodate the different earnings trajectories of manual workers, who average a decline in earning power in later life, and white-collar workers whose incomes continue to increase. Women who take time out of full-time employment to care for children would stand to benefit if pensions were based on the highest income years rather than a lifetime average or even the latest year.

Although the terms 'earnings replacement' and 'income replacement' tend to be used interchangeably, they are not, of course, synonymous. Most social security schemes are designed to replace *earnings* with the intention of reducing the fall in overall *income*. The rate of replacement may be related to either gross or net wages depending on policy objectives, the structure of the tax regime and the tax treatment of benefits. In Sweden, unemployment benefits are fixed in relation to gross earnings (80 per cent of previous daily average earnings) whereas in Germany they are based on net earnings (67 per cent or 57 per cent if no children). Quite often, minimum and maximum rates of benefits are also defined. Minima are applied so that recipients are not obliged to live on inadequate incomes (Chapter 7) and sometimes to ensure that insurance benefits are paid at a higher level than social assistance. Maxima are imposed variously to curb excessive expenditure, to ensure that paid work remains financially attractive and sometimes to foster social cohesion by reducing income disparities.

Assessing replacement rates

While benefit rates are typically fixed as a proportion of earnings, replacement rates tend to be measured in relation to income. (To revert to the thermostat metaphor, this is akin to setting two different targets and is as nonsensical in terms of evaluating a policy as it is in ensuring efficient heating.) Net income is also generally preferred to gross when measuring replacement rates. The reason for these differences stems from administrative practicability. Consider first the analytic perspective. In terms of ensuring a person can continue to enjoy an adequate standard of living, it is the comparability of income in and out of work that matters. Moreover, income net of tax and insurance contributions provides a better index of **disposable income**, what a person has to spend, and hence of living standard than does gross income. Economists also argue that net income comparisons are the most relevant for assessing the disincentive to work produced by the level of benefit. However, from the perspective of administration, it is much easier to assess a person's earnings than to calculate their total income from all sources, which would effectively entail conducting a means test (itself anathema in regimes that prioritize social insurance principles). Similarly, measuring gross earnings is typically easier than assessing net, especially if tax liabilities are determined retrospectively each year.

The estimates of the replacement rates applying to unemployed persons given in Comparison 6.1 are instructive rather than definitive. The first point to notice is that ten estimates are given for each country, varying by prior wage level and family type. The importance of this will be appreciated by recalling, as already noted, that the earnings replacement rate in Germany that applies to unemployment benefit is higher when the recipient has dependent children. Secondly, the replacement rates are based on net income with a comparison between income on benefits in the first month of receipt and income immediately prior to unemployment. Thirdly, the figures take account of *all* benefits, not just those that are fixed explicitly in relation to earnings. Fourthly, the estimates are based not on what individuals actually receive but on what they *ought* to receive if they get all the benefits and tax allowances and relief due to them. In practice, not everybody claims everything that they should and so any differences between countries in the take-up of benefit etc. will distort the comparisons.

A final consideration to bear in mind when interpreting Comparison 6.1 is the difference in national policy objectives. Policy in Sweden and Germany is to achieve high replacement rates, to maintain high levels of income in times of adversity so as to foster social cohesion and solidarity. In the other countries, perhaps the USA and Korea in particular, there is a much greater concern to ensure that work pays and that recipients are not enticed to spend long periods on benefits. So, with reference to *internal* objectives, those of the policymakers themselves (Chapter 2), high replacement rates would indicate success for Germany and Sweden and low ones success for the USA and Korea, providing the actuality of people's experiences matches the modelling reported in the comparison. An economist applying external objectives might conclude from the same comparison that the USA, Korea and, particularly Australia, have less of a problem with work disincentives than Sweden or Germany.

Compensation

As explained in Chapter 2, social security often serves as a social response to individual crises. It can compensate for additional costs incurred, such as those associated with childcare or disability. Alternatively, social security can provide compensation for losses of many kinds: a drop in income, falls in living standards or the inability fully to participate, either socially or economically. The issues raised are most easily understood with respect to disability benefits but the principles can apply to other forms of social security.

It is first necessary to address a number of pertinent but complex issues even though they are not of central concern. In many countries, different benefit systems have been established according to the cause of disability. Victims of war or industrial accidents tend to be dealt with differently from

Comparison 6.1 Net replacement rates for unemployed persons, 1999

Percentage

Earnings level	Average production worker				
Family type	Single	Married couple	Couple 2 children	Lone parent 2 children	Simple mean
Australia	33	29	62	47	43
UK	46	46	49	49	48
Korea	55	55	54	55	55
USA	58	60	57	58	58
Germany	60	56	70	71	64
Sweden	71	71	78	85	76
Earnings level	Two thirds of average production worker				
Australia	45	39	77	59	55
UK	66	64	54	55	60
Korea	54	54	54	54	54
USA	59	59	49	49	54
Germany	67	65	75	76	71
Sweden	82	82	90	93	87

Source: OECD (2002)

The table shows net replacement rates after tax and including unemployment benefits, family and housing benefits in the first month of benefit receipt for four family types at two earnings levels immediately prior to claiming.

Variation is huge – from 29 per cent to 93 per cent – but, on average, replacement rates are highest in Sweden and Germany (consistent with a commitment to promoting social solidarity) and lowest in Australia and Britain (without earnings-related unemployment benefits). Replacement rates are higher for former low-paid workers, suggesting that the objective of income replacement is tempered by a concern about adequacy and social inclusion. The same concern may help to explain why replacement rates, and the rank order of countries, vary by family type, being higher for families with dependent children.

Case Study 6.2a Pension provision in Australia

In common with many countries, pension provision in Australia is built on three pillars. However, two of the three pillars are unusual: first, the universal but means-tested state Age Pension and secondly, compulsory superannuation (private pensions) called the Superannuation Guarantee. The third pillar of pension provision is voluntary superannuation. Australia is also unusual in having no state earnings-related pension.

By being means tested, the Age Pension shares a common characteristic with most Australian social security provision. Founded in 1909, the Age Pension serves as the first pillar – the main provision for most retirement pensioners. It was never intended that the Age Pension would be the sole source of pension, but, by being means tested, the Age Pension also serves as a defence against the failure of a secondary pension to generate an adequate stream of income. The means test for the Age Pension is generous compared to social assistance schemes in other OECD countries but low in relation to comparable social insurance provision (Bateman and Piggott 2001).

Compulsory superannuation was introduced in 1992 following the failure of the government to persuade employers to make adequate voluntary contributions in the context of an accord under which the centralized national wage-bargaining process was meant to incorporate decisions about private pension provision.

The Superannuation Guarantee works by compelling employers to contribute to a fully funded superannuation fund of the employee's choice on penalty of being subject to a punitive Superannuation Guarantee Charge. The expectation is that, over a working life, the guarantee will contribute about the same income as the Age Pension for someone on 75 per cent of average earnings, three fifths more for someone on average earnings, and four times more for someone on one and a half times average earnings.

---

people who are injured in other spheres of life or who are disabled from birth. Social security schemes for the first two groups were often established earlier, typically before the middle of the twentieth century, and have generally provided benefits that are more generous. Sometimes this is because these groups are accorded higher status having suffered impairment while pursuing their duty as citizens or workers. On other occasions, it is possible to identify liability for the injury and hence to extract generous funding from those responsible. There are also ongoing debates in many countries as to the most appropriate way to share the costs and to pool the risks of disability between the state, employers and individuals and, indeed, complex questions about the extent to which the apparent costs of disability are

Case Study 6.2b Partial evaluation of Australian Superannuation Guarantee			
Characteristic		*Evaluation with respect to risk*	
Contributions	• 9% of wage by employer	**Coverage**	Adequate for employees only
Funding	• Fully funded • Individual accounts	**Replacement rate**	Adequate for continuous contributions
	• Many private funds	**Longevity**	Not covered
Benefits	• Defined contribution	**Inflation**	Not covered
	• Fully vested, portable and	**Investment**	Borne by retiree but addressed through asset diversification
	preserved to age 55	**Political**	Accumulated savings insulated but Age
	• No early withdrawals		Pension is exposed
		Gender	Likely to disadvantage women with interrupted employment
	• Lump sum, benefit or annuity		
Coverage	• All employees 18–65, not self-employed	**Expense**	Administration costs with many small funds
	• Earnings above $A450		
Taxation	• Contributions tax deductible	**Economic**	Fund assets valued at 70% of GDP in 1999; 117% by 2020
	• Income and benefit taxed at concessionary rates		
Adapted from Bateman and Piggott (2001)			

actually created by society rather than by disability *per se*. This last perspective is often termed the social model of disability (Howard 2003). While important, with one exception, these concerns here serve merely as a reminder of the simplification necessary in an introductory text.

The exception has to do with language. The social model of disability postulates that disability is imposed rather than incurred. In the USA, therefore, it is often considered appropriate to speak of 'people with disabilities' in preference to 'disabled people'. In Britain, usage has reverted to 'disabled people' to reflect the belief that people are disabled by society on account of their impairment. Current British usage is adopted.

The immediate task is to outline how the financial consequences of disability are assessed and to do so with reference to income, living standards and participation. In each case, there are two broad approaches to assessment that echo the categorical and means-testing methods of determining income (Chapters 1 and 5). One focuses on group differences: individuals who share particular impairments or other characteristics are deemed to have the same needs and incur the same costs, usually assessed relative to people without the impairment. The other method is to seek to establish the actual impact on particular individuals. Both approaches share a common underlying presumption, namely that the financial consequences arise from limitations imposed on the disabled person by their physical or mental impairments. This assumption is, as already noted, liable to challenge from the perspective of the social model of disability.

Income loss

Turning first to income loss, there is prima facie evidence of a link between disability and low income, stronger in some countries than others and more marked before payment of benefits (OECD 2003c). These associations do not determine causation – it is known, for example, that low income can trigger depression and other mental illness (DH 1998a). Nevertheless, they have been used to justify the introduction and retention of a range of disability benefits and as political ammunition to argue for benefit increases. This evidence has also informed the design of disability benefit schemes, which in many countries are graded according to severity of impairment. However, the level at which benefit amounts are set is generally a compromise between competing pressures, the most important of which are generally expense and relativities with other benefits and entry-level wages.

In some systems, the degree of impairment is measured directly by medical practitioners as a percentage loss of faculty or as the extent of incapacity incurred with respect to paid employment, again often expressed in percentage terms. These measurements are then used as weights to determine the amount of benefit to be paid on a reducing scale from the maximum payable when a person has 100 per cent loss of faculty. Medical assessments of this kind are often technically difficult to accomplish and are sometimes considered humiliating by claimants (Legard et al. 2002). The results are often contentious.

In Sweden, the amount of the disability pension (förtidspension) increases with the degree of permanent incapacity for work, with four rates equating to 25, 50, 75 and 100 per cent incapacity. Likewise, in Korea four degrees of disability are recognized, with the first defined as total loss of capacity and requiring constant attendance, the second as severe loss or incapacity, and the third and fourth as some loss. Benefit is paid for the first three levels at the rate of 100, 80 and 60 per cent of the basic pension amount, which is earnings related. In Germany, as in Sweden and Korea, benefit is earnings related but there are just two categories of incapacity (full and partial with rates for the former, based on prior earnings, being twice the latter). Neither the USA nor the UK recognize partial disability, benefit being paid only to those deemed (entirely) incapable for work, and there were plans in Australia to limit Disability Support Pension to people unable to work for more than 15 hours per week, commencing in July 2003 (ISSA 2003). In each country, different and typically more generous provisions apply to people injured at work.

As illustrated, social insurance schemes designed to compensate for income loss resulting from disability are often categorical: eligibility and entitlement are determined by the nature and degree of incapacity, broadly defined. However, claims for private accident insurance sometimes require the loss of income incurred by the insured person to be precisely specified. This requires assumptions about the future income flows that the person would have enjoyed had the accident not occurred (an individual counterfactual) and estimates of income flows likely after taking account of impairment resulting from the accident. Such procedures for assessing loss are perhaps most well developed in the field of tort law, which aims to provide relief for the harm incurred by injured parties as the result of neglectful or deliberate actions by others (LII 2003; Rose 2003). Damages may be recovered with respect to such considerations as the present and future loss of earnings capacity, pain and suffering, and reasonable medical expenses, all of which have to be assessed and given a monetary value. Amounts awarded through this legal process tend to be higher than compensation assessed by other mechanisms, but it is important to recognize that judgements reached under tort law also have to do with the apportionment of blame and can be inflated to deter others from committing the same harms.

Lowered living standards

In addition to lowering income, disability can further reduce living standards by imposing additional monetary and social costs. These include additional healthcare, mobility and personal care costs, and requirements for physical adaptations, and can be incurred by both disabled people and/or their carers.

The medical costs incurred depend both on the health condition or impairment and the nature of health provision, but may include regular and intermittent expenses. These are likely to be minimized where health provision is free at the point of use, as in Britain and Australia, but even here there are supplementary charges for certain medicines and treatments. Also, the cost of health-related consumables such as sanitary equipment can be considerable. Where healthcare is not free, as in the USA, charges for operations, in-patient care and outpatient therapies can be considerable and, without private insurance, even prohibitive.

Depending on the nature of disability, considerable non-medical costs may be incurred as part of day-to-day living. Again, some costs may be occasional, such as when a person is forced to move to accommodation that is more suitable or to have adaptations made to their home. Other expenses can be ongoing, for example additional heating for people who are housebound, transport costs for those who are mobility impaired, or the expense of employing a personal assistant. For carers, there may be income forgone due to not working (at all or as much), extra expenditure associated with the process of caring and intangible, but no less real, psycho-social stress and social isolation resulting from the demands of caring (DH 1998b).

While all the above costs are important, they are quite difficult to assess and quantify. Not only do they vary according to the type of disability or health condition, because of the nature of the service infrastructure, they also differ according to individual circumstance, the degree of family support and the level of income. Affluent disabled people tend to spend more in response to their disability than those with fewer resources. This is partly due to higher expectations with regard to consumption generally – they expect to enjoy a higher standard of living – but also because they are able to take advantage of aids and support services beyond the reach of those on lower incomes. Compensation determined under tort law will take account of this fact, as, indirectly, will earnings-related invalidity benefits.

There are no national schemes to meet the additional costs of disability in Germany, Korea or in the USA, although social assistance schemes can, in specific circumstances, meet such demands. However, in Sweden attendance allowance (*assistansersättning*) is available for persons needing personal assistance for more than 20 hours per week and a car allowance (*bilstöd*) is available for people unable to use public transport. In Britain, Disability Living Allowance and, for people aged over 65, Attendance Allowance have similar functions.

Loss of participation

Finally, it is important to note the fall in social participation that can accompany disability. Limited income curtails expenditure and participation in activities that demand or involve expenditure. Participation may also be made difficult by disabled people being denied access to various social settings because of social discrimination or barriers to physical access, which may result in social exclusion and personal isolation. In some circumstances, additional income provided by benefits may serve to enhance participation – to meet the additional costs necessary to overcome the barriers that society imposes on disabled people. In others, it may serve only to provide a degree of solace.

Ironically, benefits may actually contribute to limited social participation, partly as an unintended consequence of eligibility criteria based on a medical model of disability (Howard 2003). The medical model tends to treat disability as a status (rather than a process), to emphasize permanence and to prioritize impairment as the problem rather than lack of opportunity, and can impose rigidity on a social security system. For example, in Britain and the USA, disability benefits are available only to people who cannot work. A potential result is that a disabled person who seeks work risks losing benefit, while an employee who develops a partial disability may have to give up work entirely to receive any form of compensation. Britain has introduced a number of measures to address this problem, as has the USA, but with only limited success (Loumidis *et al.* 2001; OECD 2003c).

Assessment

This discussion on compensation has focused on the various ways of setting performance objectives related to the many forms of loss associated with disability. It is evident that the case study countries differ markedly in approach and in the targets set. Comparisons 6.2 and 6.3 further illustrate these differences.

Adequate data to assess how well each country is meeting its performance objectives have not been assembled. Remember such an evaluation would require a clear statement of the performance objectives, suitable data on outcomes and an appropriate measurement tool. To be certain that an outcome could justifiably be attributable to the policy would also require a counterfactual. Nevertheless, Comparisons 6.2 and 6.3 serve to excite the imagination.

Presumably, if people were fully compensated for loss or additional costs, they would score no differently from other people on a chosen criterion, such as standard of living. Returning to the example of disability and the criterion of after-benefits income, since this is below average for disabled people in all case study countries, full compensation does not appear to have been achieved, and certainly not in the USA, Korea and Australia (Comparison 6.3). Again, however, it is important to remember the distinction between internal and external objectives. Simply because Australia affords disabled people less income protection than Sweden does not mean that Australian policies are failing. Given that the Disability Support

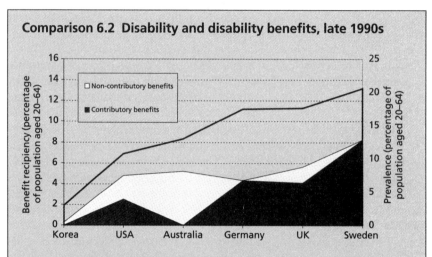

Comparison 6.2 Disability and disability benefits, late 1990s

The chart shows the number of people aged 20–64 in receipt of disability benefits in 1999 expressed as a percentage of the population of that age, and the division between contributory and non-contributory benefits. The recipiency rate varies from 3 per cent in South Korea to just over 20 per cent in Sweden; in Germany and Sweden only contributory benefits are payable exclusively on grounds of disability.

The prevalence of disability is shown for the late 1990s based on self-assessment recorded in surveys. This increases broadly in line with the incidence of benefit receipt.

Pension is means tested, one can safely presume that the Australian government did not intend to offer full compensation.

The simple measure of household income used in Comparison 6.3 probably overstates the success of compensation policies since it takes no account of the extra costs of disability and only Sweden and Britain have national policies to meet these. Comparison 6.2 indirectly addresses the dimension of participation. It is apparent that the case study countries with the most comprehensive systems of disability benefits, Sweden and Britain, also have a higher incidence of reported disability and high rates of benefit receipt. Leave aside differences in definition and whether high prevalence of disability results in more inclusive provision or vice versa (either through reducing stigma attaching to disability or by encouraging active benefit dependency): if the design of benefit presumes that disability is permanent (the medical model), few people will leave benefit and claimant numbers will rise. Certainly, fewer than one in a hundred recipients ceases to claim disability benefits in each year in Sweden, Korea and Australia, less than 2 per cent in the USA and Germany and under 6 per cent in Britain. To the extent

Comparison 6.3 Integration of disabled people

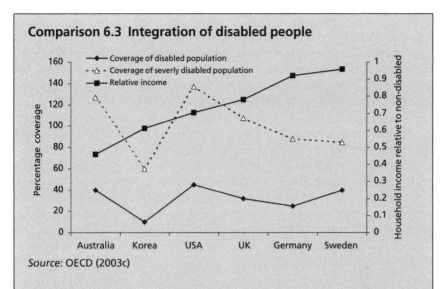

Source: OECD (2003c)

The chart plots the average household incomes of disabled people relative to that of other people (with the exception of Australia where data relate to individual income). The income data is for the late 1990s, equivalized to take account of household size and includes benefit income. Incomes of disabled people are lower in all countries, although not by much in Sweden and Germany.

The chart also records estimates of the coverage of disability benefits for people aged 20–64. This is calculated simply by dividing the number of benefit recipients by first, the total number of people with a severe or moderate disability, and secondly, by the number with a severe disability. Coverage of the disabled population varies from just 10 per cent in Korea to 45 per cent in the USA. All severely disabled people *could* be receiving assistance in the USA, UK and Australia, although this cannot be discerned from the evidence available. Even so, potentially high coverage does not necessarily translate into high incomes since relative incomes are comparatively low in Australia and only moderate in the USA and UK.

that benefit status is itself socially excluding, this could further erode social participation.

Closing summary

Asking whether social security policies work requires a clear understanding of policy objectives and the precise specification of measurable performance targets. Income replacement and compensation are examined as policy objectives.

High income replacement rates let people maintain their living standards but can create perverse incentives by making paid work financially unattractive. For reasons of administrative expediency, benefit levels tend to be fixed as a proportion of wages. However, replacement ratios are usually measured with respect to net income since this provides a better guide to living standards and work disincentives.

Sometimes social security provides compensation for losses arising or costs incurred as a result of accident, crisis or fate. Establishing the nature and extent of loss, or the order of cost incurred, is challenging for social security administrations and analysts alike. The challenges are discussed with respect to disability. In essence, the choice is to detail individual circumstances or to identify broad categories of loss or additional cost, measured relative to people who are not affected, and to impose somewhat arbitrary thresholds for the payment of additional benefit. Apparently arbitrary choices are likely to reflect prevailing paradigms and may have unanticipated consequences.

Further reading

McKay and Rowlingson (1999) provide an overview of the main topics, while Becker (2003) and Burchardt (2003) explore issues concerning compensation of specific groups in a British context.

Howard (2003) provides an excellent and detailed account of the various models of disability and their implications for social security. OECD (2003c) reviews disability benefits in a large number of countries (concluding that none has found a successful policy for disabled people).

The OECD website (http://www.oecd.org) is an Aladdin's cave of data and analysis on all matters to do with social security and much else. Particularly useful are the synoptic *policy briefs* available on http://www.oecd.org/publications/Pol_brief.

Note

Case Study 6.1 (This data on disability derives from the US Current Population Survey and is based on people reported to have 'a health problem or disability which prevents them from working or which limits the kind or amount of work they can do'.)

Tackling Poverty, Guaranteeing Sufficiency

This chapter is about poverty and the adequacy of social security and welfare benefits designed to eradicate or alleviate the problem.

While many social security systems trace their origins to a collective response to poverty, today this focus is mainly a feature of liberal welfare regimes. Nevertheless, other countries seek to ensure that families at least attain what in Nordic countries is termed a 'minimally adequate income' or to provide, in the language of the European Union, 'a guarantee of sufficient resources' (EC 2001).

The concept of poverty is contested even in those societies where it is part of the political discourse. Some propose that it is solely a rhetorical device used to mobilize forces for policy change and that its definition is arbitrary (Piachaud 1987; Walker and Park 1998). Others consider poverty simply to be an extreme materialization of inequality (Saunders *et al.* 1992). A few argue that poverty is largely synonymous with lack of income, while others propose that it is a complex multidimensional phenomenon. Certain sociologists believe poverty to be a social reality, the behavioural manifestation of a lack of resources (Townsend 1979; Gordon and Pantazis 1997); others that it exists only to the extent that citizens recognize a standard of living below which their peers should not have to live (Rein and Marris 1982). Some commentators take poverty to equate with absolute destitution; life lived at the verge of subsistence, a circumstance now largely confined to the Third World but still afflicting upwards of a billion people (Moore 1989). Most analysts (outside the USA) define poverty in relative terms, taking as the threshold the level of material well-being deemed to constitute a reasonable minimum by the standards of the society in question (Ravallion 1992).

Not all of these different conceptualizations of poverty have had an impact on policy discourse. The 1960s witnessed a growing appreciation of the concept of relative poverty in Australia, Britain and the USA, although, in the USA, governments have subsequently held to a relative measure but not uprated it in line with rises in living standards, thereby creating a quasi-absolute index (Citro and Michael 1995). In the 1980s and 1990s, leaders in Germany and Britain retreated from a European dialogue on poverty, refusing to acknowledge its existence and the term 'social exclusion' was introduced as a euphemism that facilitated their continued participation. More recently, the multidimensional nature of poverty has been stressed in Britain (Cm. 2001).

When it comes to measurement, the discourse on poverty in liberal regimes is close to that on adequacy and sufficiency in social democratic and conservative ones. Leaving aside sociologists who seek evidence for the existence of poverty in behavioural changes associated with limited income (Gordon and Pantazis 1997), what is required is a method of identifying those whose resources are so inadequate that they should be supplemented by society. Given the intent to identify a trigger for political response – namely that society will make good the shortfall in resources – adequacy, sufficiency and poverty (when defined as a performance objective) can be spoken of together. Poverty is the direct negative counterpart, or antonym, of adequacy and sufficiency; if a person's resources are inadequate, then they are deemed to be poor.

Defining adequacy

In determining adequacy, four supplementary decisions have to be taken that can conveniently be formulated as discrete questions (Veit-Wilson 1998). The first, *'adequacy for what?'*, is partially resolved by context: resources should be sufficient to support an acceptable way of life. Nevertheless, what is acceptable, and to whom, still has to be defined. In a democracy the 'to whom' is ultimately the electorate, while the level of sufficiency – the 'for what' – might be 'the minimum possible' standard of living or, perhaps, a 'modest but adequate' one. Any greater generosity is unlikely to be countenanced in a democracy. This is because people above the adequacy threshold, who would necessarily decline in number if the threshold were raised, would refuse to forgo the additional income necessary to support the greater numbers beneath the threshold. Indeed, the notion of the benefit system supporting a minimum or minimally adequate standard of living is somewhat of a distortion. Adequacy is more honestly defined as the maximum standard of living that the majority of voters are prepared to underwrite by forgoing income as taxation.

The 'adequacy for what' question prompts a secondary issue that has received comparatively little attention, namely *'adequate for how long?'*. Before 1980, the British social assistance system included a higher, long-term

Case Study 7.1 US benefits and the federal Poverty Threshold

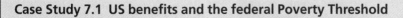

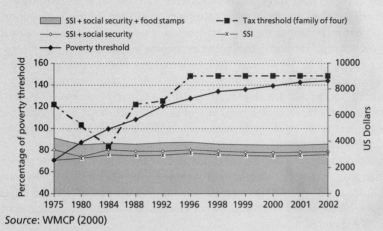

Legend:
- SSI + social security + food stamps
- —○— SSI + social security
- —◆— Poverty threshold
- —■— Tax threshold (family of four)
- —×— SSI

Source: WMCP (2000)

Unlike Australia and Britain which do not have an official poverty line (despite producing official statistics on low income), the US Poverty Threshold is accorded formal status and used as a reference point against which benefit levels are assessed.

The Threshold indexes an absolute rather than a relative living standard. It was originally set with regard to the 'lowest cost "nutritionally adequate" diet' which was multiplied by three on the basis of survey evidence that suggested families spent about a third of their income on food: 'The assumption underlying this procedure was that if a family did not have enough income to buy the lowest cost nutritionally adequate diet and twice that amount to buy goods and services, it was "poor" ' (WMCP 2000: 1281). Since 1969, the threshold has (with other minor changes) simply been up-rated in line with the US Consumer Price Index.

The graph plots the monetary value of the Poverty Threshold for single individuals from 1975 to 2002. The graph also shows the cumulative value of three benefits available to elderly Americans (Supplemental Security Income (SSI), social security (OASDI) and food stamps (see Case study 1.2 for details)); this falls short of the Threshold. Since around 1980, the benefits have maintained their level *vis-à-vis* the Threshold. However, since the Poverty Threshold is an absolute measure and will have fallen substantially behind average living standards, the value of the three benefits will also have fallen relative to living standards.

The value of the tax threshold for a family of two adults and two children is also plotted on the chart and this, too, has maintained its level against the Poverty Threshold, at least since 1996. This means that, other things remaining equal, the tax threshold has fallen relative to average earnings and that more low-income people have been brought into the tax net.

rate for recipients of 12 months or more in recognition of the additional depreciation and replacement costs that they incurred. Alternatively, though, people who have recently suffered falls in income and who may be recent or short-term benefit recipients are often obliged to continue with financial commitments transacted before their circumstances deteriorated. In Germany, the value of benefit drops from 67 per cent of former earnings to 57 per cent (for beneficiaries with dependent children) when entitlement to insurance benefit (*Arbeitslosenversicherung*) is exhausted and assistance (*Arbeitslosenhilfe*) becomes payable. This is consistent with the idea that needs fall over time although, in practice, the rationale has more to do with maintaining differentials between insurance and assistance benefits.

The second operational decision relates to *who should make the decision on adequacy* – that is, who should interpret the wishes of the electorate. The choice is generally between government officials and appointed experts acting on behalf of the electorate or the electorate themselves, as represented by people sampled in surveys.

The third decision, '*adequacy for whom?*', is more complex. It has a political dimension and a technical one. The political dimension relates to coverage and whether the commitment to ensure adequacy should apply to citizens alone, to all people resident in a jurisdiction or to a population defined in yet another way. It might be that the decision is to vary the adequacy threshold for different groups. For example, it could be that people would consider a lower standard of adequacy acceptable if the circumstances were known to be short-lived.

The more technical matter relates to definition of the **unit of assessment**, the unit for which resources and needs are measured and adequacy assessed. The unit chosen could be the individual, but larger units are generally chosen to capture economies of scale achieved through sharing resources. Units used include: **households**, people sharing a dwelling; **spending units**, people taking expenditure decisions in common; **family units**, in which people are linked by blood or marriage; or the **inner family**, comprising a single person, couple and any dependent children (Atkinson *et al.* 2002). In each case, the financial sharing is presumed to result in a common living standard (although it is acknowledged that unmeasured intra-unit differences may, and usually do, exist).

It may occasionally be necessary to assume that the needs, or consumption requirements, of everyone in the assessment unit are identical. This is the case with the World Bank's (2001a, 2001b) poverty threshold of a dollar per person per day, which is driven by the lack of more sophisticated data. Whenever possible, needs are recognized to vary: a child's requirements, for example, will generally be considered less than those of an adult. Sometimes these differences will be individually assessed. More often, **equivalence scales**, statistical weights to adjust for differences in the composition and individual needs of assessment units, will be applied to estimate the standard of living that a family or household of a particular form will enjoy from a given income (Veit-Wilson 1998). The derivation and use of equivalence scales to make comparisons between the incomes, costs or expenditures of households of differing size and composed of people of differing ages and status are discussed in more detail in Chapter 8.

The fourth decision, '*with what intent?*', is answered with respect to the aims and objectives of social security policy. The policy might be to ensure that no one falls beneath the adequacy threshold – a goal the UK has set to achieve by 2019, albeit only for children (Blair 1999). The threshold might provide a datum against which all benefits are fixed, theoretically providing adequate incomes for everyone eligible for benefit; this is partially true of the USA and Australia, although, particularly in the former, coverage is very far from comprehensive (Wiseman 2003a). Alternatively, the threshold might be a purely political aspiration.

There is a fifth supplementary consideration that differs in kind from those discussed above. It concerns the reasons *why an individual or family has low resources* and, as such, does not affect the assessment of adequacy *per se* but rather the decision as to whether or not the state should make good the shortfall in income. To oversimplify, the judgement to be made is whether, in the circumstances, the individual or family is deserving or undeserving of state support (see also Chapter 5).

In summary, **adequacy** refers to the resources necessary for a unit comprising one or more individuals to sustain a specified, usually minimal or modest, standard of living for a specified period. In social security discourse, poverty is generally taken to equate with **inadequacy**, the antonym of adequacy.

Determining the adequacy standard

There are three main ways of defining an **adequacy standard or threshold**, the ratio of resources to needs that separates assessment units with adequate resources from those without. They respectively rely on normative judgement, attitudinal assessment and arbitrary determination. Adequacy standards are variously used by governments to set benefit rates, to monitor the outcomes of individual programmes or welfare provision more generally, and occasionally to compare performance internationally (Chapter 13). They can be adopted by pressure groups and social commentators to lobby for reforms including, perhaps, higher benefits. Academics also exploit adequacy standards to evaluate the performance of programmes and systems against external objectives.

Comparison 7.1	Impact of policy on poverty measures, 1980s and 1990s		
Headcount (%)	Pre-policy	Post-policy	Percentage change
Australia (1989)	19.2	8.1	−57.7
Germany (1989)	19.8	4.8	−76
UK (1986)	21.9	5.5	−74.5
USA (1997)	22.1	15.6	−29.5
Sweden (1992)	32.7	4.7	−85.6
Poverty gap ratio (%)			
USA (1997)	50.4	30.3	−39.8
UK (1986)	59.8	32.5	−45.6
Australia (1989)	61.7	30.2	−51.1
Sweden (1992)	67.6	36.6	−45.9
Germany (1989)	74.9	24.9	−66.4
Coefficient of variation squared			
USA (1997)	0.385	0.110	−71.4
Australia (1989)	0.710	0.136	−80.9
UK (1986)	0.641	0.172	−73.1
Sweden (1992)	0.860	0.163	−81.0
Germany (1989)	1.430	0.099	−93.1

Source: DeFina and Thanawala (2002)

The data in the table derives from the Luxembourg Income Study, which collates and standardizes national survey information for the purpose of comparison and is the latest available (Korea is not included in the study). The poverty threshold is defined as 50 per cent of the median equivalent disposable income (using the OECD equivalence scale, Chapter 8). The headcount is the sum of people in households with income below the threshold, divided by the total population expressed as a percentage. The poverty gap ratio is the average shortfall in income divided by the poverty threshold, again expressed as a percentage. The squared coefficient of variation is a measure of the diversity of incomes of poor people, with a small value indexing low variation.

After tax and payment of social security, the headcount rate is lowest in Sweden and Germany and higher in the other three countries (three times higher in the USA). On average, poverty is least severe, and the living standards of poor people most homogeneous, in Germany. Although the headcount rate is lowest in Sweden, the severity of poverty suffered is relatively high. There are marked inter-country differences in the reduction in poverty achieved after tax and benefit payments, but US policies appear particularly poor at reducing the headcount rate and severity.

Normative judgement: budget standards

Budget standards are lists of expenditure items judged necessary for households of differing compositions to enjoy a given standard of living and are quite widely used to establish adequacy thresholds. Judgements about what is necessary are generally made normatively by a group of 'experts' appointed for the purpose. Budget standards have been employed in Germany, Sweden and the USA as a guide to setting social assistance rates. They have also been used by academics and pressure groups in Australia, Britain and the USA to stimulate debate about the adequacy of social security benefits (Parker 1998; Saunders 1998; Bernstein *et al.* 2000; Boushey *et al.* 2001).

The standard of living used as a reference point can be fixed at any level, but in this context seeks to capture the concept of adequacy defined above. Budget standards committees generally adopt one of two strategies. The first entails establishing a core set of expenditure items, the cost of which can be comparatively easily assessed. The items may be determined arbitrarily but account will usually be taken of the actual consumption patterns of people presumed to be at the reference standard of living. Once chosen, these items are costed and a total calculated. These core costs will then be multiplied by an empirically informed 'multiplier' to generate the total budget required to sustain the appropriate standard of living. The underlying assumption, therefore, is that the core expenditure constitutes a fixed proportion of the total, which is used to create the multiplier. Because the origins of this approach can be traced back to the nineteenth-century German social statistician, Ernst Engel, it is often called the Engel (or, occasionally, the food share) method (Engel 1895; Houthakker 1957). The Orshansky poverty line, used in the USA since the mid-1960s, calculated minimum dietary requirements and applied a multiplier of three based on the observation that, on average, US households spent a third of their incomes on food (Orshansky 1965; Citro and Michael 1995).

This approach has been criticized because there is no necessary reason why the ratio between core and other expenditures should be constant across all living standards. Indeed, Engel observed that the proportion of the household budget spent on food declined as incomes rose.

The second strategy adopted by budget standards committees – the one used in Germany and Sweden – requires that a comprehensive budget is compiled covering not just food but also housing, fuel, clothing, household goods and services, transport, leisure, health and personal care costs etc. While informed by actual expenditures, as revealed by surveys, normative judgement is still required concerning the items included, their quality and durability, the rate at which items need to be replaced and economies due to household size and composition. Like the Engel method, but more self-evidently, the comprehensive budget needs to be continuously updated to reflect increased living standards and changing lifestyles.

Attitudinal assessment

While budget standards are determined by experts, the defining characteristic of approaches based on attitudinal assessment is that the public are taken to be the best judge of adequacy. There are three major variants of this approach distinguished by how the public's attitudes are assessed. The one that has been developed most recently takes the budget standard methodology but substitutes experts with groups of citizens who develop sets of budget standards for households of differing size and composition (Walker 1987; Middleton 2000). Groups, homogenous in terms of family type and income level, first reflect on their own budgeting requirements and then decide on lists of minimum necessary requirements which are costed by researchers and then debated by groups of mixed composition to secure a consensus (Figure 7.1). This 'consensual budget standards', approach, being dependent on the views of comparatively small numbers of individuals, has been most influential in small jurisdictions. It is currently being used to inform the design of a new social assistance scheme by the States of Jersey (2001) and has been used by academics in New Zealand (Waldegrave *et al.* 1997).

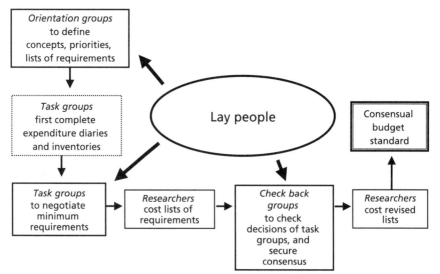

Figure 7.1 Consensual budget standards
After Middleton (2000)

The other two variants both rely on survey methods to consult the public. One, commonly called 'Breadline Britain' after a UK television programme of that name, asks respondents to identify from a list those social necessities that nobody should have to do without (Figure 7.2; Gordon and Pantazis 1997; Gordon *et al.* 2000). The list includes activities as well as goods. Those that are thought to be necessary by more than half of people in nationally representative surveys are taken forward as index necessities. Respondents who lack a specified number of index necessities because of inadequate income are then defined to be poor and a percentage poverty rate calculated.

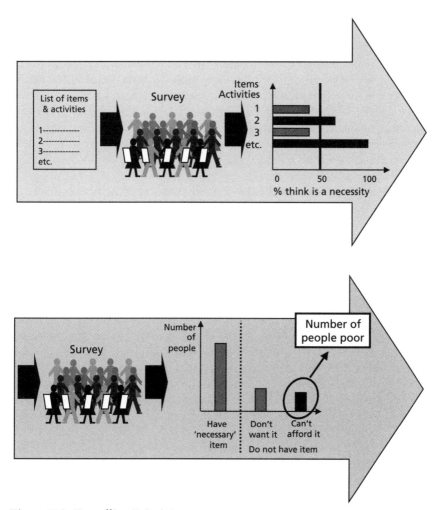

Figure 7.2 'Breadline Britain'
After Mack and Lansley (1985), Gordon and Pantazis (1997)

Unlike budget standards, the Breadline Britain approach does not automatically generate adequacy thresholds (income levels for households of given size and composition) that are necessary to establish or determine the adequacy of social assistance benefits. These have to be estimated separately based on the degree of correlation observed between income and the lack of necessities. In practice, correlations are high but seldom approach unity. This is to be expected because the Breadline Britain approach solicits views on material and, to a lesser extent, social deprivation rather than about poverty or adequacy *per se*. The concepts are similar but not identical. Indeed, a measure used on behalf of the Irish government exploits this difference, counting as poor only those people who have both low income and suffer material deprivation (Nolan and Whelan 1996; Layte *et al.* 2001).

The Breadline Britain approach has been criticized for the arbitrary choice of items and activities included in the initial list, the 50 per cent threshold for inclusion as an index necessity, the number of index necessities used to determine poverty, and the fact that no account is taken of the age or quality of the items possessed (Walker 1987; Halleröd 1994). These criticisms, though different in substance, all relate to various aspects of **measurement error**, the failure precisely to measure the concept intended. This means counting as poor, people who are not and vice versa (Atkinson *et al.* 2002).

The third variant of attitudinal assessment seeks to establish a measure of adequacy directly based on income rather than consumption. Originally developed by economists at Leyden, the direct income approach entails two stages. Respondents are first asked what income would be sufficient 'to make ends meet'. Their replies are then compared with their actual incomes, taking account of differences in household size and composition, to find the average income of people who believe that their own income equates with the level at which it is possible to make ends meet. This income – the income at which it is possible to make ends meet – is taken to be the poverty or adequacy threshold (van Praag *et al.* 1982). A variation of this approach asks respondents to say whether their income is more or less sufficient for their actual needs using a semantic differential scale ranging from 'very bad' (that is, very deficient) to 'very good' (amply sufficient). In this case, the adequacy threshold is pitched at the income level a little below the average income of respondents who choose the midpoint of the semantic differential scale (Cantillon 1998).

Both variants of the direct income approach have been criticized (Walker 1987). First, it is possible that respondents' assessments of the income required to make ends meet will be unreliable – experience from the consensual budget standards approach suggest that respondents reappraise their immediate response in the light of more thorough consideration of their own spending. Secondly, both variants are highly sensitive to the opinions of the comparatively small number of people who believe that their income is sufficient to make ends meet. In the 1980s, the Belgian government considered but rejected the possibility of adopting the second variant as an official minimum income standard (Veit-Wilson 1998).

Finally, it should be noted that each of above three approaches (budget standards, breadline and direct income) yields a relative measure of adequacy that is context specific, sensitive to the choice of equivalence scale and requires updating to reflect social change. Moreover, while each defines an adequacy threshold that is socially acceptable, none explicitly incorporates the presumption that shortfalls in adequacy should be made good by redistribution from those above the adequacy threshold. On occasion, supplementary questions have been asked to solicit this additional information (Hills 2001).

Arbitrary determination

While it is possible to criticize the above approaches to determining adequacy on the grounds of arbitrariness, the third set of approaches have no theoretical claim to be anything else; they are essentially pragmatic choices grounded in sociopolitical considerations. The commonest approaches are to define adequacy in relation to existing benefit levels, average incomes, minimum wages or a portfolio of different indices.

Fixing adequacy in relation to average household incomes requires judgements about the best measure of 'average' income, the choice of equivalence scales, and the ratio between the adequacy threshold and average income. Consideration of equivalence and the precise constituents of income is deferred to Chapter 8. Suffice to say that, because households differ in size, income has to be 'weighted' or adjusted to take account of the fact that it is shared between different numbers of people. Social security, and particularly social assistance benefits, similarly often vary in amount according to the size and composition of the assessment unit.

By convention, the adequacy threshold is set at 40 per cent, 50 per cent or 60 per cent of average income after taking account of household size. It is important to note that distributions of household income are generally characterized by a large number of households clustered around the middle with a long tail of households with high incomes.[1] This means that median income – the figure that divides the population into the top and bottom halves of the income distribution – is invariably lower than mean income. (Mean income is found by summing the income of all households and dividing the result by the number of households.) Median income is also less

---

1 In statistical terms this means that income distributions are invariably characterized by high kurtosis (pointed-ness) and positive skewness. See any basic book on statistics for the formal definition of skewness and kurtosis (e.g. Sirkin 1999).

affected than the mean by year-to-year fluctuations in the incomes of the super-rich and has increasingly come to be the preferred measure (Atkinson *et al.* 2002).

Measures of adequacy usually take account of income from all sources. However, there are examples where wage income alone has been used. In Australia, benefit levels have been fixed with reference to the Index of All Male Total Average Weekly Earnings (AWE). For example, the standard rate for Age Pensions, introduced in 1963, was set at 25 per cent of the AWE, the 'married rate' being 167 per cent of the standard. Benefits for children were fixed as percentages of the married rate. Relating adequacy to wages emphasizes the primacy of the labour market as a source of economic wealth and social status. However, there are conceptual difficulties in this. Wages are set in relation to productivity and labour supply rather than adequacy in the sense of relating income to needs. However, the counterargument is that adequacy has to do with social relativities, not absolute need, and that wages are paramount in driving social expectations with regard to consumption.

The second difficulty with linking benefit levels to wages is both practical and context specific. Different groups rely more or less heavily on wages as a source of income so that the appropriateness of an earnings-based measure of adequacy will vary between them resulting in systematic measurement error. Also, there is a trend, best exemplified in the USA, towards households deriving income from a growing variety of sources, especially investments, which is likely to reduce the appropriateness of an earnings-based measure of adequacy. Finally, in times of high inflation, linking benefits to wage rates can prove inflationary. An example of this is provided by the Netherlands, where a wide range of benefits are linked to the statutory minimum wage with adjustments made to take account of variations in family size. In the 1970s, when benefits were linked to wages net of contributions, the feedback between the fixing of wage and benefit levels helped trigger an inflationary spiral (van Amelsvoort 1984).

The attraction of defining adequacy with respect to income (or wages) is the comparative availability of data and the ease of translating results directly into cash estimates for adequate benefits levels. It is worth noting, however, that the approach is sometimes criticized on the grounds that living standards and social inclusion are better defined in terms of consumption, which can be influenced by factors other than income: home production, mutual exchange, access to credit etc. (Zaidi and Vos 2001). While true, consumption is very difficult to measure and its surrogate, expenditure, is deficient in a number of respects (Atkinson *et al.* 2002). Indeed, Atkinson *et al.*, in a contribution to the debate about the social dimension of the European Union, argue that income is preferable to expenditure when the concern is with sustaining the right to a minimum level of resources, which people are free to use as they see fit, rather than with achieved living

Case Study 7.2 Trends in the value of social assistance in Sweden and Germany, 1985–97

Source: Behrendt (2002)

The solid lines plot changes in the real value of the social assistance standard in Germany and Sweden according to an index in which the benefit level in 1985 is set at 100. The effect of inflation on consumer prices is removed by considering 'real' values, meaning that benefit with a value of 100 would buy the same basket of goods irrespective of the year. The value of social assistance in Germany (*Sozialhilfe*) rose ahead of prices with marked increases between 1985 and 1986 and in the early 1990s after reunification. The old system of fixing benefit levels in relation to a 'basket of goods' was last revised in 1985 and a new system of setting rates of benefit with reference to a statistical model of expenditures of families with incomes 10–15 per cent above the benefit level was introduced in 1990. The fall in the value of benefits since 1992 reflects a decision not to fully index in line with prices.

After a small rise in the guideline 'basic amount' (*basbelopp*) in the late 1980s, the level of social assistance benefits (*socialbidrag*) fell in Sweden and by 1992 had returned to its 1985 level where it subsequently remained. Moreover, it should be recalled that municipalities are not obliged to pay the basic amount and some set lower rates.

Wage rates tend to increase faster than prices. The broken lines therefore track the value of social assistance benefits in relation to average wages. In Germany, benefit levels have generally kept up with wages such that recipients have shared in the country's growing wealth. However, in Sweden, between 1985 and 1996, the basic amount fell by 25 per cent relative to wages.

standards. Given this emphasis on participation rights 'the fact that people with the same level of resources may have different standards of living is irrelevant' (Atkinson *et al.* 2002: 81).

Rather than relying on a single measure, a number of countries report a range. This has the attraction of appearing less arbitrary and also helps to capture the multidimensionality of deprivation. The British government, for example, has since 1999 published 38 different indicators reflecting various aspects of poverty and social exclusion. While not indicators of adequacy as such, and therefore not a direct aid to fixing benefit levels, the associated targets set performance objectives for government policy as a whole.

Dynamism

If measures of adequacy are to be used to evaluate the performance of policy over time, they need to be updated to ensure first, that from year to year like is being measured with like, and secondly (possibly at odds with the first), that the measure still retains relevance. This applies not just to relative measures but also to absolute ones, such as the US federal standard, which have to be adjusted for changes in prices.

For measures linked to average wages and incomes, the process of up-rating is automatic: as the median income rises, so the predetermined 'x per cent' of the median poverty line also increases. However, it is possible that changes in the distribution of income will distort the measure, and this is particularly the case with measures based on mean rather than median incomes. For example, if the incomes of the rich race ahead of those of other groups, the resultant increase in mean income will itself lift the poverty threshold. This, in turn, will increase the poverty rate even though many of those counted as poor will also have experienced a rise in living standards.

Other measures of adequacy have to be recalculated, which often entails the collection of new data and can be expensive. Moreover, measures based on normative judgement and attitudes are likely to entail difficult decisions about what changes should be made in the composition of any index. There might be pressure, for example, to add lack of access to the Internet for reasons of lack of finance as a measure of deprivation given the growing value attached to e-connectivity. In so doing, greater relevance may be achieved at the cost of loss of comparability. Equally, though, it might be argued that comparability is maintained since access to the Internet today is the equivalent of access to a television a generation ago. Perhaps more problematic, there is evidence of considerable instability over time in the views of laypersons as to what constitutes adequacy (Calandrino 2003). In part, this may be the result of sampling error, with different survey respondents in different years, but could be due to measurement error, reflecting unreliable questions and inherently invalid assumptions about the nature of perceived disadvantage (Walker 1987).

Finally, there can be significant challenges for interpretation, and problems for governments in presentation, if some components of a multidimensional index suggest improvement and others deterioration.

Assessing adequacy

The various policy actors can use a measure of adequacy, once established, in a number of different ways. First, it can be applied to establish benefit levels, as in Australia and the USA. For example, states in the USA, prior to 1996, were required to make Medicaid available to pregnant women and children aged less than 6 if family income was below 133 per cent of the federal guidelines, a provision that has carried over in modified form.

Secondly, certain of the measures can be used to establish the adequacy of benefits. Thus, the US Congressional Research Service produces statistical series that show the value of benefits relative to the federal poverty guidelines (Case study 7.1; WMCP 2000). Analysts outside government can also use adequacy standards to critique official policy, in this case the evaluation is with respect to external objectives rather than to the internal ones used by policymakers. Figures 7.3 and 7.4 provide examples for Britain. The first compares social assistance rates with budget standards drawn up by the Family Budget Unit, a research and lobbying organization. They show that benefit rates were below those required for 'a low-cost but adequate'

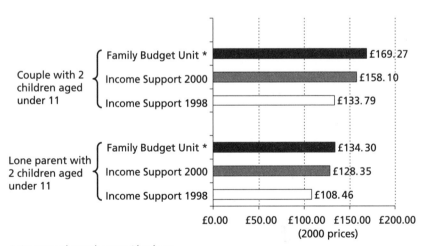

* 'Low cost but adequate' budget

Figure 7.3 Adequacy of UK social assistance in relation to a 'low-cost but adequate' budget standard
Source: Parker (1998), Bradshaw (2001)

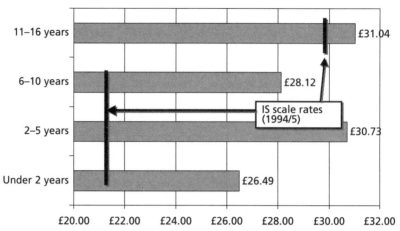

Figure 7.4 Adequacy of UK social assistance for children compared to a consensual budget standard
Source: Middleton (2000)

standard of living, although the shortfall was much reduced between 1998 and 2000. Moreover, the British government acknowledges that one motivation for raising benefits was earlier research, summarized in Figure 7.4. Based on a consensual budget standards methodology, it showed that benefit rates fell below the minimum standards, especially allowances for younger children (Middleton 2000).

Thirdly, adequacy standards can be used both to establish the number of households and individuals who have incomes below the adequacy threshold or poverty line and the number lifted above the threshold due to the implementation of social security policies. The most straightforward measure is the **headcount poverty rate**: this is simply a count of all people with incomes below the poverty (or adequacy) threshold expressed as a percentage of the total population. This is the much cited 'poverty rate'. Recent studies have refined this concept by providing separate counts of the number of people who have been poor for different periods of time, thereby recognizing the important distinctions between transient and permanent poverty (OECD 2001a; Oxley *et al.* 2001).

The headcount rate is straightforward but has limitations. It takes no account of the **severity** or *depth of poverty*, the amount by which income falls short of the poverty threshold. Moreover, it is not consistently responsive to changes in policy. If most poor people had incomes just below the poverty line, a small beneficial change in policy, or a small rise in average incomes, could bring about a marked fall in poverty. Equally, if most poverty was severe, the same beneficial change in poverty might have virtually no effect on the observed poverty rate.

Case Study 7.3 Australia and the Henderson Scales

The turn of the millennium witnessed a shrill debate in Australia on the nature of poverty (absolute or relative?) and the most appropriate method of measurement, triggered by a report (Harding *et al.* 2001) that took 50 per cent of mean income as the standard (Tsumori *et al.* 2002; Saunders 2003a).

While Australia has no official poverty line, the Australian Bureau of Statistics publishes estimates using the so-called Henderson lines, stemming from a Commission of Enquiry on Poverty in 1972. The lines, in turn, are based on a 1907 decision by the Arbitration Court which set a basic wage to provide for 'the normal needs of the average employee regarded as a human being living in a civilized country' (McDonald 1997: 8). The line for the 'standard' unit of two adults and two children was set at the 1966 basic wage (57 per cent of the seasonally adjusted average weekly earnings, AWE) plus the social security endowment for two children. The Henderson equivalence scales were derived from budget standards developed for the Community Council of Greater New York. Until the 1980s they were up-rated in line with movements in the AWE when the linkage was changed to per capita household disposable income (HDI; a net rather than a gross measure). In the figure, the *comparable* Henderson line substitutes the *true* Henderson equivalence scale with the modified OECD one.

The Henderson scales are essentially arbitrary, being relative with absolute connections. The graph shows that they are comparatively generous by international standards. For some types of household, they are also close to eligibility thresholds for receipt of benefit which makes them sensitive to relative movements in benefit scale rates.

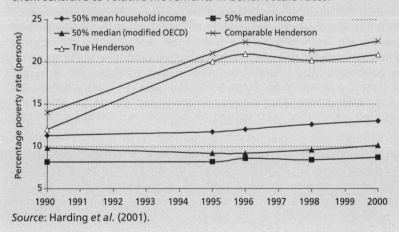

Source: Harding *et al.* (2001).

The **poverty gap** measures the total amount by which incomes of poor families fall short of the poverty threshold. The poverty gap (G) can be divided by the headcount rate (H) to provide a measure of **average severity** (S = G/H) while dividing average severity (S) by the poverty threshold (p) yields the **poverty gap ratio**, a measure of the relative poverty gap used for international comparison. While very useful, care needs to be taken in using the poverty gap measure. First, it is reliant on good data about the incomes of very poor people that is hard to obtain. Household surveys tend to miss disproportionate numbers of very low-income individuals, while there is quite often doubt about the reliability of the information collected, with some people claiming to live on implausibly low incomes. Secondly, the choice of equivalent scales can influence the results and their interpretation (Atkinson *et al.* 2002). Thirdly, the poverty gap provides no information about the concentration of poverty within the poverty population. Concentration can be of interest in itself and, when allied to information of the duration of poverty, provides insights into the distribution of different kinds of poverty experience (Walker with Ashworth 1994). Sen suggests a family of measures that take account of concentration (Sen 1976; Sen and Foster 1997); one is the squared coefficient of variation of income among the poor.

Comparison 7.1 presents different measures of poverty for five of the six case study countries and shows the combined effects of social security and direct tax policies. Perhaps not surprisingly, the countries rank differently on the three measures: headcount, poverty gap ratio and squared coefficient of variation. Sweden has the lowest headcount rate, but the highest poverty gap, suggesting that the comparatively small proportion of Swedes who are poor on average experience more severe relative poverty than elsewhere.

Care should be taken in interpreting the difference between pre-tax and benefit incomes and post-tax and benefit incomes as a direct measure of the differential effectiveness of national policies. This is because pre-tax and benefit income is a poor counterfactual since it is likely itself to be affected by national tax and benefit policies; for example, in high-tax regimes trade unions may bargain for higher wages or for non-taxable components to the employment package. Nevertheless, it is evident that, in each country, headcount poverty rates are noticeably lower after payment of benefits and taxes, but that the reduction in the variation of incomes of poor persons is even greater. This is, of course, consistent with policies that offer standardized rates of benefit. In most of the countries, the percentage change in the poverty gap ratio is less than for the other two measures, which suggests that polices are helping persons with the very lowest incomes but leaving some people below the adequacy threshold; to oversimplify, the social safety net is generally working but is set at too low a level.

Finally, while noting the caveat of an inadequate counterfactual, Comparison 7.1 suggests national differences in policy effectiveness. DeFina and Thanawala (2002), who undertook the original research using data for 17 countries, concluded that the headcount rate was highest in countries with a prevalence of low-waged workers and lowest where social transfers were high. They found no statistical associations between policy and the other poverty indices and concluded that policies are either ineffectual or not targeted on severity and variation as policy problems.

Closing summary

Many social security systems were originally established to tackle or relieve poverty and most include this as a policy objective. Designing policies to attain this objective and measuring their effectiveness requires poverty and/ or its antonym, sufficiency or adequacy, to be defined, an adequacy standard to be specified and appropriate data to be assembled.

Defining adequacy predicates answers to several questions: adequacy for what, for whom, for how long and with what intent? In the context of social security provision, the answers point to adequacy being the resources necessary for a household or family comprising one or more individuals to sustain a specified, usually minimal or modest, standard of living for a specified period.

The various means of specifying a modest standard of living include normative judgement, sounding out public opinion and arbitrary determination. Since each method has weaknesses as well as strengths, policies and measures of policy outcome will necessarily be imperfect. Understanding these imperfections is essential to avoid errors in interpreting the success of nations, or individual policies, in alleviating poverty and the resulting human suffering.

Further reading

Atkinson *et al.* (2002) provide an excellent account of the issues and choices faced when devising indices of relative poverty, while Citro and Michael 1995), updated by Short *et al.* (2002), provide corresponding accounts from a US perspective that prioritizes absolute measures of poverty. DWP (2003a) reports the conclusions of a review of poverty measures in Britain.

Leisering and Walker (1998) consider the policy implications of taking time explicitly into account in the measurement of poverty and OECD (2001a) and Bradbury *et al.* (2001) provide an international comparative analysis of poverty dynamics (the latter focusing on children).

Numerous international comparisons of poverty are available at the website of the Luxembourg Income Study: http://www.lisproject.org/

eight

Redistribution of Income

This chapter is about the redistribution of income and about how to measure the extent to which it is achieved by social security provision.

Redistribution differs from the three objectives of income replacement, compensation and the relief of poverty considered in Chapters 6 and 7 in that it is an inevitable consequence of social security provision. While redistribution is sometimes an explicit objective of social security, it is always one of its functions.

Three forms of income redistribution were considered briefly in Chapter 2. The intention (or outcome) of vertical redistribution is to transfer resources between individuals (or units of assessment, see Chapter 7) with different income levels. Horizontal redistribution entails transfers between individuals or units with different needs, while lifetime redistribution involves the transfer of resources from one period in a person's life to another. To these can be added **territorial redistribution** – the transfer of income between individuals living in different geographical areas. Each form of redistribution is discussed in turn, describing how it is specified and measured as a performance objective.

Vertical redistribution

It is helpful to distinguish between the purpose, mechanism and measurement of vertical redistribution as an objective of social security provision.

Purpose

The motivating premise underlying vertical redistribution is that incomes are insufficiently equal and that resources should be diverted from assessment units with more income to those with less. It will be recalled from Chapter 2 that this form of income redistribution is called *positive* redistribution to distinguish it from **negative** or **regressive redistribution**, the transfer of income from assessment units with less income to those with more. The terminology itself reveals a bias in favour of positive redistribution, which is frequently justified with respect to notions of redistributive justice, as again was noted in Chapter 2. From an analytic perspective, however, positive redistribution is merely the opposite of negative redistribution, not inherently better or preferable.

This point in the discussion has been reached without specifying exactly which income is considered so unequally distributed as to require remedial action. This is usually taken to be **market income**, the income that people accrue through selling their labour and/or from holding capital investments. In an ideal world, market income would constitute the counterfactual against which post-social security incomes would be compared in order to establish the degree of redistribution accomplished through the social security system.

Unfortunately, the real world is seldom ideal and market incomes provide a rather inadequate counterfactual. The reason is that incomes allocated through the market-place already reflect the existence of social security and are influenced by it. Take wages, for example. Imagine that state pensions did not exist and that employees had to save for their own retirement; it is likely that they would demand higher wages than they currently receive. The same might be true if employees could not look forward to an occupational pension provided through their employer; indeed, occupational pension contributions paid by employers are best thought of as a deferred wage. Most income surveys only record monetary wages and so understate the full remuneration received.

As a counterfactual, market wages are perhaps most likely to be downwardly biased in societies with conservative social security regimes where the social partners (government, employers and trade unions) negotiate with an eye to the social wage, and employers' social security contributions form an explicit part of the wage packet. In situations where trade unions focus on take-home pay, that is wages after deductions for income tax and social security contributions, pressures may exist to raise wages above the level that they might have been had social security not existed. Market wages are most likely to be upwardly biased in this way as a counterfactual in liberal welfare regimes. Either way, market income, while usually the only counterfactual available, is far from perfect.

Mechanisms

Turning to mechanisms, it is essential to remember that social security facilitates redistribution both through processes of fundraising, be it by insurance contributions or direct or indirect taxation, and through the allocation of benefits. The annual 'Effects of Taxes and Benefits on Household Income' analysis undertaken by the UK provides a useful insight into the processes involved (Lakin 2003; Table 8.1). '**Original income**' is the best approximation to market income and is derived from responses to a national household face-to-face survey but with population estimates adjusted to take account of the fact that response rates are relatively low among both the poorest and most affluent households. Incomes are also adjusted to take account of household size.

To original income is added income from cash benefits – the contribution to redistribution made through the allocation of social security – to yield **gross income**. Gross income is therefore the sum of all forms of monetary income, including that derived from the market-place and through social security. The first thing to note is that, in Britain, cash benefits more than double the per capita incomes of the poorest fifth of households: gross annual incomes in 2001/2 were £8,900 compared with original incomes of £3,410. Not surprisingly, given the importance of means testing in British social security, the households in the top quintile of original income on

Table 8.1 Redistribution of income in Britain, 2001/2

	Household income (not equivalized)		*Ratio of top to bottom quintile*
Quintile of disposable income	*Bottom quintile* £	*Top quintile* £	
Original income	3410	62080	18.2
PLUS cash benefits	5490	1150	0.2
Gross income	8900	63230	7.1
MINUS direct taxes/social security contributions	1040	15200	14.6
Disposable income	7860	48030	6.1
MINUS indirect taxes	2710	6660	2.5
Post-tax income	5150	41370	8.0
PLUS benefits in kind	5240	2650	0.5
Final income	10390	44020	4.2

Note: Estimates have been adjusted to ensure that they sum. In the source table final income for the bottom quintile is reported as £10,410 which is more accurate.
Source: Lakin (2003)

average receive much less in social security payments. Nevertheless, they do receive some income via social security, an average of £1,150, mostly universal Child Benefit.

The next two steps in the process of income redistribution involve the tax system. First, gross incomes are reduced by raising of direct taxation – that is, taxes on income and to a lesser extent on assets – to produce *disposable income*, the income from all sources that is available to be spent. Secondly, indirect taxes are imposed on purchases made by households, which leaves **post-tax income**, an estimate of the volume of goods and assets that can be acquired once all taxes are paid.

The difference between gross and post-tax income provides an indication of the redistribution of income attributable to mechanisms of raising revenues. However, it is important to recognize that the analysis presented in Table 8.1 takes account of the total volume of redistribution and not just that attributable to social security. Given that social security spending in Britain accounts for about 30 per cent of the total, a little under a third of the difference between gross and post-tax income might be considered to result from the existence of social security.

The difference between gross and post-tax incomes perhaps varies less than might be expected between households with original incomes in the top quintile and those with incomes in the bottom fifth. The reason is that indirect taxes tend to be regressive because low-income households on average spend a higher percentage of their income than other groups, and spend it on items that are highly taxed, notably tobacco. Thus, while direct taxes reduced the gross incomes of the poorest fifth of households by 12 per cent, half that for the top quintile (24 per cent), the first group lost 34 per cent of their disposable income to indirect taxation compared with only 14 per cent for the second, the richest fifth.

Finally, Table 8.1 allocates government spending in kind – mainly health and education but also some housing and travel subsidies, means-tested free school meals and welfare milk – on the basis of information gathered from a variety of sources on usage to yield **final income**, income after taxes and state benefits in cash and kind. Households in the lowest quintile received twice as much income in kind as those in the top, which had the effect of almost doubling their total consumption of goods and services. The difference is primarily the result of the poorer group both having more children at school and including a greater number of elderly people, making heavy demands on the health system.

To summarize, only part of the difference between original income and final income is due to social security, some is due to the provision of services and some to taxation used to fund non-social security activities. The combined effect of the fiscal system – taxes and social security benefits but not services and benefits in kind – in Britain was to allocate an average of £1,740 to that fifth of households with the lowest original incomes while deducting

£20,710 from the fifth with the highest original incomes. The implication is that the fiscal system in Britain may be progressive.

Measurement

Before it is possible to establish just how regressive or progressive any particular social security or fiscal system is, it is necessary to say more about the concept of equivalence scales (mentioned in Chapter 7) and to introduce the graphical technique called a Lorenz curve.

Equivalence scales

As already explained, income is usually measured for an assessment unit, typically the household, rather than for individuals **per se** (Chapter 7). This reflects both the reality of people's lives, in that people living together often pool at least part of their individual incomes, and the practical difficulty of assessing the financial resources available to an individual living with other people. It is much easier to measure the total income of an entire household than to trace who spends what, on what, and for what purpose. Total income is usually defined as the sum of income from employment and investment, together with income in kind such as subsidized housing and home production.

Of course, households (and most other assessment units) differ in size and the same monetary income will represent a lower living standard for a large household than for a small one. Equivalence scales are used to adjust household income to take account of differences in household size. Take a very simple example and assume that a two-person household requires twice the resources of a one-person household and a three-person household three times as much. If each household has the same total income (1000 units), the one-person household will have a living standard twice that of the two-person household and three times that of the three-person one. Alternatively, the effective or *equivalent income* of members of the two-person and three-person households is respectively only a half or a third that of the one-person household. More formally:

$$Equivalent\ income = Total\ income \times Equivalence\ quotient \qquad (1)$$

Where:

$$Equivalence\ quotient = \frac{1}{Household\ size} \qquad (2)$$

Although the rationale for equivalence scales is easy to grasp, their derivation is difficult and complex. The reasons are that households enjoy economies of scale from living together that are hard to assess and that the needs of individuals and children of different ages vary in ways that are difficult to measure and take account of. Figure 8.1 illustrates one of the least sophisticated means of deriving equivalence scales. Assume the proportion of income spent on a particular index commodity or activity depends on one's standard of living. Two people living together will require a higher income to enjoy the same standard of living but not twice as much due to economies of scale. If the two different sized households spend the same proportion of income on the index item, the difference in their incomes $(H_2 - H_1)$ will indicate the additional demands implied by the second person. Therefore, if the one-person household is given an equivalence quotient of 1, that for the two-person household will be:

$$Equivalence\ quotient = 1 + \left(\frac{H_1}{(H_2 - H_1)} \right) \qquad (3)$$

Such a method is clearly deficient not only because index items are rare but also because no account is taken of taste. In reality, the empirical derivation of equivalence scales is very complex, either based on a statistical exercise or a budget standard, and the final choice of scale is often arbitrary. In Britain, official analysis is based on the McClements scale, originally based on a statistical analysis conducted over 20 years ago that was last validated in 1993 (McClements 1978; Banks and Johnson 1993) (Table 8.2). The OECD devised an equivalence scale in 1992 for the purpose of international comparisons and Eurostat use a version of this as modified by Hagenaars *et al.* (1994).

While the choice of equivalence scale may be arbitrary it is not without consequence, sometimes changing the apparent degree of inequality or the supposed characteristics of the population in poverty. It also embraces strong assumptions about the nature of living standards within households (that they are equal) and about the degree of between-household financial

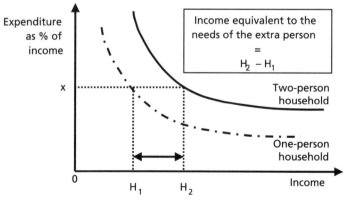

Figure 8.1 Establishing equivalence

Table 8.2 Equivalence scales compared *weights*

Living arrangements	Household member	Original (1972) OECD	Modified OECD (Hagenaars et al. 1994)	McClements	Luxembourg Income Study
'Married'	Head of household			1.00	
	Second adult			0.42	
	Other adult			0.36	
'Single'	Head of household			0.61	
	Second adult	0.70		0.46	
	Third adult			0.42	
	Subsequent adults			0.36	
	First adult	1.00	1.00		1.00
	Second adult	0.70			
	Person aged 14 or over		0.50		0.30
	Each child	0.50			
	Child aged under 14		0.30		
	Child aged 16–18			0.36	
	Child aged 13–15			0.27	
	Child aged 11–12			0.25	
	Child aged 8–10			0.23	
	Child aged 5–7			0.21	
	Child aged 2–4			0.18	
	Child aged under 2			0.09	

support (that it is zero unless captured as income transfers). Neither assumption is likely to be valid and may, therefore, systematically bias findings. In particular, the living standards of many women may be overstated since they are known to make individual sacrifices for the benefit of their family, forgoing food and personal consumption when resources are tight (Walker and Collins 2003).

Lorenz curves

The Lorenz curve is a graphical device of beguiling simplicity and great power that shows pictorially how equally or unequally income is distributed (Figure 8.2). The graph can be interpreted intuitively. The diagonal line plots absolute equality. Thus, if everybody in a society has exactly the same income, the income distribution would plot as the diagonal. Similarly, if household income is taken and equivalized using one of the techniques discussed, when every household has the same equivalized income, that, too, would appear as a diagonal. At the other extreme, take an equally unreal society in which all income is received by a single person, or all equivalized income is held within a single household, then that income distribution would follow the bottom and right-hand axes of the graph (indicated by the heavy broken line in Figure 8.2). All real income distributions lie in between these two extremes: the more equal they are, the closer they cling to the diagonal; the more unequal they are, the closer they follow the bottom and right axes.

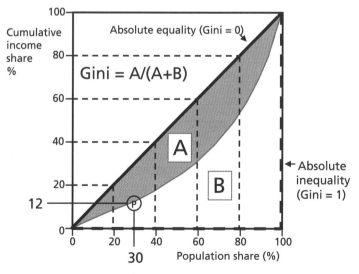

Figure 8.2 Measuring inequality: Lorenz curves

Technically the Lorenz curve plots the cumulative income share against the cumulative population. Imagine that the population of a country is arrayed in quintiles along the bottom of the Figure 8.2 graph with the poorest person at the left-hand end and the richest at the right; and that all the income received by every person in the country is arrayed cumulatively along the left vertical axis. Point P on the curved cumulative income line plotted in Figure 8.2 can then be read as showing that the poorest 30 per cent of individuals together receive 12 per cent of the total national income. If income was equally distributed, one would expect this 30 per cent of the population to receive 30 per cent of the income – the intersection with the diagonal, but of course they do not. A Lorenz curve can be interpreted in an analogous fashion if households are substituted for individuals.

There are a number of methods in which the income curve in Figure 8.2 can be characterized by a single number, a measure of income inequality. The simplest and most commonly used method is called the **Gini coefficient**. This is simply the geometric area between the income curve and the diagonal (A) expressed as a proportion of the total area beneath the diagonal (A + B). The Gini coefficient has a range from zero, absolute equality, to 1, absolute inequality. It is possible to interpret the coefficient as showing the proportion of total income needing to be redistributed in order to achieve an equal distribution.

Returning to the UK case study on redistribution, Figure 8.3 plots the distributions of original, gross, disposable and post-tax incomes as Lorenz curves and cites the associated Gini coefficients. The plot for original

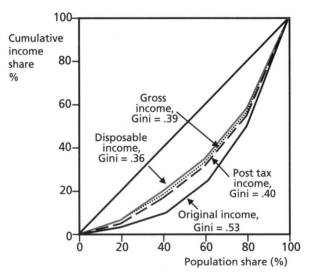

Figure 8.3 Inequality among households, 2001/2, UK
Source: Lakin (2003)

income is closest to the axes and, with a Gini coefficient of 0.53, it clearly has the most unequal distribution. Disposable income, income after receipt of benefits and the application of income tax, is the most equal with a Gini coefficient of 0.36. Interestingly, indirect taxes levied on consumption serve to increase inequality with the Gini coefficient for post-tax income rising to 0.40. Indirect taxes are therefore regressive, partly because low-income households tend to spend a higher proportion of their income, which is therefore exposed to tax, and partly because higher taxes are levied on alcohol and tobacco that are more widely used in low-income households. In total then, the combined impact of the taxation and social security systems was to reduce inequality, as measured by the Gini coefficient, from 0.53 to 0.40. In order to achieve this outcome, 13 per cent of original income was redistributed although, because benefits are paid to people who also pay tax, rather more than this amount actually changed hands.

While the Gini coefficient is very widely used, it is important to be aware of its idiosyncrasies and note that other measures of inequality exist. The coefficient is particularly sensitive to income transfers that occur around the middle of the distribution rather than at the tails, which can make it rather insensitive to redistribution brought about by social security which often occurs in the lowest third of the distribution. Atkinson (1970) has proposed an alternative measure that can give explicit weight to transfers that occur towards the bottom of the distribution. Two measures that are more intuitive include the **'Rawlsian' inequality measure**, the share of total income received by the poorest fifth of the population, and the **quintile share ratio**, which takes the Rawlsian equality measure and divides it by the income share of the richest fifth of the population. The latter measure, which clearly relates the circumstances of those at the bottom of society to those at the top, has recently been proposed as a social indicator for use by the European Commission (Atkinson *et al.* 2002).

Further Lorenz curves

The Lorenz curves presented in Figures 8.2 and 8.3 are sometimes called 'relative Lorenz curves' (Jenkins 1991). It was explained above that point 'P' on the Lorenz curve plotted in Figure 8.1 could be read to mean that the poorest 30 per cent ('p') of households collectively receive 12 per cent of the total national income. The value 'p' is the cumulative population share, which is read from the bottom horizontal axis. The value of 'P' read from the vertical axis, the proportion of the total income received by 'p' poorest households, can also be said to represent the mean (or average) shortfall in income, *relative* to the mean income for the entire population. This is because the value 'P' also equals 'p' times the mean income among the poorest 'p', divided by the mean income for the total population.

The significance of this is that if two people at different points in the income distribution both receive a 10 per cent increase in income, the Lorenz curve will remain unchanged. Assume that the poorer person initially had an income of £100 and the richer person had £1,000, £900 more than the poorer person. With the 10 per cent increase, the richer person would receive £1,100, or £990 more than the poorer person who would now receive £110. This increase in differential from £900 to £990 is not registered by a relative Lorenz curve.

An absolute Lorenz curve, such as that plotted in Figure 8.4, would reveal this increase in differentials. The horizontal axis is again the cumulative population, but the vertical axis is now defined as 'p' times the average income among the 'p' poorest households, this time *minus* the mean income for the total population. A perfectly egalitarian income distribution would, with this formulation, cling to the horizontal axis,[1] while a completely unequal distribution would follow the diagonal and the vertical axis below the horizontal.

The generalized Lorenz curve, presented in Figure 8.5, takes both relative and absolute notions of income into account. The cumulative population is once again shown on the vertical axis but, in this case, the value plotted on

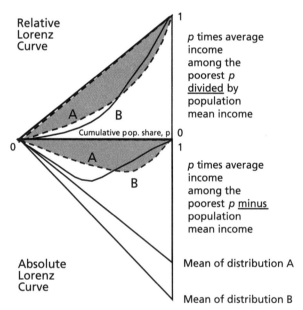

Figure 8.4 Lorenz curves: comparisons of inequality
Adapted from Jenkins (1991)

1 This is so because the mean income for each 'p' would always equal the mean income for the population. Therefore, subtracting the population mean income from the mean income for 'p' would always give a value of zero.

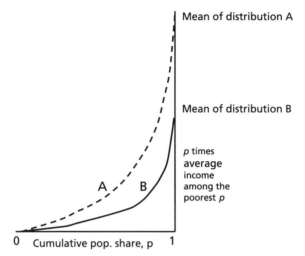

Figure 8.5 Generalized Lorenz curves: comparisons of social welfare
Adapted from Jenkins (1991)

the vertical axis is 'p' *times* the average income among the poorest 'p' households. This, then, is simply the relative Lorenz curve with each point on the curve multiplied by the mean income for the total population and plotted on the vertical axis.

The importance of these different formulations becomes apparent when one compares different income distributions. For example, one might want to contrast the income distributions of different countries or to consider how the income distribution in one country has changed over time. Gini coefficients, as noted above, provide a simple descriptive statistic to facilitate comparison and can be calculated for all three types of Lorenz curve. If the policy goal is to reduce income inequality, performance could be assessed by comparing the Gini coefficients for relative Lorenz curves calculated for different years. However, such a comparison would not indicate whether any reduction in inequality had been achieved at the expense of average incomes falling. Comparing Gini coefficients from generalized Lorenz curves could provide prima facie evidence of this, although the comparison would not in itself demonstrate either that any fall in average income was a necessary consequence of the reduction in inequality, or that a fall in average income had facilitated the reduction in inequality.

When comparing income distributions it is important to be aware of the assumptions that underlie the comparison. This is, of course, particularly important when one distribution is preferred to another. Moreover, the assumptions differ according to the type of Lorenz curve employed. The main assumption, which applies irrespective of the type of Lorenz curve, is that a transfer of income from a richer to a poorer person reduces inequality, providing that the transfer does not cause the person who was initially richer to have less income than the person who was originally poorer. (More formally, this is termed a rank-preserving income transfer.) If Lorenz curves cross, as in Figure 8.4, a further assumption is required, namely that a transfer from a richer to a poorer person reduces inequality more if it occurs between the poorer of two pairs (except when incomes are equal). Given these assumptions, distribution A can be said to be more equal than distribution B.[2]

Three further assumptions are required when interpreting generalized Lorenz curves. First, social welfare is deemed to have increased if one person's income rises and all others remain unchanged. Secondly, income distributions that are more equal and have a higher mean are to be preferred. Thirdly, while distributions where equality is lower may on occasion be preferred to those with higher mean income, and some increase in inequality may be tolerated if mean income is sufficiently higher, greater equality can never fully compensate for lower income. These assumptions are self-evidently strong and will not find favour with all readers. Some people, for example, may be prepared to prioritize greater equality over high incomes, especially in the context of concerns about the negative global consequences of continued economic growth. Nevertheless, the assumptions are required for consistent comparison of income distributions using generalized Lorenz curves and summary measures such as the Gini coefficient.

Table 8.3 illustrates insights that can result from comparing different Lorenz curves. In 1979, a right-wing government was elected in Britain under the leadership of Margaret Thatcher, who had little time for proponents of egalitarian policies and was keen to curb the role of government and to promote market forces. Without specifying cause and effect,

Table 8.3 Britain's income distribution, 1971–86: inequality and social welfare orderings from Lorenz comparisons

Rank order of year (1 = most equal/preferred)	Relative inequality	Absolute inequality	Social welfare
1	1976	1971	1986
2	1971	1976	1981
3	1981	1981	1976
4	1986	1986	1971

Source: Jenkins (1991)

2 To be true universally, the variance of income distribution A has to be less than that for distribution B.

Table 8.3 summarizes the UK income distribution in selected years around the time of the first Thatcher government. Income inequality – measured with respect to an absolute Lorenz curve – had been increasing even before the 1979 general election, and this secular trend continued unabated between 1971 and 1986. However, the trend towards increased relative equality was reversed after 1979, a development that would have been consistent with Mrs Thatcher's aspirations. Moreover, social welfare (captured in the generalized Lorenz curve with the implicit trade-offs between equality and higher incomes) continued to increase after Mrs Thatcher assumed power, presumably because increased relative inequality was more than offset by fast-rising incomes.

Comparison 8.1 Income distribution and redistribution

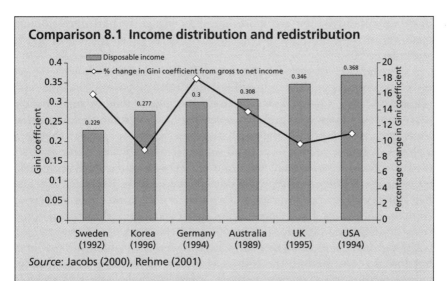

Source: Jacobs (2000), Rehme (2001)

The bars in the chart present Gini coefficients to summarize the distribution of equivalized disposable income in the six study countries. The Luxembourg Income Study equivalence scale is used. Disposable income is distributed most unequally in the USA and UK and most equitably in Sweden and Korea. The line summarizes the degree of income redistribution achieved via the direct tax system. It plots the proportionate change (reduction) in the Gini coefficient moving from a measure of gross income to one of net income (akin to disposable income). Redistribution is highest in Sweden and Germany.

Horizontal redistribution

Horizontal redistribution involves the transfer of resources between assessment units that have the same level of original income but differ in other respects. When horizontal redistribution is a goal of social security, rather than simply a consequence of it, the aim is usually to increase the incomes of people who are generally recognized, both socially and politically, to have additional needs (Chapter 7). Quite often, the justification is to counteract the tendency for the labour market generally to allocate resources to workers based on their marginal productivity rather than in relation to household needs; employees typically receive the same wage irrespective of whether or not they have children or adult dependants to care for. Indeed, sometimes people receive less in wages as a direct result of having additional responsibilities. For example, one reason sometimes given for the persistence of gender differences in wage rates is that women are more likely to prioritize care for their children over paid employment. Consequently, their productivity may possibly be lower but, more importantly, they are more likely to engage in part-time employment and to take time out of employment, thereby losing seniority in the workplace.

As in the case of vertical redistribution, the degree of horizontal redistribution is assessed by comparing either final or post-tax income with original income, and the same limitations apply in that original income is an imperfect counterfactual. However, the focus shifts to the differential experience of subgroups of the population and the extent to which they gain or lose income as a result of tax and social security policies. Most analysts tend to consider horizontal redistribution between subgroups defined in terms of age or household type, but one might equally be interested in transfers between ethnic groups, men and women or adults and children. In later sections, subgroups are defined according to geographical unit (territorial redistribution) and life-stage (life-course redistribution).

Conceptually, it is useful to distinguish between **unweighted** and **weighted** **horizontal redistribution**: the former is measured by comparing post-tax income with original income without applying equivalence scales, while the latter entails comparison of equivalized incomes. Unweighted horizontal redistribution focuses attention on differential treatment. Under an equitable fiscal system, one would expect larger families with greater needs either to gain more by way of benefits or refundable tax credits or to contribute less in taxation than other families with similar incomes. Turning to weighted horizontal distribution, if the equivalence scales used take full account of differences in need, then an equitable fiscal system is one in which households with the same equivalent income are treated identically. Differential treatment of assessment units with different characteristics would suggest unfair policies unless they could be justified on other grounds such as affirmative action. In practice, as noted above, equivalence scales only take account of differences in household size and, to a lesser extent, in household composition, and are not sensitive to other variations in need.

Case Study 8.1 Income redistribution in Australia, 1998/9

Australian dollars (A$)

Selected life-cycle groups	Original income		Fiscal policy			Final income		
	Actual	Equivalized	Direct taxes	Indirect taxes	Direct benefits	Total	Actual	Equivalized
Couple only, reference person aged less than 35 years	1209	806	−285	−90	13	−362	847	565
Couple with dependent children, eldest 15–24 years	1215	565	−297	−106	83	−320	895	416
Lone person aged less than 35 years	556	556	−136	−49	31	−154	402	402
Couple only, reference person aged 55–64 years	571	381	−115	−75	105	−85	486	324
Couple only, reference person aged 65 years or over	231	154	−31	−59	227	137	368	245
One parent with dependent children	268	185	−44	−50	213	119	387	267
Ratio of largest to smallest income in column	5.26	5.23					2.43	2.30

Source: ABS (2003)

The table illustrates income redistribution effected by the Australian fiscal system with respect to six household types. The incomes and transfers reported are averages for each household type and the analysis deliberately excludes redistribution resulting from receipt of services. Families with higher incomes tend to pay larger sums in taxation and generally receive lower benefits. Single pensioners and lone parents, households with the lowest original incomes, have their incomes increased by 60 per cent and 40 per cent respectively. The extent of vertical redistribution can be gauged by comparing the ratios of the largest to smallest incomes for original income with the corresponding ratios for final income; the ratios are more than halved irrespective of whether or not incomes are equivalized.

The modified OECD equivalence scale is used and households with children are assumed to have the average number (1.5 children). Comparing the three pairs of household types with similar original incomes suggests some horizontal redistribution. For example, the higher taxes paid by couples with children are more than offset by higher benefits.

The simplest way to determine whether unweighted horizontal redistribution occurs is to calculate, for each subgroup, the average difference between original and post-tax income. The existence of statistically significant differences between subgroups serves as prima facie evidence of horizontal redistribution. Australia provides examples and Case study 8.1 identifies three pairs of household type with similar levels of income that are treated differently by the Australian fiscal system. This is most marked with respect to the comparison between single people (aged under 35) and couples (aged 55–64). The former lose an average of 28 per cent of their original income to the state (compared to 15 per cent for the latter), paying a little more in direct taxes and receiving much less in benefits.

Comparison 8.2 Redistribution strategies

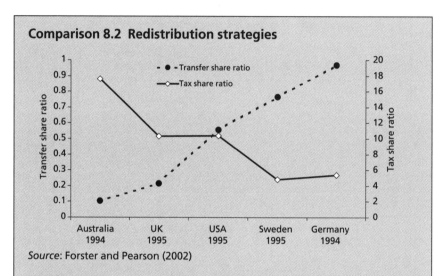

Source: Forster and Pearson (2002)

The chart contrasts the different tax and benefit treatment of the richest and poorest 30 per cent of the working age population in five of the six case study countries. Personal disposable household income is adjusted using the OECD equivalence scale. The benefit share ratio expresses the proportion of total cash benefits received by the richest 30 per cent as a ratio to the proportion received by the poorest 30 per cent. In each country, poorer people receive a larger share of benefits than the rich, but in Germany, where policy ethos emphasizes social cohesion, and to a lesser extent in Sweden, the differences are less marked than in the UK or Australia where benefits are targeted on the poor. The US benefit system is less redistributive than that in the UK or Australia because coverage of Old Age, Survivors and Disability Insurance (OASDI) dominates in an otherwise residual system. The tax share ratio reveals that, in Australia, the richest 30 per cent pay almost 18 times more tax than the poorest 30 per cent. The ratio is only 4.8 for Sweden and 5.4 for Germany, where social insurance contributions form a larger proportion of the tax bill and are made even by low earners.

The procedure can be repeated using equivalized incomes to investigate weighted horizontal redistribution. After equivalization, the original incomes of single people in Australia are very similar to couples with dependent children. The fact that their final incomes are also similar provides confirmatory evidence of equitable treatment being achieved through horizontal redistribution. On average, the Australian fiscal system reduces the equivalized incomes of young single people by 24 per cent and that of couples with dependent children by almost the same amount (22 per cent).

Territorial redistribution

Territorial redistribution is a special case of horizontal redistribution in which subgroups of interest are defined geographically to comprise individuals living in a particular region or neighbourhood. It is a necessary consequence of social security provision wherever benefit recipients are not evenly distributed geographically.

Social security is not usually used to redistribute incomes between one region or another. It occurs most often in federal countries both for positive and Machiavellian reasons. In the USA, for example, states with high unemployment rates are permitted to extend the maximum period for which claimants can receive Unemployment Insurance, thereby increasing the proportion of federally distributed resources directed to weak regional economies. In Britain, although not federal, small Employment Zones have been created in which social security payments are combined with other forms of funding to stimulate economic regeneration (Hales *et al.* 2003). More dubiously, in Germany, the *Länder*, being responsible for financing social assistance (*Sozialhilfe*), utilize activation policies to return *Sozialhilfe* clients to employment and eligibility for federally-funded unemployment assistance (*Arbeitslosenhilfe*)(Voges *et al.* 2001).

The argument for using social security as a mechanism for territorial redistribution is threefold: economic, political and pragmatic (Ravishankar 2003). The economic case is a spatial variant of that for social insurance: namely, it shares the cost of macroeconomic risk. The political rationale is that undue regional disparities give rise to political instability, even secession, while the pragmatic reasoning is that large sums of money can be mobilized without attracting much political attention. Indeed, to the extent that social security substitutes for income from the labour market, social security serves automatically to redistribute resources from the more to the less economically buoyant parts of a jurisdiction. As such, it acts as an automatic economic regulator, reducing the scale of economic fluctuation and thereby lessening its individual and social consequences in particular localities while simultaneously reducing geographic inequalities (Huby and Walker 1989; Walker and Huby 1989).

Reflecting its low profile as a policy objective, there is little analysis of the territorial redistribution of income brought about by social security. Ideally, account would need to be taken of the net effect of funding and allocation and the geographic distribution of post-tax compared with original income using the same approach as for horizontal redistribution. A couple of indices used to measure territorial redistribution warrant mention. First, the **concentration coefficient** relates the percentage of total social security expenditure spent in each area with the proportion of the total population living there. Where the proportions are the same, the coefficient takes the value of 1 (or 100 per cent if expressed as a percentage). If the coefficient is less than 100 per cent, it indicates that per capita social security spending is less than the national average. Coefficients exceeding 100 per cent show per capita spending to be above the national average. Using this methodology, Walker and Huby (1989) concluded that, in Britain, the redistribution effected by social security far exceeded that of all forms of regional economic aid.

A second, more sophisticated indicator is the **Theil index**, a measure that can be decomposed to distinguish inequality occurring between regions from that existing within regions. Like the Gini coefficient, however, the Theil index is most sensitive to changes occurring in the middle of the distribution.

Table 8.4 records the reduction in regional income inequality achieved by the fiscal systems of the three case study countries with federal structures. In each case, the analysis is based on equivalized household income and the Theil measure relates solely to inequality occurring between the regional units of government – states in the case of Australia and the USA and the

Table 8.4 Territorial redistribution in Australia, Germany and the USA

	Year	Australia 1994	Germany 1994	USA 1994	2000
Theil index of between state/*Länder* inequality	Before tax and benefit income	0.00224	0.00789	0.00642	0.00657
	After tax and benefit income	0.00101	0.048	0.00401	0.00433
	Percentage reduction in Theil index	54.9	39.2	37.5	34.1

Source: Ravishankar (2003)

Länder for Germany. The table suggests that, in the early 1990s, regional disparities in before-tax and benefit incomes were greater in the USA and post-reunification Germany than in Australia and moreover that the fiscal system did more to eradicate them in Australia than in the other two countries. Even so, it is clear that fiscal policies in all three countries have the effect of reducing regional disparities in income.

Case Study 8.2a Poverty and equivalence scales in Germany, 1993 and 1998						
						Percentages
Equivalence scale and threshold (per cent of equivalized household income)	*1993*			*1998*		
Original (1972) OECD	*All*	*West*	*East*	*All*	*West*	*East*
50% of mean household income	10.0	7.8	19.0	10.1	9.0	15.0
50% of median household income	5.2	4.2	9.4	5.7	5.3	7.7
60% of mean	19.9	15.6	37.3	19.6	17.2	29.6
60% of median	11.7	9.1	22.5	12.4	10.9	18.8
Modified OECD						
50% of mean	9.6	7.6	17.9	10.2	9.1	14.7
50% of median	5.6	4.7	9.3	6.2	5.6	8.5
60% of mean	19.0	14.8	36.2	18.7	16.3	28.9
60% of median	11.7	9.1	22.0	12.5	11.0	18.7

Source: BDG (2001)

The above table reports poverty rates for Germany using both the original (1972) and modified OECD equivalence scales (see Table 8.2). Poverty is clearly more prevalent in the old East Germany (the so-called new *Länder*) than elsewhere.

In this case, the choice of scale does not have a great effect on the observed poverty rate, although there are subtle variations that, though possibly falling within the bounds of measurement error, are consistent between the two years. Using the modified OECD equivalence scale increases the apparent incidence of poverty according to the 50 per cent of the median threshold and does so more noticeably in the new *Länder* than in the old. On the other hand, when using the 60 per cent median line, the incidence of poverty is apparently less when the modified OECD scale is employed. This suggests that there may be a concentration of families with children on incomes close to the 60 per cent median threshold.

Case Study 8.2b Inequality and equivalence scales in Germany, 1973 and 1993

The table below shows the increase in household incomes in the old *Länder* between 1973 and 1998. It is clear that average mean net incomes rose faster than the incomes of the poorest tenth of households, demonstrating an increase in inequality during this period, even after taking account of the effect of transfers. This is true regardless of the equivalence scale used. However, the modified OECD scale suggests that the poor fell further behind than is indicated by the original scale. The choice of equivalence scale matters.

Equivalence scale	Per cent change in net equivalized household income, 1973–98				Ratio of lowest decile to the mean	
	Mean income		Lowest decile			
	Nominal	Real	Nominal	Real	Nominal	Real
Original (1972) OECD	198.06	37.72	159.19	19.76	0.80	0.52
Modified OECD	188.59	33.34	144.67	13.05	0.77	0.39
Source: BDG (2001)						

Life-course redistribution

Whereas vertical and horizontal redistribution involve interpersonal transfers of income between different individuals or assessment units, life-course redistribution entails an intrapersonal transfer of resources from one individual at one period of their life to the same individual at another period. When a person saves, they are engaging in life-course redistribution. Spending is forgone in the short term and income is enhanced in the longer term by interest accruing from investments. Social security that involves the payment of contributions in return for the right to receive benefits at a later date is similarly a process of life-course redistribution. In both cases, resources are taken from the present and transferred to the future. However, it is equally possible to transfer resources from the future to the present through the process of borrowing. This increases income and the possibility of consumption in the present while reducing the scope for consumption later when the debt has to be repaid.

Saving and borrowing both serve to even out resources over the life-course and allow for the possibility of transferring resources from periods of comparative prosperity or limited need to times of relative hardship. Social security has the same effect and potential: first, by encouraging or enforcing saving and secondly by payment of non-contributory and means-tested benefits that are funded from taxation and which are analogous to borrowing, since beneficiaries are themselves usually taxpayers. However, establishing just how much life-course redistribution is achieved by social security is not easy.

There are two main reasons why it is difficult to assess the amount of redistribution that occurs over a person's life. First, the redistribution can only be known for sure once a person has died and secondly, income data covering a person's entire life is rarely available even from official records. In such circumstances, it is necessary to resort to statistical modelling to simulate likely income flows. One such model is LIFEMOD, a dynamic cohort simulation model developed at the London School of Economics. This takes a cohort of people ostensibly born in the UK in 1985 and mathematically ages it for up to 95 years based on the experiences of people who were alive in 1985 (Falkingham and Hills 1995). The lifetimes that are simulated are those that would have obtained if people had been able to live out the entirety of their lives under the economic and demographic conditions that applied in 1985.

Figure 8.6 plots the life-course redistribution implicit in the social security and fiscal regimes existing in the UK in 1985. Original income, as defined above, peaks on average between the ages of 35 and 54 and plunges after retirement, but the addition of social security payments boosts gross incomes very markedly in old age. The impact of taxation, revealed by net (i.e. disposable) income, is to cut incomes in middle age thereby helping later to pay for old-age pensions. When expenditure on education and health is added in, and the resultant final income is equivalized (using the McClements equivalence scale) to take account of differences in household

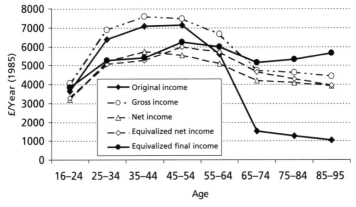

Figure 8.6 Life-course redistribution, 1985, UK
Source: Falkingham and Hills (1995)

composition, the living standards enjoyed by individuals fluctuate by no more than £1,000 per annum after the age of 24. The result of social security and other welfare provisions is therefore markedly to even out income the life-course.

A necessary by-product of life-course redistribution is a reduction in income inequality. Indeed, a considerable part of the income inequality observed in a single year is attributable to life-course factors. While the Gini coefficient for the equivalized original income in the UK in 1985 was 0.50, the corresponding value for lifetime income was 0.25. Social security payments and direct taxation further reduce the Gini coefficient for lifetime income inequality to 0.20 and benefits in kind to 0.19.

Figure 8.7 divides the simulated cohort into deciles according to the level of their equivalent net (disposable income) and indicates the average lifetime benefits accruing from social security payments and receipt of education and healthcare. While the total amount received in benefits differs very little when measured over a complete lifetime, the method of funding varies markedly. Ninety-two per cent of the welfare benefits received by the tenth of people with the lifetime highest incomes are effectively self-funded – that is, paid for by themselves either during the year in which the benefit was received or at other times in their lives. The vast majority of people in this decile are net contributors to public funds, paying over twice as much in taxes as they receive back in benefits. The reverse is true of individuals whose lifetime incomes place them in the lowest decile; benefits received by this group exceed taxes and contributions by 3.3 to 1. Even so, some 29 per cent of all the benefits received by the poorest decile are self-funded, the result of life-course redistribution. Taken across the cohort as a whole, between two thirds and three quarters of the gross lifetime expenditure on welfare benefits is accounted for by self-funding during the

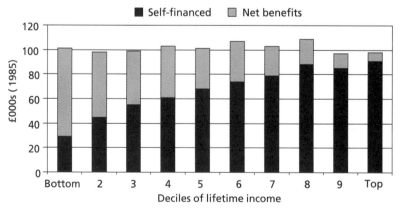

Figure 8.7 Individual life-course redistribution
Source: Falkingham and Hills (1995)

Case Study 8.3 Income redistribution in South Korea, 1996

Income sources[a]	Per cent of gross income[b]	Gini coefficient[a]	Decile ratio[c]	Gini coefficient UK (1995)
Household earnings	89.9	0.307	7.68	0.653
Property income	5.1	0.908	7.50	0.888
Market income	95.0	0.304	7.72	0.547
Public transfers	0.8	0.987	1.76	0.563
Enterprise transfers				0.896
Private transfers	4.2	0.927	0.99	0.951
Gross income	100.0	0.278	6.34	0.386
Taxes and SS contributions	4.3	0.612	2.37	0.572
Disposable income	95.7	0.277	6.56	0.344

[a] Equivalized with person weights; [b] not equivalized; [c] equivalized with household weights

Source: Jacobs (2000)

The table tracks the pattern of redistribution achieved by the fiscal system in Korea in 1996, before the economic crisis that ensued in 1997/8. For comparative purposes, it also includes Gini coefficients calculated for the UK in 1995 using the same methodology. The data in both cases were obtained from household surveys. Income is equivalized using the LIS equivalence scale (see Table 8.2).

The first column of figures reveals the components of gross income. These are dominated by market income with public transfers (social security) accounting for just 0.8 per cent (compared with 16 per cent for Britain, not shown). The volume of tax and social security contributions levied on gross income is correspondingly small: 4 per cent compared to 26 per cent in Britain. As a result, the reduction in income inequality achieved by fiscal policies in Korea is markedly limited. The Gini co-efficient for disposable income is only 0.027 different from that for market income, a reduction in inequality of just 9 per cent (compared to 37 per cent for Britain).

It may, therefore, be surprising to learn that the distribution of disposable income is noticeably more equal in Korea than in Britain (Gini coefficients of 0.277 and 0.344, respectively). This is because of the difference in the distribution of household earnings. A smaller proportion of households in Korea have either no earner or more than one earner compared with Britain. Also, the Korean labour market is characterized by two groups: core workers in secure employment and casual or contingent workers. Although earnings vary markedly between these two groups, variation within them is comparatively limited.

life-course, the reminder comprising lifetime transfers between different individuals.

The implication of this is that life-course redistribution may be a more important function of the combined UK social security, health and education systems than vertical redistribution from the lifetime rich to the lifetime poor.

Closing summary

Redistribution of income, which is an inevitable consequence of social security provision, can also be an explicit objective and take a number of forms: vertical, from rich to poor (and vice versa); horizontal, between individuals, assessment units or groups with different needs; territorial, between different geographic areas; and life-course redistribution, intrapersonal transfers across people's lifetime.

The rationale for the different forms of redistribution varies from considerations of high principle (positive vertical redistribution is required to address the unacceptable income inequality generated by market forces' demands) to practicalities and pragmatics (in order to meet current needs, resources have to be transferred between people and across time). This is achieved by means of social security contributions, direct and indirect taxation and allocation procedures (see also Chapters 4 and 5).

Assessing the extent of income redistribution is technically complex. It requires specification of a counterfactual, the distribution of income that would have obtained in the absence of social security, and the application of equivalence scales to adjust income distributions to take account of differences in the size and composition of households or other assessment units. Further conceptual tools have been introduced to aid the process of measurement: the Lorenz curve to plot income distributions, the Gini coefficient and Theil index as measures of inequality, the concentration coefficient to compare spatial distributions and simulation to try to estimate life-course incomes and redistribution.

Further reading

Atkinson et al. (2002) provide a thorough but accessible discussion of various measures of inequality, while Forster and Pearson (2002) summarize trends in income inequality across OECD states and explore the impact of policy. The Luxembourg Income Study website (http://www.lisproject.org) contains a continually growing archive of comparative research in income inequality and Timothy Smeeding offers frequent accounts of the latest findings in various publications (easily found with a web search engine such as Google).

PART 4

Efficiency

Target Efficiency

This chapter is the first of three about aspects of efficiency. Being concerned with target or targeting efficiency, it asks whether the right people receive social security. Economic and administrative efficiency are considered in Chapters 10 and 11 respectively.

The last three chapters focused on four exemplar objectives of social security and the methods used to establish policy effectiveness – that is, the extent to which objectives are achieved. To resurrect the metaphor of the thermostat, the chapters were solely concerned with whether the target temperature had been maintained, with no attention being paid to the ambient temperature, the cost of providing the heating or the reasons why the target temperature had been missed (or hit). A focus on efficiency brings these important secondary issues to the fore.

An aspiration in running any social security system is always to achieve **cost effectiveness**, to attain the desired policy objective at minimum cost. This is not a matter of meanness but of practical common sense. If costs are not minimized, then resources are by definition wasted; resources that could be used to meet other socially desirable goals. For a policy to be cost effective, all aspects of the policy design and implementation have to be fully efficient, thereby generating the maximum social benefit for a given level of input or resources. However, it should be understood that this is an aspiration rather than a practical proposition and, for the most part, the following discussion of efficiency is concerned with degrees of efficiency and the reasons for inefficiency.

Adopting and implementing a policy that is cost effective and thereby 100 per cent efficient still does not guarantee that it is the most sensible policy to pursue; other policies could generate even greater benefits for the same resource inputs. The second aspiration is therefore to achieve **social efficiency**, such that the net social benefits associated with a policy (social benefits less social costs) are maximized (Knapp 1984). Figure 9.1 illustrates the concept of social efficiency. The graph (a) plots the total social benefits and costs accruing from increased social security provision. As provision increases, so social benefit rises but at a decreasing rate; the first unit of social security may prevent people from dying but later expenditures might enable recipients to take a further, arguably unnecessary holiday. Social costs increase at an increasing rate; raising the first unit of tax may be achieved with little political opposition or economic cost, raising the umpteenth unit is likely to be much more difficult and to generate significant **opportunity costs**: output lost or utility forgone due to diverting resources from other more productive uses. The maximum social benefit occurs at the level of social security provision where the two curves are furthest apart.

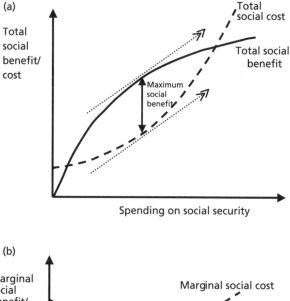

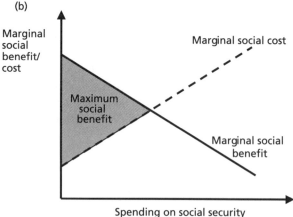

Figure 9.1 Social efficiency

The importance of this 'optimax' point is perhaps more clearly evident from graph (b) that plots the marginal social benefits and the marginal social costs derived (as the first differential) from the corresponding total social benefit and total social cost curves in graph (a). The maximum social benefit accruing from extra social security occurs where the curves cross; above that optimal level of social security provision, the marginal social cost exceeds the marginal social benefit. Increasing benefit spending beyond the optimum will lower overall social welfare. This is because the enhanced well-being enjoyed by people receiving the extra benefit will be more than offset by reductions in well-being suffered by those required to pay higher taxes. Put simply, the marginal resources would be better deployed on something other than social security.

This *Pareto optimal solution*, as economists term it, is based on several ideal-world assumptions that make it an instructive model rather than an accurate description of real policy choices (Broadway and Bruce 1984). One such assumption is that other forms of efficiency are maximized. Unless policies are perfectly designed and implemented, social efficiency cannot be attained. Hence, it is important to consider benefit targeting and target efficiency.

Concepts and measurement

Unfortunately, the term 'targeting' has ceased to be neutral when used in policy circles (Doron 2001; Gilbert 2001). In many countries it has become synonymous with attempts to reduce expenditure on social security and, in particular, with moves to curtail universal provisions based on citizenship, substituting means-tested schemes based on need (see Chapter 2). However, targeting is necessarily an integral part of the design and implementation of all social security provision and it is important to retrieve the technical content of the term from the rhetorical usage. **Targeting**, in its technical sense, is taken to refer to a range of distinguishable concepts that have to do with whether the recipients of social security benefits are those intended and the extent to which expenditure is used as anticipated.

Targeting can therefore refer to both people (actual and potential beneficiaries of social security) and resources. To take people first, the total population of a given jurisdiction is represented by the largest oval in Figure 9.2, which contains a second oval corresponding to the target population – the set of people intended to receive the social security benefit (or benefits). (This definition is deliberately less specific than that introduced in Chapter 3.) A third oval, again nested within that referring to the total population, signifies the **recipient population** or **caseload** – the set of people actually receiving the benefit. Both the target and recipient populations can be defined in one of three ways depending on the chosen level of

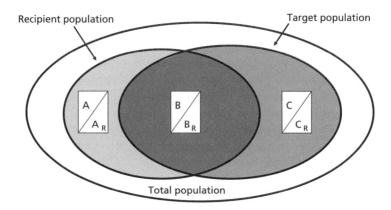

A: Recipients not in target population A_R: Resources not going to target population
B: Recipients in target population B_R: Resources going to target population
C: Non-recipients in target population C_R: Resources not received by target population

Figure 9.2 Internal targeting – basic concepts

aggregation. First, they can be defined in terms of **claimants** or **recipients**, persons to whom social security payments are made. Secondly, they can be defined with respect to **claimant units**, comprising people included in the unit of assessment; since the number of claimant units necessarily equals the number of claimants this distinction is of little practical value. Finally, benefit populations can be described in terms of **beneficiaries**, all the people included in claimant units. For simplicity, the target and recipient populations are here taken to refer to claimants or persons potentially eligible to be claimants.

It will be noted from Figure 9.2 that the target and recipient populations intersect to create three distinct subsets labelled A, B and C. 'A' refers to recipients of benefit to which they are not entitled; 'B' refers to benefit recipients who are both eligible and in receipt of benefit, while 'C' refers to persons eligible for benefit who are not receiving it. This last group are often termed 'eligible non-claimants' although 'eligible non-recipients' might be a better term since they may never have applied for the social security benefit in question.

Internal targeting efficiency

One useful measure of targeting is **horizontal targeting efficiency**: the proportion of the target population in receipt of benefit. It is formally defined, with reference to Figure 9.2, as:

$$Horizontal\ targeting\ efficiency\ (HT) = \frac{B}{B + C} \tag{1}$$

where 'B' is the number of eligible recipients of the benefit, and '$B + C$' is the number of persons who are eligible for the benefit, being the sum of the number of recipients and eligible non-recipients.

Targeting efficiency is sometimes expressed in percentage terms. This requires multiplying the expression on the right-hand side of the equals sign in equation (1) by 100. For the sake of simplicity, this extra step is also omitted from all subsequent equations in this chapter.

For reasons to be explained later, this measure of horizontal targeting efficiency is more accurately termed *internal* horizontal targeting efficiency, although it is often also called the 'take-up' of a benefit. Sometimes when measuring take-up, it is impossible to distinguish between eligible and ineligible claimants with the result that take-up is measured as follows:

$$False\ take\text{-}up = \frac{A + B}{B + C} \qquad (2)$$

where 'A' indicates ineligible recipients.

This measure of take-up exaggerates true take-up, or internal horizontal targeting efficiency, to the extent that people who are ineligible for benefit illicitly receive it.

True take-up provides a measure of the extent to which the benefit has succeeded in reaching the people for whom it was designed. In contrast, **vertical targeting efficiency**, the proportion of benefit recipients who are actually eligible, is a measure of the extent to which a benefit has missed its target and resources are thereby wasted. It is formally defined as follows:

$$Vertical\ targeting\ efficiency\ (VT) = \frac{B}{A + B} \qquad (3)$$

where 'B' is again the number of eligible recipients and '$A + B$' is the benefit caseload being comprised of the sum of eligible ('B') and ineligible ('A') recipients.

Figure 9.2 can be reinterpreted in terms of resource allocation such that horizontal and vertical targeting efficiency relate to the proportion of resources allocated to a benefit that are correctly targeted. In resource terms, horizontal targeting efficiency (HT_R) is then defined as:

$$HT_R = \frac{B_R}{B_R + C_R} \qquad (4)$$

where 'B_R' is the amount of benefit expenditure or resources received by eligible recipients and '$B_R + C_R$' is the total resources allocated to the benefit, with 'C_R' being the volume of allocated resources remaining unspent.

Likewise, vertical targeting efficiency (VT_R) becomes:

$$VT_R = \frac{B_R}{A_R + B_R} \qquad (5)$$

where 'B_R' is again the volume of resources received by eligible recipients and '$A_R + B_R$' is total benefit expenditure, being the sum of resources received by eligible (B_R) and ineligible (A_R) claimants.

All the above measures are point in time estimates, indicating targeting efficiency on any particular day. Of course, both the claimant and target populations are changing continuously as individuals move in and out of eligibility and, due to changes in their circumstances, decide whether or not to claim benefit. These dynamics impose limits on the efficiency with which benefits can be targeted (Walker 1996).

Comparison 9.1 Percentage recipiency rates of selected benefits, 1999

Percentage

	Old age	Sick-ness	Dis-ability	Mater-nity	Unemploy-ment	Social assistance	Total
USA	1.76	2.13	6.30	0.00	1.25	1.68	13.70
Australia	1.87	1.44	4.90	0.00	5.56	3.17	17.54
UK	3.38	0.84	6.38	0.27	2.88	2.80	18.39
Sweden	0.42	5.76	6.46	2.03	3.96	1.14	20.11
Germany	4.63	2.51	4.08	0.18	6.64	2.24	21.96

Source: OECD (2003d)

Recipiency rates, prepared by the OECD, express the number of benefit recipients as a percentage of the working-age population. As such, the recipiency rate may be viewed as a crude external measure of horizontal targeting efficiency. The crudeness stems from the fact that, at any point in time, only a small proportion of the working-age population experiences any relevant contingency. In this context old-age benefits generally refer to early retirement schemes and social assistance to non-categorical means-tested schemes. The total recipiency rate (that also includes survivors' benefits and labour market leave) is highest in Sweden and Germany and lowest in the US. Recipiency rates for disability benefits are comparatively high in all countries and for unemployment in Germany and Australia. It is important to recognize that the five countries were not all at the same point in the economic cycle in 1999.

External targeting efficiency

The measures of targeting efficiency introduced in the previous section were defined with respect to the specific aims of the social security scheme in question. This is the reason why they were prefaced by the adjective 'internal'. As such, the measures related to the concerns of policymakers and administrators charged with the efficient delivery of benefit. Reference was made neither to the concept of social efficiency (and the issue of whether or not the resources should have been invested in that particular scheme) nor to the matter of whether the scheme was successfully meeting other social objectives. These broader questions – which relate to external targeting efficiency – are the focus of this section.

The move from a concern with internal efficiency to one with external efficiency can be simply illustrated, as in Figure 9.3, by substituting 'needy population' for 'target population' in Figure 9.2. Need could be defined and assessed in any of the ways discussed in Chapters 6 to 8 but the criteria would not necessarily coincide with those used to define eligibility for a particular benefit. With the substitution complete, horizontal and vertical targeting efficiency would be defined as in equations 1, 2, 4 and 5 above but where:

- 'A' refers to benefit recipients who were not in need and 'A_R' is the benefit expenditure going to this group;
- 'B' signifies benefit recipients who were definitely in need prior to receiving benefit and who, depending on the level of benefit, may continue to be in need, and 'B_R' is the expenditure associated with this group; and

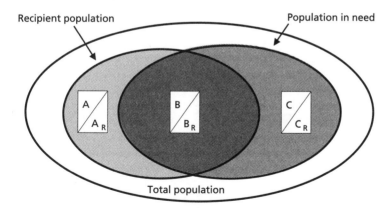

A: Recipients not in needy population A_R: Resources not going to needy population
B: Recipients in needy population B_R: Resources going to needy population
C: Non-recipients in needy population C_R: Resources not received by needy population

Figure 9.3 External targeting – basic concepts

- 'C' indicates persons in need who do not receive benefit and 'C_R' is the resource cost of meeting their needs together with those of benefit recipients ('B') that are unmet even after payment of benefits.

There are two particular circumstances when analysts would focus on external rather than internal targeting efficiency. One is when they are engaged in comparative analysis, judging the performance of one country or jurisdiction against another, and require a common yardstick. In such circumstances, a universal measure of need is likely to be defined without reference to the specific objectives of schemes in different jurisdictions. The other occasion is when the performance of a policy is being assessed against higher order, or global, policy goals. For example, in Britain since 1998, policies have been judged annually against the goal of eradicating child poverty even though many of them were designed long before the child poverty goal was established.

Figure 9.4 offers another way of conceptualizing external targeting efficiency. It shows the income of four different claimant units in relation to an externally derived adequacy threshold both before and after payment of benefit. (The adequacy threshold might have been set using techniques covered in Chapter 7.) Claimant unit 'a' has original income that exceeds the adequacy threshold but nevertheless receives benefit, 'A_a' – that is, 'wasted' (or, at least, inefficiently targeted) if the global objective is to prevent people having inadequate income. Claimant unit 'b' has before-benefit income that is below the threshold but the benefit that they receive ($A_b + C_b$) takes them above the threshold by the amount 'A_b', which again counts as inefficiently targeted benefit. By way of contrast, claimant unit 'c', also with income below the adequacy threshold, receives an inadequate amount of benefit ('C_c') that leaves them 'B_c' units of currency below the adequacy threshold.

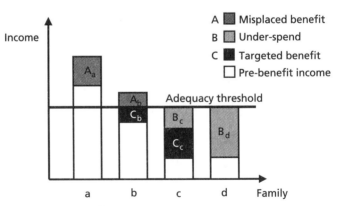

Figure 9.4 Programme efficiency

Finally, household 'd' receives no benefit at all and remains 'B_d' currency units short of the adequacy threshold.

Expenditure '$A_a + A_b$' is clearly mis-spent with respect to a global objective of ensuring that all people have adequate income. Expenditure '$C_b + C_c$' reaches the target households but fails in the case of 'C_c' to ensure adequate income. If the adequacy threshold is taken to equate with a poverty line then the amount '$B_c + B_d$' is equivalent to the post-benefit poverty gap discussed in Chapter 7 and represents the additional spending required to attain the global objective under the current policy regime. If mis-spending '$A_a + A_b$' could be entirely eradicated, the global objective could be attained at much lower cost, namely '$B_c + B_d$' plus '$C_b + C_c$' minus '$A_a + A_b$'. This illustrates the benefits of efficient targeting as a contribution to maximizing social efficiency.

The astute reader will have recognized that claimant unit 'a' in Figure 9.4 belongs to set 'A' in Figure 9.3 – that is, recipients not in need. Claimant units 'b' and 'c', being needy recipients, both initially fall into set 'B' in Figure 9.3, but whereas claimant unit 'b' is lifted above the adequacy threshold, 'c' remains in need even after payment of benefit. Household 'd' belongs to set 'C', needy non-recipients. This correspondence means that formulae for vertical and horizontal targeting efficiency take the same form as in equations 4 and 5 above and a coefficient of programme efficiency can also be computed by combining the two measures:

$$HT_R = \frac{B_R}{B_R + C_R} \qquad VT_R = \frac{B_R}{A_R + B_R}$$

$$Programme\ efficiency = \left(\frac{B_R}{B_R + C_R} \right) \times \left(\frac{B_R}{A_R + B_R} \right) \qquad (6)$$

The measure takes the value 1 (or 100 per cent if converted to a percentage by multiplying by 100) if no resources are mis-targeted to people not in need (i.e, if A_R equals zero) and if recipients receive benefit that takes their income to the adequacy threshold (i.e., C_R equals zero). Values of less than 1 (or 100 per cent) indicate less than perfect efficiency with resources being wasted, some people continuing with inadequate incomes or both.[1]

Figure 9.5 indicates just how imperfect social systems tend to be. It reports an evaluation of the external targeting efficiency of four of the case study countries during the mid-1990s. Poverty, defined as equivalized household income of 50 per cent or less than the median, is taken as the externally imposed objective. Horizontal efficiency is defined as above and

---

1 In the unusual circumstance when no social security expenditure reaches the target population, the programme efficiency quotient cannot be specified (since it would entail dividing zero).

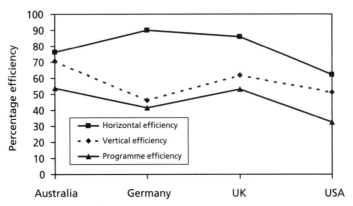

Figure 9.5 Targeting efficiency with respect to poverty, 1995
Calculated from Kim (2000)

may be interpreted as the percentage reduction in the pre-transfer poverty gap. In Germany and Britain, the poverty gap is reduced by almost 90 per cent by fiscal welfare provisions but by only 76 per cent and 62 per cent in Australia and the USA respectively. However, vertical efficiency, the proportion of resources going to reduce the poverty gap, is much less, ranging from 71 per cent in Australia, where social security is almost entirely means tested, to 46 per cent in the German conservative regime, where many benefits are based on contingency and insurance rather than financial need. Programme efficiency, being the product of the other two measures, is necessarily even lower, ranging from 54 per cent in Australia and 53 per cent in the UK and 33 per cent in the USA.

Benefits to the non-needy

Measures of targeting efficiency have been used to demonstrate that social security systems differ markedly in the efficiency with which resources are focused on the alleviation of poverty. Moreover, even the best proved to be little more than 50 per cent efficient. The remainder of the chapter is devoted to explaining why this is so, beginning with the question: 'Why are resources wasted on the non-needy?'.

Mismatch in target populations

Five sets of reasons explain why vertical targeting efficiency rarely approaches 100 per cent and why resources are therefore ill-used. Each set is now discussed in turn. First, there may be a mismatch between the policy intention and the persons actually targeted. This occurs often in external evaluations when efficiency is assessed according to targeting criteria that do

Case Study 9.1 Take-up of social assistance in Germany, 1993

Household characteristic	Take-up rate (%)	Household characteristic	Take-up rate (%)
First quartile of poverty gap (low severity)	10.1	Single person household	26.2
Second quartile of poverty gap	20.5	Single parent household	63.6
Third quartile of poverty gap	40.0	Married couple, no children	26.1
Fourth quartile of poverty gap (high severity)	78.8	Married couple, with children	44.3
New *Länder*	22.0	Cohabiting couple, no children	18.1
Old *Länder*	39.8	Cohabiting couple, with children	52.2
German households	36.8	Household head, age 30–39	46.7
Foreign households	49.1	Household head, age 40–49	45.9
Towns < 20,000 inhabitants	29.8	Household head, age 50–59	36.4
Cities > 100,000 inhabitants	43.8	Household head, age 60–69	31.9
Head schooling: 12/13 years	33.7	Household head aged over 70	27.1
Head vocational training or university degree	46.4	All poor households	37.4

Source: Riphahn (2000)

The table reports the take-up rate of social assistance benefits in Germany based on a national survey of 40,230 households conducted in 1993. The response rate was less than 40 per cent and the results were weighted to be nationally representative and therefore need to be treated with care. They suggest that, overall, the take-up of social assistance was 37 per cent, low compared to rates achieved in the UK and Australia. Take-up increased with the severity of poverty and was high among single parents, but low among the childless, very old people, rural dwellers and in the new *Länder*.

not appropriately reflect the true policy objectives. It might be argued, for example, that the above comparison between the vertical efficiency of the Australian and German social security systems is misleading because the income poverty target is more likely to coincide with the actual policy objective in Australia, where benefits are means tested, than in Germany where social cohesion has been a more important policy objective than poverty relief.

Nevertheless, there are many practical reasons why there could be a mismatch between the design target and that reached. One is administrative simplicity. Discussion in Chapters 6, 7 and 8 revealed the difficulty of operationalizing and measuring performance against policy targets. For example, instead of requiring administrative personnel to measure incomes with great precision, policy targets may be defined in terms of demographic groups thought to be more at risk of having low incomes. So, in Britain, all retirement pensioners receive a Christmas bonus irrespective of income while retirement pensioners over the age of 80 are paid a marginally higher pension on account of additional costs generally associated with late old age. Similarly, to minimize administrative effort, arbitrary deductions or additions may substitute for measures of need, income or other resources. Likewise, administrations may rely on historic rather than current evidence: Housing Benefit (*Wohngeld*) in Germany is assessed on income in the previous year as is taxable income for Earned Income Tax Credit in the USA.

Population and benefit dynamics

A second reason for the mismatch has to do with the instability of people's circumstances. In some systems, recipients are expected to report changes of circumstances immediately they occur and benefits are altered accordingly. If, for whatever reason, people fail to report circumstances that might cause them to lose benefit, vertical targeting efficiency is likely to fall. In other settings, administrations formally, and sometimes informally, ignore changes of circumstances. Since 2003, the UK's system of tax credits generally remain in payment for periods of 12 months irrespective of most changes in circumstances; this change was intended both to contain administration costs and to reduce work disincentives (see Chapter 10 for discussion of work incentives).

If the ignoring of changes in circumstances is officially sanctioned, internal efficiency is unaffected. However, this could affect an external audit since benefit would be found to be received by people who would not appear to fall in the target group of people in need. Indeed, some would argue that ignoring changes in circumstances always flatters estimates of vertical efficiency. This is because of **benefit drag**, the fact that the numerator of the efficiency fraction (equation 3) is inflated by recipients who would be ineligible based on current circumstances, while the denominator ignores

Comparison 9.2 Coverage of disability benefits, late 1990s

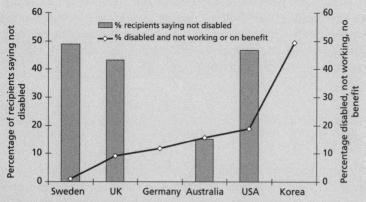

Source: OECD (2003d)

The graph indicates poor targeting of benefits on disability in the case study countries, albeit assessed on external criteria. The curve shows the percentage of disabled people who are neither working nor in receipt of benefit, a measure of horizontal targeting efficiency. The bars record the proportion of people receiving benefits who do not consider themselves to be disabled, a crude measure of vertical targeting efficiency. Sweden and, to a lesser extent, Britain have achieved high horizontal targeting efficiency at the expense of poor vertical efficiency. To a degree, the opposite situation applies in Australia, while the USA performs poorly according to both criteria when measured relative to the other case study countries (Korea excluded).

Rates of disability have been rising in most OECD countries and the lag in policy response may help to explain poor targeting. However, there are likely to be other reasons, some substantive, some structural and others reflecting difficulties of measurement. Mismatches between 'official' definitions of disability and/or incapacity used in the administration of benefit, health or social services, and between these and the understanding of the public in general and of disabled people in particular, are all likely to be important sources of explanation.

those people who were previously in the target group but no longer are due to changes in circumstance (Walker 1980, 1996).[2]

Another distorting influence of benefit dynamics is apparent in the USA. In a number of states, recipients of TANF who find employment have a proportion of their earnings disregarded. However, in a number of cases these schemes prove to be inequitable in that they provide more generously

---

2 The phenomenon of benefit drag also artificially inflates estimates of horizontal targeting efficiency and take-up unless statistically corrected for.

for working families with a history of recent welfare use than those without one. For example, in California in 1999, a working lone parent with two children would only have become eligible for TANF if her earnings had fallen to less than $900 per month, whereas an existing recipient would have retained eligibility with earnings of $1,450 per month (Giannarelli and Wiseman 2000). Again, an external audit might assume that this existing recipient fell beyond the intended target group even though legislation allowed for this eventuality.

Fraud and abuse

A third reason for vertical inefficiency arises from fraud. By its very nature, the extent of fraud is difficult to determine and the distinction between fraud and **abuse**, unintentional withholding of information or misleading of officials, is often a fine one to draw. (There are further complex distinctions between so-called organized fraud and that by individual recipients – see Chapter 11.) In the UK, the major component of individual fraud is thought to be the failure to declare earnings. Horizontal efficiency is invariably reduced by an individual's non-declaration of income if their total income exceeds the eligibility threshold, since they fall outside the target population. However, this is not so in situations in which the fraudulent claimant would remain eligible for benefit even after declaration of earnings. While horizontal efficiency measured with respect to resources would fall, no change would be registered against a measure defined in terms of population.

Mal-administration

Mal-administration generates the fourth set of factors inhibiting the attainment of perfect efficiency. Since administration is discussed more fully in Chapter 11, suffice to say that administrative errors and incorrect payments remain significant even in highly computerized systems, and that circumstantial evidence suggests that errors increase with the complexity of policy design and administration. Error can result in both overpayments, including ones to people who are in fact ineligible, and underpayments that serve to deny applicants income to which they are legally entitled. It can therefore influence both vertical and horizontal targeting efficiency. In the UK, official estimates of overpayments tend to exceed underpayments by about 1.25 to 1 (DSS 1998). However, the statistics on overpayments include fraud which is thought to account for about half. This suggests that in the UK error probably results in more underpayments than overpayments (perhaps in the region of 1.6 to 1) and, therefore, has a larger effect on horizontal than vertical targeting efficiency.

Measurement error

The final influence on estimates of targeting efficiency is measurement error. This can be substantial since estimation typically requires the integration of administrative records, providing evidence of benefit receipt, with survey evidence on the characteristics of the target population. Error arises from several sources. Administrative data, especially when subject to financial audit, can be quite reliable but is often limited in scope, being restricted to information required for processing claims. This means that there may be little detail available on the individual and household characteristics needed to assess targeting with the result that interpolation is often required. Additional errors can arise when special statistical datasets have to be compiled as an add-on to administrative procedures since front-line staff, under pressure to process applications for benefit, tend to give lower priority to such 'peripheral' tasks.

Survey data is subject to the standard problems of response rates and selection bias, with household surveys being prone to be under-representative of low-income families. Income data are notoriously unreliable unless supported by documentary evidence, while ensuring common definitions across administrative and survey records is often problematic. In addition, it is rare for survey and administrative records to be perfectly synchronized, resulting in comparability errors simply because the income and other data were collected at different times. Finally, merging data from different sources complicates calculation of the standard errors associated with sample estimates, which makes if difficult to judge the precision of the estimates of targeting efficiency.

Reasons for unmet need

Imperfect horizontal efficiency, and hence unmet need, can partially be explained by the same factors as imperfect vertical efficiency: mismatches in the specifications of the policy target, mal-administration, benefit dynamics and measurement error. However, there are two additional factors to note: inadequate benefit levels and the low take-up of benefits.

Inadequate benefit levels and limited coverage

The issue of inadequate benefits is epitomized by the experience of family 'c' illustrated in Figure 9.4. They qualify for and receive benefit but still have an income that is less than the adequacy threshold. This could be the result of administrative error leading to underpayment but is perhaps more often due to a discrepancy between the benefit scale rates and the adequacy threshold. Leaving aside a situation where an external threshold is applied that does not take account of the specific objectives of a particular scheme, there are several causes of seemingly inadequate benefits. One is the linkage of social security entitlement to contribution records, which, if incomplete, results in reduced benefits that may or may not be topped up with means-tested benefits. Another is the imposition of sanctions for failure to fulfil work or other conditions. A third is the failure by claimants to report special or extenuating circumstances, perhaps for reasons of stigma (see below), that might have resulted in higher benefits.

In each of the above examples, the benefits paid to certain individuals are less than the maximum legislated for. On other occasions, the maximum benefit levels fail to attain the kind of adequacy thresholds discussed in Chapter 7. The reasons for this can often be traced to political processes and constraints, many of which were discussed in Chapter 3. Popular support for social security provision, and especially social assistance, often falls short of the political rhetoric that claims adequate financial assistance and security for everyone. For example, it took the severe economic shock that affected Korea in 1997/8 to lever political support for the introduction of a moderately comprehensive social assistance system (MLSG, Minimum Living Standard Guarantee). Moreover, it is often exceedingly difficult to sustain popular enthusiasm to fund benefits for persons whose needs are exceptional, especially when personal failing or fault is suspected. On the other hand, a mandate for generous provision can sometimes be elicited for universal benefits, such as retirement pensions based on self-interest; in the case of Germany, an exemplar conservative regime, it is enshrined in constitutional law. Likewise, OASDI, in the USA, is unusually generous in a system that generally provides low benefits and limited coverage by international standards. However, even social security benefits have proved vulnerable to cuts, both in monetary and real terms ('real' meaning 'after inflation'), during periods of financial stringency and when the political Right has been in the ascendancy. This was evident in Britain during the 1980s, in Germany in the early 1990s and in Sweden, especially under the 1991–4 Liberal-led government (Hort 2001). Similarly, in 1998 the conservative coalition government in Australia replaced the language of 'reciprocal obligation' with that of 'mutual obligation', removing the requirement for government to provide substantial training and employment opportunities to recipients of New Start unemployment assistance (Howard 2003).

A related consideration is the imperfect coverage of benefits. Some groups may be excluded from eligibility for benefit for reasons that are technical, historical or ideological in origin and may remain so due to a lack of political will or support to rectify the omission. For example, before the 1970s in Britain, benefits designed to meet the specific financial costs associated with disability did not exist because, to the extent that they were recognized at all, they were considered to be a private family matter rather than a public responsibility (Walker with Howard 2000). Similarly, the USA and Korea do not provide generic cash benefits to assist with the cost of childrearing. In the former case, this is because the choice to have children and its consequences is considered primarily to be a personal matter while, in Korea, the influence of Confucianism, with its emphasis on the constructive influence of family ties, may support political convenience and financial stringency. In Germany, people disabled from birth were for many years denied financial support partly because of the legal and technical difficulty of paying social insurance benefits to people who had no contribution record. A not dissimilar obstacle is apparent in a number of countries concerning how best to respond to the immediate and longer-term financial needs of people who reduce or give up work to care for ill or disabled relatives.

Low take-up

A second major reason why financial needs remain unmet is that benefits go unclaimed, a possible explanation for the situation of family 'd' in Figure 9.4. **Low take-up** is the term popularly used for internal horizontal inefficiency and has featured in political debates in a number of countries, notably Britain and others that rely heavily on means-tested provision. The phenomenon has been extensively researched and a number of competing explanations for low take-up exist.

Comparison 9.3 gives estimates of take-up for a number of benefits in the exemplar countries. It is evident that rates vary markedly but fall far short of 100 per cent. However, the estimates should be treated with care because they are subject to all the uncertainties and errors discussed above. Indeed, Duclos (1997) has calculated that these imperfections mean that the actual take-up rate for UK means-tested Supplementary Benefit (80 per cent – the benefit is now called Income Support) is understated by 16 percentage points, while that for US Food Stamps (73 per cent) is underestimated by 7 percentage points. Moreover, it is not necessarily the case that households not claiming benefit will never do so; Blank and Ruggles (1996) found that 80 per cent of lone parent recipients of means-tested AFDC in the USA did not apply immediately they became eligible. Equally, though, they also discovered that only 28 per cent of all the lone mothers who became eligible for AFDC ever went on to claim it, even though the overall take-up rates lay between 62 and 69 per cent.

Comparison 9.3 Take-up rates for selected benefits in selected countries

Country	Social security scheme	Date	Take-up rate (%) Caseload	Expenditure
Australia	Age Pension	2003	78	
Germany	Sozialhilfe	1991–5	41–8	
		1993	37	
		1996	37	55
Sweden	Socialbidrag	1985	18	
		1997	23	
UK	Income support (working age)	2000/1	86–95	91–7
	Minimum Income Guarantee (retirement age)	2000/1	68–76	78–86
	Jobseekers Allowance (Income Based)	2000/1	62–71	69–78
USA*	Medicare		95–6	
	Earned Income Tax Credit		80–6	
	Unemployment Insurance		65–83	
	Food Stamps		54–71	
	SSI (elderly)		50–6	
	AFDC		45–70	

Sources: Remler et al. (2001), Andrade (2002), Behrendt (2002), Gustafsson (2002), Facs (2003), ONS (2003). * US estimates straddle years.

The take-up estimates for Britain are based on official analyses derived from a comparison of administrative data for the number of recipients and survey estimates of the size of the eligible population. The figures for Australia, which give the proportion of people over the qualifying age for Age Pension who receive it, are best interpreted as a **recipiency rate**. Some of those not claiming benefit will be ineligible on income grounds. All the other estimates are unofficial and based exclusively on survey data. The Swedish data rely on respondents to make estimates of their own eligibility for benefit. Comparisons should therefore be made with care.

The evidence on low take-up is remarkably consistent across countries (Craig 1991; van Oorschot 1994; Andrade 2002). It suggests that take-up is generally lower for means-tested benefits than for contributory and non-contributory benefits. It also reveals that people are more likely to claim benefits if they are a lone parent, in poor health, have stable circumstances or a large number of dependent children. Low take-up increases with age and the degree of social exclusion but also, perhaps counter-intuitively, with increased education, more work experience, and higher current and future wages (Andrade 2002; though see case study 9.1 for an exception). Take-up is also typically inversely related to the amount of benefit forgone.

This last finding can be interpreted in a number of ways. One line of interpretation is that it is people who are most in need that are most likely to claim; other individuals perhaps trade off the limited financial gain against the effort involved in making a claim. This suggests that measures of take-up (targeting efficiency) based on caseload exaggerate the problem of low take-up when compared to a measure based on resources. Policy-makers content with the illusion of success might therefore be tempted to rely on a resource-based measure of take-up. Alternatively, people with small entitlements may be less sure about whether or not they are eligible and therefore be less likely to apply. Administrative errors are also more likely to result in a full disallowance from benefit for people due small awards.

Econometric studies have also shown that people with high entitlement to one benefit are more likely to claim others (Dorsett and Heady 1991). Again, there are alternative possible explanations. One is that, being in greater need, people are keener to claim all the assistance available. A second possibility is that people may learn about other benefits as the result of claiming, while a third is that claiming one benefit reduces apprehension about applying for benefits in general.

To provide a coherent story about why take-up varies between benefits and in different settings and is frequently much less than 100 per cent requires strong theory. The most persuasive to date is perhaps that proposed by van Oorschot (1996) and refined by Corden (1999). Rather than focusing exclusively on individualistic explanations to do with the choices made by potential claimants, they offer a dynamic hierarchical model that also emphazises factors to do with the design and implementation of benefits.

The standard economic approach postulates that a person will claim a welfare benefit if the net utility of doing so exceeds that from not doing so (Blundell *et al.* 1988). The gains from claiming arise from the extra income received while the costs include **transaction costs**, the effort and hassle associated with claiming, and **stigma**, the negative associations attached to benefit receipt. Sometimes the take-up decision is modelled jointly with labour supply decisions in which case the marginal utility from benefit income is assumed to be less than that from an equivalent sum of earned income due to stigma (Moffitt 1983). Unfortunately, the data used to model such decisions usually lack precise measures of transaction costs or stigma and the variables used as proxies are open to interpretation. The models take for granted perfect knowledge, equate awareness with understanding, or model imperfect knowledge as the cost to potential claimants of acquiring information. They also assume that the take-up decision entails simultaneous trade-offs between the various considerations, whereas in reality the decision process may be sequential or iterative.

Van Oorschot (1996) and Corden (1999) take account of insights generated by psychologists and sociologists who have sought both to explore the content of the take-up decision and the external constraints that circumscribe it. Kerr (1982), studying British retirement pensioners claiming means-tested supplementary pensions, identified a set of barriers that he believed had to be overcome in a fixed sequence. The successful applicant had to perceive that they were in need, acquire basic knowledge about the existence of benefits, discern their eligibility for benefit and recognize a positive utility in claiming that outweighed any perceived costs and that, in the context of comparatively stable circumstances, made the effort of application worthwhile. Kerr was able correctly to predict 90 per cent of claims, though less able to predict who would remain an eligible non-claimant. His own statistical modelling threw doubt on the presumption that applicants had to follow an immutable sequence of decisions (Craig 1991) and later work by Ritchie and England (1988) with other types of claimant suggests that some people make quite complex trade-offs between the various considerations. Nevertheless, Kerr's concepts remain helpful.

Van Oorschot (1996), working in the Netherlands, finds that the first three elements in Kerr's sequence act as a threshold after which, when potential applicants believe that they may be eligible, they trade off positive and negative considerations before reaching a final decision. The process may be iterative with people leaving the decision sequence at different points on a number of occasions, and returning when circumstances trigger reconsideration (Figure 9.6). Moreover, the elements of the decision are shaped by the benefit structure and implementation.

Moving through the recognition of need to the perception of eligibility can be complex for potential applicants. Qualitative evidence suggests that the recognition by people that they are unable to make ends meet can be triggered both by crises and the gradual accumulation of financial demands. The ease with which people link the recognition of need with eligibility for a benefit depends partly on the characteristics of the scheme. Schemes that are complex, with many policy rules or vague entitlement criteria, are inherently difficult to promote; they complicate and frustrate the design of advertising and other direct communication with the target audience and inhibit

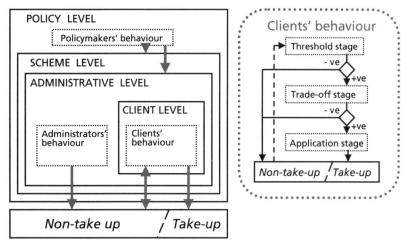

Figure 9.6 The van Oorschot model of take-up
Adapted from van Oorschot (1994, 1996)

the diffusion of clear positive messages through social networks. Potential claimants find it difficult to assess whether they might be eligible and, if so, their level of entitlement, and lay people with whom they confer for support and advice may be equally confused. These characteristics may be more associated with means-tested social assistance provision than with social insurance.

Once a person feels reasonably confident about their eligibility, van Oorschot finds them trading off competing concerns, some of which are again shaped by features of the benefit scheme and its implementation. Take stigma as an example. This has a number of forms. Felt stigma (Chapter 4) describes the sense of personal failure that can be experienced when claiming benefit. This is heightened when the benefit claim is made publicly, is accompanied by probing questioning and investigation and when applicants have to demonstrate that they have inadequate resources. **Stigma by association** arises when benefit is reserved for, or associated with, groups who are socially excluded, disadvantaged or discriminated against (Corden 1995). It has also been suggested that a form of statistical stigma exists when, rightly or wrongly, people believe that many benefit recipients are undeserving (Besley and Coate 1992). **Social stigma** occurs when benefit claimants are labelled and abused by other individuals and institutions, including the media. This can inadvertently be exacerbated by welfare institutions when, for example, policies to reduce fraud serve to tarnish the reputation of all benefit recipients. Besley and Coate suggest that social stigma can also reflect the resentment of taxpayers who are obliged to pay taxes to finance benefits that they consider too generous. **Institutional stigma** describes the attempts of welfare agencies deliberately to deter people from applying. The principle

Case Study 9.2 Take-up of social assistance in Sweden

	%	
Responses	1985	1997
1 'Receives social assistance today'	1.9	2.7
2 'I assume that I am entitled but want to manage on my own'	8.8	9.2
3 'I know that I'm not entitled'	60.9	61.0
4 'I think that I'm not entitled'	28.4	27.0
Total	100	100
Sum of rows 1 + 4	10.7	12.0
Proportion of eligible non-claimants	82.2	77.3
Take-up	17.8	22.7
Number of recipients		
Recipients as percentage of population	6.4	8.5

Source: Gustafsson (2002)

It is not easy to measure take-up. Usually the numbers of recipients are derived from administrative records and the number eligible is calculated from evidence on incomes derived from social surveys. However, in Sweden, income information collected in surveys generally relates to annual income but social assistance is assessed based on monthly income. Moreover, most claims last for less than 12 months with the result that short-term eligibility cannot be readily assessed based on survey data.

Estimates of the take-up of social assistance (socialbidrag) included in the table are derived from self-assessments made by a representative sample of people completing a postal survey (response rate: 68 per cent.). Self-assessment can result in two kinds of error: (1) people thinking themselves to be eligible for benefit when they are not; and (2) those who are eligible but who do not appreciate that they are.

Estimated take-up is very low by international standards (see Comparison 9.3). This might be taken as indicative that error type (1) is the more prevalent. However, social assistance is a benefit of last resort in a system renowned for comparatively comprehensive and generous social insurance benefits. It is also operated locally in settings prone to all forms of stigma. Hence, only 24 per cent of people responding to the survey said that they would think of claiming socialbidrag if they had insufficient money for food and housing. This is only a slightly higher proportion than is estimated actually to have claimed benefit.

The increase in take-up observed between 1985 and 1997 is not statistically significant but is consistent with increased caseloads.

of less eligibility, associated with the nineteenth-century British Poor Law administration (Chapter 1), is the definitive example, but many others still exist and continue to be created. The increasing emphasis on seeking paid employment as a condition of receipt and as a badge of active citizenship may serve to stigmatize persons unable to work (Bennett and Walker 1998; Walker 2001). According to van Oorschott, the prospective applicant weighs the costs of these various forms of stigma against the perceived financial gain from receiving benefit and against other positive and negative considerations in making a final decision to claim. The experience of the claiming process itself may influence a person's decision to pursue the claim, and whether or not to apply in future should the opportunity to do so arise.

Van Oorschot compared 14 combinations of schemes and types of applicant in the Netherlands and found that, overall, 50 to 60 per cent of non-take-up was explicable in terms of people not being adequately aware of the benefit, and another 10 to 20 per cent was due to people failing to recognize their eligibility. In some 20 to 30 per cent of cases, the failure to apply was the result of negative factors associated with receipt of benefit or the process of claiming. However, in the case of one particularly complex benefit, between 30 and 60 per cent of eligible non-claimants, depending on the type of claimant, failed to appreciate that they were eligible for benefit.

Closing summary

It is possible to spend too much as well as too little on social security, and for social security to be received by the wrong people while others fail to obtain benefits to which they are entitled. While the normative basis for who should be entitled to benefits was covered in earlier chapters, this chapter has introduced a range of technical concepts including social and targeting efficiency.

Social efficiency provides a basis for judging how much resource should be allocated to social security while targeting or target efficiency is concerned with whether resources are well spent. Measures of target efficiency are of two kinds, those that relate outcomes to the internal objectives as specified by the policy architects and those that apply external criteria, as in cross-national comparisons. Both kinds of measure can be defined with respect to the target population or to the resources consumed, and both embrace an interest in the extent to which the needs of the target population are met (horizontal efficiency) and the degree to which resources reach people not specifically targeted (vertical efficiency).

There are many reasons why benefits appear to go to the non-needy. They include poor specification of the target population, rapidly changing circumstances, fraud, mal-administration and measurement error. Likewise, the failure adequately to reach the needy and to address their needs has multiple causes, including low benefit levels and limited take-up, the latter a product of benefit design, social attitudes and reluctance to apply on the part of prospective claimants.

While social efficiency is predicated on the ability to achieve targeting efficiency, the evidence is that targeting efficiency is unlikely ever to be fully attained.

Further reading

Much of the existing literature on targeting is highly technical. Corden (1999) provides a useful review of research on take-up, while Andrade (2002) offers an economic perspective on the same topic. Kerr (1982) remains a seminal empirical study of benefit take-up.

Economic Efficiency

While this chapter is about economic efficiency, it is also about welfare – social welfare as defined in Chapter 1. Both concepts inform the two foundation questions to be addressed: 'Does social security make societies worse off?' and 'How can we know?'

Within some policy paradigms – illustrated by social democratic and corporatist regimes – the first question is almost unthinkable or asked only with rhetorical intent. It is self-evident that in meeting, if only imperfectly, the aims and objectives examined in Chapters 2, 6, 7 and 8, social security contributes substantially to social welfare and the common good.

However, as discussed in the last chapter, economic theory suggests that there is likely to be an optimal level of social security provision – the Pareto optimum – beyond which further increments of provision serve to reduce overall social welfare. It might therefore be that existing provisions reduce average well-being: for example, total household income might be below the **potential income** that would have existed with optimal provision and perfect economic efficiency, or below the **preferred income,** the product of the collectively desired trade-off between income and leisure.

In such scenarios, it is even possible that social security recipients themselves are worse off than they might have been had social security not existed. The argument, penned most eloquently by Charles Murray (1984), is that social security so erodes individual initiative that it curtails economic growth and the generation of collective and individual wealth. Figure 10.1 illustrates some of the mechanisms by which this could happen.

Even without subscribing to the Murray thesis, it is useful to formulate and empirically to investigate the questions that would need to be answered before such a thesis could be substantiated:

1 How does social security provision affect **economic structure:** the pattern of opportunities, signposts and rewards that drives the capitalist system?

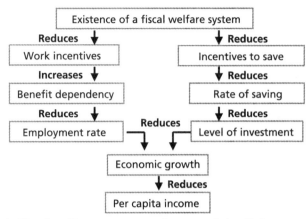

Figure 10.1 Fiscal welfare as a cause of economic inefficiency

2 How do individuals and households respond and accommodate to the economic structure?

3 How do individual responses combine to produce an overall effect?

Each of these questions is addressed in turn before considering some of the policy responses that have been proposed to limit the potential harm done by social security.

Shaping economic structures

Individuals, according to basic economic theory, are utility 'maximizers'. In all the roles they play, as consumers, workers, parents or citizens, individuals behave in ways which they believe will maximize their **utility** – the satisfaction gained from consumption of any kind, financial, social, time etc. In the simplest economic models, individuals are blessed with perfect information; they know all the options open to them and the utility that will result from pursuing each of them, and are free to choose between them. The very existence of social security, providing income at certain times in people's lives or whenever resources fall short of need, is likely to influence the utility that individuals derive from certain actions and hence affect the behavioural choices that they make.

In reality, as economists readily admit and social psychologists and sociologists are keen to document, people operate with very partial information. Individuals are rarely aware of all the possibilities available to them and many theoretical options are denied them for a multitude of reasons, often structural, that are beyond their control. They frequently find it difficult to judge the utility that will result from pursuing one option rather than another. Indeed, people almost invariably operate in conditions of great uncertainty. Moreover, it may be that people do not even try to act rationally in the way that economists might define it.

Some modern economists are much exercised with modelling real world decisions taken by individuals in conditions of uncertainty (e.g. Sarin and Wakker 1998; Cubbitt and Sugden 2001), and it is important to avoid the fallacy that individual choices will necessarily be determined by the pattern of social security provision. Nevertheless, it remains helpful to analyse how social security changes the structure of the theoretical opportunities and choices available to people, primarily by altering the pattern of **incentives**, the gains and losses associated with particular courses of action. The counterfactual in this case is a world without social security.

Altering incentives

Social security affects incentives in two principal ways: through the provision of benefit and the raising of taxes to fund spending on benefits.

Figure 10.2a presents an omniscient individual with two choices: to work or not to work – that is, to substitute work with leisure (McClements 1978; Dilnot and Walker 1989). Working generates income (recorded on the vertical axis) but reduces leisure (measured in hours on the horizontal axis) and the assumption is that increased income and leisure both add to utility. The wage rate (wr) is constant and given by the slope of line AB. At A, an individual works continuously for income A. At B, income is zero, and the person enjoys full-time leisure.

The curve CD in Figure 10.2a is an indifference curve. The individual in question is equally content with all combinations of work and leisure plotted by the curve; that is, they are indifferent to the choice of combinations. The indifference curve can also be taken to signify utility; the further the curve is away from the origin of the graph, the greater the volume of income and leisure and hence the greater the utility. The indifference curve is convex to the origin of the graph; an individual is presumed to be willing to sacrifice almost all of their leisure to attain the highest income but to give up increasingly smaller amounts of income for each additional hour of leisure they might take. The utility maximizer will choose the combination of work (income) and leisure that touches the highest indifference curve (or, strictly, is tangential to it).

Providing a universal flat rate benefit to all households raises everybody's income by the same amount and enables them to reach a higher level of utility (Figure 10.2b). It is not self-evident however, that individuals receiving the new benefit will continue with the same balance of work and leisure. For example, if they dislike work and labour only for the income, they may choose to transform the new benefit into leisure by reducing their

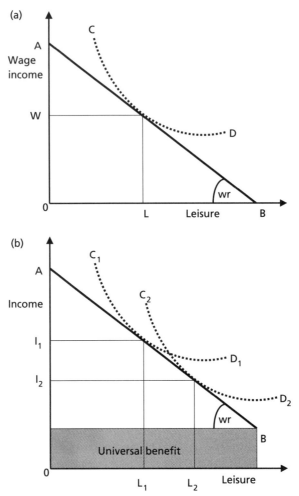

Figure 10.2 Choosing work or leisure

hours of work by an amount equal to the benefit income. Probably most people will choose to enjoy a mix of additional income and increased leisure although this is speculation. Nevertheless, the provision of the universal benefit reduces the incentive to engage in paid work and therefore probably reduces the total amount of work undertaken and, other things being equal, the total volume of economic output.

The benefit has to be paid for and, as explained in Chapter 4, resources are likely to be raised by some form of direct tax on wages. Figure 10.3 shows the effect of raising revenue for a benefit through a proportional income tax (t/wr). The effect is to reduce the income that can be generated

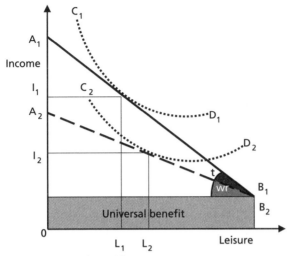

Figure 10.3 Taxation, work and leisure

by work – compare line A_1B_1 in Figure 10.3 with line A_2B_2; the person working continuously earns ((t/wr) × 100) per cent less than they would have done before the tax was introduced, as does everyone else. To receive the same income as before, people therefore have to work for longer (and those already working long hours may never be able to recoup the income on account of there being too few hours in the day). This effect of taxation, the **income effect**, is therefore to create an incentive for people to increase the hours that they work. The driving signal is the average tax rate (tax expressed as a percentage of gross income). However, introduction of the tax also means that the income forgone through not working – the opportunity cost of leisure – is reduced. This effect of taxation, the so-called **substitution effect**, is to create an incentive for people to reduce the hours that they work.

The income and substitution effects of taxation therefore create opposite incentives. Which effect dominates depends on the precise shape of the indifference curves and can only be determined by empirical analysis (McClements 1978). However, the signals to which people respond are different. In the case of the income effect, individuals respond to the **average rate of tax**, the total tax paid as a percentage of before-tax income, which is indicated by (t/wr) in Figure 10.3. The average rate of tax determines a person's take-home pay. In contrast, the signal for the substitution effect is the **marginal rate of tax**, the tax taken from the last pound or dollar of income. With a proportional tax system such as that illustrated in Figure 10.3, the average and marginal tax rates are equal. With progressive tax systems, the marginal tax rate exceeds the average rate.

Social security may also affect the incentive to save. Take preparation for old age as an example. In a cash-based society without social security in which everybody is expected to reach retirement age, people could choose between three options in old age: certain poverty; financial dependence on kin or friends; or comparative prosperity based on savings. The last option can only be achieved through saving a proportion of the (wage) income received during working life. Other things being equal, higher levels of saving secure a more prosperous retirement.

Universal social security provides a fourth option: dependence on benefit in old age. Consequently, some people may choose not to save as much (or at all) with the intention of claiming benefits in old age instead. Some may even choose more leisure at the expense of work and income during working life. Less saving generally means less industrial and commercial investment (since entrepreneurs borrow others' savings in order to invest), leading potentially to reduced economic productivity and lower economic growth.

Reality, of course, is much more complex than the provision of a fourth option. Architects of social security schemes are generally aware of the possible disincentive effects and introduce various forms of conditionality to try to minimize the problem (Chapters 4 and 5). Indeed, social security is often a response to concern among policymakers that the citizenry have too great a tendency to live for today and let the future take care of itself. So social insurance schemes, which take the form of more or less compulsory collective saving, are designed to encourage people to set money aside for distant contingencies. Nevertheless, paying into social insurance schemes may cause people to forgo other forms of personal saving, some of which may be more efficient. Similarly, tax incentives to employers and employees to provide and join occupational pension schemes have, in some countries, notably Britain, resulted in the concentration of investment decisions in the hands of large pension funds that some commentators have suggested are risk averse and detrimental to economic growth (Klumpes and McCrae 2000). Furthermore, to the extent that social security is redistributive, those people who necessarily receive less in benefits than they pay in contributions may be tempted to increase other forms of saving to compensate – the aforementioned income effect at work again.

In summary, therefore, social security influences the economic signals that individuals confront, changing the pattern of incentives to work or save. However, disincentives to work or save caused by the provision of social security can either be offset or reinforced by the requirement to raise taxation or contributions in order to pay for benefits. In reality the signals are often very complex and, indeed, sometimes confusing with the result that the impact on individual behaviour may be muted. Moreover, the structure of incentives and disincentives created by social security systems appears in different guises in different situations: when seeking employment, when considering promotion or a change of jobs, or when deciding how to spend hard-earned or surplus cash. Each situation is now considered in turn.

The unemployment trap

School-leavers or benefit recipients considering taking work may confront an **unemployment trap**, the situation in which the income available through working is not significantly greater than that received through out-of-work social security. The signal presented to the potential worker is one of caution: they are encouraged to ask themselves whether the effort of working is financially worthwhile.

Unemployment traps result from the fact that different factors determine the level of wages and social security benefits. The market for labour fixes wages. Employers seek the most productive employees at the lowest possible price. Potential employees compete with each other by acquiring skills and experience and by accepting lower wages. Employers will be prepared to pay more for labour and skills that are in short supply and compete with each other by offering higher remuneration packages. The market is imperfect because ignorance of opportunities is high and labour comparatively immobile. It is highly differentiated, with separate occupational and local markets characterized by different types of employer and worker. Moreover, labour markets vary markedly between countries. They tend to be highly regulated in countries with conservative welfare regimes with centrally negotiated agreements, but are comparatively unregulated in liberal ones. Nevertheless, irrespective of time and place, wages are rarely, if ever, fixed directly in relation to the family needs of employees.

In contrast, of course, social security benefit levels are often related to family needs or else set in relation to political arithmetic that has little if anything to do with economic productivity. The closeness of the association between benefit levels and family need varies according to the objects of the scheme and is most clear with schemes designed to alleviate poverty. For this reason, unemployment traps are generally considered most prevalent in countries that are heavily reliant on means testing, and they are most severe for large families that typically receive higher benefits on account of their size (Oorschot and Clasen 2003). However, social and political pressures to raise benefit replacement rates can generate unemployment traps in other kinds of jurisdiction. In Sweden, for example, replacement rates are in the region of 80 per cent of prior earnings (Chapter 6).

The unemployment trap is often exacerbated by dissonance between three common elements in the policy world: progressive taxation, multiple benefits and federal governance. As Figure 10.3 shows, taxation introduces work disincentives by reducing the marginal value of employment, reducing the slope A_1B_1, which indexes gross income, to A_2B_2, that is final income. Progressive taxation (rather than the proportional tax shown in Figure 10.3) would cause line A_2B_2 to become convex to the horizontal axis, with work disincentives increasing with each rise in the marginal rate of tax. In some jurisdictions, benefits are untaxed or taxed at a lower rate than wage income while, almost everywhere, they are not subject to wage taxes or deductions for social security contributions. Therefore, crossing the employment threshold can take someone instantly from a low tax world to a high tax one, substantially reducing the financial gain from working.

If taxation reduces net income in work compared to that on benefit, multiple benefits can serve to raise out-of-work income relative to that when in work. People with multiple needs can accrue a number of benefits designed for separate contingencies and thereby accumulate comparatively high out-of-work incomes. The benefits may be designed and administered by separate agencies without much attention being paid to their cumulative disincentive impact. This is particularly a feature of federal systems in which lower tiers of government have autonomy to introduce local schemes that do not necessarily dovetail well with federal schemes accessible by the same client groups.

The poverty trap

The unemployment trap is a special instance of a more generalized phenomenon, the **poverty trap**, the high marginal deduction rate caused by the interaction of income taxation and the withdrawal of income-related benefits; the **marginal deduction rate** being the proportion of any marginal addition to gross income that is lost to taxation and reductions in benefit. The term **budget constraint** is sometimes used by economists to refer to the marginal deduction rate.

The poverty trap is illustrated in Figure 10.4 with reference to provision in a theoretical jurisdiction in which a means-tested benefit is available for those on low wages and a proportional income tax is levied on all but the lowest paid. Line A_1B_1 plots gross weekly wage income. People with gross wages of less than £t per week receive a benefit of £b per week. Once their wages reach £t per week, the benefit is reduced £ for £ until all entitlement to benefit is extinguished at a gross wage of £e per week. The **tax threshold**, the income at which tax begins to be levied, is £x per week. People with wages of between £t and £e per week both receive benefit and pay income tax.

As can be seen from Figure 10.4, the system succeeds in boosting the income of all workers with wages of less than £e per week. Moreover, until a person earns £t per week they get to keep all the extra income they can earn, thereby maximizing the incentive to work and to earn additional income. However, once a person's weekly wage reaches £t, the financial

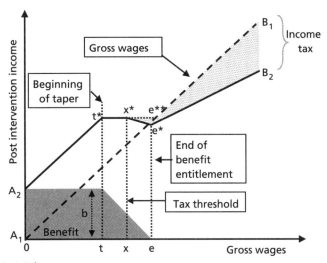

Figure 10.4 The poverty trap

incentive to earn more disappears. This is because the **benefit taper**, the amount by which benefit is reduced as other income rises, is 100 per cent – that is, each additional unit of income reduces the benefit by the same amount. The result is that a person's income remains the same however much they earn within the range between £t and £x per week. Above £x per week, which is the tax threshold, the poverty trap is even more severe because tax is now levied at the same time as benefit is withdrawn. In fact, over the range of earnings, £t to £e (the point at which entitlement to benefit is exhausted), a person will find their final income falling as their wage income increases – that is, they experience a marginal deduction rate of more than 100 per cent.

In some respects, the situation portrayed in Figure 10.4 is an extreme case. However, all means-tested benefits impose high marginal deduction rates that can be exacerbated if recipients are also subject to taxation. This is illustrated by the actual budget constraint faced by lone parents in Britain and Florida (illustrative of the USA) (Comparison 10.1). In Britain, lone parents experience marginal deduction rates of almost 70 per cent when their gross incomes are between £8,300 and £21,250 and 100 per cent when in receipt of Income Support. Even in less generous Florida, rates reach as high as 66 per cent for lone parents with gross incomes equivalent to between £5,200 and £6,400 when TANF, Food Stamps, Earned Income Tax Credit and income tax interact. Marginal deduction rates are even higher over very small bands of gross income in both countries.

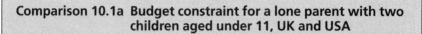

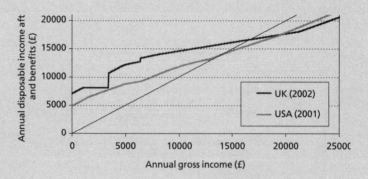

Comparison 10.1a Budget constraint for a lone parent with two children aged under 11, UK and USA

Source: Brewer and Gregg (2003)

The figure attempts a direct comparison between financial provision for lone parents with two children (both aged under 11) in the UK and USA. It plots annual disposable income (income after tax and benefits) against gross (i.e. original) annual income, both converted into £ sterling (£1 = $1.5). Some simplifications are necessary. Provision varies markedly between states in the USA; the figure portrays the situation in Florida, a relatively low-benefit state. Data for Florida omit Medicaid and state taxes while housing support and help with childcare are ignored for both countries.

The distance of disposable income above the diagonal indicates the sum by which families benefit from the mix of social security and tax credits. When disposable income is below the diagonal, tax paid exceeds income from benefits and tax credits. Support for lone parents is substantially more generous and redistributive in the UK than in the USA.

The savings trap

The poverty trap is usually illustrated with respect to earnings and its potential effect on the decision to work. The same phenomenon, of benefits substituting for other forms of income and thereby reducing the imperative to acquire such income, applies more generally in a number of different guises. The **savings trap**, when income accrued from interest on savings reduces entitlement to social security benefits, is a particularly interesting example.

The decision to save involves forgoing current consumption with the expectation of increasing future income and potential for future consumption; current living standards are sacrificed in the expectation of higher ones in the future. The savings trap means the sacrifice is less worthwhile.

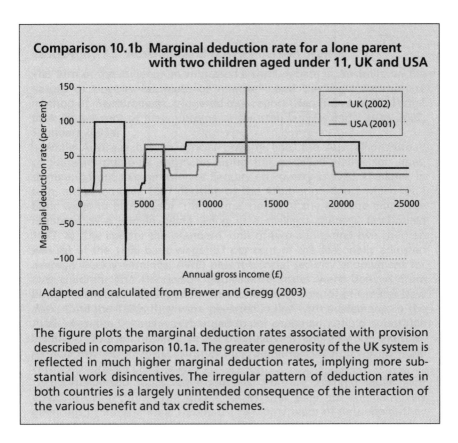

Comparison 10.1b Marginal deduction rate for a lone parent with two children aged under 11, UK and USA

Marginal deduction rate (per cent)

— UK (2002)
— USA (2001)

Annual gross income (£)

Adapted and calculated from Brewer and Gregg (2003)

The figure plots the marginal deduction rates associated with provision described in comparison 10.1a. The greater generosity of the UK system is reflected in much higher marginal deduction rates, implying more substantial work disincentives. The irregular pattern of deduction rates in both countries is a largely unintended consequence of the interaction of the various benefit and tax credit schemes.

Figure 10.5 illustrates the savings trap graphically for two individuals, I and J (the circumstances of individual K are discussed later). DD is the eligibility threshold for a means-tested benefit. An individual with original income below this threshold will receive a benefit sufficient to raise their income to DD. If their original income is above D, they are ineligible for benefit. Both individuals have non-savings income B. Individual I additionally has savings income A_iB_i but their total income is less than the threshold and they are entitled to benefit. Therefore, their income will be increased to D but they will enjoy no improvement in current living standard in return for the consumption previously forgone when accumulating their savings. The existence of the benefit would have guaranteed them an income of D even if they had spent their money rather than saving it. Individual J has higher savings income, A_jB_j, which makes them ineligible for benefit. While they gain financially from their savings, they do so by only A_jD_j rather than by the full amount A_jC_j. (Individual J may also benefit to the extent that they avoid any stigma attached to claiming social assistance.)

Received wisdom is that the savings trap disincentivizes saving; people

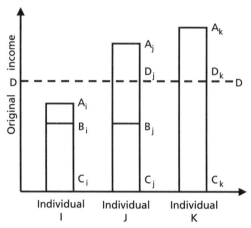

Figure 10.5 The savings trap

are encouraged to spend rather than to save. However, there is also an income effect in that earned income is taxed to pay for benefits and people therefore have to earn more than they would otherwise need to do in order to save a particular sum. Furthermore, the savings trap means that the sum of savings will need to be larger if it is to make a worthwhile difference to their future standard of living. Disincentives attributable to the savings trap may in practice also be overstated if people fail to appreciate the negative consequences of saving. Some individuals may even conclude that personal saving is more secure and therefore preferable to reliance on political promises. Others may save inadvertently, simply by not spending all that they earn. In sum, while social security inevitably changes patterns of incentives, sometimes in a fashion that may be perverse, not everyone will necessarily change their behaviour in the ways predicted by theory.

Behavioural responses

By now, it will be evident that the incentives created by social security provision are not as straightforward as implied by Figure 10.1. This, in turn, makes it difficult to ascertain the extent to which individuals respond, more or less consciously, to the signals created by social security provisions.

Case Study 10.1 Family assistance in Australia, 2000

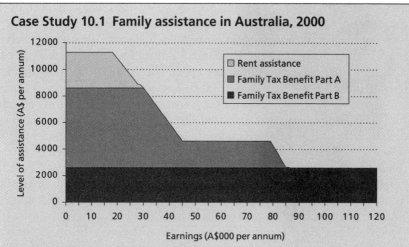

Family assistance for single income couple, private renters, one child under 5, one to 12, post July 2000

Source: Hirsch (2000)

The system of family allowances introduced in Australia in July 2000 reduced 12 benefits to 3. Like most provision in Australia, these new benefits are means tested but reach high up the income distribution. All but the richest 10–15 per cent are eligible for Family Tax Payment (FTP), Part A; almost 50 per cent, those on low to moderate incomes, receive a flat-rate benefit with the remainder receiving a rate that reduces by 30 cents per dollar (A$). Families on the highest rate are eligible for Rent Assistance. FTP is a refundable tax credit but may be taken as a cash benefit. FTP, Part B, is a fixed amount payable to families with a single earner (including lone parents); it can be paid to two-earner families but reduces once the wage of a second earner reaches a low threshold fixed according to the age of the youngest child. Part B may be thought of as a 'social wage' for childcare. In 2000, families also had access to Childcare Assistance and Childcare Cash that were replaced by Childcare Benefit in July 2002. Although benefit reduction rates were not high in 2000, when combined with the tax system families could still face a marginal deduction rate of 60 per cent.

Benefit dependency and duration

The phenomenon that has provoked most concern is **benefit** or **welfare dependency,** a term variously used to refer either to the long-term receipt of social security benefits, or to an acquired culture of long-term reliance on, and exploitation of, benefit provision. In the confusion, the existence of the former, especially among people of working age, has sometimes been cited as evidence of the latter (Murray 1984).

Interest in the duration of spells on benefits was stimulated by the arrival of longitudinal data from the US Panel Study of Income Dynamics in the 1970s and 1980s (Bane and Ellwood 1983). This showed that the majority of spells on social assistance were short, lasting weeks and months rather than years, but that a minority of recipients spent long periods on benefit. This observation has been repeated for numerous countries including Sweden, Germany and the UK (Gustafsson and Voges 1998; Krause 1998; Walker and Ashworth 1998). Moreover, the surveys revealed that the probability of a person leaving benefit declined the longer they had been in receipt. It is also sometimes presumed that the average duration of benefit claims has increased although this is difficult to substantiate because, the USA apart, longitudinal data have not been available until very recently.

Some authors (e.g. Murray 1984) argue that analyses of benefit durations provide evidence of the disincentive effects of benefit. Others (e.g. Mead 1992) interpret the results not as a rational response to perverse incentives, but rather as an indication of social pathology: long-term recipients have come to accept life on welfare, lacking the will to pursue financial self-sufficiency. Moreover, it is argued that, in certain settings where benefit recipients live in close proximity, life on welfare becomes socially acceptable and reinforced by community norms. Welfare dependency may coexist symbiotically with crime, fostering the formation of an **underclass**, a community with norms and interests that are antithetical and unacceptable to members of the wider society (Murray 1984; Wilson 1987).

In fact, it is difficult to ascribe the reduced probability of leaving benefit among long-term recipients solely, or even mainly, to a process of acculturation or negative learning – that is to **state dependency**, the process by which the experience of living on benefits in itself materially reduces the chance of self-sufficiency. This is because, over time, the cohort of recipients for which estimates of the probability of leaving benefit are calculated reduces in size and changes in composition. As people move off benefit, they leave behind others who are unable or choose not to follow them. State dependency is thus confounded by a process of selection, the so-called 'heterogeneity effect': people who remain on benefit do so simply because they have characteristics that lead them to be less likely to leave.

Ascertaining the relative importance of state dependency and heterogeneity has proved very difficult. What is clear is that it is possible to predict most, although not all, of the variation in the time that people spend on certain benefits based on the characteristics that they exhibit at the time of first claiming benefit. Limited work experience, poor education, ill-health, age, membership of a minority ethnic community and, in Britain, even the absence of a car and telephone, have all been linked to long spells on benefit (Gustafsson and Voges 1998; Smith *et al.* 2000; Green *et al.* 2003). So, too, has residence in an area of high unemployment and limited economic growth.

Reservation wages

In considering how people respond to the structure of work disincentives, it is generally presumed that people seeking work set a **reservation wage**, the lowest that they would be prepared to accept, and that the reservation wage is set above the level of benefits payable when out of work (but see Dawes 1993). In late 1997, the median reservation wage set by British jobseekers claiming benefit was £173 per week; median manual earnings were then £295 (McKay *et al.* 1999). While the reservation wage was typically between £20 and £30 less than people hoped to be able to secure, the latter was still only about three fifths of median earnings. This should not generally have been a major impediment to securing work even though return-to-work jobs tended to offer much below average wages. Moreover, the research team (Bottomley *et al.* 1997) found little evidence that benefits establish a floor to wages. Only 20 per cent said that they took account of benefit levels when fixing their reservation wage; the overwhelming majority (87 per cent) reported that they determined their minimum wage in the light of the amount that they needed to live on: almost half (47 per cent) took account of nothing else.

What people say, of course, is not necessarily what they do. However, multivariate analysis using objective measures revealed two sets of independent determinants: one was driven by family needs, while the other reflected prior work experience – former professionals and managers set the highest reservation wages (Bottomley *et al.* 1997). More importantly, the same research showed little difference in the reservation wages of claimants who found work and those who did not. In fact, 44 per cent of claimants leaving benefit took jobs paying less than their stated reservation wage. Be this as it may, when a stricter welfare regime was introduced in Britain in 1996, reservation wages fell marginally while return to work wages fell by 9 per cent for people finding work within three months of claiming benefit (Smith *et al.* 2000). There was, though, little discernible difference in the attitudes and aspirations of short- and longer-term benefit recipients.

Work-rich, work-poor families

The concept of the reservation wage focuses attention on an individual's decision to work. There is growing evidence, however, that families either take collective decisions on employment strategy or, at least, that family members are influenced in their decision by the employment and income status of other family members. This is suggested by the growing polarization between work-rich households with multiple workers and other households where nobody works. This phenomenon has been observed in a number of countries from the 1980s onwards (Sheeham 2001).

The polarization is partly a necessary consequence of the rising number of women engaged in paid work. However, policy attention has concentrated on the potential work disincentive created by the growing reliance on social assistance benefits with household means tests. If two partners are working and one loses their job, a proportion of the other's salary will serve merely to offset the unemployed person's entitlement to benefit. If the employed partner's income is less than the household means test, there will be no financial gain at all from working. Higher earning partners will benefit financially from working only by the amount that their earnings exceed the means-test threshold; if Individual K in Figure 10.5 were a working partner and the household means test was DD, they would gain just A_kD_k from working and experience an average deduction rate $(100(A_kD_k/A_kC_k))$ of about 67 per cent.

A useful measure of the impact of this incentive on employment is provided by the **employment shortfall,** the difference between the employment rate of the partners of unemployed persons and that of partners of persons in paid work. A review of the international evidence (Smith *et al.* 2000) suggests that the shortfall averages around 30 per cent. However, this shortfall cannot be entirely attributed to work disincentives created by benefits. Smith *et al.* suggest that, in Britain, about two thirds of the employment shortfall is accounted for by the fact that the female partners of unemployed men tend to be disproportionately low skilled and lacking in work experience. They also, of course, mostly reside with their partners in areas that may offer equally limited job opportunities to both partners.

Uncertainty and risk

The focus on decision-taking in families has indicated that people on low incomes tend to be risk averse; limited resources mean that families have little choice but to plan budgets meticulously while seeking to avoid the unexpected (Kempson *et al.* 1994; Duerr Berrick 1995; Walker and Collins 2003). In this context, taking a job is necessarily a risky enterprise: it might not last; take-home pay is uncertain; the time between the last payment of benefit and the first wage cheque has to be bridged (Dobson *et al.* 1994). It is possible, therefore, that perceptions of the security of income may be as important as the level in benefit recipients' decision to leave benefit for employment (Jenkins and Millar 1989).

Some supportive evidence is provided by studies of people moving off Unemployment Benefit (and its replacement, Jobseeker's Allowance) in Britain during the late 1990s (Bottomley *et al.* 1997). Respondents were asked about any worries that they had about leaving benefit and the problems that they had actually encountered when doing so. One in six were initially concerned about not knowing what their disposable income would be when working, nearly two fifths foresaw a difficulty in managing financially until the first payday and almost a quarter of those who found jobs actually did experience hardship while awaiting their first wage. A third were fearful that employment might be short-lived and, in practice, a fifth of people did have to reclaim benefit within three months of finding work (Smith *et al.* 2000).

Case Study 10.2 Family support in Wisconsin, 2000

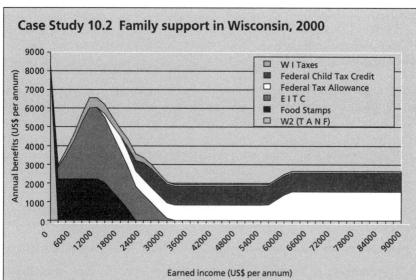

Cumulative child benefits, two parents, two children

Source: Hirsch (2000)

There is no system of universal benefit for children in the USA and the provision that exists is, unlike Australia, the product of multiple initiatives rather than grand design. Wisconsin is more generous than most US states to families with no earnings but withdraws benefit comparatively rapidly with rising income. Most financial assistance in Wisconsin is directed to families with moderate earnings. This reflects the policy objective of tackling poverty through encouraging paid work rather than by relieving poverty directly. State and federal income taxes are payable but there is a tax allowance (which is worth most to the highest tax-payers), a non-refundable credit that benefits all income groups equally and refundable Earned Income Tax Credits that aids the low paid (and is a major redistributive mechanism). 'W2' is a welfare to work or activation programme linked to TANF. Food Stamps and Medicaid are also payable, subject to a means test.

However, though uncertainty about the transition from benefit worried some recipients, just as many mentioned incentives. Two fifths were concerned about low wages and more than half were anxious about the extra costs associated with employment, such as travel and the loss of supplementary benefits to cover both housing costs and local taxes. These concerns proved to be justified in a substantial minority of cases, but far fewer people experienced financial problems leaving benefit than had anticipated them. This latter observation is consistent with benefit recipients being risk averse, but also counsels against assuming that the structure of disincentives created by the juxtaposition of wages and benefits is accurately perceived.

Policy responses

Policy responses to the disincentives created by social security provision can be divided into those that seek to change structures and the resultant behavioural signals, and those that aim to change behaviour more directly. Until very recently, attempts to change structures have seldom advanced much beyond theory and the occasional experiment. However, the imposition of conditions and sanctions directly to influence behaviour has commonly been used and variants of this strategy are discussed first.

Directing behaviour

Conditionality and enforcement

The introduction in Britain of labour exchanges in 1909, two years ahead of unemployment insurance in 1911, is symbolic of the attention given to the potentially perverse incentives created by social security. Through the system of labour exchanges, the authorities were able to validate and police the requirement on recipients of unemployment benefit to be available for and actively to seek work (Walker *et al.* 1995). Similar provisions apply to unemployment benefit systems in all jurisdictions although they vary in the vigour with which they are enforced and in the nature of the sanction. In Britain today, unemployed claimants are required to sign and pursue a 'Jobseeker's Agreement' detailing the actions to be taken in pursuit of work and may lose benefit if the agreement is not adhered to. In Australia, all unemployed Income Support recipients are similarly required to enter a 'Preparing for Work Agreement' when first claiming benefit and those aged under 34 need at the same time to choose a 'Mutual Obligation Activity', comprising some form of training or work experience.

Conditionality is not limited to unemployment benefits, although it tends to be most explicit in connection with benefits targeted on people of working age where disincentives to work apply. Sometimes conditionality can have unwelcome consequences. For example, as noted in Chapter 6, incapacity benefits in Britain and the USA are generally payable only to people who entirely disengage from the labour market even though substantial minorities of recipients would like to undertake limited amounts of paid work (Thornton *et al.* 2003). Two concerns worry administrators in both countries. The first is that without the zero employment condition unscrupulous claimants could use incapacity benefit to supplement part-time earnings – the equivalent to moving from L_1 to L_2 in Figure 10.2b. The second is that claimants might be tempted to migrate from unemployment to higher-paying incapacity benefit.

In practice, benefit conditionality is often most emphatic with respect to social assistance benefits. This may partly be because electorates fear that, unlike insurance benefits, social assistance raises the prospect of deceitful recipients receiving 'something for nothing'. However, there is also a tradition in many countries, including Sweden and Germany, of local delivery and the close involvement of social work. In such settings, the receipt of benefit is sometimes used as a tool to promote social rehabilitation and modification of behaviour that is achieved through a range of activities, including job search and work-related activities such as training, under-pinned by the potential sanction of withdrawing benefit (Hvinden 1999).

Activation and proactive welfare

The concept of **activation,** linking benefit receipt to microeconomic measures such as compulsory training to increase the supply of labour, has been traced to Sweden and other Scandinavian countries (Wilenski 1992; Lødemel and Trickey 2001). There, a combination of social security and labour market policies continued to be used to stimulate the demand for, and supply of, labour even after Keynesian demand management policies had become discredited elsewhere. **Active** or **proactive welfare,** the Anglo-Saxon twin of activation, has its origins in political concerns over the growth of welfare caseloads in the USA and, later, of unemployment in the UK. It was initially given momentum by the aforementioned analyses of Murray (1984) and Mead (1986), suggesting a direct link between work disincentives and the long-term receipt of benefits, and later by the apparent success of experiments to encourage welfare recipients into paid work (Walker 1991; Deacon 2002).

Jessop (1993) attributes the diffusion of activation policies to the trans-formation of economies from industrialized to post-industrialized modes of production and the need to move from macroeconomic means of regu-lating economic demand to microeconomic measures to improve labour supply. The diffusion was actively fostered by international organizations (Lødemel and Trickey 2001; Walker 2001). The OECD published the *Jobs Study* in 1994, which included a set of recommendations for member countries designed to advance reform of labour market and social security policies. The United Nations summit in Copenhagen in 1995 pursued a similar agenda as did the European Union Luxembourg summit in 1997 that established a process of annual employment guidelines and national action plans that promote activation as a key element in reform.

Table 10.1 summarizes some of the key elements in active welfare policies. The list is neither comprehensive nor definitive since jurisdictions have tended to adopt particular components thought best suited to local conditions. Three components warrant mention since they are direct responses to the disincentives discussed in this chapter: workfare, bridging and relative wage adjustment.

The term '*workfare*', requiring claimants to work in return for benefit, is of US origin but the policy has long been a feature of localized social assistance in Scandinavia, Germany and elsewhere in continental Europe (Walker 1991; Lødemel and Trickey 2001). It places the conditionality of benefit on a pinnacle and, if vigorously implemented across the full caseload, implies large-scale, expensive governance able to find or create employment for all welfare recipients. In reality, social assistance workfare in Europe has historically tended to be the deterrent or sanction of last resort, and to be used comparatively rarely when other less draconian options have been exhausted. For a period in the early 1990s workfare became the positive rhetoric of welfare reform in the USA but, even so, workfare was usually

Table 10.1 Proactive welfare

Strategy	*Selected components*
Encouragement and coercion	• Advice, placement and counselling contracts • Sanctions on voluntary unemployment • Enforcement and workfare • Limiting benefits
Policies to assist job search	• Job placement services • Exclusive schemes
Building human capital	• Training • Remedial education • Work experience
Bridging	• Continuing entitlement to benefit • Meeting work expenses • Minimizing the cost of failure
Relative wage adjustment	• Reducing out-of-work benefits • Minimum wages • In-work benefits and wage subsidies
Employment creation	• Labour supply policies • Direct job creation • Employer subsidies

implemented as only one of a range of work-related pathways along which welfare recipients were directed. Moreover, in most US states, only a minority of claimants participate in any of the work-related programmes available, and attempts by the Bush government to increase the rate of participation contributed to a political impasse in 2002 that prevented the passage of new welfare legislation (Walker and Wiseman 2003c).

The variant of workfare that is most often implemented comprises a set of work-related options such as skills training, remedial education and temporary work experience. The work experience may be acquired with private sector employers but more commonly involves placements with governmental and not-for-profit organizations. Provision is generally targeted on specific groups, particularly long-term recipients and those thought to be at risk of not leaving benefit early. Working literally for benefit is very rare, although workfare employment is sometimes remunerated at market rates, as on selected programmes in the UK. More often, participants receive a supplement to their benefit to cover real and notional expenses associated with employment (Lødemel and Trickey 2001). Various forms of supportive services are also frequently provided including childcare, mentoring services and special financial support to cover costs associated with job search and employment.

The precise mix of provision reflects the ideological underpinnings of the policies and their precise objectives. Some governments seek to counter economic disincentives to prevent long-term dependence on benefits, while others focus on the psychosocial and cultural correlates of welfare dependency. Some policies prioritize social exclusion and seek to foster integration and social engagement, while some schemes are designed to improve labour market attachment and yet others to enhance the human capital and employability of benefit recipients. Many schemes address a mix of objectives. At risk of oversimplification, US states tend to focus on welfare dependency with 'work-first' polices that prioritize work experience over prior training. The UK and Germany lean more towards human capital enrichment and social inclusion, while Scandinavian countries employ a mix of strategies.

Bridging mechanisms, policies to ease the move from benefits to employment, constitute a response to the uncertainty that may prevent benefit recipients from taking up work. Different measures apply before and after the move into work. Ahead of the decision to take up employment, the emphasis is on supplying benefit recipients with accurate information about their likely disposable income in work compared to that on benefit. On taking up work, policies aim to smooth the financial transition by meeting the set-up costs associated with starting work, by extending benefit entitlement to receipt of the first wage and by ensuring rapid calculation and payment of in-work benefits. Longer-term, mentoring services may be provided to assist former welfare recipients to negotiate crises that might threaten sustained employment and, for occasions when employment fails, to implement procedures to smooth the transition back onto benefit. Since 1996, Britain has introduced an extensive programme of bridging measures in response to the severity of the situation created by linking in-work and out-of-work benefits to different eligibility criteria. Other countries have introduced bridging mechanisms on a more ad hoc basis.

To summarize, enforcement and activation policies employ a mixture of sticks and carrots to encourage benefit recipients not to respond rationally to the perverse economic signals created by the interaction of tax-benefit systems that make the receipt of benefits more attractive than paid work.

Structural reform

Advocates of structural reform see this as a means by which many activation measures would become redundant. If the unemployment and poverty traps could be lessened, or better still, eradicated, then it would always be rational for people to choose paid work in preference to benefit receipt.

The four strategies discussed in this section all seek to lessen the disincentive effects of social security, three by merging the tax and benefit systems. The two boldest schemes, negative income tax and a social dividend, are almost devoid of practical examples. Tax credit schemes, on the other hand, are rapidly becoming a key component of modern welfare systems, while modification of systems to realign benefit levels and wage rates is often a continuing process.

Negative income tax

Whereas ordinary income tax reduces people's incomes, **negative income tax** aims to increase the incomes of the poorest taxpayers. At its simplest, a negative income tax scheme deducts tax from people with incomes above a defined threshold and makes payments to people with incomes below the same or some other income threshold. As originally envisaged, negative income tax replaces all welfare benefits and applies to all forms of income, although the scheme portrayed in Figure 10.6 is limited to earnings. Line A_2B_2 records the income people receive after the application of a negative tax system and is to be compared with gross earnings A_1B_1. The tax threshold is indicated by Xx^*, above which tax is taken from taxpayers; the total tax collected is given by the triangle $x^*B_1B_2$. However, anybody with a gross wage of less than x *receives* a payment of tax. The difference between the total tax taken $(x^*B_1B_2)$ and that paid out as negative income tax $(x^*A_1A_2)$ gives the resources available for non-social security government spending J.

The key feature of the negative tax system portrayed in Figure 10.6 is the smoothness of the marginal deduction rate. Line A_2B_2 is straight and

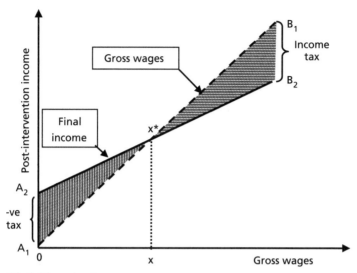

Figure 10.6 Negative income tax

sloping upwards from left to right. This indicates that everybody faces the same marginal deduction rate and that this is always less than 100 per cent: hence, each person is able to spend the same fraction of any additional gross income and the unemployment and poverty traps are entirely eradicated. Moreover, to the extent that everybody pays tax and is known to the tax authorities, then anybody who has a gross wage of less than x will receive a payment that lifts their final income to A_2 or more. Therefore, if A_2 is set at or above the poverty threshold, negative income tax should also eradicate poverty. Furthermore, negative tax schemes hold out the prospect of significant administrative savings resulting from the closure of social security offices.

While at initial reading, negative income systems may appear to be perfect, there are several political and technical problems. First, to lift everybody out of poverty is expensive, requiring additional revenue that might entail a substantial increase in the marginal tax rate. While nobody would be subject to a poverty trap, every marginal unit of income would need to be taxed at a high rate, thereby creating work disincentives for the many rather than the few. Negative income tax schemes are also inefficient, making payments to people with final incomes above A_2 (Figure 10.6).[1] Secondly, most tax systems operate on an annual basis with current tax payments fixed in relation to income in the previous year. Poverty, of course, occurs in the present and therefore requires payments to be linked to current needs. As yet, no one has provided a convincing resolution to this, the so-called, *ex post* problem. Finally, negative income tax needs to be based on a family or

1 The inefficient spending is given by the triangle $A^2 \overset{*}{x} z$ in Figure 10.7.

household assessment, otherwise, people could unfairly exploit the economies in budgeting acquired through living together (Chapter 8). This runs counter to the trend in many countries towards individualized taxation.

Negative income tax schemes are associated with the radical Right: Milton Friedman offered a minimal design as long ago as 1962. They ostensibly remove employment disincentives and eradicate poverty with the minimum of government bureaucracy. Sceptics on the Left of the political spectrum, however, dismiss negative income schemes as being 'quite simply, a universal system of means-testing' (Fitzpatrick 1999: 88). Be this as it may, experimental tests of the negative income tax idea conducted in the USA between 1968 and 1978 suggested that it was expensive, eroded work incentives and promoted family break-up (Neuberg 1995).

Basic income

If negative income tax schemes are associated with the political Right, the idea of a basic income has attracted the attention of left of centre reformers (Rhys Williams 1943; Tobin 1965; Jordan 1985; Fitzpatrick 1999). A **basic income** (sometimes called a **social dividend** or, when directed to a population subgroup, a **demogrant**) is an income paid unconditionally on a regular basis to every person as a right of citizenship. As such, it could not sound more different from a negative income tax, although, as Figure 10.7 illustrates, in economic terms the two proposals are identical. Every person receives a basic income, $A_1\dot{A}_2$, from the state that increases

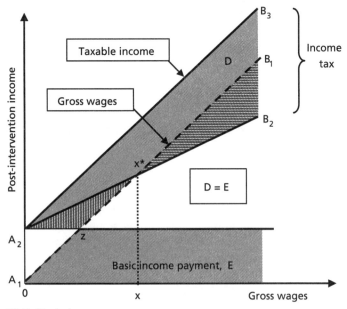

Figure 10.7 Basic income

people's initial incomes from A_1B_1 to A_2B_3. The whole of the income A_2B_3 is then subject to a constant marginal tax, which results in exactly the same post-tax income, A_2B_2, as under the negative income tax scheme portrayed in Figure 10.6. All but $x^*A_1A_2$ of the initial outlay E is recovered through taxation; again this is exactly the same net expenditure as for the negative income tax scheme.

Despite being economically isomorphic, basic income differs from negative income schemes in matters of presentation and substance. Basic income is not conditional on the receipt of earnings or other income as is negative income tax. Secondly, it offers more security in that it is paid ahead of earnings; that is, it is paid *ex ante* rather than *ex post*. Finally, it is paid to individuals rather than households. What is less clear from the writings of the proponents of basic income is how payment and taxation interact to contain costs and eradicate poverty. With basic income and taxation both individualized, the cost of eradicating poverty is likely to soar.

Only a few partial basic income schemes have ever been implemented. At one time, Canada paid demogrants to children aged less than 18 and to persons over 65. Alaska allocates a share of the royalty produced from oil sourced on state-owned land by adding an average of between 2 and 3 per cent to the personal incomes of all Alaskans. Finally, in 2003, Britain combined the child dependant additions previously paid under a range of benefits into a single tax credit that is paid alongside the universal Child Benefit and which approximates to a demogrant for dependent children.

Refundable tax credits

The recent spread of refundable tax credits is in marked contrast to the limited take-up of basic income and negative income schemes and probably reflects the fact that some of the same advantages can be achieved at a more reasonable cost. A refundable tax credit usually takes the form of a negative income tax scheme that is targeted on subgroups of the population and supplements, rather than replaces, other forms of social security. (Refundable tax credits should not be confused with non-refundable tax credits that remove certain forms of income from taxation, thereby raising the tax threshold and reducing the tax paid, but do not include payments from the tax authority to the taxpayer.) The US Earned Income Tax Credit is paid to working families with dependent children, and in Britain the Working Tax Credit is targeted at low-income workers and the Child Tax Credit is made to parents in respect of their dependent children.

Most refundable tax credits implemented to date are concerned to address the unemployment trap by increasing income in employment relative to out-of-work benefits and so apply only to earned income. The maximum credit is paid to low-paid workers with earnings below or close to benefit

Comparison 10.2   Active labour market programmes, 2000/1

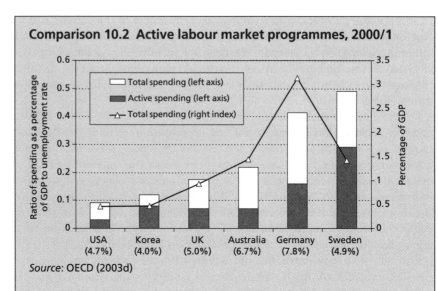

Ratio of spending as a percentage of GDP to unemployment rate (left axis)
Percentage of GDP (right index)

Legend:
☐ Total spending (left axis)
■ Active spending (left axis)
—△— Total spending (right index)

| USA (4.7%) | Korea (4.0%) | UK (5.0%) | Australia (6.7%) | Germany (7.8%) | Sweden (4.9%) |

Source: OECD (2003d)

The line plots total expenditure on active and passive labour market programmes as a percentage of GDP. In 2000/1, expenditure was highest in Germany, which also had the highest level of unemployment, and lowest in Korea and the USA, which had much less unemployment. The importance attached to active labour market policies in Sweden is illustrated by the fact that expenditure was the second highest while unemployment was only moderate.

The bars indicate the importance attached to labour market programmes after allowing for differences in unemployment and show Sweden and Germany in the lead. The height of each bar plots the ratio of spending as a percentage of GDP to the percentage unemployment rate.

The graph also shows the priority given (in terms of spending) to active as opposed to passive labour market measures. The darker bars show this to be highest in Korea and Sweden, both countries that have emphasized employment as a source of social welfare and have applied activation to mainstream policies and not just to social assistance as in the US and, until recently, in Britain.

levels and payments reduce, eventually to zero, with rising earnings. The rate at which credits are reduced determines the cost of the scheme, the number of workers who benefit financially and the number who necessarily face higher than normal marginal deduction rates as the credit is withdrawn. In theory, workers with wages high enough to exclude them from credit help to fund the cost of the scheme through higher taxes although, in practice, funding is typically drawn from general government revenue such that the cost is dissipated over a large tax base and may go unnoticed by taxpayers. Indeed, tax credits are often presented as a reduction in tax rather than as an increase in government expenditure, one reason that it has been possible politically to expand tax credit programmes (case study 2.3). However, because tax credits are but part of a complex tax-benefit system they cannot ensure that poverty traps are eradicated; indeed their interaction with other schemes can exacerbate the problem that fully-fledged negative income tax schemes aim to cure.

The extent to which tax credits are fully integrated into the tax system varies considerably. The US Earned Income Tax Credit is well integrated and paid as part of the end of year tax reconciliation based on joint tax assessment. The credit therefore reflects family needs but is *ex post* and based on last year's income. The British tax credits are social security payments packaged as tax adjustments. This reflects the fact that income tax is individualized and a separate household assessment is considered necessary. Virtues of this are that payments are based on more current income assessments than is possible in the USA, while the credit is paid through the wage packet or directly to the beneficiary at fortnightly intervals. It is assumed in government circles that tax credits attract less stigma than welfare benefits (HM Treasury 1998).

Relative wage adjustment

While the other three strategies involve substantial reform of the tax and benefit systems, **relative wage adjustment** can be characterized as 'mere tampering'. The objective of relative wage adjustment is to maximize the difference between in- and out-of-work incomes, and usually entails altering the level of existing benefits and tax rates. Often the process is semi-automatic since, if benefit levels are up-rated in line with prices but wage inflation is higher, the effect is to reduce work incentives (case study 7.1). However, during the 1980s and early 1990s, a number of countries, including Germany, Sweden and the UK, explicitly adopted a strategy of reducing the level of out-of-work benefits (notably unemployment benefit) to increase work incentives, although political constraints severely limited the scale of adjustment that proved feasible. Since the mid-1990s, the emphasis has shifted somewhat towards increasing in-work incomes, a strategy involving increases rather than falls in family incomes that is often more politically palatable, especially in social democratic and conservative regimes. The change in strategy also reflects a response to evidence that the wages of unskilled workers fell further behind those of other workers during and after the recession of the early 1990s, and support from the OECD for boosting in-work incomes through various forms of wage subsidy, notably tax credits (discussed above) and minimum wages.

In summary, therefore, policies available to address economic disincentives are of two principal kinds: one seeks to alter the structure of the incentives, the other to minimize their behavioural consequences.

Closing summary

Introducing any social security scheme alters the pattern of financial incentives. This may cause people to work more or less, to save greater or lesser sums, to borrow or forgo borrowing or even to provide more or less for their families. It would be wrong, however, to assume that social security alone shapes the choices that people make, not least because the tax-benefit system is often not well understood by lay people.

Likewise, it cannot be assumed that social security necessarily reduces economic efficiency. Social security allows national economies to adapt and restructure with less social distress than would otherwise be the case. Social assistance can enhance health and productivity, unemployment benefit may enable people to take more rational labour market decisions and pension provision may encourage savings. Equally, it would be unwise to assume that social security spending is always benign, and so this chapter has focused on some of the trade-offs between social security provisions and economic efficiency.

Disincentives take many forms. The unemployment trap means that people stand to gain little financially from taking a job, while the poverty trap limits the financial benefit accruing from extra earnings. Analogously, means testing income from investments creates a savings trap and curtails the monetary value of saving. Individuals may respond by not working or saving and, to counteract this response, benefit receipt may be made conditional, activation policies may be introduced and sanctions may be applied. Alternatively, attempts may be made to alter the structure of incentives. This can be achieved by adjusting the value of benefits downwards in relation to wages or by introducing negative income tax schemes, a basic income or refundable tax credit systems.

Further reading

McKay and Rowlingson (1999) provide an accessible introduction to the disincentive effects of social security, a topic which is covered at a slightly more technical level by Blank *et al.* (2000), who focus on US provision. Lødemel and Trickey (2001) detail activation policies in the USA and a number of European countries, while Walker (2001) discusses the limitations of a work-focused approach to welfare reform. Fitzpatrick (1999) traces the ideological rationale underpinning negative income tax and basic income schemes.

Administrative Efficiency

This chapter is about making social security happen, and about achieving the most possible with the resources available.

The generic goal of social security administration is to implement policy, delivering the correct cash benefit to every person eligible at the most appropriate time. **Administrative efficiency** demands both **technical efficiency**, attaining the aforementioned goal with the optimum combination of resources, and **price efficiency**, ensuring that the goal is achieved at minimum cost. To the generic goal, one might want to add that the service should be delivered in a way that shows respect and consideration to benefit applicants, recipients and other users. This supplementary goal – which is, of course, inconsistent with designs to promote institutional stigma (Chapter 9) – will affect both technical and price efficiency

The range of services offered within a social security system in support of the delivery of benefits is large. In Chapter 5, services were categorized into those to do with the application process (processing forms, making assessments, implementing payment, taking appeals etc.), those comprising infrastructure activities (policy development, promoting benefits, collecting contributions, staff recruitment, estate management etc.) and those offering support and employment opportunities (child support, skill enhancement, job placement etc.). The range of these services is such as to engage a large number of other end-users besides benefit recipients. These include employers, people paying social security contributions, benefit advisers and professionals having contact with current or potential benefit recipients. In addition, there are agencies, private firms, not-for-profit organizations and social partnerships that have a role in the delivery or servicing of social security.

To manage and deliver social security, social administrators have access to the same factors of production as any organization: land, labour, and capital; that is, in more modern parlance, property, staff and capital resources. All are generally in short supply, despite the vast power and resources of modern governments. That social security is more or less efficiently delivered is one of the administrative miracles that the often maligned bureaucracies achieve but which goes largely unnoticed. The aim of this chapter is to begin to explore how such miracles are brought about. The ways in which resources are organized are described, as are the processes of performance management. First, however, it is necessary to introduce the concept of intermediate outcomes and to list those appropriate to the study of social security administration.

Intermediate outcomes

The **final outcomes** of social security record a system's performance measured with respect to the aims and objectives discussed in Chapter 2. They concern the extent, for example, to which a system alleviates poverty, adequately compensates for loss or brings about the redistribution of resources desired. **Intermediate outcomes** or **outputs** correspondingly relate to performance with respect to **intermediate** or performance **objectives** that have to do with the effective delivery of benefits rather than the consequences that benefits might have for recipients and the wider society. As with final outcomes, there are often many intermediate objectives that are sometimes in conflict. Moreover, it is again possible to distinguish between primary and secondary objectives, and between intermediate objectives and intermediate functions, the latter including the unintended consequences of administrative procedures as well as the intended ones. In the interests of space, the following discussion focuses largely on objectives, emphasizing those to do with the delivery of benefits to recipients.

Delivery and volume

The predominant objective is the efficient processing of applications and delivery of benefit. The key elements involved have been considered in Chapter 5. Suffice to say that systems have to be in place that are adequate to meet the volume of business – often enormous. In the USA, for example, 46.4 million persons received benefits under the OASDI programme in 2002; 1.7 million disabled workers submitted applications of whom 750,000 were successful and had awards put into payment (WMCP 2003). In the same year, 19.1 million American families were in receipt of food stamps; in 1999, 18.2 million received Earned Income Tax Credit and, in 1998, 40.6 million made use of means-tested Medicaid, including 18.5 million to cover the cost of treatment from a physician and 4.3 million to meet in-patient fees (WMCP 2000). Failure to deal well with high volumes results in delays and often a decline in accuracy. It also adds uncertainty to people's lives that may conspire to frustrate attempts to strengthen work incentives (Chapter 10) and may even lower take-up (Chapter 9).

Speed of service

From an applicant's perspective, speed of response is important in all aspects of their dealings with a benefit system. They generally dislike having to queue and wait in offices: it is inconvenient, stressful (particularly for mothers accompanied by children), and can contribute to the use of aggressive behaviour and abusive language (Vincent *et al.* 1995). Benefit applicants want processing times to be short and payment prompt. This is not only a matter of courtesy but also reflects the limited alternative resources available to benefit recipients, especially those reliant on means-tested benefits who, by definition, will be forced to live beneath the adequacy threshold if benefits are delayed. Delay in social security payments is a major cause of social assistance applications in Germany (Leisering and Leibfried 1999) and, to a lesser extent, of social fund loans in the UK. For similar reasons, people making complaints or going to appeal also want their grievances dealt with rapidly.

From the perspective of bureaucracy, delays provoke customers to chase progress on their applications, generating additional unnecessary contacts that serve to exacerbate the problem.

Accuracy and adequacy

Benefit recipients want to be paid their correct entitlement and an adequate level of benefit. While the latter is a policy issue and the former an administrative one, recipients do not always make the distinction with obvious implications for customer satisfaction. Certainly, measures of customer satisfaction are closely linked with the outcome of an application: in Britain, the group most likely to report dissatisfaction with benefit administration are those whose claim has been rejected. They are closely followed by claimants who feel that they should have received more benefit than they did. This association between outcome and satisfaction means that benefit levels are likely to constrain the level of customer satisfaction that an administration can attain, almost irrespective of the quality of other aspects of the service.

While applicants place a premium on accuracy, when benefit rules are complicated they are unlikely to be aware of assessment errors that occur. Indeed, in such circumstances, most errors probably come to light through a generalized feeling of injustice, which leads a person to seek further advice or to appeal against the decision, rather than from an informed understanding of the benefit system or the assessment process (Sainsbury 1992). Social security administrations may also determine errors retrospectively and seek to recover overpayments from benefit recipients, a practice which can result in long-term indebtedness (Berthoud and Kempson 1992; SEU 2002).

User efficiency

User efficiency is defined from the perspective of applicants to mean obtaining the maximum benefit for the minimum effort. As such, it does not necessarily correspond with technical efficiency when defined narrowly in the short-term interests of benefit administrations. Benefit applicants require ease of application, simplicity of rules and procedures, good communications and the avoidance of repetition in providing information to agencies. In the short term, bureaucracies may be able to reduce staff costs or capital investment by burdening applicants with form-filling, additional visits etc. However, to the extent that this results in inaccurate information or incomplete evidence being provided by applicants, or generates a sense of resentment among them, it may serve to add to administration costs in the longer term.

The notion of simplicity has numerous connotations in social security and as many ramifications for administrative agencies. Applicants are likely to interpret simplicity in terms of being readily able to discover the benefits available, the level of their entitlement, and the application procedure that they need to follow. Indeed, many would often prefer the benefit to be paid automatically, as sometimes happens with tax credits. Applicants welcome an application process that is straightforward and that requires minimal information and supportive evidence to be provided. They typically abhor complex forms, multiple benefits requiring multiple applications and lengthy interviews unless well conducted and self-evidently beneficial.

Simplicity has payback for administration in terms of ease of computerization, less staff training, reduction in error and lower promotion and advertising costs. However, sometimes simplification may also substantially increase benefit costs. This can occur, for example, when programme efficiency is reduced due to the introduction of less refined targeting which, in turn, may result in accusations of 'rough justice' or unfairness if the categories of eligibility are thought to be crudely drawn. This happened in Britain with the 1987 reform of Income Support.

Access

The concept of access comprises a number of elements. One has to do with the ease of translating benefit eligibility into benefit receipt. Another concerns the maintenance of communication between the administration and benefit recipients. Others connect with the discussion of benefit take-up in Chapter 9 and the strategies adopted for enabling applicants to move rapidly to the threshold point of discerning eligibility, and then to encourage them to weigh positive considerations above negative ones in the pursuit of an application. A further dimension of access applies to methods of ensuring that members of the public can make an informed choice about the most appropriate form of provision; this is primarily an issue for the private sector but is increasingly important in the public sector too, especially in relation to old-age pensions.

Benefit applicants in Britain typically find it hard to detail how they came to recognize their eligibility, some saying that they 'just knew' and others referring to 'common knowledge'. Sometimes they have no more than a vague awareness that they need help which may be available, and this acts as the seed for further enquiry among intimates and para-professionals (Hedges and Thomas 1994). This may point to a failure of the British system to communicate the knowledge necessary for rapid, informed decision-taking but it equally echoes experience in the USA (McConnell and Ohls 2000) and other research on decision-making, notably that on the diffusion of innovation (Rogers 1962, 1976). Combining both streams of evidence suggests the need for outreach and advertising by social security administrations to convey broad messages about the availability of benefits and their general purpose, to be accompanied by more focused material to aid assessment of entitlement and to detail the application process. The latter needs to be made readily available to potential applicants and lay and professional advisers.

Choice as to mode of access – electronic, telephone, mail or personal interview – may also be important; certainly, applicants express a preference for choice although, in practice, they often tend to rely heavily on one preferred mode. Certain activities lend themselves to particular modes of contact but there is also evidence in Britain that prior dissatisfaction can cause some people to prioritize face-to-face contact because of the perception that it offers applicants and recipients more control. Applicants also tend to favour a single point of entry into the system, 'one-stop shopping', requiring that one agency deals with the full range of an applicant's needs or can provide seamless access to all benefits and services even when the provision is contracted to a range of service providers (Walker 1995; SPR 1997). Recognition of this preference has led to the recent provision of one-stop services: Centrelink in Australia, Jobcentre Plus for persons of working age, and the Pension Service for older claimants in the UK; and 'One-Stop Career Centers' in the USA provided under the Workforce Investment Act of 1998 and being expanded in some states to include employment and support services for recipients of TANF (Golonka 1999).

The choice of provision raises other issues concerning access: how to ensure that people know what is available, are able to make informed decisions about competing products, are fully aware of the true costs and likely value of different options and can trust the probity and financial security of the institutions with which they deal. This has always been an issue with private-sector provision and the state has responded with regulatory systems. Britain probably has the longest history of large-scale reliance on the private sector, especially with respect to pensions. The government has set minimum standards that pension products and companies must meet, has established regulatory bodies (ten of which were replaced in 2001 by the Financial Services Authority) and acted to prevent the mis-selling of products. The pensions industry itself has set up a pensions ombudsman service. However, a recent review (Sandler 2002) found that the savings market had to date failed to ensure the provision of simple to understand, value for money products or to stimulate an adequate level of private savings. In particular, it was judged to have failed to serve less well-off members of the public, most probably because of the high cost of servicing this segment of the market. If governments choose increasingly to rely on private-sector provision, they need to invent new ways to ensure that low-income families and individuals retain access to social security.

Access, like most aspects of administration, is constrained by policy design. The three routes to entitlement discussed in Chapter 5 (insurance, citizenship and means testing) help shape the decision process of applicants and the outreach of agencies. Means testing usually entails greater complexity of benefit design and eligibility assessment, and in many settings is associated with higher levels of stigma and lower take-up. Less stigma typically attaches to insurance benefits, and administrations are normally in touch with potential clients even before a claim is made due to a history of contributions. However, while eligibility is normally transparent, the assessment of entitlement may be complicated and, especially if dependent on investment income, unpredictable. Although citizenship benefits typically pose fewer barriers to access, increased international migration may lead to more people being excluded on the grounds of residency or foreign citizenship (Chapter 13).

Quality of treatment

Benefit applicants lay great stress on being treated with respect (Clasen *et al.* 1998). This relates to facilities – the provision of privacy, secure information storage, attractive décor and cleanliness of premises, provision of toilets and (when appropriate) facilities for children. It also pertains to the demeanour and behaviour of staff.

Social security applicants would like to receive the best quality service that they obtain in commercial organizations but frequently, depending of context and regime, do not expect to do so. High aspirations, low expectations and the associated resentments add to the challenges faced by front-line staff. Applicants hope for front-line staff who treat them with courtesy, behave professionally and who are effective. They value encouragement

Case Study 11.1   Errors in the administration of US Food Stamps, 2002

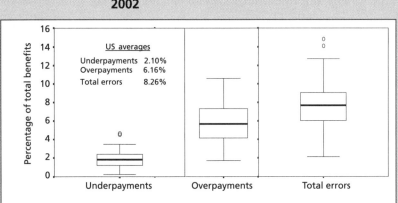

US averages

Underpayments	2.10%
Overpayments	6.16%
Total errors	8.26%

Source WMCP (2003)

The diagram reports official estimates of administrative errors made in the payment of the US Food Stamps programme in 2002. The estimates are based on a statistical sample of over 90,000 cases that were reviewed as part of a quality control programme first instigated in 1972. States are rewarded financially for exceptionally low error rates and sanctioned for unusually high ones.

The overall error rate in 2002 was 10.7 per cent of the value of benefits paid out, with overpayments running at over twice the rate of under-payments. Statistics are also gathered on the proportion of claims receiving an incorrect payment (a headcount measure) but are not reported here. Overpayments include fraudulent claims as well as administrative mistakes in determining eligibility and entitlement; about a fifth of over-payments (1.5 per cent of total benefit expenditure) is considered to be fraudulent, some $395 million annually between 1999 and 2002.

The 'box and whisker' plots indicate the variation in administrative error between states. The central horizontal line in each case indicates the median error rate and the box signifies the inter-quartile range – the 50 per cent of states with error rates closest to the median (in a normal distribution). For example, 50 per cent of states had error rates for over-payments of between 4.06 and 7.26 per cent. The two states, California and Michigan, making a very sizeable number of underpayments (4.69 and 4.56 per cent respectively, compared to the median of 1.84) also had the highest error rates overall (14.84 and 14.10 per cent respectively). However, another five states had total errors exceeding 11 per cent (Connecticut, Kansas, New Hampshire, Oregon and Wisconsin), primarily due to high numbers of underpayments.

and support from social security staff, appreciate being listened to and get angry when their word is (thought to be) doubted. These aspirations help to explain why the recent introduction of case-working in Anglo-Saxon countries has generally proved popular when resources have been sufficient for caseloads to be kept comparatively small (O'Connor *et al.* 1999; WCF 2000; Howard 2003).

The challenge for front-line social security staff is often to reconcile the aspirations of claimants for a flexible and responsive service with the demands of the policy and administration as they interpret them. In an environment of resource constraints these twin demands may often be in conflict, as Lipsky (1980) observed in his classic study of US social assistance provision. He reported front-line staff responding to these pressures by limiting the demand for services, maximizing the use of available resources and ensuring the compliance of claimants. An example of the first strategy is provided by a recent study of UK Jobcentres (Wright 2003). Staff distinguished between 'good' clients, perceived as compliant and willing to take paid work, and 'bad' ones who were differentiated by labels such as 'wasters', 'unemployables', 'nutters', 'snooty' or 'at it' (suspected of committing fraud). The first group tended to be afforded more time and support than the others.

Howard (2003) records staff in Centrelink offices in Australia who sometimes resort to the second strategy and seek to maximize available resources to assist favoured clients and bend or ignore rules in order to do so. In Britain, the administration has sought to capitalize on and control this pattern of behaviour by providing staff with discretionary budgets for them to use in exceptional circumstances (DWP 2003b). Evidence of the third strategy is provided by Mead (2001). He reports staff in US welfare offices who opine that recipients welcome being made to do what they know they should do but otherwise would not. Moreover, Mead argues that enforcing compliance is indeed important in the effective delivery of TANF. From the perspective of staff, if they succeed in ensuring compliance, they are likely to reduce the hassle that they confront on a day-to-day basis. However, success may prove elusive in settings where benefit recipients perceive rules to be unfair, punitive or counterproductive; the evidence is that recipients simply will not comply (Vincent 1998; Waller and Plotnick 2001). The challenge for supervisory staff is to ensure that their front-line colleagues retain their creativity while staying within the bounds of propriety and prioritizing the interests of clients above their own.

Interactions between staff and benefit recipients or applicants are bounded by the objectives of policy and by more or less shared presumptions about the aims of the social security system. Applicants access a residual, social assistance system with different expectations and feelings of self-worth than they would claim an insurance pension or a non-contributory war pension. They are therefore likely to behave and respond differently in their dealings with officials. Likewise, the boundaries of legitimate, possible and acceptable responses by front-line staff differ in parallel ways that are likely to have a cumulative effect on the quality of service experienced by applicants and claimants. While benefit applicants and recipients may want high-quality service, they are not frequently in a position readily to demand it. Likewise, while policymakers may on occasion aspire to providing 'customer focused' services, taxpayers may not believe that (all) social security recipients deserve high-quality provision.

Security

Fraud is perhaps inevitable in organizations that deliver billions of dollars or pounds to millions of people. Therefore, as in the banking industry, financial security has to be a central element in social security administration, aiming to minimize the opportunities for fraud by staff, agents and applicants alike. By its very nature, the scale of fraud is very difficult to estimate; attempts in the UK suggest that, in 2002/3, fraud may have accounted for between 6 and 10 per cent of total spending on Jobseeker's Allowance and about 5 per cent of spending on the main social assistance benefit, Income Support (DWP 2004). Fraud actually detected by the Centrelink administration in Australia saved AS$1 billion in 2001/2 (Centrelink 2003). The opportunity cost associated with this level of fraud is clearly substantial and, some fear, sufficient to undermine public support for social security provision (Cm. 1998; Field 1998; Saunders 2003b). On the other hand, Raper (1999: 103) has argued that Australia's anti-fraud strategy has resulted in 'a culture of mistrust at street level' that pervades the administration of benefit.

Public discussion of fraud tends to concentrate on the activities of benefit recipients, rather than staff or agents, and to connect with debates on the underclass (Chapter 10). Even so, non-claimant fraud can be very important: within the US WIC programme (Special Supplementary Nutritional Program for Women, Infants and Children), which provides food benefits in the form of vouchers, fraud among vendors providing food in return for vouchers is thought to be 30 times greater than that among recipients (GAO 1999). **Recipient fraud**, defined as the deliberate misrepresentation of circumstances with the intent of gaining financial advantage, can either be committed through commission, by actively providing false information, or through omission, knowingly withholding relevant information (Sainsbury 2003: 278). It may be deliberately organized by crime syndicates or undertaken by individual benefit recipients, sometimes initially inadvertently.

British researchers have identified four different kinds of fraudulent claimant, defined with respect to two criteria: first, the extent to which they are self-reflective about their actions and secondly the degree of anxiety they feel about the illegality of their action and its possible consequences (Dean and Melrose 1997; Haines 1999). 'Unprincipled' fraudsters experience little anxiety, are non-reflexive and see no need to justify their actions. 'Subversive' ones believe their actions to be a rational response to a mean and punitive system and, again, are unmoved by the consequences of their activities. In contrast, 'desperate' and 'fatalistic' fraudsters both suffer considerable anxiety, living in fear of being caught. The former often strongly believe that they had no other option given their circumstances and the latter tend to act impulsively and to be regretful later. Over time, some people move from one category to another, perhaps with most movement away from the high anxiety categories as the perceived risk of being caught falls.

Administrations typically attempt to tackle fraud through 'front-end' controls to prevent it occurring, and through investigative reviews and systematic systems of checking. Over the last decade or so, there has been an increased reliance on sophisticated checks of identity. The USA introduced social security enumeration at birth in the late 1980s and Germany launched a social security card in 1992. There have long been plans to bring in a similar card in Britain, although it has been strenuously opposed by civil rights organizations. Various states in the USA have experimented with fingerprint and iris recognition systems in connection with welfare administration.

Secondary systems rely on intelligence and increasingly on data-matching made possible by integrated computer systems. Over recent years repeated large-scale advertising campaigns have been run in Britain inviting members of the public to report people thought to be engaged in fraud, while Australia is encouraging people to report fraud via the internet. Australia permits data linkage for the purpose of fraud detection between Centerlink (administering benefits) and the Australian Taxation Office (ATO), Department of Veterans' Affairs, Department of Immigration and Multicultural Affairs, Department of Corrective Services and the Registrar-General's Office. Similar schemes exist in Britain, Germany and Sweden.

A more radical strategy to reduce fraud is through benefit design. The argument is that removing temptation might deter the desperate and fatalistic, while avoiding perverse incentives would at least make the activities of the subversive less easy to justify. One example is to encourage the reporting of casual earnings by increasing the period over which earnings are assessed for means testing (thereby reducing the prospect of losing all benefit in assessment periods when work is undertaken). A similar device, adopted in Germany, is provision for part-time unemployment benefit. Increasingly popular is the payment of benefit via automatic credit transfer rather than by means of cash or vouchers that can be lost or stolen, both in reality and as fraudulent pretence. This approach is safer and avoids the risk of stigmatizing law-abiding benefit recipients who do lose their cash, by presuming guilt.

To summarize, social security policy is perhaps shaped and experienced as much through implementation as design. Therefore, intermediate outcomes have to be delivered if policy objectives are to be achieved.

Management of resources

The delivery of intermediate outcomes is achieved through the effective organization and management of resources. Rather than attempt a comprehensive review of the management and administrative sciences as they apply to social security administration, the intention is to focus on a few exemplars that most directly affect intermediate outcomes.

Personnel

Despite advances in computerization, large numbers of staff remain at the core of social security operations: 131,000 in the UK Department for Work and Pensions and 24,000 in 430 Centrelink customer service centres in Australia (albeit dealing with a range of government services). Ensuring that suitable staff are recruited, retained, properly trained, well supervised and allocated appropriately to work type and workload in a constantly changing political, economic and social environment would be a challenge for any administration, but is essential to the efficient delivery of social security.

Training

Leaving aside policy development and support functions, social security administration has historically been characterized by clerical activity (assessment, benefit payment, record-keeping and financial security) with smaller numbers of staff available to offer information on benefits and, especially in social assistance, to interview applicants and validate claims. Delivery was usually at neighbourhood level and most staff were recruited locally to lower clerical grades. University graduates were usually only found in policy positions or, in Sweden and Germany, in social work related functions attached to social assistance provision.

Most functions remain clerical although computers now handle much of the routine benefit assessment, record-keeping and payment. For many staff, face-to-face contact with clients has been replaced by postal and telephone contact, the latter increasingly organized around remote telephone call-centres, sometimes contracted out to private-sector suppliers. This has resulted in some reduction in staff numbers and a downgrading of numeracy and people skills among staff, but with a greater emphasis on basic computer literacy. This trend has been evident in many countries for 20 or more years. More recently, it has been accompanied by the move from passive to active policy (Chapter 10) that has resulted in the requirement for some staff to act as case-workers or personal advisers and to acquire labour market and other expertise unnecessary before. As an example, Case Study 11.2 lists the tasks associated with the post of a

Case Study 11.2 Examples of knowledge and expertise required by personal advisers working in the UK New Deal for Disabled People pilots

Job task	Requirements	Examples of knowledge and expertise	
		Client: disabled person	*Client: employer*
Recruitment	Knowledge base	Population characteristics	Local employers
	Professional expertise	Disability awareness	Understanding of business interests and concerns
Provision of advice	Technical expertise	Marketing and publicity	Marketing and publicity
	Knowledge base	Benefit rules	Employer incentives
	Professional expertise	Eligibility calculations	Applicability of incentive schemes
	Technical expertise	Application procedures	Application procedures
Assessment	Knowledge base	Aetiology and prognosis of specific illnesses and disabilities	Business plans and recruitment history
	Professional expertise	How to identify aspirations abilities and barriers	How to assess commitment
Preparation	Technical expertise	Criteria for case-loading	Liaison criteria for employers
	Knowledge base	Range and scope of training providers	Incentives and support available to employers
	Professional expertise	Counselling and listening skills	Counselling and listening skills
	Technical expertise	Appropriateness of training and other support	Employment law

			Job requirements
Placement	Knowledge base	Details of benefit and tax credit systems	
	Professional expertise	Liaison and brokering skills	Liaison and brokering skills
	Technical expertise	Labour force placing and case management computer packages	Application and access procedures for employer support and incentives
Follow-up and in-work support	Knowledge base	Sources of in-work financial and other support	Sources of in-work support
	Professional expertise	Assessment of likely threats to employment	Conflict resolution
	Technical expertise	Ability to access or provide support	Ability to access or provide support
Management	Knowledge base	Organizational and personnel management	External relations
	Professional expertise	Team-building skills	Liaison and networking
	Technical expertise	Resource management	Quality assessment and assurance
Administration	Knowledge base	Public and private sector practices	Public and private sector practices
	Professional expertise	Stress management	Time management
	Technical expertise	Computer literacy	

Source: Loumidis et al. (2001)

The table shows the span of knowledge and expertise required by personal advisers engaged in a pilot UK activation programme for disabled people, now operating nationally, with modifications. One management response to the challenge was to introduce specialization among staff, which eroded somewhat the initial aspiration to offer one-to-one casework support to participants in the programme.

personal adviser engaged on Britain's New Deal for Disabled People, a voluntary activation measure aimed at recipients on Incapacity Benefit. The specification derives from the pilot for the programme, which was extended nationally albeit in somewhat revised form, in 2001. The programme entails personal advisers making sophisticated judgements about people's potential employment prospects and liaising with benefit recipients, employers, specialist service providers and health professionals.

A distinct, though related, development has been the growing influence of consumerism with an increased emphasis on service quality. The now defunct Benefits Agency, which was established in Britain in 1991, introduced the term 'customer' to replace the hitherto used 'claimant'. In 1997, Australia did likewise when, in creating Centrelink by merging the former Department of Social Security and the Commonwealth Employment Service, use of the term 'beneficiary' was consigned to history. Adopting a 'customer-centred' focus, Centrelink introduced a Customer Charter outlining the rights and responsibilities of customers, feedback mechanisms to discern customer opinion, a one-to-one personalized service ethos in one-stop offices branded 'customer service centres' and a commitment to make customer choice 'the primary method for determining service options' (Vardon 2000: 15, cited in Howard 2003). Similar policies have been pursued in Britain, by many US states delivering TANF and have recently been urged on the US Social Security Administration (GAO 1999). They imply a substantial shift in administrative culture, moving from rule-bound procedures to governance that is both more open and prioritizes customers, initiative and creativity.

There is evidence that the task of upgrading staff to undertake the more complex tasks associated with customer-focused provision, especially active casework, is far from complete in many jurisdictions. A report by the Australian National Audit Office (ANAO 2001: 74), following the creation of Centrelink and the implementation of the Mutual Obligation activation policy, concluded that lack of knowledge by staff was a 'risk to effective service delivery'. It pointed to excessive workloads and an anti-training culture in local offices as contributing factors. Similarly, research on personal advisers in Britain has revealed large variations in styles and effectiveness, with much confusion over roles and often feelings of inadequacy when dealing with claimants with multiple difficulties (Lewis *et al.* 2000; Kelleher *et al.* 2002; Osgood *et al.* 2002). In both these countries, staff receive training lasting days or, at most, weeks, with limited external accreditation. This contrasts markedly with the graduate intake common among social assistance caseworkers in Sweden and Germany.

Deployment

The effectiveness of social security administration depends not only on the training of staff but also on their number and how they are used and supported. There are significant constraints to what can be attained. One is the legacy of past recruitment policies that mean that staff in post may not be well fitted to current work demands; this almost certainly partly explains the slow adaptation to the demands of proactive policies. Ironically, this impediment is lessened by high staff turnover, normally viewed as a sign of failure by human resource managers. Turnover is typically greater in city locations with buoyant economies where modest public sector pay rates are especially unattractive. Another constraint, of course, is resources: activation policies were introduced in Korea with caseloads of 250; customer service officers in Australia's Centrelink have caseloads of around 160; while personal advisers in Britain's New Deal system work with between 30 and about 100 participants depending on the scheme. The nature and content of casework will inevitably differ between these settings depending on the time staff have available to devote to benefit recipients.

Different policy regimes and organizational structures mean that staff are deployed very differently in different jurisdictions and there are variations even within jurisdictions on account of the range of administrative functions entailed in delivering social security. Nevertheless, there are common issues that have to be addressed that are revealed by focusing on the three functions of verification, assessment and case management. These include the location of staff, work organization and specialization.

When procedures demand personal contact with applicants and recipients, some staff have to be deployed locally. Historically, when systems were comprised of paper-based offices, this meant locating most functions in neighbourhood offices to facilitate speedy assessment and payment. With the advent of computers, it became possible to relocate many activities, for example payment and even benefit assessment, in 'remote' offices to gain economies of scale and capitalize on lower labour costs. In the 1980s and 1990s, pressures to reduce costs and staffing led to an increased reliance on postal, telephone and, latterly, web-based contact with applicants that further reduced the requirement for local offices. Concerns about security and an emphasis on customer service and activation mean that a local presence is increasingly likely to be retained, at least for some groups of social security recipients.

In the local office setting, managers are obliged to ensure that customers are speedily directed to the most suitably trained and experienced members of staff who have access to all relevant information. They should therefore be able to deal effectively with the necessary business in the minimum time, to the satisfaction of customers and in accordance with the spirit and letter of the legislation. While the administrative challenge is obvious, the solution rarely is.

Filtering systems are frequently employed, whereby clients presenting with less complex problems are dealt with by less specialized and, typically, less expensive staff, who increasingly have access to information supplied via information technology systems. The first point of contact is particularly important for a least two reasons. First, reception staff can be used to manage demand by diverting people to more appropriate sources of assistance or, illicitly, to prevent entry for reasons including prejudice, ignorance and (arguably false) loyalty to overworked colleagues. This has been reported among staff working for both the UK Social Fund (Barton 2002) and Australia's Mutual Obligation Initiative (Howard 2003). Secondly, there are substantial costs to clients and the organization if clients are directed onto the wrong processing pathway. These problems are magnified where many different benefits and/or services are accessed through a single portal – 'one-stop shopping'.

Ensuring staff have access to the right knowledge and expertise requires training and information technology support but also appropriate working practices. There are typically trade-offs to be made between allowing staff to acquire and exploit a detailed knowledge of their clients and making sure that they are fully conversant with the legislation and aware of all the opportunities available to clients.

Caseloading, or one-to-one working, where clients deal with a named member of staff, usually best achieves maximum knowledge of the client but such systems break down when client-staff ratios are high (Howard 2002). A compromise is **team working** in which small groups of staff either deal with claims from a small geographic area (patch working) or from a sub-group of clients, often defined by family name ('alpha splits'). Maximizing substantive knowledge typically requires a degree of specialization with clients either being routed to appropriate specialist staff on a 'need-to-know' basis, or caseworkers acting as intermediaries between clients and specialists. Sometimes work is organized with teams of specialists in an attempt to square the circle.

The role of supervisors is often crucial. Interpretation of complex regulations – administrative judgement – is challenging and even experienced staff often need access to informed guidance. Where staff are charged to use discretion, they are sometimes confronted with moral and administrative dilemmas of inestimable difficulty in making real the intentions of policy-makers and the body politic. In such circumstances, they often need an authoritative sounding board. Where, as in Centrelink, management wishes to encourage innovation and entrepreneurship and to see that making mistakes in an inevitable part of service improvement (Vardon 2000), they need authority to take risks and support when they do. Good supervision – and underpinning that – good management are also critical in managing the pressures that cause front-line staff to abuse their position in the ways identified by Lipsky (1980) and others. It is important that abuse that deleteriously affects clients or undermines policy objectives is appropriately challenged by supervisors in the confident knowledge that they will be supported by more senior management.

Demand management

To make the most effective use of the resources at their disposal, social security administrations are frequently required to prioritize and manage demand. This is particularly challenging when legislation affords applicants the right to benefit and customer service agreements set standards of customer service. The strategies employed range from crude queuing and delay, to the more sophisticated. An intermediate level approach is the judicious use or non-use of advertising. Given that appropriately designed and targeted information has been shown to increase awareness and applications, not advertising might be justified at times when demand outstrips administrative resources. Certainly, administrations have become much more sophisticated in the use of advertising when changes are introduced, eschewing blanket advertising that might generate an avalanche of demand in favour of staged and targeted promotions. The matter of how long advertising should be forgone for fear of excess demand is a question of policy, morality and law as much as it is one of operations.

Another strategy is to formalize the filtering role of reception staff by encouraging potential applicants to consider alternative strategies to claiming benefit. In the USA, the strategy is given greater impetus by the time limits on length of benefit receipt, and Mead (1998) has argued that diversion is a major reason for the fall in social assistance caseloads since the introduction of TANF. In practice, however, many states condone informal as well as formal policies to divert welfare applicants away from TANF (Solomon-Fears 2003).

The targeting or rationing of resources has been formalized in the UK Social Fund although, in this case, the rationing relates to benefit payments rather than simply administrative resources. The Social Fund is a system of lump sum grants and loans to cover exceptional needs and circumstances, and is unusual in that payments are made from a fixed annual budget. This is devolved to local offices that have to apportion the budget over the year, often with reference to seasonal patterns in demand noted in earlier years. Local management is also charged with devising local priorities that determine the response to applications.

Another approach to maximizing the effective use of resources is to avoid **deadweight**, expenditure incurred in order to achieve a result that would have occurred in the absence of the expenditure. This is particularly common with regard to expensive support services such as training or remedial education. As noted in Chapter 10, most recipients of short-term benefits move off social security comparatively quickly, leaving only a small percentage of individuals who claim for long periods. Offering assistance designed to help people to leave benefits quickly to recipients who will do so anyway is an example of deadweight. One response is to limit access to special schemes solely to people who have already been on benefit for a comparatively long time. This principle applies to most New Deal activation policies in Britain, although there has been a tendency to shorten waiting periods as caseloads have fallen.

A perceived weakness of the 'wait and see' strategy is that it simply condemns the most disadvantaged recipients to longer spells on benefit. This is because skills erode and stigma increases while a person is on benefit, thus exacerbating the problem of leaving. In response, a number of administrations have sought to develop **profiling** strategies, predictive models to identify the people most at risk of long spells on benefit close to the point of application so that they alone are directed to receive appropriate services. Profiling strategies, which vary markedly in sophistication, are universally applied in the administration of Unemployment Insurance in the USA and are employed by some states in connection with the TANF social assistance programme (Rangarajan 2002). The potential of the strategy has recently been reviewed in Britain (Bryson and Kasparova 2003), and a profiling instrument for people receiving incapacity benefit has also been developed (Waddell *et al.* 2003).

Information technology

As already noted, computing capacity has long been used on a large scale in the administration of social security (Chapter 5). Its traditional function has been the calculation and payment of benefit but it is increasingly being employed to provide additional customer services, to realize activation and enforcement policies and to identify fraud and improve financial security (Kellard 2003).

The deployment of information technology is often integrally linked to the deployment of personnel, sometimes operating as a substitute, sometimes as a support. Moreover, technology often imposes constraints on policy as well as offering opportunities. As long ago as 1988, major policy reform in the UK was driven in part by information technology constraints. Committed to staff reductions, the Thatcher government believed that information technology provided an answer by eradicating the need for manual calculation of benefit. However, the existing benefit system was very complex, with entitlement being closely tailored to individual circumstances. The main social assistance benefit, Supplementary Benefit, was replaced by a simpler scheme, Income Support, which was better adapted to the demands of automated assessment.

The power and sophistication of information technology systems has advanced enormously in the last decade and a half and, while they still impose limits on benefit design, certain policy innovation is only made possible by sophisticated information technology. The large-scale implementation of activation policies is dependent on information technology systems to identify job matches, track client progress against agreed objectives and enable advisers to manage large individual caseloads. Similarly, child support policies, that track non-resident parents to enforce and recover child support payments for their children, are highly dependent on information technology. Indeed, a failure in information technology development meant that implementation of child support reform in Britain was much delayed (NAO 2002). Other examples of information technology based approaches to social security administration include large-scale telephone operations in call-centres, payment card systems and fraud detection based on data linkage.

The future contribution of information technology to the administration of social security may be most marked in terms of the provision of consumer services. The internet has opened a new mode of communication between agency and client that is already being widely used for the dissemination of information and advice, and for job search and placement. Likewise, web access is increasingly being offered as a mode of application and, in future, should provide facilities for reporting changes in circumstances, undertaking reviews and, perhaps, for monitoring compliance. However, in so doing it also introduces additional modes of exclusion with clients in most hardship being least likely to have cheap internet access.

Performance management

As stressed in the introduction to this chapter, the effective delivery of social security requires technical and price efficiency. In attempting to achieve this, social security administrations necessarily set performance objectives, develop business plans, identify and manage risk, and audit performance with varying degrees of success. Moreover, in recent years, with the growth in **managerialism**, the deployment of private sector management techniques in public and quasi-public organizations, these processes have been conducted more formally and increased attention has been paid to the need for political accountability. Further developments have produced complex networks of internal and external audit. These include the proliferation of the contracting out of services, the increased involvement of private and not-for-profit agencies in the delivery of welfare in liberal and social democratic regimes, and the continuing role of social partnerships in conservative ones. In assessing the effectiveness of delivery, therefore, it is necessary to examine performance both at the level of organizations and in terms of the system as a whole.

Internal audit

The term **internal audit** is here used generically to refer first to mechanisms employed to try to ensure that intermediate or performance objectives are achieved and secondly, to the measures used to establish the level of performance attained. Space precludes the book-length account required to do justice to the topic of audit. Nevertheless, it is important to alert the reader to processes that are often neglected in the analysis of social security but which are an increasingly important part of the administrative environment. Moreover, audit not only reflects or records administrative performance, it helps to shape it and hence to determine the characteristics of the policy delivered to, and experienced by, social security recipients. Audit also provides much of the data available to the analyst studying social security.

Until about the 1970s, audit was largely the preserve of accountants keen to ensure that resources were not used profligately or illicitly. Alongside accountants, operational researchers were required to assess how much it would cost to deliver benefits or services (most efficiently). With the arrival of managerialism came an interest in ascertaining and ensuring both that budgets were not exceeded (technical efficiency), and that the expenditure achieved what was intended, ideally at minimum cost (price efficiency). These mechanisms can be, and increasingly are being, applied to integrated systems of social security provision, to particular social security administrations, to organizations contracted to deliver benefits or services, to sections of staff within administrations and contracting organizations, and to individual officers. In the case of officers, audit takes the form of performance review (determining how efficiently members of staff perform their duties) and appraisal (assessing how their performance can be improved).

Audit is perhaps most clearly evident in the business plans of organizations, in the subcontracting of services, in the targets set for staff and in the procedures for monitoring and evaluating performance.

Business plans

Business plans are usually produced regularly, often annually, and typically specify an organization's intermediate or performance objectives and the strategies for meeting them. Sometimes the objectives are somewhat aspirational, although increasingly they are more specific and may be accompanied by **performance targets,** levels of performance to be achieved expressed in ways that facilitate measurement. Reports may also detail achievements against targets in the preceding period.

Contracts

As already noted, considerable parts of the delivery process are sometimes contracted by social security administrations to for-profit and not-for profit organizations. (In Britain, 45 per cent of administration costs are attributable to external providers, including 13 per cent for provision of services to benefit recipients seeking work, 8 per cent for information technology services and 7 per cent for benefit encashment and banking services, Cm. 2003.) The contracts are usually multi-faceted but seek to ensure that organizations deliver the services required within a specified budget. Typically, they lay down performance standards and targets for the delivery of services, and often set out structures of financial incentives (Bartik 1995). The incentives are designed to encourage contractors to prioritize those aspects of the business that the commissioning organization considers important or to deliver services in approved ways. As such, they reveal the priorities of the commissioning organizations. Unfortunately, contracts are often considered commercially sensitive and researchers may have to make do with the invitation to tender that may itself not be publicly available.

Staff targets

Increasingly, staff are set targets designed to achieve the desired volume of activity and service quality. To the extent that they are appropriately designed and monitored, targets can enhance standards of social security administration. They also reveal organizational priorities to the outside observer.

Staff targets are difficult to devise and can on occasion lead to perverse outcomes. For example, targets have frequently been set for the number of clients that staff are expected to place in employment. Such targets can result in **skimming** or **creaming**, whereby staff seek out clients who are most easy to place in order to fill their quotas (Bartik 1995; Brown *et al.* 1998). The clients helped would probably have found work quickly without assistance (a problem of deadweight) while clients who might have benefited most from support are denied access to the service.

Management information and monitoring

Assessing whether targets are met requires the collection of information. This may be collected for the specific purpose of monitoring performance – when it might be open to manipulation by anyone with an interest in boosting measured performance – or derived indirectly from information obtained in the normal process of delivering benefits and services. The widespread trend is to exploit information technology to broaden the range of information used in performance management, to enhance analytic and presentation techniques and to make the information more accessible, more rapidly to a wider range of managers and supervisors. The utility of management information is highly dependent on the quality of the initial data.

Piloting and evaluation

Social assistance and activation policies have been formally evaluated in USA since at least the early 1970s and an evaluation 'industry' has now developed worldwide (Greenberg and Schroder 1997; Walker 2004). The US model has been to test a policy idea by establishing a pilot implementation in a locality – often called a **demonstration project** – and assessing the effectiveness of the policy by comparing the outcomes for persons randomly assigned to receive the policy with those for others randomly assigned not to do so (Chapter 6). Demonstration projects focus on whether policies work, but more recently they have been accompanied by so-called '**process studies**' that focus on establishing why policies work by examining how they are delivered (Greenberg *et al.* 2000).

Although demonstration projects have attracted a lot of attention, other methodologies have been employed in a number of countries (and sometimes in the USA) to establish the effectiveness of existing policies. Instead of asking whether a policy will work, these evaluations ask whether current policies are working or need revision. Indeed, as Table 11.1 indicates, a large number of evaluative questions can be asked for auditing purposes that differ according to when in the sequence of policymaking they are asked. The challenge is to establish an appropriate counterfactual that gives

Table 11.1 Policy evaluation questions

Time perspective	Evaluation question	
	Impact evaluation	Process
Extensive past	What worked?	How did it work?
Past	Did the policy work?	How did it work/not work?
Present	Is this policy working?	How is it working/not working?
Present to future	Is there a problem?	What is the problem?
Close future	Can we make this policy work?	How can we make this policy work?
Future	Will this policy work?	How will it work/not work?
Expansive future	What policy would work?	How would it work?

Adapted from Walker (2002)

confidence that what is being assessed is the true effect of the policy as implemented (Chapter 6).

External audit

Whereas internal audit is conducted primarily to establish administrative efficiency with respect to the intermediate objectives set by social security administrations themselves, **external audit** is concerned with administrative performance assessed against externally defined criteria, such as the list of intermediate outcomes considered in the first section of this chapter.

Suffice to say that external audit is in its infancy. Social security administrations are audited in most countries by ostensibly autonomous bodies, often reporting to the legislature rather than the executive. Examples include the Australian National Audit Office, the National Audit Office in Britain and the US General Accounting Office. However, while institutionally independent, such bodies necessarily reflect the social norms that characterize the particular jurisdiction. As explained in Chapter 13, international agencies are also gradually engaging in a process of audit and producing comparative tables and occasional analyses that raise questions as to the span and construction of intermediate objectives, the range and nature of intermediate outcomes, the levels of administrative performance and efficiency attained and the most appropriate means of enhancing these.

Such questions are certainly ones that deserve to be addressed and could form part of an agenda for the systematic analysis of social security.

Closing summary

This chapter has been about delivering benefits and services efficiently and effectively. It has therefore focused on intermediate objectives and outcomes: volumes of transactions, accuracy, speed of service, access, user efficiency, quality of treatment and security etc. Attaining administrative efficiency requires attention to the efficient use of resources, notably staff, their recruitment, training and deployment; information technology; and, mentioned only in passing, buildings and property. This, in turn, entails a creative and active management that is clear about the intermediate objectives of the administration and the strategy for attaining them, and has the wherewithal appropriately to mobilize the resources at its disposal and to know, through a process of audit, how well systems are performing.

The growing recognition that policy is shaped by implementation as well as design has, together with the development of managerialism and consumerism, recently led to a greater focus on delivery, with the increasing use

Comparison 11.1 Administration costs as a percentage of total expenditure

%	Korea (1996)	Sweden (1993)	Australia (1991/2)	USA (1995)	Germany (1996)	UK (1993/4)
Old age	0.88		0.82	0.95	2.08	3.69
Survivors	9.09				2.15	3.69
Invalidity	10.0		1.42	3.28	1.9	3.69
Employment injury		3.25	3.44	3.23	13.04	3.69
Sickness			9.83	1.01	4.15	3.69
Family	N/A		2.68	N/A	2.33	3.69
Unemployment	0.67		4.54	16.13	8.24	3.69
Housing					5.88	
Social assistance				6.52	5.8	7.66
Total	2.13	2.33	2.73	2.89	3.01	4.35

Source: ILO (2003)

The table expresses the costs of administering benefits as a proportion of total expenditure on benefits and administration. Health provision in kind is omitted from the table even when funded through the social security system. The information, as can be seen, is neither comprehensive nor recent and that for British insurance benefits does not differentiate between programmes.

The major observation is that total expenditure on administration is very small in percentage terms, ranging from 2.13 per cent in Korea to 4.35 per cent in Britain, although, in absolute terms, the sums are very large. In Britain, means-tested benefits are more expensive to deliver than social insurance benefits and this, given heavy reliance on means testing, helps to explain why administration costs overall are higher in Britain than elsewhere. In the other two countries where a similar comparison is possible, Germany and the USA, the cost of administering social assistance is also high but is exceeded by certain social security schemes.

Unemployment benefit is expensive to administer relative to other benefits in Germany, Australia and especially in the USA. The cost of activation measures is not included and the expense may reflect the comparatively short time for which claimants receive benefit. Except in exceptional circumstances, eligibility for unemployment benefit is exhausted in the USA after a maximum of six months. In contrast, the cost of delivering old-age benefits is small relative to total expenditure because benefits are high, periods on benefit are long, and claimants' circumstances are stable so that review costs are low.

of targets, contracting out of services and more sophisticated methods of monitoring and evaluation. The result is more and better data for analysts to use that, alongside evidence of economic and targeting efficiency, can be exploited to establish and better understand the contribution made by social security to individual and social welfare.

Further reading

There are comparatively few systematic studies of administrative effectiveness. Most are internal audits or evaluations of particular schemes undertaken to address short-term problems (e.g. Costello *et al.* 2002; Osgood and Thomas 2002). Bolderson and Mabbett (1997) is an important, if increasingly dated, exception. Lipsky (1980), Wright (2003) and Howard (2003) take the reader into the social security office.

PART 5

Contemporary Influences

Individualization and Social Change

This is the first of two chapters concerned with context and contemporary processes.

As was emphasized in Chapter 1, context – social, economic and political – is important when seeking to understand and evaluate social security systems. Distinguishing jurisdictions according to regime type is one, albeit crude, way of taking account of context. For this reason, most of the examples used in this volume are drawn from six countries with contrasting regimes, allowing readers to acquire familiarity with each country and hence be better placed to understand the two-way interaction between social security provisions and social and political context.

The aim in this and the final chapter is to foreground context, to consider it as an active element in shaping social security policy and provision rather than as the backcloth to the policy process. Both chapters focus on change, but whereas Chapter 13 considers factors exerting influence from outside particular jurisdictions, this chapter concerns internal pressures for change. These pressures are many and likely variously to affect the demand for social security, the resources available and the mode of implementation. Those discussed are chosen for their theoretical and practical significance and readers should be aware that many others could have been selected.

Individualization

Social change is best viewed from a distance. Perusing the period from around 1870 to about 1970, it is possible to identify the antecedents of the modern welfare state, to plot the dominant trends and to isolate the developments that have most salience. It is more difficult to be sure of the essential characteristics of late modernity and their effects on social security or, indeed, if post-modernity is not a more appropriate description of today's world. This is, in fact, another variant of the counterfactual problem although one that is without an obvious solution.

This important reservation aside, many commentators point to a growth in **individualization**, prioritizing the person, their attributes and aspirations, over the social group and the statuses it confers on individuals as an essential feature of late modernity (Giddens 1991; Beck 1992; O'Brien and Penna 1998). Whereas, in traditional societies, a person's first allegiance was to the clan, caste or class that was the root of their social status, more commonly the modern individual would think of themselves as 'I am I' rather than 'I am a tailor', 'a Brahmin' or 'a woman' (Beck 1992). It is important to stress that the term individualization is here used in a sociological sense. That is, it is a description of the way that individuals behave and societies function, not a philosophical doctrine, **individualism**, which either advocates that the interests of the individual should take priority over those of the state or that individuals should be freed from government interference to pursue their economic activities (AH 2000).

To simplify greatly, the processes of **modernization** – including the structural changes associated with scientific and industrial development that entailed division of labour, differentiation of markets, social and geographic mobility and mass consumption – resulted in a lessening of structurally imposed constraints on individual action. This, according to Beck (1992), had three important consequences. First, it offered liberation by removing historically prescribed obligations and constraints and thus enabled individuals to devise and pursue their individual life plans. But, secondly, it resulted in a loss of intellectual, moral and practical security as the rules of faith, tradition and obligation were dismantled and individuals were forced to make their own way in the world, unable to rely on emotional and financial support from family or clan. Thirdly, it led, ironically, to the emergence of new forms of control. Individuals, free in the market-place, came to confront similar opportunities, constraints and risks that produced a new standardization. For example, new modes of employment required higher levels of education, training and physical and mental fitness and caused the life-course to be structured into a sequence of three stages, childhood (education), employment and retirement, with the timing of transitions being heavily influenced by government regulation.

Freed of former obligations, therefore, the modern individual is not only able to decide and act on their own initiative, they are obliged to do so. It is now a cultural requirement, Giddens (1991) argues, that people engage in a process of reflexivity and constantly monitor, assess and modify their actions in the light of their likely consequences and with respect to personal goals. Secondary institutions, such as the market-place, the media and

Case Study 12.1 Female employment and family in South Korea

Economic activity rates among Korean women have risen rapidly in the last decade and are projected to continue by 2010 and will be comparable with those in Germany. Ostensibly this change has been supported by policy changes that have promoted the development of childcare, expanded maternity and childcare leave and regulated working time. Bringing women into the labour market will also have enhanced women's access to social security provision.

Equally, Korea may be seen as a case study of the barriers that women everywhere confront in balancing paid work and childcare and securing recognition in social security systems. The diagram reveals the M-shaped curve that describes female participation rates, reflecting low rates of labour market engagement during the childrearing years. Conventional gender ideology is embedded in legislation that assumes childcare is a primary duty of women. Obligations on employers to provide workplace nurseries apply only to those employing over 300 female workers, while 60 per cent of women work in firms with less than 100 women employees. Moreover, 36 per cent of firms fail to meet their statutory obligations with respect to legislation on maternity leave entitlement and benefits, and many women are casual workers with limited access to social security.

Policy arguably draws on Confucian assumptions 'of families as patrilineal and patrilocal, family responsibility before state responsibility, a hierarchy of responsibility drawing on generation and gender, and care responsibility resting unambiguously on women' (Won and Pascall 2004: 13.) However, qualitative research suggests that the family fails adequately to support the working mother. Instead, she is frequently engaged in 'a constant battle to manage the gaps between expectations of employers and family members, to manage the gaps between working hours and childcare hours, a war – though often simmering and suppressed – between husbands and wives, and between mothers-in-law and daughters-in-law' (Won and Pascall 2004: 9).

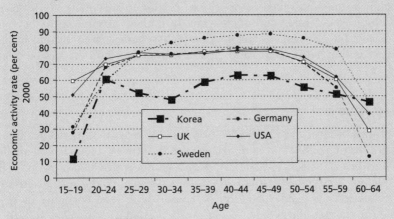

Source Won and Pascall (2004)

welfare systems (including social security), have come to replace the older institutions that once prescribed and circumscribed individual action. Individuals are required by the new institutions to choose from sets of variously constrained options those that best match their life aspirations.

With this new responsibility, individuals confront different and arguably greater risks. These include those that Giddens (1990) calls 'manufactured risks', which result from the effects of human action on the world and contribute, reinforced by extensive media coverage, to a growth of 'risk consciousness' and to unparalleled levels of social anxiety (Fulcher and Scott 2003). In addition, individuals have to confront the consequences of taking wrong decisions. Whereas, in the past, a pauper could 'justifiably' call on fate, misfortune or inheritance in their defence, a poor person today has to explain why they did not make adequate provision for themselves. Moreover, individuals are dependent, in the event of personal catastrophe, on state or commercial institutions that are not bound by altruism, reciprocity or mutual self-interest, but rather by public interest and accountability, or by the interests of shareholders and the requirement to maximize profits.

To the extent that this analysis is valid and that the process of individualization is ongoing, there are profound implications for existing social security systems that are founded on inherited institutions and concepts such as 'the family', 'the main breadwinner', and 'intergenerational solidarity'. Some of these implications are elucidated below.

Diversity

Social security systems founded in the late nineteenth century and substantially developed in the decades following World War II are underpinned by increasingly anachronistic assumptions. They typically assume homogeneity in family forms and racial composition, predominantly male workforces, high employment rates and comparatively limited survival to or beyond retirement age. In reality, late modernity is characterized by increasing diversity within nation states and, possibly, by reduced differences between them.

Gender relations

An important facet of individualization was the release of people from the 'constraints of gender' and of marriage with the latter's 'quasi-feudal attributes and givens' (Beck 1992: 105). Marriage once provided a mechanism of exchange between dynasties, circumscribed sexuality and sexual activity, and regulated the gender division of labour, with men engaging in economic production and women being primarily tied to biological and, to a lesser extent, social reproduction. With late modernity, marriage became a joint project of two people in search of mutual happiness. This, perhaps inevitably, added to the fragility of the institution that is now almost as likely to end in formal or informal dissolution as in death. Moreover, sexual activity has increasingly been separated from the institution of marriage, while the sexual and economic dependency of women on men has been challenged both in principle and practice. More recently, there has been growing social and legal acceptance of the viability of same-sex partnerships and a recognition that some same-sex couples will want to rear children.

These developments fit uneasily with social security systems that foreground marriage, pay benefits to wives and children as dependents of husbands and fathers, and make eligibility to widows' pensions conditional on the lifetime contributions of husbands when deceased. Moreover, some argue, usually from a perspective of disapproval, that the demise of the institution of marriage has been due to, or at least facilitated by, social security provisions (Horn *et al.* 1998). These, it is argued, have made divorce and lone parenthood economically viable and, on occasion, caused lone parenthood to be financially more attractive than marriage.

To date, the net result of these developments has been to increase demands on social security systems that have exceeded any consequent growth in resources. The precise sequence and scale of effects has varied between countries. In Britain, sexual behaviour changed markedly in the 1950s and 1960s but had little direct impact on social security provision. Pre- and extramarital sexual activity increased, as did pre- and extramarital births. However, most premarital conceptions were legalized through subsequent marriage, lone parenthood was rare and heavily stigmatized and since divorce was still difficult to obtain, the institution of marriage appeared to remain intact. Three decades later almost everything had changed. Legislation, in 1969, made divorce easier and the divorce rate subsequently rose by 42 per cent between 1973 and 1997 (Walker with Howard 2000). Coincident with divorce reform, the marriage rate fell, cohabitation rose and separation also increased, partly because it provided grounds for divorce. Cohabitation was, at first, the choice of people who had previously been married but, during the 1970s, cohabitation increasingly became a prelude, or an alternative, to marriage that no longer debarred participants from parenthood. During the last third of the twentieth century, the result of increased divorce, more cohabitation (which proves to be less durable than marriage) and, later, increased premarital births to unpartnered women was to triple the number of lone parents in Britain to 1.8 million. Moreover, because the proportion of lone parents who were employed fell over this period, the number dependent on social assistance benefits quadrupled and helped to increase the proportion of children in poverty to a post-War War II high.

The USA witnessed an increase in lone parenthood earlier than in Britain but the defence of the traditional two-parent family has proved more durable at a political level. The growth in lone parenthood and the associated rise in child poverty were most marked among African-Americans, which probably fed political support for policies of containment. Similar socio-demographic developments occurred slightly later in Australia than in Britain (divorce law reform occurred in 1975) but with an equivalent tripling in the number of lone-parent households (Whiteford 2001), and also in Germany, although there the rate of change was somewhat quicker. The level of lone parenthood in Sweden is slightly less than in Britain, but the proportion of lone parents who are male is double (partly due to both parents being registered as lone parents on divorce) (Bradshaw *et al.* 2000). Lone parents are disportionately likely to claim benefits, especially social assistance, and poverty rates are much higher than for other families (except in Sweden where the difference is marginal) (Bradshaw *et al.* 2000).

Policy responses to these ostensibly similar trends have been very diverse, reflecting different sociopolitical analyses of the problem and varying structural opportunities and constraints. However, there has been some recent convergence with a shared emphasis given to paid work as a defence against the financial consequences of relationship breakdown. Over the last 20 years, benefit levels for lone-parent families have both been increased as a defence against poverty (in Britain and Australia) and reduced either to lessen work disincentives (in Britain in 1997) or as an economy measure (in Sweden in 1996). Eligibility conditions have been relaxed (in Australia) and tightened (in Britain and the USA). In-work benefits and tax credits have been implemented to increase work incentives (USA) and to cut child poverty (Britain post-1998). Mandatory child support payments from parents without care have been introduced to increase lone-parent incomes (in Australia), to reduce benefit expenditures (in some US states and initially in Britain) and/or to signal public disapproval (later in Britain). Childcare has been provided and lone parents prioritized (Sweden, Germany) and/or subsidized (USA, Britain and Australia). Finally, compulsion has been introduced to change behaviour by trying, in Britain, to keep lone mothers in touch with the labour market and, in the USA, to prevent pregnancies.

The contrasting responses of Britain and the USA are especially interesting given that the pattern of provision initially looks similar: social assistance, activation policies and child support enforcement (Walker and Wiseman 2003a). The 1996 US social assistance reforms with the introduction of TANF enforced work obligations on virtually all lone-mother recipients and imposed a time limit on the state's duty to provide financial support. Neither condition applies in Britain. At present, public support in Britain would not condone policy that enforced lone parents with young children to take paid work: priority is attached to the immediate care needs of children rather than to any desire to use benefit conditionality to enforce the role model of an employed parent. The British public seems sensitive to the high levels of poverty suffered by lone parents and views lone parenthood less as a threat to the traditional family than as an outcome of its demise (Millar 2003). This may be because it is generally recognized that lone parenthood mostly arises from the breakdown of marriage or previously stable cohabiting relationships. Births to unmarried teenagers, though high in Britain by international standards and rising, are still less than in the early 1970s before contraception was widely practised (Walker with Howard 2000).

However, debate about social assistance provision contributing to the growth in lone parenthood has also been more muted in Britain than in the USA. This may be because social assistance benefits are generic rather than categorical and not just available to lone parents as was primarily the case with AFDC (that preceded TANF). Moreover, although lone parenthood is more common among certain ethnic minorities in Britain, notably those of West Indian descent, the link between race, illegitimacy and welfare receipt that features in the US debate is almost entirely absent. These considerations may also help explain why Britain has not followed the USA in introducing **family cap policies** that penalize mothers financially if they conceive while in receipt of benefit.

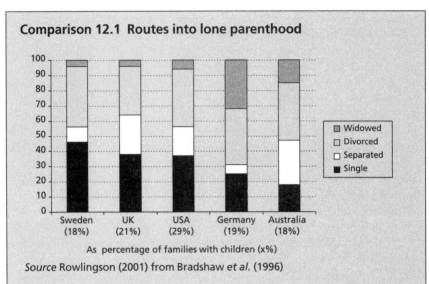

Comparison 12.1 Routes into lone parenthood

As percentage of families with children (x%)

Source Rowlingson (2001) from Bradshaw *et al.* (1996)

The graph shows the number of lone parents as a percentage of all families with children and their marital status. Marital status provides a clue to the route by which a lone parent family came into being, although care needs to be taken in interpreting the statistics. For example, a lone parent living with their child(ren) at home with their own parents in a three-generation family may not always be counted as a separate assessment unit. Another problem is that mothers who separate from cohabiting partnerships are normally treated as being 'single' although, in some cases, they may have more in common with lone mothers who are divorced or separated.

Lone mothers who have never married are most prevalent in Sweden and least so in Germany (where widowhood still seems to be a significant cause of lone parenthood) and in Australia, which has the largest proportion of lone mothers who are separated but not formally divorced.

Racial and ethnic diversity

Racial and ethnic diversity, often linked to migration, is another feature of late modernity that affects social security policy. The coincidence of the contours of disadvantage with the boundaries of ethnicity in so many societies means that ethnic minorities are frequently disproportionately represented in social assistance caseloads. As already mooted, the fact that almost three fifths of TANF recipients are either African-American or Hispanic may, given the history of racial politics in the USA, help to explain why benefit levels are so low and eligibility rules so stringent compared to European standards. However, recent migration into European countries and Australia is also beginning to influence policy and implementation.

Whereas, in the early 1980s, the proportion of social assistance recipients in Germany who were native Germans was around 80 per cent, within less than a decade this had fallen in certain *Länder*, such as Bremen, to 46 per cent. Over the same period the proportion of refugees quadrupled to 18 per cent and the number of German immigrants from Eastern Europe and the former Soviet Union increased six-fold to 28 per cent (Buhr and Weber 1998). Similarly, in Sweden, it is now common for social assistance case-loads in certain parts of larger cities to be comprised primarily of refugees and other non-natives (Gustafsson and Voges 1998). These developments fuelled debates about the generosity of benefits in both countries and, in the USA, concern about the rapid rise in the number of immigrants claiming benefit led the Clinton administration to remove from new immigrants the right to claim most social assistance benefits including TANF, food stamps and Supplemental Security Income (SSI) (Borjas 2001).

There are several reasons why foreigners and ethnic minority groups are over-represented in social assistance caseloads. These include bureaucratic rules that restrict access to social insurance benefits, higher rates of unemployment and larger family size (and, hence, greater needs). In Britain, for example, refugees are prohibited from working until accorded right of residence, a process taking many months and sometimes years. Different factors serve disproportionately to exclude minorities from eligibility for social insurance benefits. First, there may be a mismatch between eligibility requirements and the characteristics of minority communities. For example, recent migrants will have had limited opportunity to contribute sufficiently to qualify for benefit or, in the case of retirement pensions, to have accumulated enough contributions to generate an adequate pension. Others who have retained families in their countries of origin may have interrupted contribution records due to significant absences visiting relatives abroad.

Members of ethnic minorities may also be inhibited from claiming benefits due to lack of familiarity with the bureaucracy, poor language skills, and religious and cultural traditions that sometimes prioritize support provided through informal family- and community-based networks. In addition, systems may be deliberately or inadvertently discriminatory either in their design or implementation. Foreign workers in Germany under the '*Gastarbeiter*' (guest worker) scheme had restricted access to benefit provision on the assumption that they would return home during periods of economic recession; a register of foreigners still exists and full citizenship is difficult to secure. The US OASDI scheme is available only to US citizens and legal aliens (thereby excluding many millions of illegal workers that comprise substantial portions of the workforce in certain south-western states), while the British state retirement pension is generally not up-rated with inflation when paid to beneficiaries living overseas.

One consequence of this pattern of eligibility is that ethnic minority groups may experience a different kind of relationship with social security

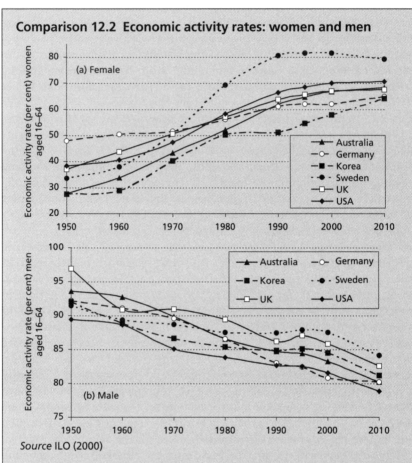

Comparison 12.2 Economic activity rates: women and men

Source ILO (2000)

The proportion of women (aged 16 to 64) who are economically active, that is who are either in paid work or looking for it, has increased markedly in all case-study countries over the last half century, but the degree and timing of change has varied markedly. In the aftermath of World War II, the number of German women who were economically active was exceptionally high, but it is expected that activity rates in other countries will equal or exceed those in Germany by 2010. Female employment in Sweden rose rapidly, especially in the 1970s, almost to attain parity with men in the 1990s. The economic activity rate of Korean women has also risen but from markedly low levels and with a pause in the growth rate in the decade before democratisation in 1987.

The secular decline in male activity rates, most marked in Britain, steadied in the 1990s (except in Germany and, to a lesser extent, in Australia and the US) but is predicted to resume a marked downward trend in the first decade of the twenty-first century.

than other people, one based on the demonstration of need rather than on the acquisition of status (Platt 2003). This may serve socially to exclude minority ethnic groups, symbolically linking them with stigmatizing benefits, exposing them to discrimination when eligibility or entitlement is dependent on staff discretion, and further marginalizing them because of low take-up and low incomes. Few countries have satisfactorily addressed these structural issues although a number have sought better to tailor delivery to the requirements of ethnic minorities. This has involved the introduction of multilingual publicity and application forms, staff drawn from minority groups and extensive cultural awareness training.

Diversity of lifestyles

Oral contraception freed women from the tyranny of childrearing, allowing them to choose motherhood as an expression of their individuality. To have or not to have children became a public statement of the depth of love between adults, a lifestyle choice and, sometimes, even a concerted attempt to salvage a relationship. The result has been that birth rates have fallen to unprecedentedly low levels that mean that some countries are now unable to sustain current population levels without substantial immigration. The age of mothers at childbirth has generally risen and average family size has fallen to the point where families with only one child have become commonplace rather than the exception.

However, counteracting the trend to smaller families has been a growth in serial relationships. Falls in the numbers of first marriages have been complemented by increases in second marriages and informal unions involving formerly married partners, often with children. This has led to an increase in the number of step-families, step-parents, step-grandparents and half siblings, falls in the number of children brought up entirely by their biological parents, and increased numbers of parents living apart from their biological children. Add to this the growth in gay partnerships, some caring for children, and it is apparent that the freedom that late modernity offers individuals to forge unique identities is also remoulding the pattern of familial responsibilities and obligations in ways that have yet to be fully realized or tested.

The assumption underlying much social security provision is that parents finance their dependent children and that adult children support their ageing and infirm parents. (Under German social assistance law, the obligation of support extends to independent children also.) These assumptions no longer universally match with social realities and yet societies generally appear loath to assume economic responsibility for care that was once securely vested in families. The resultant tensions are illustrated by recent decisions, in many countries, to introduce legislation to ensure that parents without care of their biological children nevertheless contribute financially to their upbringing. Moreover, as this example illustrates, practicalities may be as important as amorality in the decisions that parents make. A father who re-partners and fathers again acquires (or, perhaps, consciously chooses) responsibilities that have to be matched against what may be scarce resources. The decision as to whether he should adequately finance one child (and the other not at all) or provide both with inadequate sustenance is not a straightforward one and is likely to be shaped by context.

Similarly, it is not self-evident on whom the ageing generation is to depend. Increasing numbers will have few if any children to support them. Others will have both biological and step-children but some of these are likely to have step-parents with whom they may have had more recent and closer relationships. Moreover, it is not certain that, given this new web of negotiated dependencies, the incentive to save in order to pass on inheritance will be as strong as in the past. If not, this may mean that people will voluntarily save less for old age than they currently do or consume more selfishly in retirement. At this point, individualization comes perilously close to the ideology of individualism, with the interests of the self taking priority over the collective other. Either way, the implications for social security and the economy, while unclear, could nevertheless be profound.

Employment and family

Perhaps the effects of individualization on social security will turn out to be most long-lasting with respect to decisions about employment. Most change to date has resulted from the economic liberation of women: whereas once, the majority of women tended children, an increasing number now aspire to tend a career. While the degree of change that has occurred is often overstated, it has nevertheless been substantial (Walker *et al.* 2000).

What is often missing from the policy debate is recognition that poorer women were historically often forced to take paid employment to supplement family incomes even when their children were very young. Even today it is not clear what proportion of women work for reasons of intrinsic satisfaction and what proportion feel compelled to work for reasons of economic necessity or to fund a chosen lifestyle. Nevertheless, the **economic participation rate** for women, that is the proportion of all women of working age who are either employed or looking for work, has increased in every European country over the last 25 years and also in Australia, the USA and Korea.

Much of this increase in female economic participation is attributable to substantial rises in the number of women who continue in employment after they have children, juggling the roles of mother and paid worker. For this reason, large numbers work part-time but many are still reliant on increased provision of formal and informal childcare (Walker *et al.* 2000). Wages are generally substantially lower than for men. This is primarily because in most countries women tend to work in the service sector and to occupy low-skilled positions. However, gender discrimination is still rife despite the equal opportunities legislation in force in many countries. In addition, the compromises that women make in balancing employment and caring responsibilities mean that they have less opportunity fully to exploit their skill levels. They often choose to forgo promotion opportunities and lose out in competitive career situations because of taking maternity leave and career breaks to care for children. Furthermore, female employment is also characterized by insecurity, instability and (Britain excluded) a higher than average risk of unemployment.

From the perspective of social security, increased female economic participation has increased the pool of workers, thereby increasing social security contributions and the numbers entitled to receive contributory benefits. However, it has also served to lower the wage of the median contributor, and cut the average period of contributions, thereby reducing the average entitlement payable under social insurance schemes.

At the same time that more women have been working, economic participation rates among men have fallen back from very high levels, especially among those in the decade before retirement. This has occurred less as a result of direct competition from women (the labour market is often segmented into sectors that differentially recruit men or women) and more from processes of deindustrialization that have reduced employment in manufacturing industries that employ mostly men to be replaced by new service sector jobs that have disproportionately been filled by women. Male unemployment and economic inactivity rates have fluctuated, reflecting global and local reversals such as the trade recession of the early 1990s, the economic crash in Asian 'tiger economies' in 1997 and the long-term consequences of German reunification. Nevertheless, a secular upward trend is evident in male unemployment and inactivity that has yet to be reversed in Australia, Germany or the USA. This, together with increased female employment, has produced a new economic polarization between households with two or more workers, which set the aspirational norms for living standards, consumption and lifestyles, and those with none, that risk economic and social exclusion (Chapter 11).

Taken overall, these developments could shift the balance of advantage from social security systems based on the notion of a family with a single breadwinner and dependents, as characterized by conservative and liberal regimes, to a social democratic or Scandinavian model designed to support full adult employment. They also strengthen arguments for the **individualization of social security benefits,** that is for linking eligibility and entitlement to the circumstances of individuals, rather than to familial benefit units comprised of individuals deemed to be financially responsible for, and/or dependent upon, each other.

The historical rationale for assessment of families rather than individuals dates to a (possibly mythical) time when marriage was universal and wives were not employed. It allowed wives to gain from social insurance schemes by receiving benefits on the basis of their husband's contributions and reduced costs by paying lower per capita benefits to couples than to single people on account of the economies of scale gained from living together. The increased cost of rewarding adults the same benefit irrespective of family circumstances still acts as an impediment to moves towards the full individualization of assessment.

However, the sociodemographic trends described above make the concept of a family with one breadwinner increasingly anachronistic. They also mean that it can no longer be assumed that sexual intimacy occurs only within marriage or that matrimony is the appropriate basis on which to assess benefit entitlement. Furthermore, in a society where most adults both expect, and are expected, to engage in employment through to retirement age, familial assessment of benefits often creates the kinds of employment disincentives for second workers described in Chapter 10 (Figure 10.5).

There are also arguments in favour of individual assessment that have to do with strengthening or equalizing the position of women (McLaughlin *et al.* 2002). For example, individualization of benefit assessment promotes individual financial control and autonomy within families. It also helps to ensure that resources are directed more equitably within households and fosters social inclusion by extending individual financial rights.

All these reasons have proved influential in the tentative moves towards individualization recently introduced in Australia's largely means-tested social security system (Millar 1998). These have included the introduction of a partial disregard of a partner's earnings for Jobseekers' Benefit and two benefits, Parenting Allowance for those caring for children and Partner's Allowance for older wives without recent employment experience, which are both individually assessed but which partially reflect the working partner's income.

Comparison 12.3 Old-age dependency ratio, 1980–2050

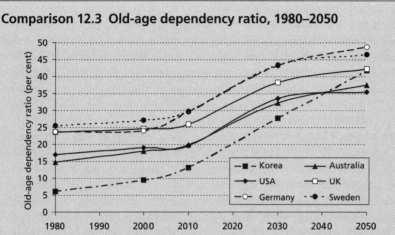

The graph plots the old-age dependency ratio (that is, the ratio of the population aged older than 64 to that aged 15–24 expressed as a percentage) for the six case study countries. The values from 2000 through to 2050 are projections and become less reliable at later dates. The ratio provides an indication of the size of the intergenerational transfers required for the working population to support those who are retired.

The old-age dependency ratios varied markedly between the six countries in 2000. They indicate, for example, that there were 18 Koreans of working age for each person of retirement age whereas the corresponding figure for the USA was 5.9 and, for Sweden, just 3.9.

The projections suggest a marked deterioration in the age dependency ratio in all countries over the period between 2010 and 2030. However, this is most marked (indicated by the slope of the curves) in Korea, Germany and the USA. By 2030, the old-age dependency ratio for Korea will be 27.7, a 294 per cent increase compared with 2000. The corresponding increase for Germany is 180 per cent, 177 per cent for the USA and 156 per cent for Britain.

Solidarity

If individualization emphasizes the 'I' and the personal project of self, it is essential to ask, in the context of social security, 'what of the "us" and the "them"?'.

It is evident from the above discussion that individualization increases the risks faced by individuals that, perhaps ironically, require collective solutions. Individuals build their own histories from sequences of decisions – economic, moral and social. Because these decisions are, by definition, based on partial information about unknowable futures, errors are inevitable. Moreover, the consequences are potentially severe, especially given the insecure nature of reciprocity created by the new kinds of extended families. Add to this greater geographic mobility and a flexible labour market, which now arguably offers less security for greater numbers of people than in the past, and the case for the continuation of social security seems assured. The 'I' and the 'us' and the 'we' all confront similar risks and the logic of insurance still applies.

However, this positive response is an oversimplification. People have to reflect on the individual projects that are their lives, to recognize that they share risks with other persons, and to make a reality of this by voting for a collective response. Moreover, while the risks that people face are ontologically similar, the degree of risk faced by individuals varies markedly. As explained in Chapter 4, insurance against differential risk is only possible if those who are least at risk are compelled to participate. Furthermore, the processes of modernity themselves conspire to make both the arithmetic of risk and the funding equations more difficult to solve.

Take, for example, the fall in the birth rate. This frees women to pursue paid work, increases the number of workers, boosts living standards and increases national wealth that, in turn, allows public spending to rise or taxation to fall. However, this good news story is offset, in the longer term, by the consequent ageing of the population and the replacement of large cohorts who move into retirement by smaller ones entering the labour market. Population ageing increases the **old-age dependency ratio** (the number of pensioners divided by the number of workers) and causes the **old-age support ratio**, the number of workers divided by the number of pensioners, to fall (Chapter 3). This, in turn, forces hard political choices.

These choices are best illustrated with reference to PAYG (pay-as-you-go pension) schemes (Chapter 4) and a simple financial model (Hancock 2003). The model comprises five elements:

$p =$ the amount of state pension paid to each pensioner
$T =$ a proportional tax levied on the earnings of workers solely to finance pensions
$D =$ the number of pensioners (D standing for Dependants)
$L =$ the number of workers (L standing for Labour force)
$W =$ the average gross wage of workers

For the pension budget to balance, the total cost (p times D) has to equal the total income raised (t times w times L). At any one time the number of pensioners, the size of the labour force and the average wage are all fixed so that the budget can only be balanced by raising or lowering the size of pension or by adjusting the tax rate. Given a fixed pension, the tax rate necessary to achieve a balanced budget is defined as:

$$t = \frac{p/w}{L/D} \qquad (1)$$

L/D in Equation 1 is, of course, the old-age support ratio while p/w is the ratio of the pension to the gross wage and, hence, a measure of the generosity or adequacy of the pension relative to wages. With an ageing population, the support ratio would fall which means one of two things: either the relative generosity of the pension would have to go down or the tax rate would need to rise. This is illustrated schematically in Table 12.1. In the top half, the relative value of the pension is maintained at 30 per cent of average wages which means that, if the support rate were halved, the tax rate would have to double from 7.5 per cent to 15 per cent. Keeping the tax rate constant (lower half) would, given the same ageing of the population, require the pension to be halved as a proportion of wages.

The model demonstrates both the solidarity required between generations for PAYG pensions schemes to work and the extra pressures created by falling birth rates. The so-called pensions crisis that affects many countries, notably Germany, is really a crisis in confidence that future generations will be prepared to pay proportionally more than earlier ones to provide equivalent relative living standards for retirement pensioners. Moreover, a funded rather than a PAYG regime, with workers asked to forgo current consumption to save for their own retirement, would not remove the requirement for intergeneration solidarity: all pensions represent a charge on the economy at the point when they are paid. Furthermore, funded schemes, based as they are on the insurance principles, can neither achieve the substantial redistribution necessary to protect the low paid against

Table 12.1 Demography and pension provision

Support ratio L/D	Ratio of pension size to gross wage p/w	Tax rate t
Constant ratio of pension size to gross wage		
4	0.3	0.075
3	0.3	0.10
2	0.3	0.15
Constant tax rate		
4	0.3	0.075
3	0.225	0.075
2	0.15	0.075

Source: Hancock (2003)

Case Study 12.2 Employment subsidies for older workers

Falling economic activity rates among older workers is a cause of concern in many countries and has stimulated policy innovation (OECD 2003d). Korea and Sweden provide targeted subsidies to employers recruiting older workers (age 55 and older, and 57 and older in each country respectively). However, Germany and Britain have, *in addition to* employer subsidies, introduced new social security benefits for certain older workers to supplement in-work incomes.

Provision in Germany is made under a labour law enacted in 2003 and is targeted on insured persons who are either unemployed or at risk of becoming unemployed, aged 50 or older, and have a residual entitlement to at least 180 days of unemployment benefit. The wage safeguard has two components. The first is a tax free grant that covers 50 per cent of the difference in the net wage received before and after a spell of unemployment and is tax free and not subject to social insurance contributions. The second component serves to reduce the consequence of lowered wages on subsequent entitlement to old-age pension. This is achieved by boosting nominal social insurance contributions to 90 per cent of those paid in the previous job. The wage safeguard is restricted in duration to the maximum period for which there is an entirlement to unemployment benefit. The provision is due to expire on 31 December 2005 (although benefits may be paid until 31 August 2008).

In Britain, a tax free employment credit is available for persons aged over 50 and who have been unemployed for at least six months. Since 2003, this has been incorporated into Working Tax Credit (a tax credit for low-waged workers employed for 16 or more hours weekly) as a special element that increases the value of the tax credit payment. It is payable for a maximum of 12 months but can be taken for a series of shorter periods separated by spells of 26 weeks or less to support people who take up casual work or who, for other reasons, experience a broken re-entry into employment.

Schemes in both countries reward a spell of unemployment when making a transition to lower-paid work in later working life although, as explained, the German scheme is also open to people threatened by unemployment. Persons moving directly to a lower-paying job, perhaps from choice or possibly reflecting lower productivity, are not eligible for the wage subsidy. As well as raising issues of equity, this differential risks creating perverse incentives and measures are in place to deny the subsidy to people considered voluntarily unemployed.

poverty in old age nor shield people against inflation (an uninsurable risk since it affects everyone). Germany is currently seeking to liberalize its immigration policy to cope with a declining labour force and skills shortage although, like the earlier *Gastarbeiter* (guest worker) programme, this is seen as a short-term imperative (Dekkte 2001; Roth 2002). Were the immigration to become permanent, it might help ease the pension crisis.

In sum, the individualistic decisions made as part of individuals' life projects have collective consequences that call for collective solutions that can only be secured through individuals' consent. The presence or absence of collective solutions, realized in the structure of social security systems, in turn help to define the set of choices that frame the individual decisions that shape people's lives. Thus, the future of social security depends on the nature of the social and political reflexivity that accompanies the individual reflexivity that, in turn, characterizes late modernity and drives the iterative process of engagement between individual agency and social structure.

Closing summary

This chapter has focused on some of the social and demographic developments that are characteristic of late modernity and which are reshaping social security: individualization, diversity and the individualistic challenge to social solidarity.

Freed from the social norms and structures that once fixed a person's place in society, individuals are now obliged themselves to plan their lives and to assume the attendant risks. This leads to increased social diversity, with multiethnic communities, varying family forms, diverse patterns of employment and a plethora of different lifestyles coexisting within a single jurisdiction. It also generates new challenges for social security and different constraints on the structure of provision.

It may no longer be appropriate, for example, to prioritize marriage as a bureaucratic device, to assume families have a single worker, to expect that people will remain employed for life, or to ignore cultural diversity in the delivery of benefits. Equally, it cannot necessarily be assumed that familial and social solidarity will be adequate to protect people against the new risks associated with the new freedoms.

Further reading

Giddens (1991) remains the classic sociological account of the impact of modernity on the individual and Beck's (1992) analysis of modern risks has been amazingly influential given that it is difficult to read. Good comparative analyses include Millar and Rowlingson (2001) on lone parents, Vleminckx and Smeeding (2001) on child welfare, and Marmor and De Jong (1998) on ageing. Walker with Howard (2000) provide an analysis of social and economic change in the British social security system.

Globalization and Internationalism

This last chapter is about external influences on the social security policies of national jurisdictions.

It is an oversimplification to suggest that the origins and development of social security systems in the nineteenth and twentieth century were exclusively a response to national problems. The fact that the foundations of social security systems were laid in so many countries in the decades adjacent to the start of the twentieth century points to external influences. So, too, does the coincidence of reforms in the 1940s and 1950s, expanding provision in the 1960s and early 1970s, and retrenchment in the 1980s and 1990s. Welfare provision both reflects and shapes national identities but is generally the product of national concerns and international influences and reference groups.

However, it is at least arguable that external influences have grown in importance with the closer integration of the global economy and the creation of trans-national policy forums such as the United Nations, the European Union, the World Bank and the OECD. It may be that national governments are increasingly likely both to confront common problems and to be less able to act unilaterally than in the past. This possibility and its potential consequences constitute the focus of this final chapter, looking first at the hypothesis of globalization.

Globalization

Globalization is an over-identified term, meaning different things to different authors (Reich 1998). For some, it suggests a historical epoch commencing either towards the beginning or the end of the 1970s. Those accepting the earlier date tend to view globalization as the response to major structural disjunction with *détente* between the USA and the former Soviet Union and the breakdown of the social contract that had underpinned the welfare state (Hirst and Thompson 1996). This contract, ostensibly now ended, had represented a historic compromise between labour and capital in the context of mass production in the Fordist mode. The state's role was as mediator committed to full employment, demand management, trade union representation, generous welfare provisions and wage moderation. Commentators placing the start of globalization a little later point not to historical inevitability, but to a series of perhaps unrelated events. Notable among these were the second oil crisis, declining global growth rates and the election of Ronald Reagan to president in the USA, Margaret Thatcher to prime minister in the UK and Helmut Kohl to chancellor in the Federal Republic of Germany (Solomon 1994).

However, most commentators agree that, as a minimum, globalization describes an increased interdependency in economic production that spans national borders. This is characterized by globally integrated production processes that entail manufacturing facilities, sales and supportive services being spread internationally across geographically and functionally segmented but interdependent labour markets. When supported by major cross-border flows of investment, these processes allow production costs to be minimized through a global division of labour. Trans-national firms seek an intra-firm division of labour, with different products and even components of a finished product being manufactured in different countries. Multinational corporations, on the other hand, are characterized by the replication of production within a number of regions to enable production to be tailored to local circumstances (although with decision-making, research and development typically remaining home-based).

The international integration of production is facilitated by technological advance and diffusion but is also dependent on political structures and social institutions. It requires the liberalization and deregulation of markets to facilitate capital flows and maximize sales, political stability to minimize economic risk, liberal democratic systems to limit political interference in commercial decisions and flexible labour markets to enable firms to respond rapidly to changing market situations. Some also argue that state expenditures should be reduced to minimize tax rates and that state assets should be privatized (Reich 1998). Certainly, the sale of state industries in the former Soviet bloc and privatization of public utilities across much of the European Union has almost certainly added momentum to the globalization of production. Indeed, some authors see globalization not so much as a technological phenomenon, but more as the hegemony of American values. The latter, in turn, is variously presented as either the fulfilment of modernization, with the benign diffusion and assimilation of capitalism and democratic institutions (Fukuyama 1992), or the product of unfettered US economic power and the existence of a trans-national class of elites who export US values (Gill 1990).

Policy competition

There is still debate about the consequences of these developments for employees in industrial countries although Standing (2002) suggests that they have added to labour market insecurity in six respects. First, the political commitment to full employment has dissipated and secondly, employment security has been eroded with moves away from traditional employment contracts. Thirdly, job insecurity has increased as the duration of jobs has fallen with a corresponding emphasis by employers and governments on the employability of the person. Fourthly, skills have become obsolescent more quickly. Fifthly, security at work has decreased while stress at work has risen in response to increased competition and falling profit margins. Finally, representational security has fallen as labour market changes have eroded the membership and influence of trade unions.

To the extent that the processes of globalization and the concomitant changes in labour market security are real – and there is debate about this, especially with respect to the scale and uniqueness of the changes entailed (Walker *et al.* 2000) – they pose significant challenges for social security. If global industry is now footloose, able to move at will to where labour costs are lowest or regulation is least intimidating, nation states are placed in competition. They need to compete to attract the largest share of commercial investment and to boost job creation or minimally, to minimize job losses. It often used to be opined that this competition would result in 'a race to the bottom' through a process termed **social dumping**, that entailed countries cutting back on welfare expenditures in an attempt to run low tax economies (Greider 1997; Gray 1998).

There is, in fact, little evidence that welfare expenditures have fallen in line with these expectations and considerable speculation about why this might be. Pierson (1996), examining expenditure trends in the USA, UK, Sweden and Germany, concluded that because significant groups of voters benefited from welfare expenditure, governments were unable to pursue across-the-board retrenchment and had only achieved piecemeal cuts in those areas where they could establish all-party consensus or otherwise divert blame so as to avoid negative electoral consequences. Clayton and Pontusson (1998) suggested that expenditures had held up because retrenchment was offset by increased entitlement spending driven by increased unemployment, disability and ageing. However, Castles' (2001) analysis of expenditures in 19 countries belonging to the OECD did not substantiate this thesis, at least for the period 1984 to 1997 (Table 13.1). Instead, he found that, if anything, expenditure on entitlement-based

Table 13.1 Public expenditure in selected countries, 1984–98

| | Percentage of GDP (1997) | | | | Change 1984–1997 (percentage points) | | | |
| | Social expenditure | | | | Social expenditure | | | |
	Entitlement	Non-entitlement	Total	Non-social expenditure	Entitlement	Non-entitlement	Total	Non-social expenditure
Australia	6.8	11.3	18.1	15.1	1.2	3.2	4.4	−7.6
UK	9.7	11.9	21.6	19.3	1.0	−0.5	0.5	−6.7
USA	6.8	9.2	16.0	15.4	−0.2	2.1	1.9	−3.6
Sweden	12.5	20.8	33.3	25.7	2.4	0.9	3.3	−3.5
Germany	13.0	13.6	26.6	21.5	0.8	2.2	3.0	−2.3
Mean for 19 OECD countries	10.6	12.7	23.3	21.9	1.1	1.5	2.6	−3.6

Adapted from Castles (2001)

social security had risen slightly less than expenditure on non-entitlement programmes as a proportion of GDP. Castles did, however, identify a marked change in the composition of public expenditure that was apparent in every country. This resulted from spending on cash benefits, active labour market programmes and health rising while other forms of public expenditure fell relative to national wealth.[1] Moreover, although growth in public expenditure was least in those countries that were most exposed to international trade (measured as the ratio of imports to GDP), this relationship disappeared when other factors were taken into account.

It would appear from Castles' analysis that OECD countries are not yet competing with each other by reducing the level of their social security expenditures relative to overall wealth. Instead, countries that substantially expanded expenditure during the 'golden age' of the welfare state did not increase spending as markedly in the 1980s and 1990s as those that had not. The result has been a convergence in levels of expenditure although, in 1998, substantial differences remained as evidence of different regimes and institutional designs. Moreover, while overall public expenditure has tended to grow relatively slowly in the countries with the highest economic growth, social spending (possibly driven by health expenditures) has tended to increase in line with growing affluence. This suggests that political support exists for the idea that better social services (and possibly more generous benefits) contribute positively to higher living standards. It should be noted, though, that social security expenditure rose most quickly in countries suffering the largest rises in unemployment, revealing that benefits continue to be important in providing protection against labour market risk.

The 'race to the bottom' thesis is based on the idea that countries compete largely through tax rates. However, there is evidence that some countries compete by means of high productivity by investing in education and the social infrastructure, a strategy that usually entails higher levels of public expenditure. This strategy has been pursued energetically in Britain since 1997, albeit starting from a comparatively low base, and has been followed over the long-term by Sweden and Germany (though, in the latter case, with less success since reunification). Some analyses have compared the low wage, low productivity approach pursued in the USA with the higher wage, high social investment model advocated in Europe and conclude that they afford similar levels of growth and employment generation (Goodin *et al.* 1999).

---

1 Social spending in Belgium and the Netherlands fell between 1984 and 1997, but other forms of spending contracted by more such that, as in other OECD countries, social spending increased as a proportion of the total (Castles 2001).

Flexible labour markets

While OECD countries do not seem to have responded to globalized production processes by reducing public expenditure, there is more evidence that they have moved towards deregulating the labour market in order to encourage flexible production (Greiner 2000). This has entailed controlling trade unions, reducing obligations on employers that might inhibit the engagement or laying off of staff, softening restrictions on fixed-term employment, agency work, telework and home working and introducing legislation and regulations to promote flexibility (Standing 1999). Activation policies have also been implemented on a large scale to assist people more rapidly to acquire employment (Lødemel and Trickey 2001).

The largest quantitative change has been brought about by changes in structural flexibility associated with **de-industrialization**, the decline of manufacturing employment relative to work in the service sector that sometimes involves the 'export' of jobs from economically advanced countries to newly-industrializing ones (Chapter 3). This, in turn, has been associated in economically developed countries with the decline in male employment and increased economic activity among women discussed in Chapter 12. Social spending on social security lessened the personal costs of de-industrialization and the provisions themselves remained largely intact with two important provisos. First, the conditionality threshold for receipt of benefit was raised in a number of countries (Chapter 10). In particular, greater emphasis was placed on ensuring that benefit recipients engaged in active job search. The intention was to curtail the growth in unemployment and to place a brake on benefit expenditure while, at the same time, seeking to improve the efficiency of the labour market by encouraging people to return to employment more quickly. The result was that the average proportion of unemployed people who received benefits in the European Union fell from 42 per cent in 1992 to 37 per cent in 1999 with especially dramatic falls in Britain (from 62 per cent to 41 per cent) and Sweden (from 71 per cent in 1995 to 55 per cent in 1999) (Standing 2002). A similar tightening of eligibility occurred in the USA and in Australia. In part, the apparent falls in the coverage of benefits were due to administrative redefinitions with, for example, participants in activation programmes no longer being counted as unemployed.

The second consequence of de-industrialization is that a greater proportion of the financial cost of economic recession and structural change is now carried by social assistance rather than social insurance (Hanesch 1998; Ditch and Oldfield 1999). This is the result of the tightened eligibility criteria for insurance benefits together with an increase in the average length of unemployment.

Moves towards greater labour market flexibility also potentially affect social security by changing the nature of employment. In fact, to date, the number of people engaged in 'flexible' or 'atypical' work that differs markedly from the traditional model of permanent, full-time and contracted employment is relatively small, although it varies by country and according to the type of employment contract. The growth in part-time work is the most notable. Over 40 per cent of women in both Britain and Sweden work less than 30 hours each week. Moreover, in Britain 58 per cent of these part-timers work less than 20 hours (the corresponding figure for Sweden is only 31 per cent). However, part-time working among men is rare: less than 4 per cent in Germany and around 8 or 9 per cent in Britain and Sweden.

Likewise, while the growth in temporary, fixed-term contract work has been strong in recent years, it still generally accounts for less than 15 per cent of employment. (Spain is exceptional among European countries with 33 per cent of men and 37 per cent of women working on temporary contracts.) Trends in self-employment are very variable. Self-employment has grown rapidly in Sweden and in the UK (where it has fallen back in recent years). It has grown, too, in Korea where self-employment is exceptionally high due to the large amount of casual employment in urban areas. On the other hand, in the USA and Australia the amount of self-employment has changed very little in recent years. The prevalence of other forms of atypical work, such as home working where individuals work from home for one or more employers, is difficult to assess, as is work in the informal economy in which workers (and their employers) seek to avoid tax and social insurance payments.

There is a possibility that the growth in atypical work has been understated. Annual statistics on temporary employment necessarily under-record the number of people on contracts of less then one year and people who move seamlessly from one short contract to another can remain invisible. Home workers may also be undercounted especially as a proportion of this work is of a somewhat clandestine nature (Pelekanos 2000). On the other hand, some people may have jobs that exhibit more than one atypical feature that would serve to overstate the total number of people affected.

The significance of flexible employment for social security is threefold. First, some forms of atypical work may be products of existing social security provision rather than the result of changes in global production or the ideal preferences of employers and employees. Part-time employment is a case in point. In both Britain and Germany, social security contributions are levied on employers and employees only once a person's earnings reach a specified threshold. The rationale is to avoid taxing the lowest paid who are the least able to pay, while also reinforcing work incentives. Clearly, however, this creates an incentive for employers to package employment in units of time that pay less than the contribution threshold. This did not matter when employment was largely the preserve of the male breadwinner who expected to be employed full-time but can leave secondary wage earners without the protection of social security. In Britain, there is a marked peak in the earnings distribution around the national insurance threshold (Smith *et al.* 2000).

Similarly, insurance contributions are generally less for self-employed people than for employees since the potential for moral hazard means that some risks encountered in self-employment are not readily insurable (unemployment and sickness being two). This creates an incentive to maximize current income and consumption by taking up self-employment at the cost of forgoing social security protection. Subcontracted and casual workers also forgo certain employment rights, including social security, which attach to the standard employment contract.

Secondly, flexible employment is almost certainly creating groups of workers with very limited access to social security. The lack of access afforded to self-employed and some part-time workers has already been noted. Likewise, people in temporary or insecure employment may find it difficult to accumulate adequate periods of contributions. Similarly, they may not enjoy career progression with associated increases in pay and thereby lose out on earnings-related benefits. Indeed, some have argued that if secure employment continues to decline, it may cease to provide an appropriate route by which to acquire rights to social security. Fitzpatrick (1999) and Standing (2002) have both proposed variations of the basic income scheme discussed in Chapter 10 since these would provide individuals with a secure, if necessarily comparatively limited, income stream within an insecure labour market. More widely advocated is the belief that social security provisions need to be changed to accommodate atypical work, extending to it the entitlements and contribution requirements of traditional employment (Pieters 2000). This would protect people who either choose or are compelled to take atypical employment and might serve to erode perverse incentives that may have contributed to its growth.

Finally, to the extent that atypical work is highly concentrated, social solidarity is likely to be eroded. This is because increased polarization between those in secure employment and those who are not serves to obscure the communality of self-interest. It is no coincidence that countries that have pursued flexible labour market policies most energetically (the USA, Britain and, to a lesser extent, Australia) have also witnessed the largest growth in wage inequality, albeit alongside higher than average growth rates (OECD 1996). Moreover, in the USA there is already little popular public support for social assistance, as opposed to social insurance, while in Britain 'scroungerphobia', the widespread denigration of benefit recipients that is often promoted by newspapers, is rarely much below the surface in popular debate. In both societies, political support for benefit expenditure is highly conditional on recipients being 'deserving'.

More generally, Standing (2002) argues that the demands of globalization for labour market flexibility serve simultaneously to increase income insecurity, erode social security and fragment the labour force. The result is a new occupational hierarchy comprising, in order of increasing insecurity:

- the *elite*, 'wealthy global citizens' with little immediate need for social security;
- the *salariat* with high personal savings;
- *proficians* able to survive in the labour market with a portfolio of skills;
- *core workers*, a dwindling group with declining industrial muscle;
- *flexiworkers* with only a fragile adherence to mainstream regulatory and social security systems;
- the *long-term unemployed* reliant on benefit and subject to activation polices;
- *the detached*, who exist outside the formal labour market and with limited legitimate access to state provision. (Standing 2002: 280–9)

To the extent that Standing is correct in his characterization of this new hierarchy, it militates against the social solidity and cohesion built on shared self-interests that have hitherto underpinned social security.

Migration

While migration in search of work and improved living standards is not new (55–60 million people are estimated to have left Europe between 1820 and 1940) (King 1990), the evidence is that international migration is increasing (OECD 2001b). This is, of course, not solely a consequence of economic globalization, which can, in fact, sometimes reduce migration flows by transferring jobs from advanced industrial countries to newly industrializing ones. It is also a product of political events and other social developments (Roberts 2000).

The consequences of migration for social security in the host country are multifarious and mediated by cultural, political and social factors. As discussed in Chapter 12, adverse movements in the age dependency profile are causing countries, such as Germany, to take policy measures to increase in-migration, usually into temporary employment. Such migration can also introduce flexibility into the labour market and relieve sectoral labour shortages. In contrast to these positive economic effects, immigrant populations are typically more prone to unemployment than the host population for reasons that include the temporary nature of their employment, language difficulties and employment discrimination. This can cause immigrants to be more reliant on social security which may, together with the immigration itself, precipitate resentment among the host population that can, in turn, be exploited for political purposes, usually, though not exclusively, by right-wing parties.

Given these sensitivities, it may come as little surprise to discover that the access of immigrants to social security, while varying between countries, is generally more restrictive than for the host population. Immigration status itself generates a hierarchy of access, with asylum seekers and those granted exceptional leave to remain located at the bottom and those who have been naturalized placed at the top. Asylum seekers generally fall outside mainstream social security provisions. In Sweden, they are housed in reception centres and provided with pocket money. In the UK, where asylum seekers are generally not permitted to work, vouchers replaced benefits between 2000 and 2002 and, although benefits have now been reinstated, they are paid by the National Asylum Support Service rather than the Department for Work and Pensions. In countries where asylum seekers are allowed to work, they are unlikely to accrue entitlement to social security benefits, while workers on short-term permits may be required to leave the country in the event of unemployment, sickness or accident.

Nationality and residency conditions also often apply (Chapter 5). For example, while no country in the European Union makes receipt of contributory benefits conditional on nationality, almost half restrict at least some non-contributory benefits to nationals and residency conditions attach to tax-financed benefits in many countries (Roberts 2001). To overcome these problems a series of bilateral and multilateral agreements have been put in place, the first in 1882 between France and Belgium and 401 others between 1946 and 1966 (Holloway 1981). These typically employ one or more of five major devices. First, they ensure equality of treatment under each country's system. Secondly, they guarantee that migrant workers are not uninsured in any of the national systems. Thirdly, periods of insurance in each country are aggregated when calculating benefit entitlement. Fourthly, countries agree to **proratorization**, which means that each country pays a proportion of the benefit determined by the duration of contributions made in each country. Fifthly, the countries allow benefits to be **exported**, that is to be payable in the country of destination (Roberts 2001).

While such agreements have value, they are time-consuming to negotiate and reform, complex to explain and administer, and generally exist only between countries with similar systems of provision, leaving migrants from most of the major labour exporting countries in Africa and Asia without the protection afforded by either bilateral or multilateral agreements. Moreover, the majority of the bilateral agreements that have been negotiated have become redundant since they existed between member states of the European Union and have been superseded by EEC Regulation 1408/71 (Roberts 2001).

To summarize, while difficult to measure, recent developments in the global economy have probably changed the level of risk to which individuals and economies are exposed. Employment, certainly in the industrially developed world, has been made more precarious. This has resulted from global commercial integration but has also been influenced by the policy of certain governments to create flexible labour markets that are ostensibly better able to respond positively to global competition. Social security has facilitated these changes and been used as a policy tool to bring them about. Some commentators advocate improved social security to compensate for increased labour market insecurity, possibly to be achieved through international collaboration (see below), but others argue that social fragmentation is likely to undermine social and political support for such reforms.

Comparison 13.1 Part-time and temporary employment, 1991–2001

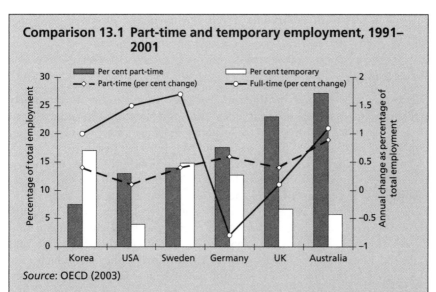

Source: OECD (2003)

The bars in the chart indicate the prevalence of part-time (less than 30 hours per week) and temporary employment as a percentage of the total. Obviously, a person can have a job that is both part-time and temporary and so would contribute twice; however second and subsequent jobs are ignored. Part-time work is especially common in Australia and Britain although it still contributes less than a third to the total. Temporary work is high in Korea (17 per cent are employed daily and another 34 per cent have other kinds of temporary job) (Jung and Shin 2002) but also in Sweden and, to a lesser extent, in Germany. However, the vast majority of workers in all the countries have permanent employment if not 'a job for life'.

The lines indicate the annual average change in full-time and part-time employment, averaged between years 1991 and 2001, expressed as a percentage of the total employment. In Germany, full-time employment fell (minus 0.8 per cent per year) during the decade but was almost offset by an increase in part-time employment (a rise of 0.6 per cent per year). In Britain, part-time employment rose faster than full-time employment but in the other four countries full-time employment rose much more markedly than part-time employment. This casts doubt on any notion that full-time jobs are everywhere being replaced by part-time jobs due to the advance of a flexible labour market driven by globalization.

Internationalism

Increased economic interdependency on a global scale serves to heighten awareness of common interests and shared problems at least among countries with similar economies and welfare regimes. This provides stimulus to policy learning and on matters such as migration, where joint action is necessitated, to cooperation. Indeed, alongside economic globalization, there is evidence of embryonic developments in the direction of global governance.

Policy learning

While the idea of one jurisdiction learning from another is intuitively straightforward, a little thought reveals that the phenomenon is quite complex (Rose 2001). Moreover, while policy learning certainly takes place, convincing evidence of when it has occurred is hard to come by.

The archetypal form of policy learning is **policy transfer**, when one government borrows an entire policy from another: its objectives, content, institutions and mode of implementation (Table 13.2). This is likely to be a rare occurrence since governments are more likely to adopt or adapt those elements of a policy that fit best with the local environment and expectations. They may take elements and combine them in ways that radically alter some or all aspects of the original policy, in which case the source of the new policy will not be evident from simple inspection. Similarly, there is little or no evidence that learning has taken place when a government reviews the policy of another and either decides against reform

Table 13.2 Forms of policy learning

Type of policy learning
0   Policy objectives, philosophy, rhetoric, content, institutions, mode of implementation
1   Adoption of all of (0) above
2   Adaptation of all of (0) above
3   Selective adoption/adaptation of (0) above
4   Hybridization (combining compatible elements of (0))
5   Synthesis (combining elements of (0) in a distinctive way)
6   Appraisal of all or part of (0) above
7   Inspired by all or part of (0) above
8   Acknowledgement of all or part of (0) above
9   Rejection of all of (0) above

Adapted from Rose (2001)

Table 13.3 Global spread of pensions policies

	Europe/Antipodes/USA/CA	Latin America/Caribbean	Africa/Middle East	Asia
		Pension system adoption, 1889–1994		
1880s	***DE***			
1890s	***DK, NZ***			
1900s	***AU, AT, BE, IS, UK,*** CS, IE			
1910s	***FR, IT, NL, SE, ES, RO,*** *LU*			
1920s	CA, BG, EE, HU, LV, LT, **PL, RU,** VU, GC	CL, EC	ZA	
1930s	***FI, NO, US,*** GR, PT	**BR,** PE, TT, UY, BB		
1940s	AL, CH, TR, MC	AR, CO, CR, DO, GY, MX, PA, PY, VE	DZ, GQ	*JP*
1950s	CV, JE, LI, MT. SM	BO, HN, JM, NI, SV, BS	**BI,** EG, IQ, GN, IR, IL, LY, MU, MA, **RW,** SY, **ZR,** CV	CN, ID, IN, MY, PH, SG, LK, TW
1960s	AD	CU, HT, GT, BM, GD	BF, CM, CF, CG, CI, ET, GA, GH, **KE, LB,** MG, ML, MR, NE, NG, SA, TG, TN, TZ, UG, ZM	NP, VN, FJ, FM, MH, PW
1970s		AG, BZ, DM, LC, VC, VG	**BJ, TD, JO, KW, LR, OM,** SD, SN, SZ, BH, SC, ST	HK, **KR, PK,** KI, SB, WS
1980s			GM, YE	PG, VU
1990s			ZW, BW	

Multi-pillar pension reform, 1981–2001

1980s	CH, NL, UK	CL	
1990s	DK, SE, AU, HU, PL	AR, CO, PE, UY, BO, MX, SV	
2000s	BG, HV, LV	CR	HK

Notes: Bold indicates country with over 1m population in 2000. Italics indicates high-income OECD country. Countries listed alphabetically by category.

Country codes: AD = Andorra, AG = Antigua, AL = Albania, AR = Argentina, AT = Austria, AU = Australia, BB = Barbados, BE = Belgium, BF = Burkina Faso, BG = Bulgaria, BH = Bahrain, BI = Burundi, BJ = Benin, BM = Bermuda, BO = Bolivia, BR = Brazil, BS = Bahamas, BW = Botswana, BZ = Belize, CA = Canada, CF = Central African Republic, CG = Congo, CH = Switzerland, CI = Ivory Coast, CL = Chile, CM = Cameroon, CN = China, CO = Colombia, CR = Costa Rica, CS = Czechoslovakia, CU = Cuba, CV = Cape Verde, CY = Cyprus, DE = Germany, DK = Denmark, DM = Dominica, DO = Dominican Republic, DZ = Algeria, EC = Ecuador, EE = Estonia, EG = Egypt, ET = Ethiopia, FI = Finland, FJ = Fiji, FM = Micronesia, FR = France, GA = Gabon, GC = Guernsey, GD = Grenada, GH = Ghana, GM = Gambia, GN = Guinea, GR = Greece, GT = Guatemala, GQ = Equatorial Guinea, GY = Guyana, HK = Hong Kong, HN = Honduras, HT = Haiti, HU = Hungary, HV = Croatia, ID = Indonesia, IE = Ireland, IL = Israel, IN = India, IQ = Iraq, IR = Iran, IS = Iceland, IT = Italy, JE = Jersey (my abbr.), JM = Jamaica, JO = Jordan, JP = Japan, KE = Kenya, KI = Kiribati, KR = South Korea, KW = Kuwait, KZ = Kazakhstan, LB = Lebanon, IC = St Lucia, LI = Liechtenstein, LK = Sn Lanka, LR = Liberia, LT = Lithuania, LU = Luxembourg, LV = Latvia, LY = Libya, MA = Morocco, MC = Monaco, MG = Madagascar, MH = Marshall Islands, ML = Mali, MR = Mauritania, MT = Malta, MU = Mauritius, MX = Mexico, MY = Malaysia, NE = Niger, NG = Nigeria, NI = Nicaragua, NL = Netherlands, NO = Norway, NP = Nepal, NZ = New Zealand, OM = Oman, PA = Panama, PE = Peru, PG = Papua New Guinea, PH = Philippines, PK = Pakistan, PL = Poland, PT = Portugal, PW = Palau, PY = Paraguay, RO = Romania, RU = Russia, RW = Rwanda, SA = Saudi Arabia, SB = Solomon Islands, SC = Seychelles, SD = Sudan, SE = Sweden, SG = Singapore, SM = San Manno, SN = Senegal, ST = St Tome & Prmcipe, SV = El Salvador, SY = Syria, SZ = Swaziland, TD = Chad, TG = Togo, TH = Thailand, TN = Tunisia, TR = Turkey, TT = Trinidad and Tobago, TW = Taiwan, TZ = Tanzania, UG = Uganda, UK = United Kingdom, US = United States, UY = Uruguay, VC = St Vincent, VE = Venezuela, VG = Virgin Islands, VN = Vietnam, VU = Vanuatu, WS = Samoa, YE = Yemen, YU = Yugoslavia, ZA = South Africa, ZM = Zambia, ZR = Zaire, ZW = Zimbabwe.

Adapted from Orenstein (2003)

or is inspired to implement change but not directly to borrow any specific components.

Evidence of policy transfer is sometimes available from the geographic diffusion of policy. The top and lower panels in Table 13.3 respectively show the spread of state insurance pensions from the 1880s through to the 1990s, and the more recent adoption of pension reforms consistent with the World Bank's preference for stimulating private pension markets by dismantling state provision and replacing it by personal savings channelled through private financial institutions. In the first case, pension policies first spread in Europe and Anglo-Saxon countries in the decades adjacent to 1900, were then taken up in Latin America and the Caribbean between 1920 and 1970 and then in Africa, the Middle East and Asia, mainly during the 1950s, 1960s and 1970s. The geographic clustering is suggestive of policy learning but it is also notable that richer countries implemented policies before poorer ones (true also of the retreat from non-funded, state provision in the 1980s and 1990s) and large ones before small (Orenstein 2003). The fact that similar countries adopted similar policies approximately contemporaneously does not prove the existence of policy learning; they might simply have developed similar policies to meet common challenges.

Another example of diffusion is the adoption of labour market activation and proactive welfare policies by numerous industrial countries, including Sweden, the USA, Britain, Germany and Australia, from the mid-1980s on. A number of authors have pointed to the influence of US ideas on Britain, and via Britain and the OECD, on European countries (Walker 1998; Peck 2001; Walker and Wiseman 2003a). The writings of Charles Murray and particularly Lawrence Mead are often cited (Deacon 2002) and were actively promoted by right of centre US think-tanks such as the Heritage Foundation and the Cato Institute, working with the UK Institute for Economic Affairs (now Civitas), in the 1980s and 1990s. As important, the incoming 1997 Labour government had close links with the Clinton administration. Others (Wilenski 1992; White 2000; Lødemel and Trickey 2001), however, have pointed to the influence of Scandinavian countries. Sweden, in particular, has a long history of activation policies developed to support the high rates of economic activity necessary to fund generous welfare provision. A meeting of European ministers took place in 1995 that fed ideas on activation into the United Nations social summit held in Copenhagen later that year. Then, in 1997, a European Union summit (the so-called 'Jobs Summit') set targets for the coverage of activation policies among unemployment benefit recipients.

The complex pattern of influences on the diffusion of activation policies is illustrated by interviews recently undertaken with British policymakers about the origins of New Deal welfare to work policies introduced by the 1997 Labour government (Cebulla 2002). Their accounts confirm that policy learning took place at the level of ideology, rhetoric, design and implementation. Some of the learning was active – for example, Labour ministers and senior officials visited implementations in Wisconsin and California in 1998. Some was more passive with the parameters of the policy debate shifting as if by osmosis in regular intergovernmental meetings. Officials in the then Department for Education and Employment emphasized the influence of Scandinavia, while their colleagues in the then Department of Social Security stressed the importance of US and Australian experience. Policy papers produced by the Labour Party before the 1997 election also explicitly drew on the Australian Working Nation and JET programmes which were, in turn, influenced by US ideas and the 1994 OECD *Jobs Study* (Howard 2003). Britain's New Deal policies were the result of both **policy synthesis**, selecting appropriate elements and **hybridization**, combining them in novel ways. However, the addition of new components and emphases created a unique policy formulation that may itself become a source of inspiration for other jurisdictions (Walker and Wiseman 2003b).

International organizations and supra-national governance

The importance of international organizations in policy learning will already have become apparent with the OECD, United Nations and European Union all being cited in connection with the diffusion of activation policies. They constitute nodes in international policy networks that serve to generate and communicate ideas and information. However, their influence is not solely as facilitators; they have, in varying degrees, the power to cajole, instruct and compel national governments to comply. Policy learning, or transfer, is not always voluntary.

It is useful to characterize supra-national organizations in a number of ways: whether they have a global or regional remit; whether they rely on moral persuasion or financial or legal leverage; and whether or not social security is central to their mission.

Global persuasion

There are three global organizations that embrace social security and that seek to influence through persuasion. The International Social Security Association (ISSA) was established in 1927 to provide training, advice and research to national policymakers and administrators. The United Nation's International Labour Office (ILO), which shares its building in Geneva with the ISSA, was founded in 1919 to promote, according to its constitution, policies to achieve 'full employment and the raising of living standards'. The OECD is a policy forum of the 29 richest countries that, as noted above, has been particularly influential in stimulating debate about proactive policy. Its

Case Study 13.1 Potential for policy learning on activation policy, Britain and the USA

	USA to the UK, 1990s	Possible lessons for the USA, 2000s	Opportunities for mutual learning
Ideology/rhetoric	• Proactive policies • Personal responsibility and social obligation • Dependency/underclass	• Include security as policy objective • Link policies to social inclusion • Target child poverty • Link reform to modernization • Promote the programme	• Reinforcement of reform momentum • Legitimization of area targeting and community development strategies
Strategy	• Welfare to work • Work first • Casework/guidance • Tax-based earnings subsidy • Minimum wage • Geographic targeting • Business alliance	• Join up government • Integrate tax and benefit systems around assistance to and in work • Enhance accountability • Identify models • Link education and training programmes to lifelong learning • Promote evidence-based policymaking • Reach out to include needy without children	• Development of job retention and career advancement support • Exploration of trade-off between local discretion and equity • Integration of process and impact evaluation
Implementation	• Piloting/prototyping/demonstration projects • One-stop service delivery • Public-private partnerships in delivery • Recipient-agency contracts	• Welfare/employment agency merger • Best practice roll-out • Personal adviser resources • Targets and accountability	• Information systems • Performance standards • Case management • Public housing • Coping with scale • effective client targeting

Source: Walker and Wiseman (2003d)

1994 *Jobs Study* was prescriptive in arguing that social security should be redesigned to support rather than to obstruct the creation of flexible labour markets:

'counties should legislate for only moderate levels of benefit, maintain effective checks on eligibility, and guarantee places on active programmes as a substitute for paying passive income support indefinitely' (p. 48).

Of the three organisations, only the ISSA has a prime focus of social security although the ILO has acquired considerable social security expertise due to its focus on labour market issues (Yeates 2003).

The interests and stance of the OECD reflects the viewpoint of the world's most economically powerful countries, notably the USA. Moreover, any influence that the OECD secretariat has on the views of its member governments is not much paraded in public.[2] In contrast, the ILO has an advocacy role and a constitution that links its activities to an explicit concern with social justice. It has more clearly defined policy goals, repeatedly articulated in the public domain, and argues that the primary objective of social security should be to ensure access, as of right, to a minimum standard of living. Moreover, the ILO anticipates that over time coverage should be extended and the minimum increased. To achieve this it has adopted over 30 conventions and 20 recommendations that deal exclusively with social security (Yeates 2003), which countries are encouraged to ratify. Reflecting the time when they were adopted, most of the conventions protect the traditional full-time worker. However, because they generally do not explicitly exclude atypical work, they can be used to extend minimum standards (Pelakanos 2000). Moreover, Convention 175 seeks to provide protection for part-time workers and Convention 177 offers equivalent protection to home workers.

Recently, following on from the aforementioned Copenhagen social summit in 1995, the ILO has pursued an agenda to promote **decent** (or dignified) (Standing 2002) **work**, work that is productive and secure, upholds labour rights, provides adequate income, offers social protection and facilitates collective bargaining, free trade unions and worker participation, underpinned by social dialogue between employers, employees and governments. The summit emphasized the links between employment, gender inequality and poverty in the context of globalization and the ILO is promoting decent work as the principal path out of poverty. It rejects the view that the poor countries should 'grow first, distribute later', arguing that 'distribution has been slow in coming – threatening social cohesion and

---

2 There are exceptions to this behind the scenes diplomacy as when, in January 2004, high-profile coverage was given to an OECD report that offered policy support to a beleaguered Labour government seeking to reform university finance.

making people lose faith in governments, institutions and those with the power to change things' (Somavia 2003: 6–7). Instead, the ILO is intent on linking decent work with:

'new ways to provide social protection and reclaim the role of the state in this sphere. Women's capacity to renegotiate the distribution of unpaid work caring for family needs is crucial. Support for people unable to work because of age, illness or disability is essential' (Somavia 2003: 7).

Global leverage

The World Bank, the International Monetary Fund and the World Trade Organization all, on occasion, take an interest in social security matters, especially pensions, and have the financial leverage lacked by the ILO. Moreover, they have often taken a radically different view of the objectives of social security. Indeed, the ILO's current policy stance can be seen as a rejection of the so-called 'Washington Consensus' that has characterized World Bank thinking. At risk of oversimplification, the Washington Consensus holds that, in the early stages of economic development, social insurance is a luxury or even an impediment to advancement, and that social assistance is a major work disincentive. Such thinking is evidenced by the World Bank's previously mentioned preference for stimulating private pension markets; a preference that it was able to promote by disbursing financial and institutional resources in Latin America, Central and Eastern Europe and China. (There is, though, debate about the extent to which the Bank was successful in persuading countries to follow its policy prescription – Fultz and Ruck 2001; Holtzmann *et al.* 2003b; Yeates 2003.)

There is, however, also debate about the continuing robustness of the Washington Consensus. Holtzmann *et al.* (2003b) argue that the World Bank is increasingly giving greater priority to social protection. This change in stance appears to have two main causes. First, the East Asian crisis in 1997 showed that high growth rates, while necessary, were insufficient for lasting poverty reduction. Secondly, there is also a growing recognition of increased risks created by globalization and a deeper understanding of poverty dynamics and the long-term effects of seemingly transitory shocks. Consequently, the World Bank is now advocating 'social risk management' to prevent the occurrence of risk events, to reduce their effects and to relieve their impact through informal, market-based and public arrangements. The reader will note the striking correspondence between the World Bank's new focus on prevention, mitigation and coping strategies and the goals and generic aims of social security discussed in Chapters 2, 6, 7 and 8 above. Moreover, Holtzman *et al.* (2003b: 8) and colleagues in the World Bank also rehearse the various advantages and limitations of different modes of funding and delivering social security (discussed in Chapters 4 and 5) and conclude that 'in the real world, all risk management arrangements will play important roles that are likely to change over time'. Even so, Yeates (2003: 65) remains unconvinced that the World Bank views social security as much more than 'a social safety net for the critically poor', when commercial provision and family support prove inadequate.

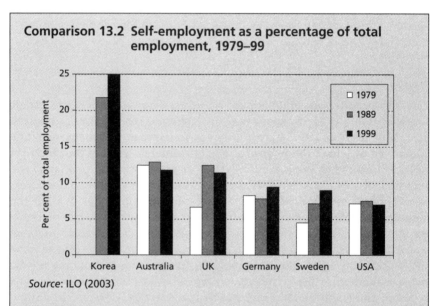

Comparison 13.2 Self-employment as a percentage of total employment, 1979–99

Source: ILO (2003)

Some self-employment is thought to be generated by firms seeking to reduce their employment costs by passing the responsibility for insurance on to workers who would otherwise have been recruited as employees. Sometimes this is suggested to be a response to increased global competitiveness. In addition, activation policies, especially in Britain, have encouraged people to create their own employment by becoming self-employed. Such workers are often excluded from full social security protection. For example, they may be denied unemployment benefit because of the threat of moral hazard. Therefore, the effect of a trend can be to reduce the coverage of contribution-based benefits, leaving people potentially reliant on social assistance.

However, self-employment is a very diverse employment category, embracing the self-employed professional and the casual worker prevalent in Korea. Also, as the graph illustrates, there is no uniform upward trend in the volume of self-employment.

Regional international governance

Most regional international organizations rely on persuasion to influence national social security policy. This is certainly the case with the Association of South-East Nations (ASEAN) and the Southern African Development Community (SADC), although the Southern Core Common Market (MERCOSUR, comprising Argentina, Brazil, Paraguay and Uruguay) has implemented a supra-national law providing for mutual recognition of social security rights. Even within the European Union, social security and taxation remain the legal responsibility of member states. Founded as the European Iron and Steel Community in 1951, the European Union is perhaps the most politically developed of the regional economic organizations. However, early ambitious aspirations to harmonize national policies have generally been replaced by the more pragmatic goal of convergence. There is, though, recurring discussion about the desirability of making social security a community responsibility, most recently in the context of the debate concerning the European constitution required to facilitate the 2004 enlargement from 15 to 25 members.

Nevertheless, the influence of the European Union on the social security policies of member states has been profound. It has shaped system aims and programme objectives, often by the mechanism of judiciously creating political opportunities in return for imposing policy constraints. Although founded primarily as an economic community, the ideology underpinning continental European social security systems contrasts markedly with that of the Washington Consensus. There is strong adherence to the idea of a European social model, which was initially merely a description of the approach adopted by European countries but is now increasingly viewed as a badge of Union membership. The social model places social protection a close second to economic development and is continually being refined. As enunciated at an informal meeting of ministers at Nafplio in January 2003, it comprises four 'common principles': Europe's success must not exclude anyone; solidarity should be linked to economic success; there is neither dilemma nor contradiction between economic and social progress; and the welfare state is a factor of production not a luxury or a byproduct of economic development.

In reality, national social security policies have to date been driven by the prosaic requirement to support community economic policy. European law has been established to facilitate labour mobility, ensuring migrant workers retain rights to social security throughout the Union. Likewise, initial concerns that different provisions on equal pay would result in unfair competition between member states fed community legislation to outlaw direct and indirect sex discrimination in national employment and social security policies. However, new forms of governance are being developed that actively promote convergence, and may add another tier of external political influence and constraint on the social security policies of nation states. Notably among them is the Open Method of Coordination (OMC) that applies to employment strategy and policies on social protection and social inclusion.

OMC depends on so-called 'soft' law, transparency and commitment to activism, as opposed to the 'hard' law of regulation:

> The main institutional ingredients of the OMC are common guidelines, national action plans, peer reviews, joint evaluation reports and recommendations. None of these instruments has a binding character underpinned by legal enforcement powers. Moreover, while providing policy actors with a relatively clear agenda, the mix of these ingredients leaves ample room for national contextualization. The new approach remains 'soft' and 'national state friendly': two features that greatly facilitate the making of coordinated decisions.
>
> (Ferrera *et al.* 2002: 227)

Through the peer review and joint evaluation reports the OMC explicitly encourages policy learning, helping nation states to develop their own policies informed by an understanding of what works best elsewhere. The aspiration is that the process of comparison and review, the results of which are open to media and public scrutiny, will foster a common commitment to seeking improvement rather than policy competition and social dumping.

It is too early to determine the results that follow from adoption of OMC (Buechs 2003). It may be, for example, that the number of member states adopting refundable tax credits since the 1997 launch of the European Employment Strategy is simply coincidence. Nevertheless, OMC serves as a powerful example of nation states seeking to respond to global economic forces by acting together as equals to enhance social security protection.

Social security on a global scale?

The classic welfare state may be viewed as a collective twentieth-century response to the individual risks created by the processes of industrialization and modernity, organized within the jurisdiction of the nation state. Late or postmodernity, and the growing importance of global economic processes in heightening individual and social risk, may eventually forge new systems of social security that are structured and perhaps operate on an international scale. Certainly, to take one example, it is inconceivable that the continued economic integration of Europe will not precipitate further convergence in social security provisions, if only to facilitate labour mobility and market competitiveness.

Nevertheless, more effective international governance will only be achieved at the cost of eroding national sovereignty by placing additional limits on the prerogatives and power of individual governments. Currently, in almost all matters to do with social security, the balance of power favours national states. For example, it is for member states of the United Nations to select which labour conventions to sign and it transpires that, in the context

Comparison 13.3 Labour market competitiveness

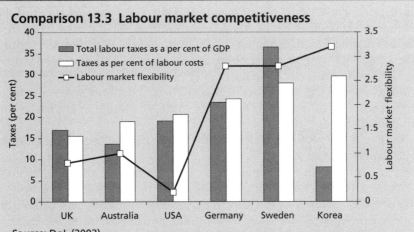

Source: DoL (2003)

The white bars indicate the percentage of labour costs attributable to social insurance and other compulsory labour taxes. High values suggest that a country is relatively uncompetitive in attracting inward investment in jobs although no account is taken of differences in labour productivity. In addition to social insurance and labour taxes, labour costs include direct pay for time worked and taken as leave (excluding sick leave), bonuses and payments made in kind. The measure relates to production workers in manufacturing and differences in hours worked is accounted for by calculating hourly rates. Values are lowest in the Anglo-Saxon countries and highest in Korea, which funds an unusually high proportion of its public expenditure from labour taxes.

The grey bars express workers' and employers' social security contributions and other payroll taxes together with personal income tax as a percentage of GDP. Again high values of this broader based measure also indicate relative lack of competitiveness. A dramatic 'improvement' is evident in the position of Korea since personal income tax is comparatively low.

The line is a summary measure of labour market flexibility relating to the strength of employment protection legislation – the ease with which employers can hire and fire workers. It covers the procedures required with respect to dismissals, notice, severance pay and the regulation of temporary work and ranges from 0 (no restrictions) to 6 (very restrictive). Anglo-Saxon countries, the USA in particular, are notably more flexible than the other countries, offering workers less protection.

of migration, the conventions that could be of most assistance to migrants have been signed by the fewest countries. Only three member states of the European Union have signed the ILO Convention 143 and none has signed the International Convention for the Protection of the Rights of All Migrant Workers and Their Families (Roberts 2000). Even the Universal Declaration of Human Rights is circumscribed in that the right to social security is conditional upon being 'a member of society', which national states can interpret in terms of citizenship, residency or some other more or less exclusionary formulation.

In sum, it will probably be a long time before the choice made in Chapter 1 to define the nation state as the jurisdiction of relevance in the study of social security ceases to be appropriate. In the meantime, the social security systems of nation states can be judged by the treatment accorded to the majority of citizens and to the most vulnerable members of society. Patriotism and ignorance may lead citizens in many states to believe that their social security system provides the most generous provision of all. Using concepts and techniques introduced in this volume, it should be possible to begin to challenge such beliefs with evidence.

Further reading

Yeates (2003) offers a short and very accessible account of social security in a global context while Standing (2002) provides an agenda for action from a personalized ILO perspective. Turning to policy transfer, Lødemel and Trickey (2001) describe the diffusion of 'workfare' policies in Europe, Ashworth *et al.* (2004a, 2004b) examine international influences on New Labour's welfare policies in Britain, and Walker and Wiseman (2003) encourage the USA to look to the UK for policy ideas.

Postscript

The end of this book is hopefully only the beginning.

The book has introduced the reader to concepts and techniques with which it is possible to begin to frame and to answer questions that are of profound importance for the future of modern democratic society:

- Is social security successful in fulfilling its socially approved aims and objectives?
- If so, is it achieving them as effectively and efficiently as possible and in ways that are both consistent with majority social values and respectful of the legitimate claims and aspirations of minority groups?
- If unsuccessful, in what ways is the social security system and/or its constituent parts defective and how might they be improved?
- Are more resources required for social security, to what purpose and would this additional expenditure be money well spent?
- Would it be possible, and indeed preferable, to reduce expenditure on social security?
- Are systems in other jurisdictions comparable and, if so, are they more effective and/or more efficient and do they offer scope for policy learning?
- Alternatively, do other systems differ so much with respect to their aims and social priorities, and/or in terms of their welfare regimes, that attempts at policy learning would be doomed to failure?

It should be apparent after reading this book, if not beforehand, that to obtain secure answers to such questions is no easy task. However, difficult does not always mean impossible and the combination of intellectual challenge and political importance makes the quest for answers urgent, often frustrating, sometimes rewarding and almost infinitely fascinating. The topics and themes introduced provide crude tools that can be further refined and improved through additional study and practical application.

Some readers will wish to exploit these conceptual tools in the process of policy evaluation and development, while others will be content to use them to hone their understanding of, and participation in, the social security system as citizen, financier and claimant. Everyone should at least acknowledge the importance of framing appropriate questions and seeking reliable answers. If not, the author has failed, an opportunity has been missed and democratic society stands to be a mite less secure.

Nevertheless, none of the above questions can be satisfactorily answered merely by recourse to policy analysis, no matter how sophisticated. The answers are profoundly political. At heart, they have to do with people's aspirations for themselves and for each other, today and for the foreseeable future and beyond. While it is a statement of faith, not fact, that better-informed politics is better politics, the argument that basing policymaking on ignorance is not only easier but also preferable to rational, informed analysis is difficult to countenance.

Glossary

abuse the unintentional withholding of information or misleading of officials.

activation policies linking benefit receipt to microeconomic measures such as compulsory training in order variously to enhance the employability of benefit recipients, increase the supply of labour and reduce benefit caseloads.

active stigma the attitudes and actions of people not claiming benefit that reveal their contempt for benefit recipients.

active welfare an Anglo-Saxon term for **activation**; see also **proactive welfare**.

adequacy the resources necessary for a unit comprising one or more individuals to sustain a specified, usually minimal or modest, standard of living for a specified period.

adequacy standard or threshold the ratio of resources to needs that separates assessment units with adequate resources from those without.

administrative efficiency a measure of the extent to which **technical efficiency** and **price efficiency** are attained and the associated concept.

adverse selection when people who are objectively more at risk disproportionately take out insurance, typically because they have prior knowledge of the extra risk that they face.

agency relationship the role and status of an organization (usually a dependency relationship *vis-à-vis* government).

aims the purposes of a social security system.

amelioration partially making good an income loss at a higher level than the basic minimum; see **income support**.

applicant a person who makes an application for benefit.

atypical work remunerated work that departs from the traditional model of permanent, full-time and contracted employment; also termed **flexible work**.

average rate of tax the total tax paid as a percentage of before-tax income.

average severity the **poverty gap** divided by the number of poor persons.

basic income (see also **social dividend** and **demogrant**) an income paid unconditionally on a regular basis to every person as a right of citizenship.

beneficiary a member of a **claimant unit**; a person gaining (usually defined in terms of standard of living, or more generally, **utility**) from an award of benefit.

benefit according to context, a programme of cash payments or a cash payment awarded under such a programme. A benefit programme is the lowest-level discrete component in a hierarchy of social security provision.

benefit dependency unnecessarily long-term reliance on benefits. The term is also variously used by authors to refer simply to the long-term receipt of social security benefits, or to an acquired culture of long-term reliance on, and exploitation of, benefit provision.

benefit drag a phenomenon that biases estimates of **take-up** or **horizontal targeting efficiency** upwards because the numerator of the defining fraction is inflated by recipients who would be ineligible for benefit based on circumstances current at the time of estimation, while the denominator is reduced due to the omission of people who were previously in the target group but no longer are due to changes in circumstance.

benefit taper the amount by which benefit is reduced as other income rises; it is usually expressed as a percentage.

benefit (tax credit) scheme a group of benefits or tax credits that are administered together under a common rubric.

bridging mechanism a mechanism or mechanisms to ease the transition from benefit to employment.

budget constraint a term sometimes used by economists to refer to the **marginal deduction rate.**

budget standard the cost of a set of expenditure items judged necessary for a household of a specified composition to enjoy a given standard of living. The time period over which expenditure is to be incurred may or may not be made explicit. Sometimes the term is used to refer to the set of items rather than the associated cost.

capability the reason or reasons why a person is unable to access sufficient funds of their own and which legitimate their claim for benefit.

caseload the set of people receiving a benefit; the same as the **recipient population.**

caseloading a system of administration in which claimants primarily deal with one named member of staff (hence, it is sometimes referred to as one-to-one working).

categorical (benefit) a benefit for which eligibility depends on membership of a status group defined in terms of age, disability, employment etc.

claimant unit the **beneficiaries** of a single benefit claim. The claimant unit usually equates with the assessment unit but not always (e.g. social assistance schemes in Germany and Korea).

claimant person to whom a social security payment is made; also termed a **recipient.**

collective transfer transfer of income that occurs when two or more individuals agree to make a payment to one or more of their number when a particular circumstance or contingency arises; the agreement may be informal or enforced by contract or by government.

concentration coefficient a measure of spatial inequality defined as the ratio of the proportion of total (social security) expenditure spent in a specific geographic area to the proportion of the total population living there.

constraints factors that limit the set of possible policy designs or reduce the effectiveness of benefits.

contribution payment made in order to receive benefit in the event of the occurrence of a pre-specified contingency; also called a premium, especially in relation to private insurance.

contributory benefit a benefit for which eligibility depends on a record of contributions; also termed a social insurance (or in the US a social security) benefit.

cost effectiveness the degree to which a desired policy objective is attained at minimum cost.

counterfactual the situation that would obtain if the policy being evaluated did not exist.

covert objectives: internal objectives that are not made public.

creaming activation staff seeking out clients who are most easy to place (sometimes in order to meet targets); also termed **skimming**.

creative justice principle of pursuing a flexible response to individual human needs and to the immense variety of complex individual circumstances, usually in the context of discretionary assessment of eligibility and/or entitlement; sometimes termed individualized justice.

de-industrialization the decline of manufacturing employment relative to work in the service sector, sometimes involving the substitution of jobs in economically advanced countries by additional employment in newly industrializing countries.

deadweight expenditure incurred in order to achieve a result that would have occurred without the expenditure.

decent or **dignified work** work that is productive and secure, upholds labour rights, provides adequate income, offers social protection and facilitates collective bargaining, free trade unions and worker participation underpinned by social dialogue between employers, employees and governments. A concept promulgated by the ILO.

decentralization situation where responsibility for the design or delivery of benefits is devolved to a sub-national tier of government; sometimes also used to refer to national policies delivered on an agency basis by local government or other organizations.

decommodification services or resources that are allocated and often delivered by the state rather than the market.

defined benefit schemes a term, usually applied in the context of old-age pensions, to describe policies in which the amount of benefit is fixed as a proportion of previous earnings (final salary prior to retirement).

defined contribution schemes a term, often applied in the context of old-age pensions, to describe policies where the level of pension is dependent on contributions and subsequent returns on investment and annuity rates at the point of claiming benefit (usually at retirement).

demogrant a basic income scheme that is directed to one or more population subgroups.

demonstration project a local pilot implementation designed to assess the effectiveness of a policy, usually by comparing the outcomes for persons randomly assigned to receive the policy with those for others randomly assigned not to do so.

dependency ratio the ratio of the number of children and people above retirement age, to the number of working-age persons.

devolution when a sub-national tier of government is responsible for varying aspects of the design and/or financing of social security.

discretion process of decision-making in which an official (or institution) chooses between two or more equally valid courses of action, observing the spirit of the legislation but unfettered by rules determining decisions in particular circumstances.

disposable income personal or household income from all sources that is available to be spent.

earnings-related (benefit) a benefit for which entitlement (benefit level) is fixed as a proportion of previous earnings.

economic participation rate the proportion of a social group (usually of working age) that is either employed or looking for work.

economic structure the pattern of opportunities, signposts and rewards that drives the capitalist system.

eligibility a person is *eligible* for a benefit if they meet all the qualifying conditions and *ineligible* if they do not.

employment shortfall the difference between the employment rates observed for the partners of unemployed and employed persons.

entitled an eligible person will be entitled to the benefit in question if they apply for it.

entitlement the amount of benefit that a person eligible for benefit would receive on application.

equivalence scales statistical weights used to adjust for differences in the composition and individual needs of households (or assessment units).

etatism the attempt by nineteenth-century European monarchs to foster national allegiance as a bulwark against socialist ideas.

exported (benefit) benefit payable to migrants in the country of destination on the basis of rights acquired in the country of origin.

external audit measures to assess administrative performance against criteria defined outside the social security administration or jurisdiction.

external objectives objectives attached to a policy by stakeholders and others not responsible for its design.

family cap policies policies that penalize mothers financially if they conceive while in receipt of benefit.

family unit a set of persons linked by blood or marriage defined for the purpose of social security policy and/or implementation.

felt stigma the sense of worthlessness, personal failure or worse that some people feel because of claiming benefit.

filtering system administrative system that gives applicants with the most complex problems access to specialized staff and greater resources with the corollary that clients with less complex problems are dealt with by less specialized staff and have access to fewer resources.

final income personal or household income after all taxes and receipt of state benefits in cash and kind.

final outcome effect (or performance) of a social security benefit or system measured with respect to the objectives and aims.

flexible work remunerated work that departs from the traditional model of permanent, full-time and contracted employment; also termed **atypical work**.

fraud the deliberate misrepresentation of circumstances with the intent of gaining financial advantage, either through commission, by actively providing false information, or through omission, knowingly withholding relevant information.

function an outcome of policy, either intentional or unintentional.

funding saving and investing premiums (contributions) paid today to accumulate assets from which future liabilities can be met.

GDP gross domestic product, a measure of the total values of goods and services produced by a nation during a given period (usually a year).

Gini coefficient a measure of inequality; when applied to personal or household income it can be interpreted as showing the proportion of total income needing to be redistributed in order to ensure that income is equally distributed.

globalization (increased) interdependency in economic production that spans national borders and/or the processes generating such interdependency.

government insurance: insurance provided by the state, quite often financed on a **pay-as-you-go** basis.

gross income the sum of all forms of personal or household income, including that derived from the market-place and through social security; income in kind is normally ignored.

headcount poverty rate the number of people (or households) in poverty expressed as a proportion of the total population (or total number of households).

heterogeneity effect appertains to people who remain on benefit solely because they have characteristics that lead them to be less likely to leave.

hoarding holding on to money in the form of cash or marketable assets.

horizontal redistribution the transfer of resources between people who have different demands on their budgets irrespective of their incomes.

horizontal targeting efficiency the proportion of the target population in receipt of benefit (also termed take-up). The prefix *internal* or *external* indicates that it is measured with respect to **internal objectives** or **external objectives**.

household people sharing a dwelling, usually assumed to be sharing other resources.

hybridization combining policies derived from different jurisdictions.

hypothecated tax tax that is earmarked for spending for specific purposes such as social security.

iatrogenic problem problem caused by the existing policy.

in-kind benefits social security provision delivered in the form of goods or services rather than in cash.

incentives the gains and losses associated with particular courses of action; there is debate about whether or not the gains and losses need to be consciously recognized by policy actors.

income effect signal provided by the average rate of tax (or average deduction rate) that creates an incentive for people to increase their gross income to maintain their disposable income (e.g. by working longer hours).

income support sometimes used synonymously both with income maintenance (and confusingly) with **amelioration.**

individual welfare individual well-being or **utility,** defined by economists in terms of an individual's preferences as revealed by the choices they make within a given income and price regime.

individualism philosophy that advocates that the interests of the individual should take priority over those of the community or state; individuals should be free from government interference in the pursuit of their economic activities.

individualization behaviour and attitudes whereby priority is given to the person rather than the social group in terms of attributes, status and aspirations.

individualization of social security benefits linking eligibility and entitlement to the circumstances of individuals, rather than to the circumstances of the households or families of which they are part.

inner family a single person or couple and any dependent children.

institutional stigma the process, or consequences, of actions by social security agencies to deter people from applying for benefit (**purposive stigma**) or of the failure proactively to promote the status of benefit recipients.

insurance system under which a third party agrees to pay one or more sums of money to an individual (or claimant unit) in the event of a pre-specified contingency in return for one or more prior payments (called contributions or premiums).

intermediate objective a goal relating to the effective delivery of a social security benefit or system.

intermediate outcome or **output** effect (or performance) of a social security benefit or system measured with respect to intermediate objectives.

internal audit mechanisms to ensure that intermediate or performance objectives are achieved, and the measures used to establish the level of performance attained.

internal objectives the policy objectives of those responsible for the design of the policy.

interpretative judgement the following of rules to choose between two or more courses of action.

investment lending money (the '*principal*') to others to invest in profitable activities with a view to gaining interest.

jurisdiction the territory over which the authority of a government is exercised.

life-course redistribution the transfer of income from periods of relative prosperity in a person's life to times of comparative shortage.

Lorenz curve a graph plotting the cumulative income share against cumulative population.

low take-up the more usual term for internal horizontal inefficiency.

managerialism the deployment of private sector management techniques in public and quasi-public organizations.

marginal deduction rate the proportion of any marginal addition to gross income that is lost to taxation and reductions in benefit; sometimes called the **budget constraint**.

marginal rate of tax the rate of tax applying to the last unit of income.

market income the income that people accrue through selling their labour and/or from holding capital investments.

means-tested benefit a benefit for which eligibility and entitlement depend on an applicant's resources falling below a prescribed standard; often termed **social assistance** especially in continental Europe.

measurement error the (degree of) failure to precisely measure the concept intended.

modernization the structural changes associated with scientific and industrial development that involve the division of labour, differentiation of markets, social and geographic mobility and mass consumption.

moral hazard situations in which policies to reduce the consequences of a risk event increase the likelihood that the event will occur.

mutual organizations organizations owned by their members.

negative income tax a direct tax scheme that deducts tax from people with incomes above a defined threshold and makes payments to others with incomes below this or some other income threshold.

negative redistribution the transfer of income from assessment units with less income to those with more; also termed **regressive redistribution**.

non-contributory benefits benefits in which entitlement is based on the occurrence of a contingency (such as a disability) irrespective of the level of income and other resources (or not dependent on the payment of contributions).

objective a purpose of a social security benefit or scheme.

occupational benefits benefits forming part of the employment package provided by an employer (but sometimes funded in part by additional contributions from employees and tax subsidies).

old-age dependency ratio the number of pensioners (or persons of retirement age) divided by the number of workers (or persons of working age).

old-age support ratio the number of workers (or persons of working age) divided by the number of pensioners (or persons of retirement age).

open objectives: internal objectives that are known publicly.

opportunity cost output lost or utility forgone due to diverting resources from other more productive uses.

original income an approximation to market income, usually calculated from information derived from household face-to-face surveys.

outcomes observable products of a policy implementation.

outdoor relief cash payments to people living outside the workhouse in Victorian Britain.

path dependency the propensity for welfare systems to be self-perpetuating because existing institutions and prevailing values limit policy choices.

pay-as-you-go financing mechanism by means of which today's contributors and/or taxpayers meet the cost of benefits paid to today's recipients.

performance objective a precisely specified policy target against which current outcome can be measured.

performance targets levels of performance to be achieved expressed in ways that facilitate measurement.

policy a collective term covering social security schemes and benefits.

policy effectiveness a measure of the extent to which a social security scheme or system attains its objectives.

policy synthesis a type of policy learning in which selected elements from the policies of a number of jurisdictions are integrated and implemented in a new policy.

policy transfer a form of policy learning in which a policy is implemented that is very closely modelled on a policy from another jurisdiction.

positive horizontal redistribution the transfer of resources to people who have high demands on their budgets irrespective of their incomes.

positive vertical redistribution the transfer of income from people with higher living standards to others with a lower standard of living (the state usurping Robin Hood's mythical role in stealing from the rich to give to the poor).

post-tax income an estimate of the volume of goods and assets that can be acquired once all taxes are paid.

potential income the level of collective and individual income that would have existed with optimal provision and perfect economic efficiency.

poverty gap a measure of the amount by which the incomes of poor households (or assessment units) fall short of the poverty threshold.

poverty gap ratio a measure used in international comparisons of the relative poverty gap that is calculated by dividing average severity by the poverty threshold.

poverty rate see **headcount poverty rate.**

poverty threshold see **adequacy threshold.**

poverty trap the high marginal deduction rate caused by the interaction of income taxation and the withdrawal of income-related benefits.

preferred income the product of the collectively desired trade-off between income and leisure.

prescribed needs the needs that social security is designed to meet.

prevention policies to ensure that people's income does not fall below a prescribed standard or which make good any shortfall that does occur.

price efficiency a measure of the extent to which a policy objective is achieved at minimum cost (and the associated economic concept).

primary objectives: objectives that would provide sufficient cause to establish a benefit scheme where none existed.

principal objective a policy objective that is accorded great importance.

proactive welfare an Anglo-Saxon term for **activation;** see also **active welfare.**

process studies evaluations that focus on establishing why policies work by examining how they are delivered.

profiling predictive models used at the point of application (or close thereafter) to identify applicants most at risk of remaining on benefit in order to offer special treatment.

proportional justice requires that two or more persons whose circumstances are identical will be treated identically, while others whose circumstances are different will be treated differently but to a degree that is proportional and explicit.

proratorization agreement under which countries pay a proportion of the benefit payable to a migrant determined by the duration of contributions made in each country.

purposive stigma stigma created by institutions in order to deter applications.

quintile share ratio ratio of the share of total income received by the poorest fifth of the population to the income share of the richest fifth of the population.

Rawlsian inequality measure the share of total income received by the poorest fifth of the population.

recipiency rate the number of benefit recipients as a percentage of the target population, often defined fairly imprecisely with a reference to, for example, an age band.

recipient population see **caseload.**

refundable tax credit a form of partial negative income tax scheme; payments are made to a person if the tax credit to which they are entitled exceeds their tax liabilities. Refundable tax credits are analogous to social assistance.

regressive redistribution see **negative redistribution**.

relative wage adjustment policies to maximize the difference between in- and out-of-work incomes.

relief policies to increase personal or household income to a socially acceptable minimum standard.

replacement ratio the ratio of benefit receipt or entitlement to a reference income (sometimes former earnings).

reservation wage the lowest wage that a person (on benefit) would be prepared to accept.

risk pooling sharing the cost of responding to the occurrence of a contingency between a group of people (e.g. members of an insurance scheme).

savings trap the reduction in entitlement for means-tested benefits resulting from having savings.

scroungerphobia the widespread denigration of benefit recipients (often evidenced in the popular media).

secondary objectives objectives associated with rectifying deficiencies in current provision.

selective providing benefits only to people in or at risk of poverty; usually entails means testing (see **means-tested benefits**).

self-sufficiency securing an income above the means-tested threshold through paid work or other legitimate means without reliance on means-tested (or, according to some authorities, any social security) benefit.

skimming see **creaming**.

social assistance see **means-tested benefits**.

social citizenship the ability fully to participate.

social cohesion a stable national collective, often defined around a nested hierarchy of social groups, with the family at the bottom and nation state at the apex.

social dividend a form of **basic income** scheme.

social dumping policy of reducing welfare expenditures in order to run a low-tax (and arguably more competitive) economy.

social efficiency a measure of the extent to which net social benefits (social benefits less social costs) are maximized (and the associated concept).

social security broadly defined, includes all cash or near cash benefits provided through government contributory, non-contributory and social assistance schemes together with similar benefits provided by occupational, for-profit and not-for-profit organizations; narrowly defined, it equates with social insurance.

social security system the full set of social security provisions operative within a jurisdiction.

social stigma the negative associations attached to benefit receipt that occur when benefit claimants are labelled and abused by other individuals and institutions, including the media.

social welfare the sum of individual welfare.

spending unit people taking expenditure decisions in common.

state dependency the process by which the experience of living on benefits in itself materially reduces the chance of self-sufficiency.

stigma the negative associations attached to benefit receipt.

stigma by association negative associations attached to benefit receipt that arise when benefit is reserved for, or associated with, groups who are socially excluded, disadvantaged or discriminated against.

subordinate objective a policy objective deemed to be less important than another.

subsidiarity principle that responsibility should be allocated to the lowest group in an administrative (or social) hierarchy that is capable of bearing the risk in question.

subsitution effect signal provided by the marginal rate of tax (or marginal deduction rate) that creates an incentive for people to reduce the hours that they work, thereby substituting leisure for work.

target population the set of people intended to receive the social security benefit (or benefits).

targeting a range of distinguishable concepts that appertain to whether the recipients of social security benefits are those intended and the extent to which expenditure is used as anticipated.

targeting efficiency see **vertical targeting efficiency** and **horizontal targeting efficiency.**

tax allowance a stipulated amount of income that is not taxed (or is taxable at a differentially low rate) which serves to reduce a person's tax liability.

tax credit nominal or actual payments made to taxpayers by the tax authority.

tax threshold the income at which tax begins to be levied.

team working organizational form in which staff work together in small groups to process claims (or otherwise deal with clients). Clients may often be grouped by geographic area (patch working) or by family name ('alpha splits').

technical efficiency measure of the extent to which an objective is attained with the optimum combination of resources (and the associated concept).

territorial justice equal treatment irrespective of place of abode.

territorial redistribution the transfer of income between individuals living in different geographical areas.

Theil index a measure of inequality that can be decomposed to distinguish between inequality occurring between groups or regions and that existing within them.

transaction costs from the perspective of (potential) applicants, the effort and hassle associated with claiming benefit.

underclass a community or group with norms and interests that are antithetical and unacceptable to members of the wider society.

unemployment trap the situation in which the disposable income available from working is not significantly greater than that achieved when receiving out-of-work benefits.

unit of assessment the unit comprising one or more people for which resources and needs are measured and adequacy assessed.

universalism: system under which benefits are available to all in prescribed circumstances irrespective of their particular characteristics such as income and social position; also ideology that believes in the superiority of universalism over other modes of benefit allocation.

unweighted horizontal redistribution: horizontal redistribution measured by comparing post-tax income with original income without applying equivalence scales.

user efficiency obtaining the maximum benefit for the minimum effort (defined from the perspective of applicants).

utility satisfaction gained from consumption of any kind: financial, social, time etc.

vertical targeting efficiency the proportion of benefit recipients who are actually eligible for the benefit. The prefix *internal* or *external* indicates that it is measured with respect to **internal** or **external objectives.**

weighted horizontal redistribution: horizontal redistribution measured by comparing of equivalized post-tax income with equivalized original income.

welfare variously taken to relate to the goals of a social security system; to utility (individual and summed across all people in a jurisdiction); and to measures of the performance of social security systems and schemes or programmes.

welfare to work (programme) an Anglo-Saxon term for an activation programme.

work disincentives the reduction in the additional income, personal utility and/or welfare accruing from (extra) paid work due to the existence of social security, and associated economic signals.

work-first policies: activation policies that prioritize work and work experience over prior training.

workfare schemes in which receipt of **social assistance** is made conditional upon participation in specified programmes of work or work experience; the term is sometimes restricted to schemes that require claimants to work in return for benefit.

Bibliography

ABI (2002) The Association of British Insurers at www.abi.org.uk.

ABS (2003) Economic resources – income distribution: taxes and government benefits, the effect on household income, in *Australian Social Trends 2003*. Canberra: Australian Bureau of Statistics.

Adema, W., Gray, D. and Kahl, S. (2003) *Social Assistance in Germany*. Paris: OECD Labour Market and Social Policy Occasional Paper No. 58.

Adler, M. and Henman, P. (2001) e-justice: a comparative study of computerisation and procedural justice in social security, *International Review of Law, Computers and Technology*, 15(2): 195–212.

AH (2000) *The American Heritage Dictionary of the English Language*, 4th edn. Boston, MA: Houghton Mifflin.

ANAO (2001) *Learning for Skills and Knowledge – Customer Service Officers*. Canberra: Australian National Audit Office.

Andersen, J.G. (2002) *Different Routes to Improved Employment in Europe*. Presentation to a seminar on Interaction Between Labour Market and Social Protection, European Foundation for the Improvement of Living and Working Conditions, Brussels, 16 May.

Andrade, C. (2002) The economics of welfare participation and welfare stigma: a review, *Public Finance and Management*, 2(2): 294–333.

Arts, W. and Gelissen, J. (2002) Three worlds of welfare capitalism or more? A state of the art report, *Journal of European Social Policy*, 12(2): 137–58.

Ashworth, K., Cebulla, A., Greenberg, D. and Walker, R. (2004a) Meta-evaluation: discovering what works best in welfare provision, *Evaluation*, forthcoming.

Ashworth, K., Cebulla, A., Davis, A., Greenberg, D. and Walker, R. (2004b) *Welfare-to-Work: What Britain Should Have Learned from the US*. Aldershot: Gower.

Aspalter, C. (ed.) (2003) *Neoliberalism and the Australian Welfare State*. Hong Kong: Casa Verde.

Atkinson, A.B. (1970) On the measurement of inequality, *Journal of Economic Theory*, 2: 244–63.

Atkinson, T., Cantillon, B., Marlier, E. and Nolan, B. (2002) *Social Indicators: The EU and Social Inclusion*. Oxford: Oxford University Press.

Autor, D.H. and Duggan, M.G. (2003) The rise in the disability rolls and the decline in unemployment, *Quarterly Journal of Economics*, 118(1): 157–205.

Bane, M.J. and Ellwood, D. (1983) *The Dynamics of Dependency: The Routes to Self-sufficiency*. Cambridge, MA: Urban Systems Research and Engineering Inc.

Banks, J. and Johnson, P. (1993) *Children and Household Living Standards*. London: Institute for Fiscal Studies.

Bartik, T.J. (1995) *Using Performance Indicators to Improve the Effectiveness of Welfare-to-Work Programs*. Kalamazoo: UpJohn Institute Staff Working Paper.

Barton, A. (2002) *Unfair and Underfunded: CAB Evidence on What's Wrong with the Social Fund*. London: National Association of Citizens Advice Bureaux.

Bateman, H. and Piggott, J. (2001) *Australia's Mandatory Retirement Saving Policy: A View from the New Millennium*. Washington, DC: The World Bank, Social Protection Discussion Paper Series No. 108.

BDG (2001) *Lebenslagen in Deutschland: Der erste Armuts- und Reichtumsbericht der Bundesregierung*, Berlin: Bundesregierung.

Beck, U. (1992) *Risk Society: Towards a New Modernity*. London: Sage.

Becker, S. (2003) 'Security for those who cannot': Labour's neglected welfare principle, in J. Millar (ed.) *Understanding Social Security: Issues for Policy and Practice*, pp. 103–22. Bristol: Policy Press.

Behrendt, C. (2002) *At the Margins of the Welfare State: Social Assistance and the Alleviation of Poverty in Germany, Sweden and the United Kingdom*. Aldershot: Ashgate.

Beltram, G. (1984) *Testing the Safety Net*. London: Bedford Square Press.

Bennett, F. and Walker, R. (1998) *Working with Work*. York: YPS for the Joseph Rowntree Foundation.

Bernstein, J., Brocht, C. and Spade-Aguilar, M. (2000) *How Much is Enough: Basic Family Budgets for Working Families*. Washington, DC: Economic Policy Institute.

Berthoud, R. and Kempson, E. (1992) *Credit and Debt: The PSI Report*. London: Policy Studies Institute.

Besley, T. and Coate, S. (1992) Understanding welfare stigma: taxpayer resentment and statistical discrimination, *Journal of Public Economics*, 48: 165–83.

Birkmaier, U. and Laster, D. (1999) *Are Mutual Insurers an Endangered Species?* Zurich: Swiss Reinsurance Company, Sigma series.

Blair, T. (1999) Beveridge revisited: a welfare state for the 21st century, in R. Walker (ed.) *Ending Child Poverty: Popular Welfare for the 21st Century*, pp. 7–18. Bristol: Policy Press.

Blank, R.M. and Ruggles, P. (1996) When do women use Aid to Families with Dependent Children and Food Stamps? The dynamics of eligibility versus participation, *Journal of Human Resources*, 31(1): 57–89.

Blank, R.M., Card, D.E. and Robins, P.K. (2000) Financial incentives for increasing work and income among low-income families, in R.M. Blank and D.E. Card (eds) *Finding Jobs: Work and Welfare Reform*, pp. 373–419. New York: Russell Sage Foundation.

Bloom, H., Hill, C.J. and Riccio, J.S. (2003) Linking program implementation and effectiveness: lessons from a pooled sample of welfare-to-work experiments, *Journal of Policy Analysis and Management*, 22(4): 551–76.

Blundell, R., Fry, V. and Walker, I. (1988) Modelling the take-up of means-tested benefits: the case of Housing Benefit, *The Economic Journal*, 98: 58–74.

Bolderson, H. and Mabbett, D. (1997) *Delivering Social Security: A Cross-national Study*. London: HMSO, Department of Social Security, Research Report No. 59.

Borjas, G.J. (2001) Welfare reform and immigration, in R. Blank and R. Haskins (eds) *The New World of Welfare*, pp. 369–85. Washington, DC: Brookings Institute Press.

Bottomley, D., McKay, S. and Walker, R. (1997) *Unemployment and Jobseeking*. London: HMSO, Department of Social Security, Research Report No. 62.

Boushey, H., Brocht, C., Gunderson, B. and Bernstein, J. (2001) *Hardships in America: The Real Story of Working Families*. Washington, DC: Economic Policy Institute.

Bradbury, B., Jenkins, S.P. and Micklewright, J. (2001) *The Dynamics of Child Poverty in Industrialized Countries*. Cambridge: Cambridge University Press.

Bradshaw, J. (ed.) (2001) *Poverty: The Outcomes for Children*. London: Family Policy Studies Centre.

Bradshaw, J. and Finch, N. (2002) *A Comparison of Child Benefit Packages in 22 Countries*. London: Department for Work and Pensions, Research Report No. 174.

Bradshaw, J. et al. (1996) *Employment of Lone Parents: A Comparison of Policy in Twenty Countries*. London: Family Policy Research Centre.

Bradshaw, J. et al. (2000) *Lone Parenthood in the 1990s: New Challenges, New Responses?* Paper presented at the International Social Security Association conference 'Social Security in a Global Village', Helsinki, September.

Brewer, M. and Gregg, P. (2003) Eradicating child poverty in Britain: welfare reform and children since 1997, in R. Walker and M. Wiseman (eds) *The Welfare We Want*, pp. 81–114. Bristol: Policy Press.

Broadway, R.W. and Bruce, N. (1984) *Welfare Economics*. Oxford: Blackwell.

Brown, A., Buck, M.L. and Skinner, E. (1998) *How to Involve Employers in Welfare Reform*. New York: Manpower Demonstration Research Corporation.

Bryson, A. and Kasporova, D. (2003) *Profiling Benefit Claimants in Britain: A Feasibility Study*. London: HMSO, Department of Social Security, Research Report No. 196.

Buechs, M. (2003) *The Open Method of Co-ordination as a Model of European Social Policy: The Effects of the European Employment Strategy on Labour Market Policy in Germany and the United Kingdom*. Paper presented at the young researchers' workshop of the ESPA net and the Marie Curie Training Site, Stirling, 16–17 May.

Buhr, P. and Weber, A. (1998) Social assistance and social change in Germany, in L. Leisering and R. Walker (eds) *The Dynamics of Modern Society: Poverty, Policy and Welfare*, pp. 189–98. Bristol: Policy Press.

Burchardt, T. (2003) Disability, capability and social exclusion, in J. Millar (ed.) *Understanding Social Security: Issues for Policy and Practice*, pp. 145–66. Bristol: Policy Press.

Burchardt, T. and Hills, J. (1997) *Private Welfare, Insurance and Social Security: Pushing the Boundaries.* York: York Publishing Services and Joseph Rowntree Foundation.

Calandrino, M. (2003) *Low-Income and Deprivation in British Families.* London: Department for Work and Pensions, Working Paper No. 10.

Callan, T., Nolan, B. and Whelan, C.T. (1993) Resources, deprivation and the measurement of poverty, *Journal of Social Policy*, 22(2): 141–72.

Cantillon, B. (1998) *Poverty in Advanced Economies: Trends and Policy Issues.* Florence: European University Institute, conference paper No. WS/11.

Castles, F. (1996) Needs based strategies of social protection in Australia and New Zealand, in G. Esping-Andersen (ed.) *Welfare States in Transition*, pp. 88–115. London: Sage.

Castles, F.G. (2001) On the political economy of recent public sector development, *Journal of European Social Policy*, 11(3): 195–211.

CBO (2003) *Utilization of Tax Incentives for Retirement Saving.* Washington, DC: Congressional Budget Office.

Cebulla, A. (2002) *The Road to Britain's New Deal.* Paper presented at a UK/US 'Workshop on Welfare to Work' funded by the Economic and Social Research Council and Rockefeller Foundation, London, 10–11 January.

Cebulla, A. and Ford, J. (2000) Confronting unemployment: families' management of risk in a flexible labour market, *Risk and Human Behaviour*, (8): 2–6.

Centrelink (2003) Fraud statistics: www.centrelink.gov.au/internet/internet.nsf/about_us/fraud-stats.htm, accessed 12 August 2003.

Citro, C. and Michael, R. (1995) *Measuring Poverty: A New Approach.* Washington, DC: National Academy Press.

Clasen, J. and Freeman, R. (eds) (1994) *Social Policy in Germany.* Hemel Hempstead: Harvester.

Clasen, J., Gould, A. and Vincent, J. (1998) *Voices Within and Without: Responses to Long-term Unemployment in Germany, Sweden and Britain.* Bristol: Policy Press.

Clayton, R. and Pontusson, J. (1998) Welfare state retrenchment revisited, *World Politics*, 51(1): 67–98.

Cm. (1998) *Beating Fraud is Everyone's Business: Securing the Future*, Cm. 4012. London: The Stationery Office.

Cm. (2001) *Opportunity for All: Making Progress, Third Annual Report*, Cm. 5260. London: The Stationery Office.

Cm. (2003) *Department for Work and Pensions, Departmental Report 2003*, Cm. 5921. London: The Stationery Office.

Cmnd. (1942) *Social Insurance and Allied Service*, Cmnd. 6404s (The Beveridge Report). London: HMSO.

Corden, A. (1995) *Changing Perspectives on Benefit Take-Up.* London: HMSO.

Corden, A. (1999) Claiming entitlements: take-up of benefits, in J. Ditch (ed.) *Introduction to Social Security*, pp. 134–55. London: Routledge.

Costello, M., Davies, V., Johnson, C., Sirett, L. and Taylor, J. (2002) *Qualitative Research with Clients: Longer Term Experiences of a Work-focused Service.* London: Department for Work and Pensions, Research Report No. 171.

Coudouel, A., Henstchel, J.S. and Wodon, Q.T. (2001) Poverty measurement and analysis, in *Poverty Reduction Strategy Sourcebook: Volume 1: Core*

Techniques and Cross-cutting Issues, pp. 29–74. Washington, DC: The World Bank.

Craig, P. (1991) Costs and benefits: a review of research on non-take-up of income-related benefits, *Journal of Social Policy*, 20(4): 537–65.

Cubbitt, R.P. and Sugden, R. (2001) Dynamic decision-making under uncertainty: an experimental investigation of choices between accumulator gambles, *Journal of Risk and Uncertainty*, 22: 103–28.

Curry, C. and O'Connell, A. (2003) *The Pension Landscape*. London: Pensions Policy Institute.

Dawes, L. (1993) *Long-term Unemployment and Labour Market Flexibility*. Leicester: Centre for Labour Market Studies.

Deacon, A. (2002) *Perspectives on Welfare*. Buckingham: Open University Press.

Dean, H. and Melrose, M. (1997) Manageable discord: fraud and resistance in the social security system, *Social Policy and Administration*, 31(2): 103–18.

DeFina, R.H. and Thanawala, K. (2002) *International Evidence on the Impact of Transfers and Taxes on Alternative Poverty Indexes*. Luxembourg: Luxembourg Income Study, Working Paper No. 325.

Dekkte, D. (2001) *Germany's New Immigration Policy*. Washington, DC: Friedrich Ebert Foundation.

DH (1998a) *Independent Inquiry into Inequalities in Health: Report* (Chairman: Sir Donald Acheson). London: Department of Health.

DH (1998b) *Caring About Carers: A National Strategy for Carers*. London: Department of Health.

Dickens, R. (2002) Is welfare to work sustainable?, *Benefits*, 10(2): 87–92.

Dilnot, A. and Walker, I. (1989) Introduction: economic issues in social security, in A. Dilnot and I. Walker (eds) *The Economics of Social Security*, pp. 1–15. Oxford: Oxford University Press.

Ditch, J. and Oldfield, N. (1999) Social assistance: recent trends and themes, *Journal of European Social Policy*, 9(1): 65–76.

Dobson, B., Beardsworth, A., Keil, T. and Walker, R. (1994) *Diet, Choice and Poverty*. London: Family Policy Studies Centre.

DoL (2003) *A Chartbook of International Labor Comparisons: United States, Europe, Asia*. Washington, DC: US Department of Labor.

Donnison, D. (1982) *The Politics of Poverty*. Oxford: Martin Robertson.

Doron, A. (2001) Retrenchment and progressive targeting: the Israeli experience, in N. Gilbert (ed.) *Targeting Social Benefits: International Perspectives and Trends*, pp. 99–128. New Brunswick: Transaction Publishers, International Social Security Association.

Dorsett, R. and Headey, C. (1991) The take-up of means-tested benefits by working families with children, *Fiscal Studies*, 12(4): 22–32.

DSS (1998) *Beating Fraud is Everyone's Business: Securing the Future*. London: Department of Social Security.

Duclos, J.-Y. (1997) Estimating and testing a model of welfare participation: the case of supplementary benefits in Britain, *Economica*, 64: 81–100.

Duerr Berrick, J. (1995) *Faces of Poverty: Portraits of Women and Children on Welfare*. New York: Oxford University Press.

Duvå, V. (1976) Social welfare, in M.K. Bjorsen and E. Hansen (eds) *Facts About Denmark*. Copenhagen: Politikens Forlag.

DWP (2003a) *Measuring Child Poverty*. London: Department for Work and Pensions.

DWP (2003b) *Jobcentre Plus to Spearhead Drive for Local Jobsearch Solutions*. London: Department for Work and Pensions, press release, 9 April.

DWP (2004) *Fraud and Abuse in Income Support and Jobseeker's Allowance from April 2002 to March 2003*. London: Department for Work and Pensions, Information and Analysis Directorate.

Eardley, T., Bradshaw, J., Ditch, J., Gough, I. and Whiteford, P. (1996) *Social Assistance in OECD Countries*. London: Department of Social Security, Research Reports Nos 46 and 47 (two vols).

EC (2001) *Social Protection in the EU Member States and the European Economic Area 2001*. Luxembourg: Office for Official Publications of the European Communities.

Eklind, B. and Löfbom, E. (2002) *Reducing the Need for Social Assistance by Fifty Per Cent – A Goal for Sweden Between 1999 and 2004*. Paper presented at 27th Annual Conference of the International Association for Research in Income and Wealth, Stockholm, 18–24 August.

Ellwood, D. (1986) *Targeting 'Would-be' Long-term Recipients of AFDC*. Princeton, NJ: Mathematical Policy Research Inc.

Ellwood, D. (1988) *Poor Support*. New York: Basic Books.

Emmerson, C. and Tanner, S. (2000) A note on the tax treatment of private pensions and individual savings accounts, *Fiscal Studies*, 21(1): 65–74.

Engel, E. (1895) Die Lebenskosten belgischer Arbeiterfamilien frueher und jetzt. Ermittelt aus Familienhaushaltsrechnungen und vergleichend zusammengestellt, *Bulletin of the International Institute of Statistics*, (9): 57.

Esaiasson, P. and Heidar, K. (eds) (2000) *Beyond Westminster and Congress – The Nordic Experience*. Columbus, OH: Ohio State University Press.

Esping-Andersen, G. (1990) *The Three Worlds of Welfare Capitalism*. Princeton, NJ: Princeton University Press.

Esping-Andersen, G. (1999) *Social Foundations of Post-industrial Economies*. Oxford: Oxford University Press.

Eurostat (2003) *Social Protection Expenditure in Europe*. Luxembourg: Eurostat News Release STAT/03/17, 13 February.

FaCS (2003) *The Australian Government Department of Family and Community Services Annual Report 2002–03*. Canberra: Government Department of Family and Community Services.

Falkingham, J. and Hills, J. (1995) *The Dynamic of Welfare: The Welfare State and the Life Cycle*. Hemel Hempstead: Prentice Hall/Harvester Wheatsheaf.

Ferrera, M. (1996) The southern model of welfare in social Europe, *Journal of European Social Policy*, 6(1): 17–37.

Ferrera, M., Matsaganis, M. and Sacchi, S. (2002) Open coordination against poverty: the new EU 'social inclusion process', *Journal of European Social Policy*, 12(3): 227–39.

Field, F. (1995) *Making Welfare Work*. London: Institute of Community Studies.

Field, F. (1998) *Benefit Fraud is Theft from the Nation*. London: Department of Social Security, press release, 13 July.

Fitzpatrick, T. (1999) *Freedom and Security: An Introduction to the Basic Income Debate*. Houndsmill: Macmillan Press.

Fitzpatrick, T. (2003) Cash transfers, in J. Baldock, N. Manning and S. Vickerstaff (eds) *Social Policy*, pp. 329–61. Oxford: Oxford University Press.

Forster, M. and Pearson, M. (2002) *Income Distribution and Poverty in the OECD Area: Trends and Driving Forces*. Paris: OECD, Occasional Studies No. 34.

Friedman, M. (1962) *Capitalism and Freedom*. Chicago: Chicago University Press.

Fukuyama, F. (1992) *The End of History and the Last Man*. New York: Free Press.

Fulcher, J. and Scott, J. (2003) *Sociology*, 2nd edn. Oxford: Oxford University Press.

Fultz, E. and Ruck, M. (2001) Pension reform in central and eastern Europe: emerging issues and patterns, *International Labour Review*, 140(1): 19–43.

Gallagher, L.J., Uccello, C.E., Pierce, A.B. and Reidy, E.B. (1999) *State General Assistance Programs 1998*. Washington, DC: Urban Institute.

GAO (1999) *Food Assistance: Efforts of Control Fraud and Abuse in the WC Program can be Strengthened*. Washington, DC: Report to Congressional Committees by the US General Accounting Office, GAO/RCED-99-224.

Giannarelli, L. and Wiseman, M. (2000) *The Working Poor and the Benefit Door*. Washington, DC: George Washington University.

Giddens, A. (1990) *The Consequences of Modernity*. Cambridge: Polity Press.

Giddens, A. (1991) *Modernity and Self-Identity*. Cambridge: Polity Press.

Gilbert, N. (ed.) (2001) *Targeting Social Benefits: International Perspectives and Trends*. Somerset, NJ: Transaction Publishers, International Social Security Association.

Gilbert, N. and Parent, A. (eds) (2004) *Welfare Reform: A Comparative Assessment of the French and US Experiences*. Somerset, NJ: Transaction Publishers.

Gill, S. (1990) *American Hegemony and the Trilateral Commission*. Cambridge: Cambridge University Press.

Golonka, S. (1999) *Designing One-Stop Career Centers*. Washington, DC: National Governors Association.

Goodin, R., Headey, B., Muffels, R. and Dirvan, H.-J. (1999) *The Real Worlds of Welfare Capitalism*. Cambridge: Cambridge University Press.

Gordon, D. and Pantazis, C. (1997) *Breadline Britain in the 1990s*. Aldershot: Ashgate.

Gordon, D. *et al.* (2000) *Poverty and Social Exclusion in Britain*. York: Joseph Rowntree Foundation.

Gray, J. (1998) *False Dawn: The Delusions of Global Capitalism*. New York: Simon & Schuster.

Green, H., Marsh, A., Connolly, H. and Payne, J. (2003) *The Medium-term Effects of Compulsory Participation in ONE*. London: Department for Work and Pensions, Research Report No. 183.

Greenberg, D. and Schroder, M. (1997) *Digest of Social Experiments*, 2nd edn. Washington, DC: Urban Institute Press.

Greenberg, D., Mandell, M. and Onstott, M. (2000) The dissemination and utilization of welfare-to-work experiments in state policymaking, *Journal of Policy Analysis and Management*, 19(3): 367–82.

Greenberg, D., Ashworth, K., Cebulla, A. and Walker, R. (2004) Do welfare-to-work programmes work for long? *Fiscal Studies*, forthcoming.

Greider, W. (1997) *One World Ready or Not: The Manic Logic of Global Capitalism*. New York: Simon & Schuster.

Greiner, D. (2000) Atypical work in the European Union, in Danny Pieters (ed.) *Yearbook of the European Institute of Social Security, 1999*, pp. 45–62. London: Kluwer Law International.

Gustafsson, B. (2002) Assessing non-use of social assistance, *European Journal of Social Work*, 5(2): 149–58.

Gustafsson, B. and Voges, W. (1998) Contrasting welfare dynamics: Germany and Sweden, in L. Leisering and R. Walker (eds) *The Dynamics of Modern Society: Poverty, Policy and Welfare*, pp. 243–63. Bristol: Policy Press.

Hagenaars, A., de Vos, K. and Zaidi, A. (1994) *Poverty Statistics in the Late 1980s.* Luxembourg: Eurostat.

Haines, F. (1999) *A Few White Lies.* York: Unpublished MA dissertation, University of York.

Hales, J., Taylor, R. Mandy, W. and Miller, M. (2003) *Evaluation of Employment Zones.* Sheffield: Department for Work and Pensions.

Halleröd, B. (1994) *A New Approach to the Direct Measurement of Consensual Poverty.* Sydney: Social Policy Research Centre Working Paper No. 50, University of New South Wales.

Hamilton, G. (2002) *Moving People from Welfare to Work: Lessons from the National Evaluation of Welfare-to-Work Strategies.* New York: MDRC.

Hancock, R. (2003) *Pensions Policy: The Principles and Practice.* Paper presented to the Department for Work and Pensions Summer School, Cambridge, July.

Hanesch, W. (1998) The debate on reforms of social assistance in Western Europe, in M. Heillila (ed.) *Linking Welfare and Work.* Dublin: European Foundation for the Improvement of Living and Working Conditions.

Hansmann, H. (1998) *The Ownership of Enterprise.* Cambridge: Harvard University Press.

Hantrais, L. (1996) France: 'squaring the welfare triangle', in V. George and P. Taylor-Gooby (eds) *European Welfare Policy*, pp. 51–70. Basingstoke: Macmillan.

Harding, A., Lloyd, R. and Greenwell, H. (2001) *Disadvantage in Australia 1990–2000: The Persistence of Poverty in a Decade of Growth.* Camperdown: The Smith Family.

Hartfree, E., Kellard, K., Adelman, L. and Middleton, S. (2001) Budgetary requirements for disabled people in Jersey, *Briefings*, 17: 3–4 (Loughborough University).

Hayek, von F.A. (1949) *Individualism and Economic Order.* London: Routledge & Kegan Paul.

Hedges, A. and Thomas, A. (1994) *Making a Claim for Disability Benefits.* London: Department of Social Security, Social Research Branch.

Hill, M. (1990) *Social Security Policy in Britain.* London: Edward Elgar.

Hills, J. (2001) Poverty and social security: What rights? Whose responsibilities?, in R. Jowell *et al.* (eds) *British Social Attitudes: The 18th Report.* London: Sage.

Hirsch, D. (2000) *A Credit to Children: The UK's Radical Reform of Children's Benefits in an International Perspective.* York: Joseph Rowntree Foundation and YPS.

Hirst, P. and Thompson, G. (1996) *Globalization in Question: The International Economy and the Possibilities of Governance.* Cambridge: Polity Press.

HM Treasury (1998) *The Working Families Tax Credit (WFTC) and Work Incentives: The Modernisation of Britain's Tax and Benefit System, 3.* London: HM Treasury.

HM Treasury (1999) www.hm-treasury.gov.uk/docs/1999/creditunion.html.

Holloway, J. (1981) *Social Policy: Harmonisation in the European Community.* Farnborough: Gower.

Holman, B. (ed.) (1998) *Faith in the Poor.* Oxford: Lion Publishing.

Holtzer, H. (2002) Employers and welfare recipients: what their interactions imply for public policy, *Focus*, 22(1): 71–5.

Holtzmann, R., MacKellar, L. and Rutkowski, M. (2003a) Accelerating the European pension reform agenda: need, progress and conceptual underpinnings, in R. Holtzmann, M. Orenstein and M. Rutkowski (eds) *Pension Reform in Europe: Process and Progress*, pp. 1–45. Washington, DC: The World Bank.

Holtzmann, R., Sherburne-Benz, L. and Tesliuc, E. (2003b) *Social Risk Management: The World Bank's Approach to Social Protection in a Globalizing World.* Washington, DC: The World Bank.

Horn, W.F., Blankenhorn, D. and Pearlstein, M.B. (1998) *The Fatherhood Movement: A Call to Action.* Lanham, MD: Lexington Books.

Hort, S. (2001) From a generous to a stingy welfare state? in N. Gilbert (ed.) *Targeting Social Benefits: International Perspectives and Trends*, pp. 187–210. New Brunswick: Transaction Publishers.

Houthakker, H.S. (1957) An international comparison of household expenditure patterns: commemorating the century of Engel's Law, *Econometrica*, 25: 532.

Howard, M. (2003) *An 'Interactionist' Perspective on Barriers and Bridges to Work for Disabled People.* London: IPPR. http://www.ippr.org.uk/research/files/team24/project90/Marilyn%20Paper%20Final.pdf

Howard, P. (2003) *The Promise and Performance of Mutual Obligation.* Canberra: Australian National University, PhD thesis.

Huby, M. and Walker, R. (1989) Social security spending in the inner cities, *Public Money and Management* (9)1: 39–43.

Hvinden, B. (1999) Activation: a Nordic perspective, in M. Heikkila (ed.) *Linking Welfare and Work.* Dublin: European Foundation for the Improvement of Living and Working Conditions.

ILO (2000) *World Labour Report, 2000.* Geneva: International Labour Office.

ILO (2003) *ILO Statistical Databases.* Geneva: International Labour Office, http://www.ilo.org/public/English/bureau/stat/info/dbases.htm.

ISSA (2003) *Social Security Worldwide.* Geneva: International Social Security Association, http://www-ssw.issa.int/sswen.

Jacobs, D. (2000) *Low Inequality with Low Redistribution? Analysis of Income Distribution in Japan, South Korea and Taiwan Compared to Britain.* London: Centre for the Analysis of Social Exclusion, CASE paper No. 33.

Jawad, R. (2002) A profile of social welfare in Lebanon: assessing the implications for social development policy, *Global Social Policy*, 2(3): 319–35.

Jenkins, S. and Millar, J. (1989) Income risk and income maintenance: implications for incentives to work, in A. Dilnot and I. Walker (eds) *The Economics of Social Security*, pp. 137–52. Oxford: Oxford University Press.

Jenkins, S.P. (1991) Income inequality and living standards: changes in the 1970s and 1980s, *Fiscal Studies*, (12)1: 1–28.

Jessop, B. (1993) Towards a Schumpterian workfare state? Preliminary remarks on a post-Fordist political economy, *Studies in Political Economy*, 40: 7–19.

Jones, M. (1996) *The Australian Welfare State: Evaluating Social Policy*. St Leonards, NSW: Allen & Unwin.

Jordan, B. (1985) *The State: Authority and Autonomy*. Oxford: Blackwell.

Jung, Y. and Shin, D.-M. (2002) Social protection in South Korea, in A. Erfried, M. van Hauff and M. John (eds) *Social Protection in Southeast and East Asia*, pp. 269–312. Singapore: Friedrich Ebert Stiftung Project.

Kautto, M., Fritzell, J., Hvinden, B., Kvist, J. and Uusitalo, H. (2001) *Nordic Welfare States in the European Context*. London: Routledge.

Kellard, K. (2002) Job retention and advancement in the UK: a developing agenda, *Benefits*, (10)2: 93–8.

Kellard, K. (2003) Changing delivery: wired-up welfare, in J. Millar (ed.) *Understanding Social Security: Issues for Policy and Practice*, pp. 297–315. Bristol: Policy Press.

Kelleher, J. *et al.* (2002) *Delivering a Work-Focused Service: Interim Findings from ONE Case Studies and Staff Research*. London: Department for Work and Pensions, in-house report No. 84.

Kempson, E. (1996) *Life on a Low Income*. York: York Publishing Service.

Kempson, E., Bryson, A. and Rowlingson, K. (1994) *Hard Times? How Poor Families Make Ends Meet*. London: Policy Studies Institute.

Kerr, S. (1982) Deciding about supplementary pensions, *Journal of Social Policy*, 11(4): 505–17.

Kim, H. (2000) Anti-poverty effectiveness of taxes and income transfers in welfare states, *International Social Security Review*, 53: 105–29.

Kim, M. (2003) *Social Security and Social Safety Nets in Korea*. Washington, DC: The World Bank.

King, R. (1990) The social and economic geography of labour migration: from guestworkers to immigrants, in D. Pinder (ed.) *Western Europe: Challenge and Change*. London: Belhaven.

Klumpes, P.J.M. and McCrae, M. (2000) *Short-termism in the Performance Management of Pension-Funds: UK Evidence*. Paper presented at the European Accounting Association Annual Congress, Munich.

Knapp, M. (1984) *The Economics of Social Care*. London: MacMillan.

Krause, P. (1998) Low income dynamics in unified Germany, in L. Leisering and R. Walker (eds) *The Dynamics of Modern Society: Poverty, Policy and Welfare*, pp. 161–80. Bristol: Policy Press.

Kwon, H.-J. (2002) Welfare reform and future challenges in the Republic of Korea: beyond the developmental welfare state, *International Social Security Review*, 55(4): 23–38.

Kwung-Suk, I. (1998) *The Korean Welfare State: Ideals and Realities*. Seoul: Nanam Publishing Corp.

Lakin, C. (2003) The effects of taxes and benefits on household income, *Economic Trends*, (594): 33–79.

Lange, T. and Shackleton, J.R. (eds) (1998) *The Political Economy of German Unification*. Oxford: Berghahn.

Layte, R., Nolan, B. and Whelan, C.T. (2001) *Reassessing Income and Deprivation: Approaches to the Measurement of Poverty*. Dublin: ESRI.

Le Grand, J. (1999) Conceptions of social justice, in R. Walker (ed.) *Ending Child Poverty: Popular Welfare for the 21st Century*, pp. 65–7. Bristol: Policy Press.

Lee, W.R. and Rosenhaft, E. (eds) (1997) *State, Social Policy and Social Change in Germany, 1880–1994*, 2nd edn. New York: Berg.

Legard, R. *et al.* (2002) *Evaluation of the Capability Report: Identifying the Work-related Capabilities of Incapacity Benefits Claimants*. London: Department for Work and Pensions, Research Report No. 162.

Leibfried, S. (1992) Towards a European welfare state: on integrating poverty regimes in the European Community, in Z. Ferge and J.E. Kolberg (eds) *Social Policy in a Changing Europe*, pp. 245–80. Frankfurt: Campus Verlag.

Leisering, L. and Leibfried, S. (1999) *Time and Poverty in Western Welfare States: United Germany in Perspective*. Cambridge: Cambridge University Press.

Leisering, L. and Walker, R. (eds) (1998) *The Dynamics of Modern Society: Poverty, Policy and Welfare*. Bristol: Policy Press.

Lewis, J. *et al.* (2000) *Lone Parents and Personal Advisers: Roles and Relationships*. London: Department of Social Security, Research Report No. 122.

LII (2003) *Tort Law: An Overview*, http://www.law.cornell.edu/topics/torts.html.

Lipsky, M. (1980) *Street-level Bureaucracy: Dilemmas of the Individual in Public Services*. New York: Russell Sage Foundation.

Lødemel, I. and Trickey, H. (eds) (2001) *'An Offer You Can't Refuse': Workfare in an International Perspective*. Bristol: Policy Press.

Loumidis, J. *et al.* (2001) *Evaluation of the New Deal for Disabled People Personal Adviser Pilot*. London: Department of Social Security, Research Report No. 144.

Mack, J. and Lansley, S. (1985) *Poor Britain*. London: Allen & Unwin.

Marmor, T.R. and De Jong, P.R. (eds) (1998) *Ageing, Social Security and Affordability*. Aldershot: Ashgate, Foundation for International Studies on Social Security.

Marmor, T.R., Mashaw, J.L. and Harvey, P.L. (1990) *America's Misunderstood Welfare State: Persistent Myths, Enduring Realities*. New York: Basic Books.

Marshall, T.H. and Bottomore, T. (1992) *Citizenship and Social Class*. London: Pluto Press.

McClements, L. (1978) *The Economics of Social Security*. London: Heinemann.

McConnell, S. and Ohls, J. (2000) *Food Stamps in Rural America: Special Issues and Common Themes*. Paper presented at the 'Rural Dimensions of Welfare Reform' Conference, Washington, DC, 4 May.

McDonald, M.K. (1997) *Poverty Measurement and Poverty Statistics in Australia*. Paper presented at a seminar on 'Poverty Statistics', Santiago, 7–9 May.

McKay, S. and Rowlingson, K. (1999) *Social Security in Britain*. Houndmills: Macmillan.

McKay, S., Walker, R. and Youngs, R. (1997) *Unemployment and Jobseeking Before Jobseeker's Allowance*. London: Department of Social Security, Research Report No. 73.

McKay, S., Smith, A., Youngs, R. and Walker, R. (1999) *Unemployment and Jobseeking After the Introduction of Jobseeker's Allowance*. London: Department of Social Security, Research Report No. 87.

McLaughlin, E., Yeates, N. and Kelly, G. (2002) *Social Protection and Units of Analysis, Issues and Reforms: A Comparative Perspective*. London: TUC, Welfare Reform Series No. 44.

Mead, L. (1986) *Beyond Entitlement*. New York: Free Press.

Mead, L. (1992) *The New Politics of Poverty*. New York: Basic Books.

Mead, L. (1998) *The New Welfare: Diversion, Sanctions, Time Limits*. Paper delivered at a conference on 'Welfare Reform: What Happens After Time Limits, Sanctions, and Diversions', Welfare Reform Academy, Washington, DC, 6 February.

Mead, L. (2001) Welfare reform in Wisconsin: the local role, *Administration and Society*, 33(5): 523–54.

Mead, L. (2003) *State Governmental Capacity and Welfare Reform*. Paper presented at the Fall Conference of the Association of Policy Analysis and Management, Washington, DC, 6–8 November.

Middleton, S. (2000) Agreeing poverty lines: the development of consensual budget standard methodology, in J. Bradshaw and R. Sainsbury (eds) *Researching Poverty*, pp. 59–76. Aldershot: Ashgate.

Millar, J. (1998) Reforming welfare: the Australian experience, *Benefits*, 23: 32–4.

Millar, J. (2003) The art of persuasion? The British New Deal for lone parents, in R. Walker and M. Wiseman (eds) *The Welfare We Want*, pp. 115–42. Bristol: Policy Press.

Millar, J. and Rowlingson, K. (2001) *Lone Parents, Employment and Social Policy: Cross-national Comparisons*. Bristol: Policy Press.

Minas, R. and Stenberg, S.-Å. (2000) *På tröskeln till bidrag Mottagningen av nya socialbidragsansökningar på sju socialkontor i Sverige*. Stockholm: Centre for Evaluation of Social Services.

Minford, P. with Davies, D., Peel, M. and Sprague, A. (1983) *Unemployment: Cause and Cure*. Oxford: Martin Robertson.

Moberg, E. (2003) *A Theory of Democratic Politics*, http://www.moberg-publications.se/theory/theory.html.

Moffitt, R. (1983) An economic model of welfare stigma, *American Economic Review*, 73(5): 1023–35.

Mommsen, W.J. (ed.) (1981) *The Emergence of the Welfare State in Britain and Germany, 1850–1950*. London: Croom Helm.

Moore, J. (1989) *The End of the Line*. Speech given by the Secretary of State for Social Security, Greater London Area CPC, 11 May.

Murray, C. (1984) *Losing Ground*. New York: Basic Books.

NAO (2000) *The Cancellation of the Benefits Payment Card Project*, HC 857. London: The Stationery Office.

NAO (2002) *Government on the Web 11*, HC746. London: The Stationery Office.

NAPF (2002) National Association of Pension Funds at www.napf.co.uk.

Nelson, M.K. and Smith, J. (1999) *Working Hard and Making Do*. Berkeley, CA: University of California Press.

Neuberg, L. (1995) *What Defeated a Negative Income Tax? Constructing a Causal Explanation of a Controversial Historical Event*. New York: New York University, Robert F. Wagner Graduate School of Public Service.

Nolan, B. and Whelan, C.T. (1996) *Resources, Deprivation and Poverty*. Oxford: Clarendon Press.

O'Brien, M. and Penna, S. (1998) *Theorising Modernity: Reflexivity, Environment and Identity in Giddens' Social Theory*. London: Longman.

O'Connell, A. (2003) *Guide to State Pension Reform*. London: Pension Policy Institute.

O'Connor, W., Bruce, S. and Ritchie, J. (1999) *New Deal (for Young People): Pathfinder Follow-through, Findings from a Qualitative Study Amongst Individuals*. Sheffield: Employment Service, Research and Development Report ESR29.

OECD (1994) *The OECD Jobs Study: Facts, Analysis, Strategies*. Paris: OECD.

OECD (1996) *Employment Outlook*. Paris: OECD.

OECD (2000) *Labour Market Reform and Social Safety Net Policies in Korea*. Paris: OECD.

OECD (2001a) When money is tight: poverty dynamics in OECD countries, *OECD Employment Outlook*, June: 37–87.

OECD (2001b) The employment of foreigners: outlook and issues in OECD countries, *Employment Outlook*, June: 167–206.

OECD (2002) *Benefits and Wages, OECD Indicators*. Paris: OECD.

OECD (2003a) *Labour Force Statistics 1982–2002*. Paris: OECD.

OECD (2003b) *OECD Social Expenditure Database*. Paris: OECD.

OECD (2003c) *Transforming Disability into Ability: Policies to Promote Work and Income Security for Disabled People*. Paris: OECD.

OECD (2003d) *Employment Outlook*. Paris: OECD.

Olsson, S.E. (1993) *Social Policy and Welfare State in Sweden*. Oslo: Arkiv Forlag.

ONS (2003) *Work and Pension Statistics 2003*. London: Office for National Statistics and Department for Work and Pensions.

Oorschot, W. Van (1994) *Take It or Leave It: A Study of Non-take-up of Social Security Benefits*. Tilburg: Tilburg University Press.

Oorschot, W. Van (1996) Modelling non-take-up, in W. van Oorschot (ed.) *New Perspectives on the Non-take-up of Social Security Benefits*, pp.7–59 Tilburg: Tilburg University Press.

Oorschot, W. Van and Clasen, J. (2003) Classic principles and designs in European social security, in D. Pieters (ed.) *European Social Security and Global Politics*. The Hague: Kluwer Law International.

Orenstein, M.A. (2003) Mapping the diffusion of pension innovation, in R. Holzmann, M. Orenstein and M. Rutkowski (eds) *Pension Reform in Europe: Process and Progress*, pp. 171–93. Washington, DC: The World Bank.

Orr, L.L. (1999) *Social Experiments: Evaluating Public Programs with Experimental Methods*. Thousand Oaks, CA: Sage.

Orshansky, M. (1965) Counting the poor: another look at the poverty profile, *Social Security Bulletin*, 28(1): 3–29.

Osgood, J., Stone, V. and Thomas, A. (2002) *Delivering a Work-Focused Service: Views and Experiences of Clients*. London: Department for Work and Pensions, Research Report No. 167.

Oxley, H., Dang, T.T. and Antolin, P. (2000) Poverty dynamics in six OECD countries, *OECD Economic Studies*, 30: 7–49.

Pahl, R. (1984) *Divisions of Labour*. Oxford: Oxford University Press.

Parker, H. (ed.) (1998) *Low Cost but Acceptable: A Minimum Income Standard for the UK: Families with Young Children*. Bristol: Policy Press.

Peck, J. (2001) *Workfare States*. New York: Guildford Press.

Pelekanos, D. (2000) International social security instruments and alternative work patterns, in D. Pieters (ed.) *Yearbook of the European Institute of Social Security, 1999*, pp. 133–48. London: Kluwer Law International.

Piachaud, D. (1987) Problems in the definition and measurement of poverty, *Journal of Social Policy*, 16(2): 147–64.

Pierson, P. (1996) The new politics of welfare state, *World Politics*, 48(2): 143–79.

Pieters, D. (ed.) (2000) *Yearbook of the European Institute of Social Security, 1999*. London: Kluwer Law International.

Plant, R. (1999) Social justice, in R. Walker (ed.) *Ending Child Poverty: Popular Welfare for the 21st Century*, pp. 55–64. Bristol: Policy Press.

Platt, L. (2003) Social security in a multi-ethnic society, in J. Millar (ed.) *Understanding Social Security: Issues for Policy and Practice*, pp. 255–76. Bristol: Policy Press.

PPG (1998) *We All Need Pensions: The Prospects for Pension Provision*. London: The Stationery Office.

PPI (2003) *State Pension Models*. London: Pension Policy Institute.

Rafferty, A. and Walker, R. (2003) Lone mothers are women third, paid workers third – targeting employment, in D. Thurley (ed.) *Working to Target: Can Policies Deliver Paid Work for Seven in Ten Lone Parents*, pp. 34–41. London: National Council for One Parent Families.

Rainwater, L., Rein, M. and Schwartz, J.E. (1986) *Income Packaging in the Welfare State: A Comparative Study of Family Income*. Oxford: Clarendon Press.

Rangarajan, A. (2002) The road to sustained employment: lessons from a US job retention strategy, *Benefits*, 10(20): 99–104.

Raper, M. (1999) Centerlink – viewed from the community sector, *Australian Journal of Public Administration*, 58(3): 101–8.

Ravallion, M. (1992) *Poverty Comparison: A Guide to Concepts and Methods*. Washington, DC: The World Bank.

Ravishankar, N. (2003) *Regional Redistribution: Applying Data from Household Income Data*. Syracuse: Maxwell School of Citizenship and Public Affairs, Syracuse University, Working Paper No. 347.

Rehme, G. (2001) *Redistribution of Personal Incomes, Education and Economic Performance Across Countries*. Darmstadt: Technische Universtät Darmstadt.

Reich, S. (1998) *What is Globalisation? Four Possible Answers*. Notre Dame: Helen Kellogg Institute for International Studies, University of Notre Dame, Working Paper No. 261.

Rein, M. and Marris, P. (1982) *Dilemmas of Social Reform: Poverty and Community Action in the United States*. Chicago: University of Chicago Press.

Rejda, G.E. (1994) *Social Insurance and Economic Security*. 5th edn. Englewood Cliffs, NJ: Prentice Hall.

Remler, D.K., Rachin, J.E. and Glied, S.A. (2001) *What Can the Take-up of Other Programs Teach Us About How to Improve Take-up of Health Insurance Programs?* Cambridge: National Bureau of Economic Research, Working Paper No. 8185.

RGWF (2000) *Participation Support for a More Equitable Society, Final Report of the Working Group on Welfare Reform*. Canberra: Family and Community Services (The McClure Report).

Rhys Williams, J. (1943) *Something to Look Forward To*. London: Macdonald.

Riccucci, N., Meyers, M.K. and Lurie, I. (2004) The implementation of welfare reform policy: the role of public managers in front line practice, *Public Administration Review*, in press.

Riphahn, R.T. (2000) *Rational Poverty or Poor Rationality? The Take-up of Social Assistance Benefits*, Bonn: Institute for the Study of Labor, IZA Discussion Paper No. 124.

Ritchie, J. and England, J. (1988) *The Hackney Benefit Study*. London: Social and Community Planning Research.

Ritchie, J. and Lewis, J. (2003) *Qualitative Research Practice*. London: Sage.

Ritchie, J. and Matthews, A. (1982) *Take-up of Rent Allowances: An In-depth Study*. London: Social and Community Planning Research.

Roberts, S. (2000) *Crossing Frontiers: Migration and Social Security*. Paper presented at the Seventh International Research Seminar on 'Issues in Social Security', Sigtuna, Sweden, 17–20 June.

Roberts, S. (2001) *Migration Social Security: Parochialism in the Global Village*. Paper presented at the Year 2000 International Research Conference on 'Social Security', Helsinki, 25–27 September. Revised version, October.

Rogers, E.M. (1962) *Diffusion of Innovations*. New York: The Free Press.

Rogers, E.M. (1976) New product adoption and diffusion, *Journal of Consumer Research*, 2(March): 290–301.

Rose, F.D. (2003) *Statutes on Contract, Tort and Restitution 2003–2004*. Oxford: Oxford University Press.

Rose, R. (2001) *Ten Steps in Learning Lessons from Abroad*, Hull: ESRC Future Governance Paper No. 1 (www.hull.ac.uk/futgov).

Roth, A. (2002) Germany's cold shoulder, *The Nation*, 9 May (http://thenation.com).

Rowlingson, K. (2001) The social, economic and demographic profile of lone parents, in J. Millar and K. Rowlingson (eds) *Lone Parents, Employment and Social Policy: Cross-national Comparisons*, pp. 169–88. Bristol: Policy Press.

Rowntree, B.S. (1901) *Poverty: A Study of Town Life*. London: Thomas Nelson & Sons.

Sainsbury, R. (1992) Understanding social security fraud, in J. Millar (ed.) *Understanding Social Security: Issues for Policy and Practice*, pp. 277–95. Bristol: Policy Press.

Sainsbury, R. (2003) Understanding social security fraud, in J. Millar (ed.) *Understanding Social Security: Issues for Policy and Practice*, pp. 277–96. Bristol: Policy Press.

Sandler, R. (2002) *Medium and Long-term Savings in the UK: A Review*. London: HM Treasury.

Sarin, R. and Wakker, P. (1998) Dynamic choice and nonexpected utility, *Journal of Risk and Uncertainty*, 17: 87–119.

Saunders, P. (1994) *Welfare and Inequality: National and International Perspectives on the Australian Welfare State*. Cambridge: Cambridge University Press.

Saunders, P. (2003a) *Getting Poverty Back onto the Policy Agenda*. Camperdown: The Smith Family, Briefing Paper No. 10.

Saunders, P. (2003b) Help and hassle: do people on welfare really want to work?, *Policy*, winter.

Saunders, P., Smeeding, T.M., Coder, C., Jenkins, S., Fritzell, J., Hagenaars, A.M., Hauser, R. and Wolfson, M. (1992) *Noncash Income, Living Standards, Inequality and Poverty: Evidence from the Luxembourg Income Study.* Sydney: Social Policy Research Centre Working Paper, University of New South Wales.

Schmid, J. (ed.) (2002) *The German Welfare State: Dimensions, Innovations, Comparisons.* Tübingen: University of Tübingen, WIF Occasional Paper No. 17, http://w210.ub.uni-tuebingen.de/dbt/volltexte/2002/541/pdf/WIP-17.pdf.

Scriverner, S. *et al.* (1998) *National Evaluation of Welfare-to-Work Strategies: Implementation, Participation Patterns, Costs, and Two-Year Impacts of Portland (Oregon) Welfare-to-Work Program.* Washington, DC: US Department of Health and Human Services, Administration for Children and Families, Office of the Assistant Secretary for Planning and Evaluation and US Department of Education, Office of the Under Secretary, Office of Vocational and Adult Education.

Sen, A. (1976) Poverty: an ordinal approach to measurement, *Econometrica*, 44(2): 219–31.

Sen, A. and Foster, J. (1997) *On Economic Inequality.* Oxford: Clarendon Press.

SEU (2002) *Reducing Re-offending by Ex-prisoners.* London: Social Exclusion Unit.

Sheeham, P. (2001) The causes of increased earnings inequality: the international literature, in J. Borland, B. Gregory and P. Sheehan (eds) *Work Rich, Work Poor: Inequality and Economic Change in Australia,* pp. 40–59. Melbourne: Centre for Strategic Economic Studies.

Shin, D.-M. (2000) Financial crisis and social security: the paradox of South Korea, *International Social Security Review*, (53)3: 83–107.

Short, K., Iceland, J. and Dalaker, J. (2002) *Defining and Redefining Poverty.* Paper presented to the American Sociological Association Annual Conference, Chicago, 16–19 August, available at: http://www.census.gov/hhes/poverty/povmeas/papers/define.pdf.

Shugart, M.S. and Carey, J.M. (1992) *Presidents and Assemblies – Constitutional Design and Electoral Dynamics.* Cambridge: Cambridge University Press.

Sirkin, M.R. (1999) *Statistics for the Social Sciences,* 2nd end. Thousand Oaks, CA: Sage.

Smith, A., Youngs, R., Ashworth, K., McKay, S. and Walker, R. (2000) *Understanding the Impact of Jobseeker's Allowance.* London: Department of Social Security, Research Report No. 111.

Smith, G. and Cantley, C. (1985) Policy evaluation, in R. Walker (ed.) *Applied Qualitative Research,* pp. 156–74. Aldershot: Gower.

Solomon, R. (1994) *The Transformation of the World Economy, 1980–1993.* London: Macmillan.

Solomon-Fears, C. (2003) *Welfare Diversion Policies.* Washington, DC: Congressional Research Service, Domestic Social Policy Division.

Somavia, J. (2003) *Working Out of Poverty.* Geneva: Report of the Director General, International Labour Organisation, International Labour Conference, 91st session.

Spicker, P. (1993) *Poverty and Social Security.* London: Routledge.

SPR (1997) *Creating Workforce Development Systems That Work: An Evaluation of the Initial One-Stop Implementation Experience.* Oakland, CA: Social Policy Research Associates.

Stafford, B. (2003) Service delivery and the user, in J. Millar (ed.) *Understanding Social Security: Issues for Policy and Practice*, pp. 213–34. Bristol: Policy Press.

Standing, G. (1999) *Global Labour Flexibility: Seeking Distributive Justice*. London: Palgrave, Macmillan.

Standing, G. (2002) *Beyond the New Paternalism: Basic Security as Equality*. London: Verso.

Swenson, P.A. (2002) *Capitalists against Markets: The Making of Labour Markets and Welfare States in the United States and Sweden*. Oxford: Oxford University Press.

Thornton, P. *et al.* (2003) *What Works and Looking Ahead: A Comparative Study of UK and US Policies and Practices Facilitating Return to Work for People with Disabilities*. Paper presented at the UK/US 'Pathways to Work in the 21st Century' seminar and workshop, Washington, DC: 1–2 May.

Timonen, V. (2003) *Restructuring the Welfare State: Globalization and Social Policy Reform in Finland and Sweden*. Cheltenham: Edward Elgar.

Titmuss, R.M. (1963) *Essays on the Welfare State*. London: Allen & Unwin.

Titmuss, R.M. (1971) Welfare 'rights', law and discretion, *Political Quarterly*, 42(2): 113–32.

Titmuss, R.M. (1974) *Social Policy: An Introduction*. London: Allen & Unwin.

Tobin, J. (1965) On improving the economic status of the Negro, *Daedalus*, 94(4): 878–97.

Townsend, P. (1979) *Poverty in the United Kingdom*. Harmondsworth: Allen Lane.

Tsumori, K., Saunders, P. and Hughes, H. (2002) *Poor Arguments: A Response to the Smith Family Report on Poverty in Australia*. Sydney: Centre for Independent Studies, Issues Analysis, www.cis.org.au

Twigg, J. and Atkin, K. (1994) *Carers Perceived: Policy and Practice in Informal Care*. Milton Keynes: Open University Press.

UK Archive (2003) *Central Government Expenditure by Department, (1) 1992–93 to 1998–99*, http://www.archive.official-documents.co.uk/document/cm39/3901/tbl-5–1.htm.

UKSIF (2001) *Response of UK Pension Funds to the SRI Disclosure Regulation*. London, UK Social Investment Forum.

van Amelsvoort, A.A.M. (1984) The Netherlands: minimum wage and unemployment policies, in R. Walker, R. Lawson and P. Townsend (eds) *Responses to Poverty: Lessons from Europe*, pp. 119–35. London: Heinemann.

van Praag, B., Hagenaars, A. and van Deeren, H. (1982) Poverty in Europe, *Review of Income and Wealth*, 28: 245–359.

Vardon, S. (2000) *One-to-One: The Art of Personalized Service*, paper presented to a conference entitled 'Case Management: Fact or Fiction', University of Melbourne, 11 February.

Veit-Wilson, J. (1998) *Setting Adequacy Standards: How Governments Define Minimum Standards*. Bristol: Policy Press.

Vincent, J. (1998) *Qualitative Research on Disallowed and Sanctioned Claimants*. London: Department for Education and Employment, Research Report No. 86.

Vincent, J., Leeming, A., Peaker, A. and Walker, R. (1995) *Choosing Advice on Benefits*, Department of Social Security Research Report No. 35, p. 88. London: HMSO.

Vlemincx, K. and Smeeding, T.M. (2001) *Child Well-being, Child Poverty and Child Policy in Modern Nations*. Bristol: Policy Press.

Voges, W., Jacobs, H. and Trickey, H. (2001) Uneven development – local authorities and workfare in Germany, in I. Lødemel and H. Trickey (eds) *'An Offer You Can't Refuse': Workfare in an International Perspective*, pp. 71–104. Bristol: Policy Press.

Waddell, G.A., Burton, K. and Main, C.J. (2003) *Screening to Identify People at Risk of Long-term Incapacity for Work: A Conceptual and Scientific Review*. London: The Royal Society of Medicine Press.

Waldegrave, C., Frate, P. and Stephens, B. (1997) An overview of research on poverty in New Zealand, *New Zealand Sociology*, 12(2): 213–59.

Walker, R. (1980) Temporal aspects of claiming behaviour: renewal of rent allowances, *Journal of Social Policy*, 9(2): 207–22.

Walker, R. (1987) Consensual approaches to the definition of poverty: towards an alternative methodology, *Journal of Social Policy*, 16(2): 213–25.

Walker, R. (1988) Syllogism based on licensed premises, *The Times Higher Educational Supplement*, 17 March.

Walker, R. (1991) *Thinking about Workfare: Learning from US Experience*. London: HMSO.

Walker, R. (1993) How Family Credit works, *Benefits*, 1(7): 27–8.

Walker, R. (1995) *Benefits Agency Customers and the 1994 Review of the Benefits System*. Leeds: Department of Social Security.

Walker, R. (1996) Benefit dynamics, targeting and take-up, in W. van Oorschot (ed.) *New Perspectives on the Non-take-up of Social Security Benefits*, pp. 97–127. Tilburg: Tilburg University.

Walker, R. (1998) The Americanisation of British welfare: a case study of policy transfer, *Focus*, 19(3): 32–40. Reprinted in the *International Journal of Health Services*, 29(4): 679–97, 1999.

Walker, R. (2001) Can work work? A preliminary assessment of the 'welfare to work' strategy, *Zeitschrift fuer Sozialreform*, 47(3): 437–63.

Walker, R. (2002) *A Comprehensive Poverty Index: A Response to the Measuring Child Poverty Consultations Document*. Nottingham: Mimeo.

Walker, R. (2004) Evaluation: evidence for public policy, in OECD (ed.) *Evaluating Policies for Local Economic and Employment Development*. Paris: OECD, forthcoming.

Walker, R. with Ashworth, K. (1994) *Poverty Dynamics: Issues and Examples*. Aldershot: Avebury.

Walker, R. and Ashworth, K. (1998) Welfare benefits and recessions in Britain, in L. Leisering and R. Walker (eds) *The Dynamics of Modern Society: Poverty, Policy and Welfare*, pp. 199–220. Bristol: Policy Press.

Walker, R. and Collins, C. (2003) Families of the poor, in J. Scott, J.K. Treas and M.P. Richards (eds) *Blackwell Companion on the Sociology of the Family*. Malden: Blackwell Publishers Inc.

Walker, R. with Howard, M. (2000) *The Making of a Welfare Class? Benefit Receipt in Britain*. Bristol: Policy Press.

Walker, R. and Huby, M. (1989) Social security spending in the UK regions: bridging the north-south divide, *Government and Policy*, 7: 321–40.

Walker, R. and Park, J. (1998) Unpicking poverty, in C. Oppenheim (ed.) *An Inclusive Society*, pp. 29–52.

Walker, R. and Wiseman, M. (1997) The possibility of a British earned income tax credit, *Fiscal Studies*, 18(4): 401–25.

Walker, R. and Wiseman, M. (eds) (2003a) *The Welfare We Want*. Bristol: Policy Press.

Walker, R. and Wiseman, M. (2003b) Making welfare work: UK activation policies under New Labour, *International Social Security Review*, 56(1): 3–29.

Walker, R. and Wiseman, M. (2003c) Leaving it be: the 2002 US debate on welfare reform, *Social Policy and Society*, 2(2): 161–70.

Walker, R. and Wiseman, M. (2003d) *Refreshing Reform: Ideas from British Welfare Strategy*. Paper presented at a conference on 'Political Economy of Policy Transfer, Learning, and Convergence', Tulane University, New Orleans, 11–12 April.

Walker, R., Shaw, A. and Hull, L. (1995) Responding to the risk of unemployment, in ABI, *Risk, Insurance and Welfare: Changing the Balance Between Public and Private Protection*, pp. 37–52. London: Association of British Insurers.

Walker, R., Goodwin, D. and Cornwell, E. (2000) Work patterns in Europe and related social security issues: coping with the myth of flexibility, in D. Pieters (ed.) *Yearbook of the European Institute of Social Security, 1999*, pp. 5–43. London: Kluwer Law International.

Waller, M.R. and Plotnick, R. (2001) Effective child support policy for low-income families: evidence from street level research, *Policy Analysis and Management*, 20(1): 89–110.

Wavelet, M. and Anderson, J. (2002) Promoting self-sufficiency: what we know about sustaining employment and increasing income among welfare recipients and the working poor, *Focus*, 22(1): 56–62.

WCF (2000) *What Welfare Recipients Know About the New Rules and What They Have to Say About Them*. Baltimore: Johns Hopkins University, Welfare Children and Families: A Three City Study, Policy Brief No. 00–1, July.

Weaver, R.K. (2000) *Ending Welfare As We Know It*. Washington, DC: Brookings Institution Press.

Weil, A. and Finegold, K. (eds) (2002) *Welfare Reform: The Next Act*. Washington, DC: Urban Institute Press.

White, G. and Goodman, R. (1999) Welfare orientalism and the search for an East Asian welfare model, in R. Goodman, G. White and H.-J. Kwan (eds) *The East Asian Welfare Model: Welfare Orientalism and the State*, pp. 3–24. London: Routledge.

White, M. (2000) Evaluating the effectiveness of welfare-to-work: learning from cross-national evidence, in C. Chitty and G. Elam (eds) *Evaluating Welfare to Work*, pp. 57–70. London: Department of Social Security.

Whiteford, P. (2001) Lone parents and employment in Australia, in J. Millar and K. Rowlingson (eds) *Lone Parents, Employment and Social Policy: Cross-national Comparisons*, pp. 61–86. Bristol: Policy Press.

Wilenski, H. (1992a) *The Welfare State and Equality*. Berkley, CA: University of California.

Wilenski, H. (1992b) Active labour-market policy: its contents, effectiveness, and odd relation to evaluation research, in C. Crouch and A. Heath (eds) *Social Research and Social Reform*. Oxford: Clarendon Press.

Wilson, W.J. (1987) *The Truly Disadvantaged*. Chicago: Chicago University Press.

Winston, P., Burwick, A., McConnell, S. and Roper, R. (2002) *Privatization of Welfare Services: A Review of the Literature*. Princeton, NJ: Mathematica for the Department of Human Services.

Wiseman, M. (2003a) Welfare in the United States, in R. Walker and M. Wiseman (eds) (2003) *The Welfare We Want*, pp. 25–64. Bristol: Policy Press.

Wiseman, M. (2003b) *Disability and Incapacity: Finding Common Concerns and Shared Opportunity*. Paper presented at a US/UK Seminar of 'Exchange, Pathways to Work in the 21st Century', Washington, DC, 1–2 May.

WMCP (2000) *2000 Green Book*. Washington, DC: Committee on Ways and Means, US House of Representatives, WMCP 106–14.

WMCP (2003) *2003 Green Book*. Washington, DC: Committee on Ways and Means, US House of Representatives, WMCP 108–6.

Won, S.-Y. and Pascall, G. (2004) A Confucian war over childcare? Policy and practice in childcare and their implications for understanding the Korean gender regime, *Social Policy and Administration*, forthcoming.

World Bank (2001a) *Globalization, Growth, and Poverty: Building an Inclusive World Economy*. New York: Oxford University Press for the World Bank.

World Bank (2001b) *World Development Report 2000/2001: Attacking Poverty*. New York: Oxford University Press for the World Bank.

Wright, S. (2003) The street level implementation of unemployment policy, in J. Millar (ed.) *Understanding Social Security: Issues for Policy and Practice*, pp. 235–54. Bristol: Policy Press.

Yeates, N. (2003) Social security in a global context, in J. Millar (ed.) *Understanding Social Security: Issues for Policy and Practice*, pp. 53–74. Bristol: Policy Press.

Zaidi, A. and de Vos, K. (2001) Trends in consumption based poverty and inequality in the European Union during the 1980s, *Journal of Population Economics*, 14: 367–90.

Index

Abuse, 190, 303
Activation
  Australia, 47
  bridging mechanisms, 221–2
  definition, 303
  entitlement, 91
  Europe, 7, 46, 220
  Germany, 167
  incentives, 219–22
Active stigma, 53, 303
Active welfare, 7, 46, 303
Additional welfare regimes, 17–18
Adequacy
  assessment, 138–41, 145–9
  decision-making, 134
  definition, 303
  democracy, 132
  deserving poor, 135
  determination, 132–5
  inadequacy, 135
  intention, 135
  over time, 134
  political considerations, 135,
    192
  technical issues, 134–5
Adequacy standard/threshold
  arbitrary determination, 141–4
  attitudinal assessment, 138–41, 144
  average household incomes, 141

breadline approach, 139–40
budget standards, 137–9
definition, 303
determination, 133–45
direct income approach, 140–1
dynamism, 144–5
make ends meet, 140
necessities, 139, 140
normative judgement, 137–8
savings, 66, 67, 68
targeting efficiency, 184–5
up-rating, 144
wage income, 142
Administration
  administrative constraints, 58–9
  appeals, 108
  Australia, 65, 103–4, 252
  benefits, 102–8
  costs, 106, 108, 252
  devolution, 94, 96
  entry and application, 102–4
  error, 190–1, 195, 231–2, 235
  Germany, 70, 94, 97, 106, 108, 252
  information technology, 58, 59, 104,
    106, 190, 238, 246–7, 249–50
  infrastructure, 103
  institutions, 93–102
  maladministration, 53, 190–1
  payments, 106–7

simplicity, 188
social assistance, 102
South Korea, 92, 108, 252
subsidiarity, 94
support/employment services, 103
Sweden, 94–5, 101, 103, 252
United Kingdom, 95, 104, 109, 252
United States, 85, 95, 104, 108, 252
user efficiency, 232
verification/decision-making,
    104–6
Administrative efficiency
access, 232–4
adequacy/accuracy, 231–2
business plans, 248
contracts, 249
definition, 303
delivery/volume, 230–1
demand management, 245–6
external audits, 251
intermediate outcomes, 230–8
internal audit, 248–51
management information, 249–50
management of resources, 239–47
one-stop shopping, 233, 244
performance management, 247–51
personnel, 234–6, 239–46
piloting/evaluation, 250–1
policy implementation, 229–53
quality of treatment, 234–7
security, 237–8
simplicity, 232
speed of service, 231
staff, *see* Staffing
Adverse selection
definition, 49, 303
insurance, 49, 73, 74, 89
Agency relationship, 100, 303
Aims
behavioural change, 35–6
compensation, 34–5
definition, 23, 303
economic efficiency, 35
examples, 29–36
income maintenance, 30–1
redistribution, 32–4
risk pooling, 32
social cohesion, 31

social ownership, 38, 42
welfare regimes, 13, 23–4
Alpha splits, 244
Amelioration, 68, 303
Appeals, 108
Applicants, 89, 303
Asia
economic crisis, 54, 56, 269
kinship, 79–80
South East Asia, 17–18
welfare state, 80
Assessment
adequacy, 138–41, 145–9
attitudinal assessment, 138–41, 144
disabled persons, 127–9
functions, 44
income replacement, 119–20
units, *see* Units of assessment
Association of British Insurers (ABI), 64
Attendance Allowance, 126–7
Atypical work, 283, 303
Audits
external, 251
internal, 248–51, 308
Australia
activation, 47
administration, 65, 103–4, 252
aims, 24
Centrelink, 47, 104, 233, 236,
    237, 239, 242, 243, 244
child support, 213
contracting-out, 102
disabled persons, 124–5, 127–9
eligibility thresholds, 5, 17
employment, 17, 18, 102
equity, 17
Family Tax Payment (FTP), 213
funding, 83
GDP, 12, 28
Henderson scales, 147
income distribution, 163
labour market policies, 226
means-tested benefits, 5, 17, 32, 47,
    82
medical costs, 125
mutual obligation, 6, 192, 218, 242,
    244
occupational pensions, 73

pensions, 122–30
policy design, 103–4
population, 9
poverty alleviation, 136, 186
recipiency rates, 182
redistribution, 17, 32, 163, 165, 166–7
Rent Assistance, 213
replacement ratios, 121
residency, 91
retirement income, 86
single parents, 264
social cohesion, 17
social security spending, 28, 50, 59
social security system, 47
stigma, 83
Superannuation Guarantee, 122–3
take-up, 194
targeting efficiency, 186
territorial redistribution, 168, 169
unemployment benefit, 192, 218
wage income (AWE), 142, 147
workfare, 46
Automatic credit transfer, 5
Average rate of tax, 205, 303
Average severity, 148, 303

Basic income, 224–5, 303
Behaviour
benefit dependency, 213–15
responses, 212–18
Behavioural change
aims, 35–6
conditionality/enforcement, 218–22
direction, 218–22
functions, 48–9
incentives, 49
social constraints, 57
social workers, 6
United Kingdom, 36
Belgium, 141
Beneficiaries, 180, 303
Benefit dependency
behaviour, 213–15
definition, 117, 304
income replacement, 117–8
Benefit drag, 188–9, 304
Benefit dynamics, 188–90
Benefit schemes, 23, 206, 304

Benefit taper, 209, 304
Benefits
actuarial probity, 97
administration, *see* Administration
cash benefit systems, 4
contributory, *see* Contributory
benefits
definition, 304
imperfect coverage, 185, 192
inadequate levels, 191–3
long-term recipients, 214
misplaced, 184–5, 186–91
optimax, 178–9
scale rates, 192
social assistance, *see* Means-tested
benefits; Social assistance
underpayment, 190, 192
universal, 203–5
vulnerability, 192
Beveridge Report (1942), 8, 24, 99
Birth rates, 36
Bismarck, Otto von, 31, 33, 35–6, 48
Borrowing, 170
Breadline Britain, 139–40
Bridging mechanisms, 221–2, 304
Budget constraints, 208, 210–11, 304
Budget standards
consensual, 137–8, 146
definition, 304
low cost but adequate, 145
standard of living, 137–8

Canada, 225
Capabilities, 44, 117, 304
Capitalism, 13
Case-working, 236
Caseloading, 244, 304
Caseloads
definition, 179, 304
disabled persons, 116
United States, 116
Categorical benefit, 304
Charities, 29, 30, 80
Child Benefit, 32–3, 153
Child support
absent parents, 58
adequacy, 135
Australia, 213

France, 45
income maintenance, 45–6
South Korea, 193
United Kingdom, 57–8, 135, 146,
153, 184, 225
United States, 193
Child Tax Credit, 22, 23
Children
dependant liability, 49, 57–8
Germany, 57–8, 119, 120
Choice
mode of access, 233
work/leisure, 203–5
Circumstances changed, 189
Citizenship
arbitrary exclusions, 90
entitlement, 89, 90, 91, 179
social citizenship, 15, 311
South Korea, 48
Civil society, 44
Claimant units, 180, 184, 304
Claimants, 180, 304
Collective transfer
community initiatives, 80–1
definition, 304
funding mechanisms, 78–84
government transfers, 82–4
income shortfall, 71
informal transfers, 79–80
occupational welfare, 81–2
Community initiatives
charities, 29, 30, 80
credit unions, 80–1
informal exchanges, 80
Compensation
aims, 34–5
disabled persons, 34–5, 124–5
disadvantage remedied, 51
effectiveness, 120–9
horizontal redistribution, 32–3
Concentration coefficient, 168, 304
Conditionality
behavioural change, 218–22
deserving poor, 91
eligible persons, 88
insurance benefits, 89, 90
ongoing conditions, 108
qualifying conditions, 88, 89, 90

sanctions, 192
social assistance, 91, 108, 219
supplementary conditions, 90, 91
Confucianism, 17, 55, 80, 193, 259
Conservative welfare regimes, 13, 14,
16–17, 32–3, 44, 48, 71, 81, 117,
151, 186, 207, 227
Constraints
administrative, 58–9
aims and objectives, 42
definition, 304
economic, 56–7
political, 55–6
social, 57–8
types, 53–9
Consumption, 142, 170
Context, importance, 13–18
Contractors, 100, 102, 249
Contributions
contribution record, 4, 89–90, 192,
193
defined, 100, 305
definition, 305
entitlement, 89–90
funding comparison, 83
Germany, 97
income-related, 117
marginal contribution, 15
occupational pensions, 81, 82
Contributory benefits
definition, 305
Germany, 4, 90
United Kingdom, 4, 22, 90
Corporatist welfare regimes, 13, 14,
16–17
Cost effectiveness, 177, 305
Council Tax Benefit, 95
Counterfactuals
definition, 114–15, 305
impairment, 124–5
market income, 151
original income, 164
Covert objectives
definition, 305
negative redistribution, 51
open objectives distinguished, 39
Creaming, 305
Creative justice, 106, 305

Credit unions, 80–1
Customer satisfaction, 231, 242

Damages, tort, 125
De-industrialization, 57, 282, 305
Deacon, Alan, 49
Deadweight, 245, 305
Decent work, 294, 305
Decentralization, definition, 94, 305
Decision-making
   adequacy, 132
   administration, 104–6
   democracy, 55
Decommodification, 14, 15–16, 305
Defined benefit schemes, 100, 305
Defined contribution schemes, 100, 305
Democracy
   adequacy, 133
   collective decision-making, 55
   performance objectives, 115
   South Korea, 54
Demogrant, 224, 305
Demographic groups, 188
Demonstration project, 250, 305
Denmark, 71
Department of Work and Pensions, 4, 8,
   24, 93, 107, 109
Dependency
   benefits, 117, 213–15, 304
   dependent children, 119, 120
   dependent liability, 49
   path dependency, 18, 309
   ratios, 52–3, 271, 305, 309
   state dependency, 214, 311
Deserving poor
   adequacy, 135
   politics, 284
   stigma, 37
   supplementary conditions, 91
Devolution, 94, 96, 306
Difference, liberation, 9–10
Dignified work, 305
Disability Living Allowance, 126
Disabled persons
   assessment, 127–30
   Australia, 125, 128, 129
   caseloads, 116
   compensation, 34–5, 125

Germany, 125, 126, 128, 129, 193
income loss, 124–5
injuries, *see* Impairment
labour markets, 127, 219
medical model, 127, 128
performance objectives, 127–30
social insurance, 125
social model, 123
social participation, 126–7
South Korea, 125, 126, 127–8
standard of living, 125–6
stigma, 128
Sweden, 59, 124, 125, 126, 127, 128,
   129, 188
United Kingdom, 82, 83, 124, 125,
   126, 127, 128, 129, 189, 193, 219,
   240–2
United States, 116, 123–4, 125, 126,
   127, 128, 129, 189, 219
Disadvantage
   gender differences, 52
   migrants, 52
   misadministration, 53
   production, 52–3
   remedied, 51–2
   reproduced, 51–2
   social divisions, 52
Discretion, 105, 106, 306
Disposable income, 119, 153, 306
Diversity
   contemporary influences, 260–8
   gender, *see* Gender differences
   lifestyles, 267–8
   race/ethnicity, 264–6

Earnings replacement, 118–9
Earnings-related benefits
   definition, 306
   income maintenance, 30–1, 45, 117
   unemployment, 51
Economic constraints, 56–7
Economic efficiency
   aims, 35
   fiscal welfare, 202
   welfare, 201–28
Economic needs, 30
Economic participation rate
   definition, 306

gender differences, 268
Sweden, 26
Economic performance
detriment, 44, 56
employment, 44
investments, 100, 206
pay-as-you-go, 77
welfare regimes, 48
Economic structures
definition, 306
shaping structures, 202–18
Economy, tripartite management, 16–17
Education
employment, 32, 34
equality of opportunity, 34
South Korea, 45
United States, 45
Educational Maintenance Allowance,
50
Effectiveness
compensation, 120–30
income replacement, 117–20
Efficiency
administrative, *see* Administrative
efficiency
economic, *see* Economic efficiency
insurance, 71
price efficiency, 229, 310
programme efficiency, 184, 185, 186,
232
social efficiency, 177–8, 185, 311
targets, *see* Targeting efficiency
technical efficiency, 229, 312
user efficiency, 232, 312
Eligibility
Australia, 5, 17
behavioural change, 48
conditions, *see* Conditionality
definition, 306
non-claimants, 180
perception, 196
Sweden, 26
target populations, 22, 43–4
United Kingdom, 233
see also Entitlement
Employers, social insurance costs, 78
Employment
Australia, 17, 18, 102

benefits, *see* Occupational benefits
capabilities, matching, 117
economic performance, 44
education, 32, 34
families, 268–70
Germany, 18
part-time/temporary, 287
policies, *see* Labour market policies
South Korea, 18
subsidies, older workers, 274
Sweden, 18
United Kingdom, 18
United States, 18
see also Unemployment
Employment shortfall, 216, 306
Engel method, 137
Entitled, definition, 88, 306
Entitlement
achievement-orientated societies, 91
applicants, 89
citizenship, 89, 90, 91, 179
conditions, *see* Conditionality
contributions, 89–90
definition, 306
evidence, 89, 104, 105
insurance, 89–90
means-tested benefits, 89, 91
review, 107–8
routes, 88–91
social insurance, 89
see also Eligibility
Equality
opportunity, 34
territorial justice, 94
welfare, 15
welfare regimes, 34
Equity, Australia, 17
Equivalence scales
comparison, 156
definition, 134–5, 306
Germany, 169–70
horizontal redistribution, 164
Luxembourg Income Study, 136, 156
McClements scale, 155, 156, 171
OECD, 136, 155, 165, 166, 169–70
poverty gap, 147
standard of living, 135
vertical redistribution, 154–5

Error
   administration, 190–1, 195, 231–2, 235
   measurement, *see* Measurement error
Esping-Anderson, G., 13, 17–18, 82
Etatism, 16, 31, 306
Europe
   activation, 7, 46, 220
   poverty, 131, 132
   regional international governance, 296–7
   social dimension, 142
   social model, 48
   welfare state, 7
   workfare, 46, 220
European Commission
   additional welfare regimes, 17
   quintile share ratio, 159
   social protection, 7
Exported benefit, 286, 306
External objectives, 306
External targeting efficiency, 183–6

Families
   employment, 268–70
   extended family, 79, 272
   informal transfers, 79–80
   inner family, 134, 308
   interest-free loans, 79
   non-monetary exchange, 80
   nuclear family, 57
   shared income trajectories, 69
   social constraints, 57–8
   solidarity, 45
   units of assessment, 134
   work-rich/work-poor, 215–16
Family cap policies, 36, 263, 306
Family Credit, 27, 39
Family units, 134, 306
Felt stigma, 53, 306
Field, Frank, 49
Filtering systems, 244, 306
Final income, 153, 165, 306
Final outcomes, 230, 306
Financing, *see* Funding
Flexible work, 283, 306
France, 32, 45
Fraud

benefit design, 238
definition, 307
front-end controls, 238
recipient fraud, 237
reduction, 199, 237–8
United Kingdom, 237–8
vertical inefficiency, 190
Functions
   aims and objectives, 27–8
   behavioural change, 48–9
   comparative assessment, 44
   conservative welfare regimes, 44, 48
   definition, 23, 307
   developing potential, 46–8
   disadvantage remedied, 50–1
   income maintenance, 45–6
   outcomes, 27–8, 42
   policy analysts, 42
   provision for needs, 43–4
   social democratic welfare regimes, 44
   types, 43–53
Funding
   collective transfer, 78–84
   contributions, *see* Contributions
   definition, 307
   importance, 63–6
   insurance, 71–8
   mechanisms, 69–71

Gender differences
   disadvantage, 52
   economic activity, 266
   economic participation rate, 268
   policy responses, 262–3
   relations, 261–3
   South Korea, 259
   standard of living, 157
   Sweden, 52
   wage income, 164
Germany
   activation, 167
   administration, 70, 94, 97, 106, 108, 252
   adult children, 57
   citizenship, 91
   conservative welfare regime, 14, 48, 80, 186
   contributions, 97

contributory benefits, 4, 90
Credit unions, 80
dependent children, 119, 120
direct relatives, 80
disabled persons, 125, 126, 128, 129, 193
employment, 18
equivalence scales, 169–70
etatism, 31
funding, 82
GDP, 12, 28
government insurance, 33, 81
housing benefit, 108, 188
income distribution, 163
income maintenance, 45
insurance, 33, 74, 81
labour market policies, 35, 36, 107, 226
migrant workers, 265, 275
objectives, 120
old-age pensions, 35
pay-as-you-go, 33
pensions institutes, 95, 97
population, 9
poverty alleviation, 135, 136, 186
poverty rates, 169–70
recipiency rates, 182
redistribution, 163, 166, 167
refugees, 52, 265
replacement ratios, 53, 120, 121
retirement income, 86
single parents, 264
social assistance, 82, 94, 100, 134, 143, 167, 187, 214, 265
social cohesion, 31, 48, 120, 188
social insurance, 33, 81, 90, 134, 193
social partnerships, 95, 97, 98
social policy, 9
social security spending, 28, 50, 59, 64
social security system, 31, 33
social workers, 6, 106, 107, 219, 239
take-up, 187, 194
targeting efficiency, 186, 188
territorial redistribution, 167, 168, 169

tripartite agreements, 33
unemployment benefit, 22, 23, 102–3, 119, 120, 227
Giddens, A., 258–60
Gini coefficients
  definition, 158, 307
  life-course redistribution, 172
  Lorenz curves, 157–9, 161, 162, 163
Global leverage, 295–6
Global persuasion, 292–5
Globalization
  definition, 307
  internationalism, 277–300
  policy competition, 279–81
Government insurance
  compulsion, 75–7
  definition, 307
  funding mechanisms, 75–7
  Germany, 33, 81
  pay-as-you-go, 77, 84
  private insurance compared, 76
  Sweden, 26
  see also Social insurance
Governments
  policy design, 93
  transfers, 82–4
  underwriting/rescue, 74, 78, 97
Great Britain, see United Kingdom
Gross domestic product (GDP)
  comparisons, 12
  social security spending, 28, 50, 57, 59, 64
Gross income, 152, 307

Headcount poverty rate
  definition, 146, 307
  policy impact, 135, 136, 146
Health insurance, 81
Heterogeneity, 214, 307
Hill, Michael, 4
Hoarding, 66–7, 307
Horizontal redistribution
  compensation, 34
  household income, 164
  measurement, 163–7
  positive, definition, 32, 307
  social adequacy, 77
  taxation, 164

unweighted, 164, 166, 312
weighted, 164, 312
Horizontal targeting efficiency
  definition, 307
  maladministration, 190–1
  measurement, 180–1, 185–6, 189
Household income
  average, 141
  horizontal redistribution, 164
  investments, 142
  total, 154
Households
  definition, 307
  economies of scale, 154, 155
  units of assessment, 134, 141,
    154
Housing benefit, 95, 102, 108, 188
Hybridization, 292, 307
Hypothecated tax, 84, 307

Iatrogenic objectives, 36, 51
Iatrogenic problem, 307
Identity checks, 104
Immigrants
  economic migrants, 285–7
  refugees, 52, 265
  United States, 52, 265
Impairment
  injuries, 120–4, 124–5
  measurement, 124
  medical costs, 125–6
  see also Disabled persons
In-kind benefits
  definition, 307
  food stamps, 6, 11, 52, 64, 104, 133,
    193, 194, 209, 230, 235
  United Kingdom, 6, 107
Incentives
  activation, 219–22
  alteration, 203–7
  behavioural change, 48–9
  definition, 203, 307
  income effect, 205
  occupational pensions, 99, 206
  personal pensions, 74
  perverse incentives, 214, 218, 238
  savings, 206
  taxation, 205

Income
  basic, 224–5, 303
  disposable, 119, 153, 306
  effect, 205, 307
  gross, 152, 307
  loss, 124–5
  market income, 151, 152, 308
  mean/median, 141–2, 144
  non-declaration, 190
  post-tax, 153, 164, 168, 309
  potential, 201, 309
  preferred, 201, 310
  redistribution, 150–74
  shortfall, 68, 69, 71
  verification, 104
Income maintenance
  aims, 30–1
  child support, 45–6
  earnings-related benefits, 31, 45, 117
  functions, 45–6
  Germany, 45
  social cohesion, 45, 117, 119
  standard of living, 31, 117, 118
Income replacement
  assessment, 119–20
  determination, 117–19
  effectiveness, 117–20
  maxima/minima, 119
  measurement, 117–18
  net income, 119
  ratios, see Replacement ratios
  reference income, 118
  unemployment benefit, 120, 121
  vertical redistribution, 117
Income support, 68, 307
Income Support (UK), 193, 194, 209,
    237, 246
Indifference curves, 203
Individual welfare, 307
Individualism, 258, 308
Individualization
  definition, 258, 308
  social change, 257–76
  social security benefits, 269, 308
Industrial achievement models, 13
Industrialization, economic risk, 31, 32
Inflation, 142
Inner family, 134, 308

Institutional stigma, 197–9, 308
Institutions
  administration, 93–102
  contractors, 100, 102
  national governments, 93–4
  private insurance, 99–100
  private pensions, 99–100
  social partnerships, 95, 97–8
  sub-national government, 94–5
  welfare regimes, 93
Insurance
  accidental injury, 90, 125
  adverse selection, 49, 73, 74, 89
  commercial insurers, 64, 71
  compulsion, 73, 75–8, 206
  consumer protection, 99, 100
  definition, 308
  documentation, 89
  efficiency, 71
  entitlement, 89–90
  financial cost, 77–8
  funding mechanisms, 71–8
  Germany, 33, 74, 81
  government, see Government
    insurance
  government underwriting/rescue, 74,
    78, 97
  health insurance, 81
  income shortfall, 68, 69, 71
  insured risk, 90
  moral hazard, 48–9, 73, 89
  not-for-profit, 69, 71, 74–5, 77, 78,
    95
  over-insured, 77
  payments, 106–7
  premiums, 71, 72, 73, 74
  principles, 71, 72
  private, 71–4, 76
  redundancy, 49
  risk pooling, 71–3
  savings, 67
  social, see Social insurance
  unemployment, 49, 74, 75
  United Kingdom, 4
  United States, 4, 11
Intermediate objectives, 308
Intermediate outcomes, 230–8, 308
Internal audit, 248–51, 308

Internal objectives, 120, 308
International Labour Organization
  (ILO), 4, 292, 294, 295, 300
International organizations, 292–300
International Social Security Association
  (ISSA), 292
Internationalism, 288–300
Interpretative judgement, 105, 308
Invalidity benefit, 90
Investments
  definition, 66, 308
  economic performance, 100,
    206
  household income, 142
  market income, 151
  risk, 67, 206
Ireland, 140

Jersey, 138
Jobseeker's Allowance, 22, 23, 216
Jurisdiction
  definition, 3, 308
  social policy, 9–10
Justice
  creative, 106, 305
  proportional, 105–6, 310
  social, 34
  territorial, 94, 312

Korea, see South Korea

Labour market policies
  Australia, 226
  developing potential, 46
  Germany, 35, 36, 107, 226
  South Korea, 226
  Sweden, 26, 36, 107, 219, 226
  United Kingdom, 27, 35, 226
  United States, 226
Labour markets
  disabled persons, 127, 219
  flexibility, 282–5
  inequality, 45
  policy competition, 279–81
  unemployment traps, 207
Liberal welfare regimes, 13, 14, 15, 34,
  69, 70, 132, 207
Liberation, difference, 9–10

Life-course redistribution
definition, 308
Gini coefficients, 172
income inequality, 172
measurement, 170–3
Moses principle, 34
savings, 170–1
subgroups, 164
United Kingdom, 171–2
LIFEMOD, 171
Lorenz curves
absolute equality, 157, 158
definition, 308
further Lorenz curves, 159–63
generalized, 160–1, 162
Gini coefficients, 157–9, 161, 162, 163
measurement, 157–63
social welfare, 161, 162
Low income, personal/social stress, 117
Low take-up, 193–9, 308
Luxembourg Income Study, 136, 156, 163

Managerialism, 308
Marginal deduction rates
definition, 208, 308
negative income tax, 223
poverty traps, 208–11
Marginal rate of tax, 205, 223, 308
Market income, 151, 152, 308
Marshall, T.H., 44
Mead, Lawrence, 49, 219, 236, 245
Means-tested benefits
Australia, 5, 17, 32, 47, 82
definition, 4, 308
economic cycles, 44
entitlement, 89, 91
marginal deduction rates, 208–11
South Korea, 91
supplementary conditions, 91, 108
thresholds, 5, 17, 91
unemployment traps, 207
see also Social assistance systems
Measurement
average severity, 148, 303
horizontal redistribution, 163–7

horizontal targeting efficiency, 180–1, 185–6, 190
impairment, 124–5
income replacement, 117–8
life-course redistribution, 170–4
Lorenz curves, 157–63
territorial redistribution, 167–9
vertical redistribution, 154–63
vertical targeting efficiency, 181–2, 186
Measurement error
Breadline Britain, 140
definition, 308
invalid assumptions, 144
targeting efficiency, 191
Migrant workers
economic migrants, 285–7
Germany, 265, 275
international conventions, 52
Modernization, 35, 258, 308
Moral hazard, 48–9, 73, 89, 309
Murray, Charles, 49, 50, 201, 214, 219
Mutual organizations, 74–5, 77, 95, 309

National Association of Pension Funds (NAPF), 64
National Insurance Fund, 22
Negative income tax, 58, 222–4, 309
Negative redistribution, 51, 151, 309
The Netherlands, 142, 198
New Deal
activation, 291, 292
caseloads, 243
disabled persons, 240–2
youth unemployment, 6, 25
New Zealand, 17, 132, 138
Non-contributory benefits, 82, 309
Non-needy, misplaced benefit, 184–5, 186–91
Northern Ireland, 8
Not-for-profit
advisory/advocacy services, 100
insurance, 69, 71, 74–5, 77, 78, 95
mutual organizations, 74–5, 77, 95

Objectives
covert, see Covert objectives
definition, 23, 309

external, 306
Germany, 120
intermediate, 308
intermediate outcomes, 230
internal, 120, 308
open, 38–9, 309
performance, 114, 309
policies, 24–7, 36–40
policy evaluation, 44
policymakers, 25, 38, 120
primary, 36, 310
principal, 37, 310
secondary, 36, 37, 311
subordinate, 311
Sweden, 120
United Kingdom, 39
Occupational benefits
collective transfer, 81–2
deferred wages, 82, 151
definition, 309
remuneration, 5
risk pooling, 72
Occupational pensions
Australia, 73
contributions, 81, 82
incentives, 99, 206
United Kingdom, 5, 8, 51–2, 81, 99,
206
Old-age dependency ratio, 271, 309
Old-age pensions
disadvantages, 52–3, 206
Germany, 35
intergenerational bonds, 46
pay-as-you-go, 77, 272
South Korea, 32, 54
Sweden, 26, 32
Old-age support ratio, 272, 309
Open Method of Coordination (OMC),
297–8
Open objectives, 39, 309
Opportunity cost, 178, 205, 309
Organization for Economic
Cooperation and Development
(OECD)
case management, 102
disabled person, 189
equivalence scales, 136, 156, 165,
166, 169–70

recipiency rates, 182
relative wage adjustment, 227
social assistance, 4, 122
social security spending, 54, 279–81
Original income
counterfactuals, 164
definition, 309
market income, 152
redistribution, 152, 164, 168
Orshansky poverty line, 137
Outcomes
comparisons, 115
definition, 309
final, 230, 306
functions, 27–8, 42
intermediate, 230–8, 308
Outdoor relief, 29, 309

Pareto optimum, 179, 201
Passive benefit schemes, 6
Path dependency, 18, 309
Patriarchal societies, 16
Pay-as-you-go
definition, 309
economic performance, 77
Germany, 33
government insurance, 77, 84
mutual organizations, 74
old-age pensions, 77, 272
Payments
electronic transfer, 6, 107
insurance, 106–7
tax credits, 107
Pensions
access, 234
Australia, 122–30
occupational, *see* Occupational
pensions
old age, *see* Old-age pensions
personal, *see* Personal pensions
Performance management, 247–51
Performance measurement, 25
Performance objectives
aspirations, 25
definition, 114, 309
disabled persons, 126–30
policy targets, 114
Performance targets, 248, 309

Personal pensions
  private pensions, 72, 99–100, 122–30
  stakeholder pensions, 100
  subsidies/incentives, 74
Perverse incentives, 214, 218, 238
Policies, definition, 23, 309
Policy design
  Australia, 103–4
  cost effectiveness, 177
  devolution, 94
  governments, 93
  TANF, 95
Policy effectiveness
  all objectives, 114
  counterfactuals, 114–15
  definition, 113, 309
  policy experiments, 115
Policy learning, 288–92
Policy objectives, *see* Objectives
Policy synthesis, 292, 309
Policy transfer, 288, 309
Politics
  adequacy, 132, 134, 135, 192
  constraints, 55–6
  electoral practices, 17
  negative income tax, 224
  unemployment traps, 207
  United Kingdom, 55, 162–3, 192
Poor Law
  dependant liability, 49
  less eligibility, 49, 199
  outdoor relief, 29, 309
  policy model exported, 29, 37
  stigma, 83, 91
  workhouse, 29, 91
Population, United Kingdom, 9
Positive horizontal redistribution,
  definition, 309
Positive vertical redistribution,
  definition, 32, 151, 309–10
Post-tax income, 153, 164, 168, 310
Potential income, 201, 310
Poverty
  depth of poverty, 146
  discourse, 131–2
  severity, 146
Poverty alleviation
  aims, 29–30

Australia, 136, 186
charities, 29, 30
Germany, 135, 136, 186
liberal welfare regimes, 15,
  132
policy impact, 135–6
social assistance, 30–1
Sweden, 135, 136
United Kingdom, 8, 22, 27, 29–30,
  135–6, 186
United States, 135, 136, 186
Poverty gap
  definition, 148, 310
  equivalence scales, 147
  post-benefit, 185, 186
Poverty gap ratio
  definition, 147, 310
  policy impact, 136
Poverty line
  de facto, 30
  minimum benefit, 37
  Orshansky poverty line, 137
  United States, 133, 137
Poverty rates
  Germany, 169–70
  headcount, *see* Headcount poverty
    rate
  measurement, 114
  Sweden, 148
Poverty traps
  definition, 53, 310
  disadvantage, 53
  work disincentives, 208–12
Preferred income, 201, 310
Prescribed needs, 44, 310
Prevention
  definition, 310
  income shortfall, 68
Price efficiency, 229, 310
Primary objectives, 36, 310
Principal objectives, 37, 310
Proactive welfare
  definition, 310
  incentives, 219–22
  recent trends, 6
  United States, 6, 46
Process studies, 250, 310
Profiling, 246, 310

Programme efficiency, 184, 185, 186, 232
Proportional Justice, 105–6, 310
Proratorization, 286, 310
Purchasing power parities, 12
Purposive stigma, 53, 310

Quintile share ratio, 159, 310

Rawlsian inequality measure, 159, 310
Recipiency rates, 182, 194, 310
Recipient population *see* Caseload
Redistribution
    aims, 32–4
    Australia, 17, 163, 165, 166–7
    final income, 153, 165
    Germany, 163, 166, 167
    horizontal, *see* Horizontal redistribution
    income, 150–74
    life-course, *see* Life-course redistribution
    negative, 51, 151, 309
    post-tax income, 153, 164, 168
    South Korea, 163, 173
    strategies, 166
    Sweden, 163, 166
    taxation, 16, 64–5, 153–4
    United Kingdom, 162–3, 166, 167, 168
    United States, 163, 166, 167, 168
    value bias, 51
Refundable tax credits
    Child Tax Credit, 22, 23
    definition, 5, 310
    policy responses, 225–6
Regional international governance, 296–8
Regressive redistribution, *see* Negative redistribution
Relative wage adjustment, 227, 311
Relief, definition, 311
Religious charities, 29
Replacement ratios
    Australia, 121
    definition, 311
    Germany, 53, 120, 121
    past earnings, 118–19

South Korea, 54, 121
Sweden, 26, 53, 120, 121, 207
United Kingdom, 121
United States, 121
Reservation wages, 215, 311
Retirement age, 53
Retirement income, 86
Retirement pensions
    earnings trajectories, 119
    United Kingdom, 4
    see also Old age pensions
Review, 107–8
Risk
    economic risk, 31, 32
    insured risk, 90
    investments, 67, 206
    leaving benefit, 216–17
Risk pooling
    compulsion, 76
    definition, 311
    differential premiums, 73
    high risk, 73, 74
    insurance, 71–3
    subsidiarity, 16
    unemployment, 32
Roman Catholicism, 16, 17
Rowntree, Benjamin Seebohm, 69

Sanctions, 108, 192, 220
Savings
    accumulation/ retention, 66–7
    adequacy standard/threshold, 66, 67, 68
    economic performance, 44
    incentives, 206
    individual, limits, 66–9
    life-course redistribution, 170–1
    ratios, 44
Savings traps
    definition, 53, 210–11, 311
    disadvantage, 53
    work disincentives, 211–12
Scotland, 8
Scroungerphobia, 284, 311
Secondary objectives, 36, 37, 311
Selective, definition, 31, 311
Self-sufficiency, 46, 311
Sickness benefits, 5

Skimming, 305
Social assistance
  administration, 102
  Australia, 17
  decommodification, 16
  definition, 4
  duration, 214
  Germany, 82, 94, 100, 134, 143, 167,
    187, 214, 265
  poverty alleviation, 30–1
  South Korea, 54, 56, 192
  stigma, 83
  Sweden, 82, 143, 198, 214
  systems, 21
  United Kingdom, 145–6, 214
  United States, 30, 57, 82, 95, 214, 236
  see also Means-tested benefits
Social citizenship, 15, 311
Social cohesion
  aims, 31
  Australia, 17
  conservative welfare regimes, 48, 117
  definition, 16, 311
  Germany, 31, 48, 120, 188
  income maintenance, 45, 117, 119
  objectives, 37
  social insurance, 78
  Sweden, 120
Social constraints, 57–8
Social democratic welfare regimes, 13,
    14, 15–16, 34, 44, 71, 132, 227
social deprivation, 140
Social dividend, 224, 311
Social dumping, 279, 311
Social efficiency, 177–8, 185, 311
Social exclusion, 27, 132, 144, 195, 221
Social Fund, 38, 244, 245
Social inclusion, 31, 142
Social insurance
  costs, employers, 78
  disabled persons, 125
  entitlement, 89
  funding mechanisms, 75–7
  Germany, 33, 81, 90, 134, 193
  government transfer, 82
  social cohesion, 78
  Sweden, 26
  see also Government insurance

Social justice, 34
Social partnerships
  Germany, 95, 97, 98
  government accountability, 98
  institutions, 95, 97–8
  social wage, 151
  Sweden, 95
Social pathology, 214
Social policy, 9–10
Social protection, 7, 16
Social security
  definition, 4, 6, 311
  policy responsibilities, 4
Social Security Advisory Committee, 29
Social security spending
  gross domestic product (GDP), 28, 50,
    57, 59, 64
  rationale, 66–9
Social security systems
  aims, 23–4
  Australia, 47
  definition, 21, 311
  Germany, 31, 33
  global scale, 298–300
  schemes compared, 21–3
  South Korea, 54
  Sweden, 26
  United Kingdom, 8
  United States, 4, 11
Social solidarity, 31, 32, 71, 120
Social stigma, 199, 311
Social welfare
  definition, 7, 311
  Lorenz curves, 161, 162
  marginal contribution, 15
  United Kingdom, 163
  see also Welfare
Social work roles, 6, 106, 107, 108, 219,
    239
Solidarity
  contemporary influences, 271–5
  families, 45
  social solidarity, 31, 32, 71, 120
South Korea
  administration, 92, 108, 252
  child support, 193
  citizenship, 48
  contributory benefits, 4

democracy, 54
disabled persons, 125, 126, 128, 129
economic recession, 28, 30
economic shock, 192
education, 45
employment, 18
funding, 83
GDP, 12, 28
gender differences, 259
health insurance, 81
income distribution, 163
labour market policies, 226
means-tested benefits, 91
Minimum Living Standard Guarantee
    (MSLG), 54, 192
old-age pensions, 32, 54
population, 9
redistribution, 163, 173
replacement ratios, 54, 121
retirement income, 86
social assistance, 54, 56, 192
social security spending, 28, 50, 59
social security system, 54
trade unions, 54
Speenhamland system, 49
Spending unit, 311
Staffing
    attitudes, 236
    deployment, 243–5
    filtering systems, 244
    front-line staff, 234–6
    resource management, 239–46
    targets, 249
    training, 239–42
Stagflation, 35, 52
Standard of living
    adequacy, 132
    budget standards, 137–8
    consumption, 142
    disabled persons, 125–6
    equivalence scales, 135
    gender differences, 157
    income maintenance, 31, 117, 118
    threshold, *see* Poverty line
State dependency, 214, 311
State earnings-related pensions, 99
Stigma
    active, 53, 303

association, 197–9, 311–2
Australia, 83
definition, 195–6, 311
deserving poor, 37
disabled persons, 128
felt, 53, 306
institutional, 197–9, 308
purposive, 53, 310
social, 199, 311
social assistance, 83
types, 53
unmet need, 192
Structural reform, 222–7
Subordinate objectives, 312
Subsidiarity
    administration, 94
    definition, 312
    risk pooling, 16
Substitution effect, 205, 312
Supra-national governance, 292–8
Sweden
    administration, 94–5, 101, 103, 252–3
    contributory benefits, 4
    disabled persons, 59, 124, 125, 126,
        127, 128, 129, 189
    economic participation rate, 26
    economic recession, 26
    eligibility, 26
    employment, 18
    funding, 83
    GDP, 12, 28
    gender differences, 52
    income distribution, 163
    income packages, 79
    insurance, 25–6
    labour market policies, 26, 36, 107,
        219, 226
    numerical targets, 25
    objectives, 120
    old-age pensions, 26, 32
    population, 9
    poverty alleviation, 135, 136
    poverty rates, 148
    recipiency rates, 182
    redistribution, 163, 166
    refugees, 265
    replacement ratios, 26, 53, 120, 121,
        207

retirement income, 86
single parents, 264
social assistance, 82, 143, 198,
214
social cohesion, 120
social partnerships, 95
social security spending, 28, 50, 59,
64
social security system, 26
social workers, 6, 106, 107, 219, 239
take-up, 194, 198
trade unions, 26, 75, 103
unemployment, 26
unemployment benefit, 75, 103, 119,
227

Take-up
comparisons, 120, 194
false take-up, 181
internal horizontal targeting
efficiency, 181
low take-up, 193–9, 308
transaction costs, 195
true take-up, 181
Target populations
definition, 312
eligibility, 22, 43–4
mismatch, 186–8
recipient population distinguished,
179–80
Targeting
definition, 179, 312
external, 183
internal, 179–80
Targeting efficiency
adequacy standard/threshold, 184–5
comparisons, 184, 186
external, 183–6
horizontal, see Horizontal targeting
efficiency
imperfect social systems, 185
internal, 180–2
needy recipients, 183, 185
programme efficiency, 184, 185, 186
social security, 177–200
vertical, see Vertical targeting
efficiency
Tax allowances, 5, 312

Tax credits
benefit schemes, 23, 304
definition, 312
payments, 107
refundable, see Refundable tax credits
United Kingdom, 22, 23, 27, 39, 108,
189, 225
United States, 39, 94, 107, 188, 194,
209, 225, 227, 230
Working Families Tax Credit
(WFTC), 27, 38, 39, 225
Tax threshold
definition, 208, 312
poverty traps, 208, 209
Taxation
average rate of tax, 205, 303
benefits, 119
cash benefit systems, 5
credits, see Tax credits
horizontal redistribution, 164
hypothecated tax, 84, 307
incentives, 205
marginal rate of tax, 205, 223, 308
negative income tax, 58, 222–4,
309
post-tax income, 153, 164, 168, 310
poverty traps, 53
private pensions, 74
progressive, 205, 207–8
proportional, 204, 205, 208
redistribution, 16, 64–5, 153–4
work disincentives, 56, 205
Team working, 244, 312
Technical efficiency, 229, 312
Telephones, administration, 104
Territorial justice, 94, 312
Territorial redistribution
definition, 150, 312
measurement, 167–9
subgroups, 164, 167
Theil index, 168, 312
Titmuss, Richard M., 13, 46, 52, 105,
106
Tort, damages, 125–6
Total income, 154
Trade unions
conservative welfare regimes, 151
South Korea, 54

Sweden, 26, 75, 103
United Kingdom, 35
Transaction costs, 67, 195, 196, 312
Transitional Assistance for Needy
    Families (TANF)
    administration, 102, 103
    benefit dynamics, 188–90
    contracting-out, 102
    customer satisfaction, 242
    demand management, 245, 246
    deterrence, 91, 106
    family cap provisions, 36
    lifetime limits, 11, 30, 91, 106, 117,
        262
    means-tested benefits, 5
    objectives, 25, 36–7
    policy design, 95
    proactive welfare, 6
    staff attitudes, 236
    work activities, 11
Transparency, 106

Uncertainty, 202–3, 216–18
Underclass, 214, 312
Undeserving poor, 15, 37, 91
Unemployment
    economic cycles, 35, 44, 75
    insurance, 49, 74
    risk pooling, 32
    social costs, 35
    Sweden, 26
    youth unemployment, 6, 25
    see also Employment
Unemployment benefit
    Australia, 192, 218
    earnings-related, 51
    Germany, 22, 23, 102–3, 119, 120,
        167, 227
    income replacement, 120, 121
    Jobseeker's Allowance, 22, 23, 216,
        237
    supplementary conditions, 90,
        108
    Sweden, 75, 103, 119, 227
    United Kingdom, 22, 23, 216, 218,
        227
Unemployment traps
    definition, 207, 312

labour markets, 207
work disincentives, 207–8
United Kingdom
    adequacy, 145–6
    administration, 95, 104, 109,
        252
    asylum seekers, 52
    behavioural change, 36
    Breadline Britain, 139–40
    child support, 57–8, 135, 146, 153,
        184, 225
    contracting-out, 102
    contributory benefits, 4, 22, 90
    credit unions, 81
    Department of Work and Pensions, 4,
        8, 24, 93, 107, 109
    dependent liability, 49
    disabled persons, 82, 83, 124, 125,
        127, 128, 129, 189, 193, 219,
        240–2
    eligibility, 233
    employment, 18
    Employment Zones, 167
    executive agencies, 93, 104
    fraud, 237–8
    funding, 83
    gross domestic product (GDP), 12, 28,
        57
    habitual residency, 91
    health insurance, 81
    in-kind benefits, 6, 107
    income distribution, 162–3
    income packages, 79
    Income Support, 193, 194, 209, 237,
        246
    insurance, 4
    insurance companies, 99
    Jobcentre Plus, 93, 104, 233
    Jobcentres, 236
    labour exchanges, 218
    labour market policies, 27, 35, 226
    lifetime receipts, 64
    local government, 95, 100
    marginal deduction rates, 209–11
    medical costs, 125–6
    modernization, 35
    non-contributory benefits, 82
    objectives, 39

occupational pensions, 5, 8, 51–2, 81, 99, 206
parliamentary democracy, 55
polygamy, 57–8
Poor Law, *see* Poor Law
population, 9
poverty alleviation, 8, 22, 27, 29–30, 135–6, 186
poverty indicators, 144
recipiency rates, 182
redistribution, 162–3, 166, 167, 168
replacement ratios, 121
retirement age, 53
retirement income, 86
single parents, 57, 261–3, 264
social assistance, 145–6, 214
Social Fund, 38, 244, 245
social security spending, 28, 50, 59, 64
social security system, 8
social welfare, 163
staff attitudes, 236
state retirement pensions, 4
take-up, 193, 194
targeting efficiency, 186
tax credits, 22, 23, 27, 39, 108, 189, 225
trade unions, 35
unemployment benefit, 22, 23, 216, 218, 227
vertical redistribution, 152–4, 158
welfare to work, 7
United States
adequacy, 132–3, 145
administration, 85, 95, 104, 108, 252
Aid for Families with Dependent Children (AFDC), 5, 37, 193, 194, 263
caseloads, 116
child support, 193
contractors, 100, 102
disabled persons, 116, 124–5, 126, 127, 128, 129, 189, 219
Earned Income Tax credit, 39, 94, 107, 188, 194, 209, 225, 227, 230
education, 45
employment, 18

family cap policies, 36, 263
family support, 217
food stamps, 6, 11, 52, 64, 104, 133, 193, 194, 209, 217, 230, 235, 265
funding, 83
GDP, 12, 28
General Assistance, 11
GPD, 12
health insurance, 81
household income, 142
illegitimate births, 25, 36, 37
immigrants, 52, 265
in-kind benefits, 6, 11, 52, 64, 104
income distribution, 163
income packages, 79
labour market policies, 226
marginal deduction rates, 209–11
Medicaid, 11, 145, 210, 217, 230
medical costs, 126
Medicare, 11, 194
Old Age, Survivors and Disability Insurance (OASDI), 4, 11, 133, 166, 192, 230, 265
One-Stop Career Centers, 233
Panel Study of Income Dynamics, 214
population, 9
poverty alleviation, 135, 136, 186
poverty line, 133, 137
recipiency rates, 182
redistribution, 163, 166, 167, 168
replacement ratios, 121
residency, 91
retirement age, 53
retirement income, 86
self-sufficiency, 46
single parents, 57, 261–3, 264
social assistance, 30, 57, 82, 95, 214, 236
social policy, 9–10
Social Security Administration (SSA), 85, 93–4, 104
Social Security Disability Insurance (SSDI), 116
social security spending, 28, 50, 59, 64
social security system, 4, 11
Supplemental Security Income (SSI), 11, 91, 116, 133, 194, 265

take-up, 194
TANF, *see* Transitional Assistance for Needy Families
targeting efficiency, 186
territorial redistribution, 167, 168, 169
verification, 104–5
welfare, 5, 7
WIC programme, 237
Wisconsin, 217
work activities, 11
work ethic, 11, 57
workfare, 46, 221
Units of assessment
claimant units, 180, 184, 304
definition, 312
households, 134, 141, 154
types, 134
vertical redistribution, 150–1
Universalism, 31, 312
Unmet need, 191–9
Unweighted horizontal redistribution, 164, 166, 312
User efficiency, 232, 312
Utility
definition, 312
indifference curves, 203
maximization, 202, 203

van Orschot, W., 195–9
Verification, 104–6
Vertical redistribution
equivalence scales, 154–5
income, 117, 150–63
measurement, 154–63
mechanisms, 151–4
positive, definition, 32, 151, 309
purpose, 150–1
quintile share ratio, 159
Rawlsian inequality measure, 159
social adequacy, 77
United Kingdom, 152–4, 158
Vertical targeting efficiency
benefit drag, 188–9
definition, 312
maladministration, 190–1
measurement, 181–2, 186

Wage income
Australia, 142, 147
deferred wages, 82, 151
gender differences, 164
relative wage adjustment, 227, 310
reservation wages, 215, 311
return to work, 215
social wage, 151
Wales, 8
Washington Consensus, 295
Weighted horizontal redistribution, 164, 312
Welfare
active *see* Active welfare; Proactive welfare
definition, 7–8, 313
economics, 7, 8
equality, 15
handmaiden role, 46
individual, 7, 307
social, *see* Social welfare
United States, 5, 7
Welfare regimes
additional, 17–18
aims, 13, 23–4
conservative/corporatist, 13, 14, 16–17, 34, 44, 48, 71, 81, 117, 151, 186, 207, 227
decommodification, 14, 15–16
economic needs, 30
economic performance, 48
equality, 34
funding mechanisms, 69, 71
institutions, 93
liberal, 13, 14, 15, 34, 69, 70, 132, 207
social democratic, 13, 14, 15–16, 34, 44, 71, 132, 227
welfare state, 14
Welfare state
Asia, 80
collective schemes, 32
Europe, 7
welfare regimes, 14
Welfare to work
definition, 313
entitlement, 91
United Kingdom, 7

Words
 disabled persons, 123–4
 glossary, 303–13
 importance, 4–8
Work disincentives
 benefit schemes, 206
 definition, 48, 313
 objectives, 120
 policy responses, 218–27
 poverty traps, 208–12
 reservation wages, 215
 savings traps, 210–12
 short-term benefits, 118–9
 taxation, 56, 205
 unemployment traps, 207–8
Work ethic, 11, 36, 57

Work-first policies, 221, 313
Workfare
 Australia, 47
 definition, 313
 Europe, 46, 220
 sanctions, 220
 social assistance, 220–1
 United States, 46, 221
Working class, 31, 32
Working Families Tax Credit (WFTC),
 27, 38, 225
World Bank, 134, 295, 296
World Wide Web
 access, 144
 administration, 104
 policy changes, 3